DOLORES DEL RÍ

DOLORES DEL RÍO

Beauty in Light and Shade

Linda B. Hall

Stanford University Press

Stanford, California

Stanford University Press
Stanford, California

Printed in the United States of America on acid-free, archival-quality paper

Library of Congress Cataloging-in-Publication Data

Hall, Linda B. (Linda Biesele), author.

Dolores del Río : beauty in light and shade / Linda B. Hall.
    pages cm
Includes bibliographical references and index.
  ISBN 978-0-8047-8407-8 (cloth : alk. paper)
  ISBN 978-0-8047-9946-1 (pbk. : alk. paper)
  ISBN 978-0-8047-8621-8 (electronic)
 1. Del Rio, Dolores, 1905-1983. 2. Motion picture actors and actresses--Mexico--Biography.
 3. Motion pictures--Social aspects--United States--History--20th century. I. Title.
PN2318.D4H35 2012
791.4302'8092--dc23   2012035992
  [B]

Typeset by Bruce Lundquist in 11/15 Bell MT

For Luís Martín
Mentor and Inspiration

Contents

Acknowledgments

This manuscript has benefited from the enormous help of a number of people. Dolores del Río's own archive, which was given to the Centro de Estudios de Historia de México CARSO by her husband Lewis Riley after her death, is the major source for my work. Violeta Sánchez organized that archive when it came to the center, and I am grateful to her for having made it accessible to me and for her constant guidance as to its contents. Josefina Moguel of the same center was also generous with her time and advice. I also want to thank CEHM CARSO and its director, Manuel Ramos Medina, for permission to use the photographs from del Río's private collection in the work that follows, and José Gotiérrez Pérez for his efforts to put together the requisite documents. The Cineteca Nacional also permitted me to use their collections, and in particular to reproduce a number of the photographs that appear in these pages. Also in Mexico, conversations with my friends Eugenia Meyer and Norma Mireles de Ogarrio gave me ideas and led me to new materials. Luisa Riley and Carmen Parra, del Río's nieces by marriage, and family member Luciana Corres Tames all offered ideas and help. Del Río-Riley family friend Jaime Chávez permitted me to see his collections of memorabilia for both del Río and her fellow Mexican star and rival, María Félix, and provided me with clippings and photographs. In particular, I want to thank Alfredo de Batuc and Amalia Mesa-Bains, whose artistic creations focused on del Río were early inspirations for my own interest.

I also want to express my appreciation to Lauren Buisson, who day-to-day has made the film collection in the UCLA Performing Arts Special Collections available to researchers. She helped me find new sources and gain access to those that require special permission; her knowledge of the film industry and her ideas about it have been enormously helpful to me. The staffs of the Bibliothèque du Film in Paris, which also provided some of the illustrations printed herein, and of the Margaret Herrick Library at the Academy of Motion Picture Arts and Sciences in Los Angeles led me to some significant and exciting material.

During the writing process, I was fortunate to be able to work with two groups, the Santa Fe Seminar and the writing workshop at the University of New Mexico. My friends and colleagues in the former—Sandra Lauderdale Graham, Richard Graham, Richard Flint, Shirley Flint, Shirley Barnes, Kurt and Polly Schaafsma, Suzanne Stamatov, Peter Linder, Barbara Sommer, and Jim Dunlap—read the early chapters of the work and provided ideas, editing suggestions, and encouragement. The writing workshop in the Department of History at the University of New Mexico also read many of the chapters over the last five years, and I am grateful for their thoughtful commentaries and suggestions. In particular, the members of the latest incarnation of this workshop with whom I was privileged to work—Sue Taylor, Chad Black, Joseph Lenti, Margarita Ochoa, and Brian Stauffer—helped me through chapter by chapter as I was completing the manuscript. Joseph Lenti read the entire final draft, and I am grateful for his suggestions. At a later stage, Robert Corrigan looked at the manuscript with his usual eye for the appropriate word, strengthening and clarifying. Chad Black, in particular, helped me with Internet issues. Blair Woodard, in Los Angeles, gathered information that I was not able to find at a crucial last moment, and Alice J. Topjon provided two beautiful unpublished photographs. My colleague Paul Hutton also furnished treasures from his collection, some of which appear as illustrations. Xayo Meunphalangchai was an enormous help with formatting issues. As I was completing the final revisions, University of Arizona students Natasha Warner, David Wysocki, Abel Cota, Marco Macías, Rocio Gómez, Shayna Mehas, Josh Salyers, Pete Soland, Adrian Mendoza, and Rodrigo Parral Durán and University of New Mexico students Brett Alexander, Matthew Berch, Joseph García, Alejandro Jara, and Luke Smith, participating in a seminar taught by Professor William Beezley and myself, read the manuscript and offered insights and suggestions.

Ronald L. Davis, professor emeritus at Southern Methodist University, originally suggested this topic to me; I am very glad he did, as it has been one of the most compelling that I have worked on in many years. I thank him for thinking of me for this project.

Finally, my gratitude to Luís Martín, also professor emeritus at SMU, who first showed me that a vocation for history could be fulfilling and, just as importantly, fun. Luís, this book is for you.

Note on Translation
and Orthography

The investigation of this topic has involved not only English but also French and particularly Spanish sources. When the translations are from Spanish or French and the original language is provided in the notes, they are my own. If translations from any language are given only in English, they are the translations of the authors or translators cited. As for Spanish orthography, I have done my best to record any quotations accurately in the way they appear in the source that I used and that is acknowledged in the citations. In most English sources, particularly newspapers, diacritical marks for names and other Spanish words were generally omitted, and I have kept the orthography as it appears in the original. In particular, Dolores del Río's name was, throughout her career and up to the present, written as "Dolores Del Rio" in almost all English-language publications and documents. The *New York Times* and a few other sources used "Dolores del Rio," with the lower case "d" but without the accent. These usages have been kept throughout. Whenever I use del Río in other parts of the text, I use the lowercase "d" and the accent. I have avoided the use of *[sic]* except where most necessary, so as not to impede the reader unnecessarily.

DOLORES DEL RÍO

1   Beauty, Celebrity, and Power in Two Cultures

These famous are symptomatic and symbolic, the large-screen projection of those human possibilities a culture believes are the most fascinating and perhaps useful for its survival.

> Leo Braudy, *The Frenzy of Renown: Fame and Its History*[1]

Only after Valentino could a blonde leading lady accept and return the ardent kisses of a screen lover with dark coloring.

> Emily Leider, *Dark Lover: The Life and Death of Rudolph Valentino*[2]

ONLY AFTER DOLORES DEL RÍO could a blond leading man make passionate love on the Hollywood screen to a dark female lover. She herself believed that she had established a new phenotype for female beauty in Hollywood—a dark-haired, dark-eyed, dark-skinned ideal—to match that established for men by Rudolph Valentino. Yet on arrival in California in 1925, she agonized over her brunette loveliness, faced with the "fairy-tale" stars with blonde hair and blue eyes.[3] At the same time she became a celebrity in the United States, she became a source of national pride for Mexico. On the day of his assassination in 1928, former Mexican President and President-Elect Alvaro Obregón asked for a showing of her film *Ramona* that evening, or so the London press claimed. The pleasure was denied him when he was shot and killed by a religious fanatic at a political luncheon. Later she became one of the country's great divas when she returned and participated in its Golden Age of cinema.

"The female Valentino." Centro de Estudios de Historia de México CARSO. Credited hereafter as CEHM CARSO, all reproduced by permission.

Who was this extraordinary woman, and what were the qualities that made her compelling to so many? How was this woman able to appeal so completely to two nations and two cultures, simultaneously gaining international fame?

Is it possible that, as Leo Braudy said of celebrated individuals, she was "symptomatic and symbolic" of her times and her places, was "fascinating" to those who saw her films and followed her life story (both the real and created), and found her public persona somehow "useful?"[4] She began her career in the post–World War I United States; renown and wealth followed almost immediately, if not always happiness. She seemed to provide on the screen and in her private life a vision of "human possibilities" that would begin to shift important markers of racial and ethnic division within U.S. society. Later she returned to Mexico, where again she seemed to provide more "projections" useful to a society still in transition after its bloody revolution of 1910–1920.

The Mexican actress Dolores del Río was the first major Latina crossover star in Hollywood, and thus subject to two cultures, rather than the single one envisioned by Braudy's quotation. Departing the economic and social changes of her home country that followed its violent civil war, 1910–1920, in which dictator Porfirio Díaz was overthrown by a cross-class alliance that included peasants bent on land reform and other revolutionaries who threatened and then in fact affected and diminished the position of the upper class, she arrived in Los Angeles in 1925. Under the sponsorship of director Edwin Carewe, she very quickly rose to the height of stardom and personal wealth and remained both popular and employed for over a decade. When good roles diminished and her personal life took a turbulent and unexpected turn in the early 1940s, she returned to Mexico to join an artistic and literary renaissance that was already flourishing. There she was able to take more control over her life, in both personal and professional aspects, and went on to become one of the most celebrated actresses in that nation's history and a key participant in Mexican film's Golden Age. This progression toward autonomy and personal control had been going on for a long time, and interpretations that see her as a largely passive victim of the Hollywood milieu or of the men in her life are surely mistaken. She was sometimes disappointed or distressed even to the point of illness, setbacks she was able to overcome though with difficulty. Yet del Río, at least from the early 1930s on, was aware of her interests and took an active part in charting her own course. Her success at doing so varied over time, but she was never simply a tool for powerful men.

A number of issues arise in looking at her life and career, but by far the one most commonly and notoriously associated with her is that of her physical beauty. Contemporaries as well as later viewers of her photographs and films reacted with dazzled admiration. Her friends and fellow great foreign beauties in Hollywood, Greta Garbo and Marlene Dietrich, considered her the most beautiful of all. Dietrich even called her "the most beautiful woman who ever set foot in Hollywood."[5] Other closely related themes have to do with the questions of gender and relationships with men, power, sexuality, race, age, and social position. These things played out in various concrete ways: the creation of an image (she started in Hollywood, after all); the corporeal creation of beauty, ranging from cosmetics and hairstyles to plastic surgery; and the re-creation of her bodily actions, that is, her voice, her movements, her acting. As with most Hollywood stars, then and now, among her roles was her own self-creation. Within that self-creation, major questions emerge: How much of what resulted was her own choice or was indeed a part of her "real" self, whatever that might mean, and what was imposed or forced on her, either by mentors or the market or both?

However difficult it may be to separate the woman Dolores del Río from the Hollywood creation and then later from her film images in Mexico, she was nevertheless a real human being with a background, a personality, a will. Joanne Hershfield, in her fascinating analysis of del Río's films, has argued: "A movie star has no 'personal identity' (even though the person who inhabits the star's body may claim such an identity). In other words, she is a figure composed of a presence and a set of discourses that symbolize an *iconic* identity."[6] Although I understand Hershfield's point and admire her book on del Río, I cannot accept it as an exclusive guide in this work. Such a view robs the individual of both agency and humanity. Rather, the actual person is in continuing interaction with the constructed image—including her publicity and her acting roles—but nevertheless continues to be a living, breathing individual. It is in the neighborhood of the interaction between the individual and the constructed image that I have looked to find the biography of this celebrated woman.

Del Río's beauty is sometimes seen as making her a victim and a commodity, but her beauty, charm, talent, and energy gave her enormous power to shape her own fate as well, and she realized this power more fully over time. Psychologist Rollo May defines *power* as "the ability to cause or prevent change," and he goes on to say that in psychology, "power means the ability to affect, to influence, and to change other persons (or oneself)." Further, he considers personal power as "self-realization and self-actualization."[7] Del Río was able to be powerful in the ways that May suggests. Moreover, much of her power came precisely from her beauty. One definition of beauty is "the quality that gives pleasure to the mind and senses and is associated with such properties as harmony of form or color, excellence of artistry, truthfulness, and originality."[8] Yet another sees it as "the quality of being very pleasing, as in form, color, etc.," or in another choice, "good looks."[9] Most definitions of female beauty equate it with sexual attractiveness.[10] In particular, beauty seems to be associated with the female face and body, and it is no surprise that Dolores's male biographers often include the word "face" in their titles.[11] In this particular case, images of del Río were ubiquitous in both countries for decades, and whether in person or on the screen or in still photographs or painted portraits, she was certainly sexually appealing. Yet her popularity— and even more important, her career—extended throughout her lifetime, far beyond the age at which most experts would believe that this erotic attraction was the only (or even the major) source of her power. In this case, perhaps, her beauty, though still physical, extended into areas associated more with manner and way of being—and, certainly, with memories and nostalgia for the young Dolores in those who had seen her work years earlier or those who saw these images replayed in various formats in later decades. She was a celebrity in both countries within months of her arrival in Hollywood, and though her fame and popularity waxed and waned, she remained one until her death. Yet the nature of this celebrity differed significantly north and south of the border.

Moreover, the perception of her beauty was enhanced by her very celebrity, defined here as fame or the quality of being well known across a large public. Celebrity is rarely earned simply because one is "great and talented and virtuous" or even very, very beautiful; it is almost always accompanied by a "publicity apparatus" and a great deal of luck.[12] Celebrity was a major key to certain kinds of power that del Río achieved, beyond the power that beauty carries to those who are attracted by or enamored of that quality. Celebrity from her publicity and her films brought far more attention— indeed, international notice—to Dolores than had she exerted that power only with others who knew her personally, though this aspect of power was certainly important to her throughout her life and career. Yet celebrity had an additional economic advantage: it made her projects bankable, and she was able to use her power in the realm of filmmaking to bring people of talent into her endeavors, particularly in Mexico.

In this case, her very beauty and social class diminished the significance of her Mexican background and her somewhat darker rather than lighter skin, and a good publicity machine and good fortune in her early directors and roles helped a great deal.[13] Her success, however, was not inevitable, and its achievement was, for her, personally costly. Though her ability and re- solve increased as she grew older, her marketability in U.S. films declined. This phenomenon had far more to do with age than race. It also had to do, to some degree, with a reaction against foreign stars, both male and female. Still, she seems to have known from her midtwenties onward that she did not need a male mentor, though at that time she still seems to have wanted a protective husband. She always recognized and appreciated working with talented and perceptive directors. When she returned to Mexico in the 1940s, in her late thirties and in considerable emotional distress, she was paradoxically both alone and in control.

Gender is significant throughout her life. She was able to engage in behaviors not initially acceptable for young women of her social class in Mexico—working as an actress for more than fifty years, making her own money, divorcing two husbands—but she did not engage in overt po- litical activity as a rule. The changes she may have inspired in Mexico in regard to women's roles had more to do with her example, particularly as she achieved increasing autonomy in her personal life and her professional endeavors. During the 1920s, in Hollywood, she was an almost quintes- sential model for the "chica moderna," working, wearing cloche hats and shorter skirts, and eventually cutting her long hair into a more fashion- able bob.[14] Although it would be hard to tell to what degree acceptance of these styles in Mexico had to do with her, her publicity photos showed her as a very elegant version of a modern young Mexican woman with her own money, and it seems likely that she was emulated as well as envied. Though she came into criticism for breaking from tradition, particularly among the high upper class to which her first husband's family belonged, it may be that she also was an example to other women of what was pos- sible. Criticism of her in Mexico, strongest when she was first in Holly-

Del Río as a model for 1920s Mexican women. CEHM CARSO.

wood, was no doubt partly based on envy of the freedom and renown that she had achieved.

The issue of age itself is in dispute, and she tried to conceal her actual birthdate from the beginning of her Hollywood career. At that time, the perception was that an actress could count on being attractive to audiences only through her midtwenties. She insisted from her arrival in California that she had been born on August 3, 1906, which would have made her barely fifteen at the time of her wedding in 1921 and nineteen at the beginning of her film career. She was, in fact, born in 1904 and celebrated her twenty-first birthday just before she arrived in Los Angeles.

By the time she reached the claimed age of twenty-four (actually twenty-six) and was married to her second husband, Cedric Gibbons, there were speculations in the press that she was "washed up." She was already saying that she was hopeful her career might last three or four years longer.[15] It lasted, in fact, almost until her death, but by no means always in Hollywood.

Power is also an important theme in her life story. Her extreme youth at the time of her first marriage (whether she was fifteen or seventeen) relative to the age of her spouse, Jaime Martínez del Río, who was about two decades her senior and from a wealthier and more prominent family, indicated an initial, very significant power differential. When she and her husband were brought to California by Edwin Carewe, the director was eager to take over her life along with her career, and conflicts inevitably developed. The story that then unfolded was very different from what Jaime, Dolores, and Carewe himself initially envisioned, and power shifted.

Other issues arise from context, particularly those of celebrity and race. These important factors were clearly entwined in Dolores's life story. The growth of the mass-market press, both newspapers and magazines, taking off in the latter part of the nineteenth century, led to the "development of celebrity journalism as a specific genre."[16] Immediately upon arrival in Hollywood, Dolores became a person of enormous interest in this new type of reporting, and Hollywood, of course, was a perfect venue for fostering celebrity and celebrities. The possibility of placing stories that would lead to the fame and therefore employability of their protégés gave directors, studio heads, and others involved in film production an incentive to employ a new breed of journalists—press agents—operating from outside newspapers and magazines themselves. Early on, Dolores had a particularly effective one, Harry D. Wilson. He worked with her from the moment she arrived in Hollywood, and he spun stories that would show her in what he felt was a favorable light and keep her before the public. Enormous interest in the famous led to the emergence of another group of journalists working for newspapers and magazines who specialized in following film stars, especially those who were beginning to enjoy wide popularity as they appeared on the silver screen. Some of these were gossip columnists; others produced stories for the society pages; and some, of course, were film critics. They focused on del Río from her earliest days in the United States. The *Los Angeles Times* alone covered her extensively, with 101 mentions of appearances in that first year in Hollywood (August 25, 1925–August 25, 1926) and 221 in the subsequent year (August 25, 1926–August 25, 1927). Even the relatively stodgy *New York Times*, which focused more on actors and actresses from the theater than on Hollywood stars, mentioned her five times in her first year in the United States and fifty-seven times in the second.[17] She began to appear as a specifically Mexican celebrity just over a month after arrival, in a *Los Angeles Times* layout of caricatures of prominent Mexicans including President Plutarco Elías Calles. She was the only woman.[18] She had not yet appeared in a film. Hollywood reporters covered her constantly throughout her career, even after she returned more or less permanently to Mexico, among them gossip columnist Hedda Hopper, society writer Grace Kingsley, and feature writer Gladys Hall. Although male writers often mentioned her as well, female journalists took a more consistent and insistent interest. Still, Mexican racial status was ambiguous. It is probable, in my view, that her popularity as a romantic leading lady was enhanced by the tension of being *almost* forbidden. This exoticism was played up more in her Hollywood roles of the 1930s than in those of the 1920s, particularly in the film *Bird of Paradise*.[19]

The case of race is more complex. Hershfield, for example, makes it a major issue, as she discusses the roles in which Dolores was cast, particularly early in her career. However, Hershfield points out that the publicity designed by Wilson and Carewe actually emphasized her "ethnic and racial characteristics" and notes that she was described in *Photoplay*, one of the first movie magazines and certainly the most important at that time, as "the raven-haired, olive-skinned, sinuous-limbed Carmen."[20] This emphasis on the part of Dolores's handlers seems contradictory both to Hershfield's analysis and to their own stress on her as rich and of European descent, but it played into the vision of del Río as exotic and foreign, maybe even, subliminally, a little more appealing because just on the edge of dangerous. Later on, Hershfield sees evidence of the "whitening" of Dolores, still performing exotic roles but looking more and more European. Of course, casting will always depend a great deal on appearance, and in film the actor must appear believable in the role. Only occasionally on the stage, and very occasionally at that, will an actor be cast as a character in which facial features or skin color make her or him implausible. Yet Dolores's very beauty led producers and directors to seek out or create roles for her in which she would be convincing, and later she herself would do the searching. Far from losing parts because of her race, she found roles were being created for her because of her beauty. Certainly, accounts of Dolores and her success reflected awareness that she was Mexican, but they consistently emphasized her high social status and the wealth of her family and her husband's. Race and ethnicity, in this case, were significantly modified by class.

Hershfield indicates that "feminine beauty in the United States has always been conceived as 'white' beauty," and she searches for an explanation of why women such as Dolores could be acceptable in that context.[21] But the facts reflect that not only was Dolores acceptable, she herself set a new standard of physical appearance and sexual attraction, as Valentino did for male stars, and Carewe almost certainly selected her for this very purpose. In 1930, six years after her first screen appearance, *Photoplay* searched for "the most perfect feminine figure in Hollywood," using a panel of "medical men, artists, designers" as judges. Del Río was "their unanimous selection." Though Hershfield is aware of this assessment, she rejects the explanation that "American celebrities can rise above the color line."[22] In this case, it seems, Dolores not only could but did, if indeed she was ever perceived by U.S. whites as racially other. In yet another *Photoplay* article four years later, when she was thirty, the most eminent fashion photographer of the time, George Hoyningen-Huene, named her as the second most beautiful actress in Hollywood, following only Garbo, stating that, "She wears less makeup than any of the stars I have met, yet her vividness is breathtaking. The bone structure of her head and body is magnificent. Her skin is like ripe fruit. She has sinuous yet artless grace; her face is so perfectly constructed that she can be photographed in any light from any angle. Wherever the light falls, it composes beauty."[23] And the light in photographs of del Río could significantly change the appearance of her skin in her portraits, with the elegance of her apparel and jewelry providing cues to her personal wealth and social status.

She was shifting the definition of *other*, and Carewe—himself of Native American descent and, more than that, raised in close proximity to if not immersed in Native American culture—seems to have selected her specifically to move those lines. Given the associations that many in the United States made between the categories "Mexican" and "Indian," it was a risk.

Certainly, she was seen as exotic, but I find no evidence that she was demeaned or placed in an inferior category in this regard, although some

Sincerely
Dolores Del Rio

An early publicity photograph shows lighting and makeup to lighten del Río's skin.

of her roles are jarringly offensive to twenty-first-century sensibilities in their depiction of gender. The men who encountered her constantly testified to her extraordinary loveliness, and it is clear that many of them fell hopelessly in love with her. Possible notions of her race as manifested physically do not seem to have mattered in terms of male response. Beauty and class trumped any attempts to view her as nonwhite, but the tactics employed by Carewe were dangerous, despite the fact that powerful men were eager to help her and the U.S. public was eager to accept her. Defying the notion that lighter skin was better, in early screen tests and beauty pageants, Carewe and her other handlers dressed her in white, the better to emphasize her dark loveliness. Dolores herself became a kind of social experiment, and in her early years in Hollywood it was she who paid the price emotionally for this audacity. Moving the racial and ethnic lines for acceptable romantic female stars—portrayed more than life-size on the silver screen—was not without its dangers. Though Valentino paved the way for men, his own acceptance was not unequivocal, and she herself was vulnerable to sexual, gender, and racial judgments, occasionally on the printed page or from those viewing her larger-than-life presence on the movie screen.

Race and ethnicity, for del Río, a dazzling Mexican woman, were highly complicated. After all, when she came to Hollywood in 1925 the country was less than eighty years away from the Treaty of Guadalupe Hidalgo, which had given more than half of Mexico's national territory to the United States. In the wake of that agreement, full citizenship of Mexicans in the region acquired seemed to be clear: the treaty itself promised that all Mexican citizens irrespective of race were entitled to the political status of whites. Yet most government officials believed that Mexicans who were predominantly of Indian ancestry should have the same status as detribalized Indians north of the border, leaving them in a liminal status dependent on whether they seemed to be of European ancestry or more indigenous. California and Arizona moved early to disenfranchise Mexicans considered Indian, with only Mexicans of European descent attaining political rights. In any case, many Mexicans, regardless of legal argument, were refused these rights.[24] Even Secretary of Labor James J. Davis admitted the confusions about Mexican race in 1929, at the height of del Río's movie fame. He stated, after years of considering the question of preventing Mexicans from immigrating into the United States, that "The Mexican people are of such a mixed stock and individuals have such a limited knowledge of their racial composition that it would be impossible for the most learned and experienced ethnologist or anthropologist to classify or determine their racial origin."[25]

Moreover, in the 1920s, when Dolores arrived in California, the issue of Mexican race was being debated in regard to school segregation; in 1927, the year of her first big movie success, the attorney general of California offered the opinion that Mexican students should be classified as Indians, and thus subject to de jure segregation, reiterating this point of view in 1930. By 1931, 85 percent of Mexican students in the California public school system were in segregated facilities.[26] In the 1920s as well, miscegenation—mixing of races—was an issue directly related to del Río's potential success as a female film star performing with white male romantic leads. It was a major theme of discussion, political and otherwise. U.S. congressional representatives John Box and Thomas Jenkins were at that time arguing publicly that Mexicans were already the products of racial mixing among Indians, blacks, and whites, a process they called "mongrelization." According to them, Mexicans on both sides of the border were entirely too casual about interracial liaisons and likely to contribute to continued racial mixing.[27] Yet the issue was almost always framed as a problem of Indian versus white blood, and Mexicans considered to be white were in theory exempt from stigma, social or otherwise. They were nevertheless in a precarious situation. Despite the attention given to these issues by Hollywood censoring agencies, del Río was unusually exempt. As noted by one of the foremost historians of the film world and race, "Even though Dolores Del Rio vehicles like *Wonder Bar* (1934), *I Live for Love* (1935), and *In Caliente* (1935), as well as the trade reviews of them clearly marked the Mexican actress as 'a Latin stage star' paired with white men, no mention is made of such differences in the PCA [Production Code Administration] files on these films."[28] Del Río simply did not trigger the same kinds of racial biases as many other dark-skinned actresses did.

In 1944, five states—Arizona, Nevada, North Carolina, South Carolina, and Virginia—prohibited "the American Redman" from marrying "Caucasians," though none of the states explicitly named Mexicans as being of a race "separate from whites or Caucasians." An article in the *California Law Review* at the time indicated that it might be possible for Indians to be considered "Mongolian" for purposes of miscegenation, and thus the prohibition might extend to that state as well.[29] Determinations of race were largely made as judgments of physical appearance by the clerks authorizing the unions. Only in 1948 did California begin to issue marriage licenses regardless of race. Until that time, Mexicans hoping to marry those designated white might be denied legal authorization on the basis of miscegenation, though by that date it rarely occurred and Mexicans in California were generally considered to be white. Still, Mexican racial status was ambiguous, liminal, and nervous-making. The case that broke through the legal barrier in California was *Perez* v. *Lippold* (1947), in which Perez was held to be white and Lippold "Negro." Using the equal protection clause of the Fourteenth Amendment of the U.S. Constitution, three judges of the California court found in favor of the couple, while another concurred on the grounds of religious freedom.[30] Yet it was not until 1967 that miscegenation statutes were finally declared unconstitutional by the U.S. Supreme Court.[31] Dolores, with her dark skin, hair, and eyes, was vulnerable. Almost paradoxically, Carewe and Wilson emphasized these characteristics, pushing them as "exotic" and, at least in the case of Wilson, "Spanish." Dolores herself never glossed her ethnicity as Spanish, however, always claiming quite clearly her Mexican nationality.

Social class emerges as another important issue here. Though Dolores was Mexican, she was in many ways much more sophisticated than most Americans, even those of similar economic means. Both her family and that of her spouse were well-to-do. Although they had suffered losses in the Revolution, they still maintained lifestyles that included European tours and homes of beauty and, in the case of the Martínez del Ríos, considerable grandeur. She and Jaime were also both strongly connected in the Mexican artistic world, including a nascent avant-garde that was developing rapidly after the turbulent upheavals of the Revolution and ensuing political changes. It was an era of new social and cultural freedoms and forms. Dolores's ties with artists and writers and others in this creative postrevolutionary movement would be lifelong.

This Mexican cultural and social elite had contacts with the movie business in the United States, and they mingled with some of its leaders. In fact, these connections were pursued by Mexicans, particularly after the economic and social changes of the Revolution impeded their access to the lifestyles that had been supported previously by their control over the land, agriculture, and mining. Hollywood was, after all, in Southern California, close to the Mexican border though a fair distance from Mexico City. Mexican elites were sophisticated and creative; it made sense that they would be sought out by those in the U.S. movie industry and that they themselves would seek creative space there. Moreover, Mexico constituted a large market for U.S. films in the 1920s and 1930s. In the first few years of the talkies, a number of films were made in two versions, English and another language (often Spanish). Sometimes producers used the same actors for the two productions, depending on language skills. More than one filmmaker in the 1920s searched for a female counterpart to the exotic male actor, Rudolph Valentino, who himself had made dark skin and eyes acceptable in male romantic leads, and Mexico was a good potential source for such a figure. Carewe framed Dolores's possibilities in precisely that light, insisting that she could be the female Valentino. He lured Dolores and her husband to Hollywood, where within a short time she gained enormous popularity. The legend has it that she was reluctant; the evidence shows that she welcomed the opportunity and took full advantage of it.

Whether or not Dolores sought out a career or fame, she later regarded the move as a liberation. According to her, "it was there, in Hollywood, that I began my life. That is to say, I found myself." She was beginning to sense her own power. As she stated, she followed a *"Straight Line*, driven by a single desire . . . to become known Worldwide as the *Most Important Actress of Mexico*."[32]

There are also issues of sexuality surrounding her story. Rumors still abound in Mexico that her first two husbands were gay. What is certain is that she never had children and was therefore unencumbered in her career and never faced the changes to her body that pregnancy would have caused. Whatever the nature of her own sexual life, it is also clear that she furthered the fantasies of both those who knew her and those who saw her on the screen. Certainly she experienced sexual tension with powerful men in the entertainment industry on both sides of the border. Throughout her Hollywood and Mexican careers, she was followed by rumors of her affairs with men as well as women, the men including some of the most prominent actors, directors, and artists of her time, the women including Greta Garbo, Marlene Dietrich, and Frida Kahlo. Whether or not these rumors were true, more than one man who fell in love with her screen image later became her lover. Yet many of the claims and gossip perhaps have to do with wishful thinking, or perhaps even wishful bragging. Moreover, despite all the rumors, she retained a reputation as a lady—again, perhaps, a class-based judgment—unlike her less-fortunate fellow Mexican, Lupe Vélez, whose unwanted pregnancy led her to commit suicide.[33] In any event,

Dolores finally married for a third time, but not until 1959. At that time, she was fifty-five years old, and she and her third husband, Lewis Riley, had been companions for more than a decade.

The problems of beauty and sexuality lead directly to issues of the body. There are a number of questions that revolve around Dolores and her physical being. Among them are pregnancy and motherhood, or in this case their absence; use of cosmetics, costumes, and other appearance-altering devices; and plastic surgery. Clothes and hairstyles were other constant concerns. Of course, each role required a particular persona, an altered appearance. Interestingly, her earliest publicity stills showed her as sophisticated, elegantly dressed, her hair pulled back tightly to emphasize the extraordinary symmetry of her face and her enormous eyes. The poses were tightly controlled, almost never showing her in any kind of movement. Yet her movie stills, reflecting her casting, often show her as young, open, outgoing, animated, and by no means upper-class. In her publicity coverage, balancing her film roles, emphasis on her sophistication was echoed by constant references to her own high social status, the wealth of her family, and her trips to Europe.

She also refuted the U.S. (not to mention European) idea of what most Mexicans were like. She distanced herself from Mexicans who were lower-class and unruly, such as those who had fought in the Revolution—and some of these people were actually in Hollywood—or those who had earlier protested the U.S. takeover of California.[34] Although she occasionally was shown dressed in the stereotypical flamenco costume, most of these photographs are from the time when she was dancing in Mexico, before she came to Hollywood. An exception was in her first film, *Joanna*, in 1925, when she appeared cavorting with a Spanish shawl. Even here, however, she was wearing a high-style European gown, elegant jewelry, and glamorous high-heeled shoes. She also had a fiery Latin role in the *Loves of Carmen* in 1927, but the still photographs continued to emphasize her sophisticated Europeanness and the publicity her upper-class status. Never, in her early years in Hollywood, was she portrayed as a Mexican peasant woman, though she played a very romanticized version of a California mixed-race orphan—of an indigenous mother and a European father raised in a Spanish family—in *Ramona*, one of her most popular portrayals. But *Ramona* followed her role as a French innkeeper's daughter in *What Price Glory?* and as a Russian peasant in *Revenge* and *Resurrection*. Specifically, roles as explicitly "Indian," in both Mexican and U.S. films, came mostly after she returned to Mexico to live.

In terms of cosmetics, she always emphasized her eyes, which were extraordinarily large and dark. David Román says that she was concerned about her dark skin and Indian features as a child, and that she had done her best to use powders to make herself look lighter.[35] If she did, she was following in the footsteps of Mexican President Porfirio Díaz, who used the same technique on his dark skin for his portraits, perhaps to impress his Mexican contemporaries and his European and U.S. counterparts. It is also possible that her still photographs were altered to make her skin look lighter. Indianness, however beautiful it might have been in the eyes of others, was not pleasing to her own high class in Mexican society, and it obviously had to be handled carefully, regardless of Carewe's desires, in the United States.

Yet another controversial issue is plastic surgery. This profession was taking hold rapidly in the United States in the 1920s, as the medical techniques developed in World War I for reconstruction of faces was refined and commercialized.[36] If, indeed, Dolores on her own merits was already considered dazzling in Hollywood when she arrived in 1925, why did she almost immediately undergo plastic surgery on her face? Obviously, there is no mention of such surgery in the press or in documents, but a careful (or even not-so-careful) study of her portraits over time makes clear that she underwent several operations. The first was probably in 1926. The stills from *What Price Glory?* show her nose as rather wide; when *Loves of Carmen* was filmed in 1927, it was notably narrower. It seems likely, as well, that by the time *Wonder Bar* was filmed in 1934, she had undergone yet another operation on her nose, this perhaps the last on that part of her face but by no means her last surgery, and stills taken at about this time are simply dazzling.

It is possible, of course, that these surgeries reflect a racialized or whitening change in her appearance. Yet del Río's Latinness was never denied in Hollywood, by herself or her publicists. Indeed, it was emphasized as an advantage. *Photoplay* commented after the release of *Loves of Carmen* that she was "the present leader of the Latin invasion. Her sudden success has been equaled only by the Scandinavian Greta Garbo and the American Clara Bow."[37] It seems reasonable to suggest that the ideals of beauty that were developing in Hollywood, or rather the exemplary figures of ideal beauty, were exotic foreigners with slender noses. Very quickly, Dolores was considered the very model of loveliness. Indeed, her friends' faces and

Dolores in about 1934, her dark skin emphasized by her white dress and her nose perceptibly narrowed from her early Hollywood publicity photographs.
CEHM CARSO.

those of other aspiring actresses began to reflect her own, slightly altered, countenance. And this vision or perhaps model continued for at least three decades. Strikingly, the cover of a novel called *The Magic Scalpel*, published in 1960 by plastic surgeon Maxwell Maltz, shows a doctor unwrapping the bandages from a woman with a beautiful new face. The patient looks exactly like Dolores, arching eyebrows, high cheekbones, narrow nose and all. Although I do not know who selected the image, whether doctor or artist or editor, the likeness is obvious and indicates selection by someone seeking to illustrate the beautiful ideal.[38]

Although she was a passable and sometimes very fine actress and always enormously charming, it was principally her physical beauty and celebrity, and the power they gave her, that made it possible for her to achieve fame and celebrity, and finally a significant measure of control over her personal and professional lives. Questions arise throughout her career of who might be using whom. Early in her Hollywood years, caught in a conflict between her husband and her director/mentor, she suffered confusion and distress, sometimes even misery. Later, with more experience and maturity, her power and control increased. What might have made this power possible, particularly in comparison to other young women coming to Hollywood at about same time, and for many decades thereafter, who were quite clearly used and abused?

Certainly, the self-confidence that was derived from the approval her beauty and charm elicited in those around her must have helped, as did the devotion of her mother. She later told a niece that her extraordinary poise and self-assurance came directly from always knowing she was loved, and her mother was certainly the most important figure giving her consistent affection, approval, and support.[39] Early successes led to her being in high demand by producers, directors, and studios through the late 1920s. In the 1930s, her career waned as she aged, but a move back to Mexico in the early 1940s led to her becoming one of the great divas of Mexican film, and from the 1950s onward she was active in the theater and in television. She also seems to have been very good at managing her money; and whether or not she needed it when she got to Hollywood, she always seems to have had it thereafter and to have looked after it carefully. There is no question, looking through her papers, that she maintained a direct hand in supervising her own interests, delegating to others where possible but deciding major issues on her own. If indeed her image was whitened or racialized, she herself was significant in establishing an image of beauty in which foreign and exotic were not only accepted but splendid.

Moreover, if she submitted to physical changes—cosmetics, changing hair styles, adornment, costuming, even plastic surgery—these seemed to be changes she not only acquiesced in but in some cases relished. The facial alterations moved her beyond youthful attractiveness to a classic aesthetic that made her even more powerful, as an image of beauty both on the screen and in her personal life. The appropriate question here, it seems to me, is for whom she made these changes and who benefited. Several other questions are explored in the following chapters. How did her beauty and Mexican nationality affect her career? How did these factors affect relationships with others in her personal, professional, and public lives? How did her life and career and image differ in Hollywood and in Mexico? Why was she able to continue her career almost until her death, when so many beautiful women saw their careers fade even as they moved into their thirties? What were her important professional contributions? How did her career fit into other trends in the artistic world, on both sides of the border, in films and in relation to literature and the other arts? What impact did her beauty have on the power to chart her own life course? And, finally, two larger questions: why and how was she able to shift the racial and ethnic ideas in the United States in regard to Mexicans, and why was she able to defy social attitudes toward the proper roles of upper-class Mexican women in that country, to become the iconic, respected, and idolized great lady of Mexican film and culture? In the next chapters, we investigate the interactions of celebrity and fame, expressed nationally and internationally, with issues of social change, evolving technologies of communication, and movement across borders, all expressed in the life of a beautiful and powerful but not invulnerable woman.

2   Mexican Princess

[T]he theater of modern fame is frequently an alternative to the
more restrictive roles of the social world.

Leo Braudy, *The Frenzy of Renown:*
Fame and Its History[1]

Once upon a time, at the beginning of the [twentieth] century, in a
city—Durango—luxurious stone dwellings of two or three stories,
European-style mansions, symbols of wealth inhabited by powerful
and aristocratic families, filled the center of town and many of its
principal streets.

David Ramón, *Dolores del Río*[2]

D OLORES DEL RÍO was born on August 3, 1904, though
she claimed later dates at various times. Her family usually gave a date of 1906, although as she aged she would sometimes shave
off a few more years, even on official documents. The question of age, apparently, was an important one, as when she first went to Hollywood—in
1925—it was expected that a young actress's career would not last into her
thirties. Regardless of age, however, her career lasted as long she wanted it
to, almost until her death in 1983. So did her beauty. Two of her biographers,
David Ramón and Paco Ignacio Taibo, believe that she was born in 1904,
and extant documents confirm that date.[3] Most current websites list 1905.[4]
The 1904 date seems to me likely; if we accept 1906 we also accept that her
family permitted her to marry at the age of fifteen, rather than seventeen.

What is not at issue is that she was born into highly respectable Mexican
society, though her parents do not seem to have been dazzlingly wealthy.

Her birthplace was the city of Durango, in Durango state. A beautiful place with many lavish buildings dating from its wealth and importance as a center of mining and cattle raising in the colonial period and into the present, Ramón describes it as "an idyllic world filled with landaus, carriages, and flags." Del Río herself later remembered that her family had a coach with two horses, "the envy of my cousins. I would climb up in the carriage and I felt like a princess. My mother sat in the back part and I accompanied her to church, on visits, to the seamstress. . . . I loved the gifts of necklaces, bracelets, earrings! My mother's friends gave me sweets while they had tea."[5] Given the profession that Dolores eventually pursued, it is interesting that the city's beauty remains and is now used often as a setting for motion pictures. Her parents were Jesús Leonardo Asúnsolo and Antonia López Negrete y López, both well-connected and well-to-do. Her father came from a family of cattle ranchers and businessmen in the state of Chihuahua to the north; her mother's family, residents of Durango, were proud of the documents showing that their lineage went back to the nobility of the viceroyalty of New Spain, as Mexico was known in the colonial period. When Dolores was baptized a few days after her birth, as María Dolores Asúnsolo López, the archbishop of Durango, a relative of her mother's, presided.[6] Her nickname, for the rest of her life, was Lolita.

Another thing that was not at issue was her close connection to her mother. In a 1966 interview with a leading Mexico City newspaper, she was asked what she remembered. Her immediate response was, "My mother. The most luminous memory of my life, next to which the others turn into foam and disappear, is that of my mother, who fills my life and also my remembrance."[7] She was an only child—an only daughter—enormously treasured. Throughout her life, her mother, her beloved "Mumy," would stay close to her, even when it meant leaving her father alone. This presence, as Dolores wove in and out of marriages, contracts, triumphs, and difficult moments, was of enormous importance to her. It was a trusting presence. As dear friend Salvador Novo later noted, "'her family' consists of her mother; and a mother that lived exclusively for her only daughter's happiness, and left to Dolores's excellent judgment the form of her happiness."[8] Without her mother's support, she might never have become the strong, confident, successful, and famous woman that she was.[9] Her father, in contrast, was a much more distant figure, appearing rarely in her reminiscences.

Lolita, already a beauty. CEHM CARSO.

She remembered the first years of her life in Durango with enormous nostalgia. The family had a house in town, and land with gardens and orchards just outside of it. She remembered when she was small playing in the beautiful park called "Las Moreras" ("the mulberry trees") and being taken to church and to other social events in a horse-drawn carriage. She also remembered afternoons at the family estate on the edge of the city, walking around with her dog Soroca. She would have more dogs in the future; in fact, she always had dogs as pets, and later, when she opened in a play or film, "*tus perritas*" (your puppies) sent her telegrams of encouragement, via, no doubt, her mother.[10] She loved playing with her dolls but denied they had anything to do with a maternal instinct. Rather, she used them as actors in little plays she invented. As she put it, "My vocation as an actress comes from my first memories, how I would look at myself in front of the mirror, how I would smile or make faces, studying myself. In these moments, I was already acting."[11] This idyllic world of her early childhood came crashing to an end, however, in about 1910. As she noted in the 1966 interview, "I remember . . . the sudden Revolution that brought an *explosive* end to that peaceful existence."[12]

When revolutionary forces attacked Durango, her mother pulled her out of bed, hid her in a big basket, and then rushed her to the railroad station to catch the last train for Mexico City just ahead of arrival of the revolutionaries. As she described it, "We fled early in the morning with the other important people of Durango, because at the shout 'Here comes Pancho Villa!' everyone ran. They said that Villa was putting all the bankers into jail and that nobody ever saw them again. My mother fixed food for my father, who crossed the Sierra Madre Mountains on the way to the United States. We caught the last train from Durango to Mexico City."[13] Dolores recounted that they both dressed humbly to avoid attracting attention. They left behind toys, dog, orchards, "everything that until that instant had constituted my first small world."[14] She was able to bring along only a rag doll that she treasured for the rest of her life. Her father did not rejoin the family in Mexico City until almost two years had passed.

Del Río later claimed to remember seeing the women of the Revolution "wrapped in their shawls, the soldiers with their widebrimmed hats, their cartridge belts, their rifles, their ammunition, their horses. In the stations I encountered, at each stop, the Emilio Fernándezes, the Pedro Armendárizes with mustaches and white cotton pants, with whom I would later film . . . so many movies of the Revolution."[15] Ironically, the revolutionary forces that drove Dolores and her family out of Durango brought to the presidency her mother's cousin, Francisco Madero. An early memory of the years in the Mexican capital was of meeting the president, of sitting on his lap and being presented with a beautiful red balloon. She later recalled "the tender light" of his eyes, the light that indicated his love of "peace, justice, and beauty."[16] She also claimed to remember with horror the days in February of 1913 when Madero was betrayed and murdered amid violent disorders in Mexico City. According to her account, she and her family hid in the basement until the disorders ceased, and then came out to see broken windows and corpses spread around the streets.[17]

Two slightly different stories connect her extended family with the famous Mexican revolutionary Pancho Villa. Both involve a male relative, the owner of a hacienda where Villa was working under his own name, Doroteo Arango, and the rape or attempted rape of his sister, Martina. One version says it was on the estate of El Gorgojito, which belonged to Dolores's mother's family, the other that the attacker was none other than Dolores's grandfather and that the hacienda was Sombreretillo, but both agree that Villa shot at the rapist and then fled to a life of raiding and cattle rustling that eventually led him into the Revolution. Dolores herself was unwilling to address these rumors. Whatever the truth of these stories, Villa became a major figure in that great upheaval, and given his Durango origins and the significance of Dolores's family in the region, it is likely that there were connections of some sort between them in the prerevolutionary period.[18] Interestingly, as of 2009 a Wikipedia entry on Durango notes Pancho Villa and Dolores del Río as numbers one and two among Durango's most "notable people."[19]

Although the violence of the Revolution and the economic chaos that it spread caused significant financial reversals for the family, they continued to live well once they arrived in Mexico City. Their house was located at no. 8 Berlin Street, in the fashionable Juárez neighborhood. At that time, French culture was very much admired by the Mexican upper classes, and Dolores herself recalled that elite families would order special volumes from France at a small bookstore run by a Monsieur Buret at 14 Calle Cinco de Mayo.[20] Dolores, child of the upper classes, was sent to a boarding school run by French nuns. The school had been founded in 1903 and had already begun to serve an elite clientele. The Convent of San José was located in the Ribera de San Cosme, between the major thoroughfare of Insurgentes North and the street now called Dr. Atl, in honor of the well-known painter and revolutionary.[21] Dolores noted that she was confronted there with a "new world. I learned to adapt, to have friends and *responsibilities*." She was concerned, as an only daughter, that she might disappoint her parents.[22] Meanwhile, she was obtaining an education highly focused on France and its culture, and acquiring the language as well, as the instruction was entirely in French. According to one report, she was a little shy, perhaps because on arrival she spoke no French at all, but she immediately became attached to a Spanish teacher who was not a nun, a woman named Torres. She remembered her, years later, with great affection. By her own account, she spent most of her time trying to be invisible. Despite her rather fragile appearance, she was intelligent and reportedly had a great deal of backbone.[23] Certainly this seems to have been the case, as from the beginning of her career in films she took considerable interest in the details of every arrangement and was insistent in making her wishes known. But it was also said that she was a little embarrassed about her dark skin and slightly indigenous features.[24] Her cousin, the actress Andrea Palma, later recalled that Dolores was a sort of "ugly duckling" and said that their mothers worried that if they dressed the girls in pink they would look like "servants" and if in white, like "flies in milk."[25] If Dolores was self-conscious as a child about her skin color, she would discover on entering adolescence that in fact she was quite beautiful and that her dramatic coloring and lovely features, particularly her enormous dark eyes, were assets, not disadvantages. Her parents commissioned a portrait of her by the well-known artist Alfredo Ramos Martínez when she was about eleven years old, which showed clearly her incipient beauty. Dressed in pale pink and looking nothing like a servant, with lace and bows on her dress but no other ornaments to distract from her stately pose and fine features, the stunning woman she was to become could be discerned in the child.[26]

Dolores was also developing a great love for movies, which she considered a magical treat, and for the ballet. Her parents arranged for her to study with a woman named Felipa López, who taught her Spanish-style dances in particular, beginning, according to her recollection, when she was eight years old. This early encounter was lodged in her memory as of great significance. Her recollection was that Felipa was very old, but she herself recognized that this assessment probably reflected only her own youth. López's repertoire was largely Spanish—"jotas, sevillanas, zapateados . . ." Her mother also took her to see Anna Pavlova, sometime around 1919, and the effect of watching her dance *Swan Lake* and later of seeing the Argentine Antonia Mercé, perhaps during a visit to Spain with her parents or in 1917 when the famous ballerina visited Mexico City, persuaded her that she wanted to pursue a similar career. Naturally graceful, she was made even more so by her instruction. Although dancing was not considered a proper profession for a woman of her social status, her parents encouraged her, no

doubt thinking that she would give it up later to marry and follow a normal life for an upper-class Mexican woman. Her little successes as a dancer,
which were based on stories that she choreographed herself and designated
later as "ingenuous," pleased her mother as much as they pleased Dolores.
When she was dancing, she felt happy; if she was not, according to her own
account, she became timid and shy again. Later, after her marriage, her new
husband read her palm and told her, quite mistakenly, that an artistic career
was not indicated for her; she felt terribly disappointed.[27]

Adolescent stunner. Collection of Luciana Corres Tames. Reproduced by permission.

It was precisely her talent for dancing that brought her to the attention of her future husband. In July 1920, a group of women from Mexico City's upper class led by Doña Barberita Martínez del Río organized a benefit at the Teatro Esperanza Iris for a local hospice. This refuge, described as "an asylum for the terminally ill," was founded by a Frenchwoman, Louise Dauverre, who had been governess to some of the Martínez del Río children, including a bachelor son, Jaime. Dolores, whose dance studies were known in those circles, was asked to participate in this charity performance. Of course, she needed her parents' permission, but it is said they agreed after finding out what the nuns thought, and the nuns thought it was fine. Jaime Martínez del Río y Vinent, at age thirty-four one of the most eligible bachelors in Mexican high society, served as one of the two artistic directors for "The Cruel Orchid," a pantomime in two acts divided into six scenes, written largely by Joaquín García Pimentel, son of a renowned bibliographer and historian. Jaime was one of the two artistic directors. The accompanying music was from Grieg, Paderewsky, Kreisler, Chopin, and Rimsky-Korsakoff. Dolores played a character called "Una Doliente," the Sorrowing One. Her credit was the second listed, just after the "Princesa" or Princess, played by another young society woman. "Princess," however, was what she was in Mexican terms, if not in the particular role she was playing. Jaime himself had a part, "Principe Pugnacio," the Contentious Prince. Roberto Montenegro, who later became a very successful artist and who painted a stunning portrait of Dolores, did the scenery and costume designs. The program for this first public appearance is preserved in her own clipping archive, with a note in her hand saying, "My first program, Teatro Esperanza Iris, July 21, 1920."[28] Reports were that Dolores was charming. Interestingly, Montenegro would become involved in the developing Mexican movie industry in the late 1920s, as would fellow-artist Adolfo "Fito" Best Maugard, who would soon become Dolores's great promoter.[29] She was already in the midst of Mexico City's postrevolutionary cultural scene.

Excelsior, one of Mexico City's leading newspapers, confirmed the significance of the event. On the society page, it provided the major story, raving that "The spectacle offered last night in the Teatro Iris was stunning," "a complete success," with the sizable auditorium being "a brilliant sight, as there one found congregated the 'elite' of our society. . . ." Jaime wrote one of the sketches, "Harlequinade," which, the reporter gushed, was "interpreted by beautiful and distinguished young ladies of our society."

The performance was attended by important members of the diplomatic corps, among them George Summerlin of the United States, and Mexico City's finest—with the notable exception of major government officials. This gathering, quite clearly, was composed of members of Mexico's pre-revolutionary upper class, not the newly emerging government leaders of the postrevolution. The article noted that the "brilliant festival" ended after 2:00 A.M. Yet there were indications in the same journal that things were unsettled. Rebellion still loomed; on another page in the same newspaper, there was an announcement that Lucio Blanco, formerly a collaborator with the revolutionary forces who were now running the government, had reentered the country with a group of men with rebellion on their minds and was currently hiding in the northern state of Coahuila. Meanwhile, another story confirmed that the National Agrarian Commission was continuing to carry out land distributions to countryfolk and indigenous groups—a concern to those in attendance, as many of them based their wealth on rural landholdings, which were now imperiled. And only the day before, a fire had destroyed a warehouse full of cotton, with the news report raising the specter of foul play stemming from social unrest. The report would have indicated a direct threat to the Martínez del Ríos, as their own fortune was based largely on cotton-producing plantations.[30]

For the moment, however, Lolita and Jaime were mutually enchanted and apparently untroubled. Andrea Palma remembered that Jaime, on first seeing her lovely cousin, said "I will marry that woman or I will die." Dolores later characterized his attitude toward her as paternal. As for her feelings, she said she immediately admired him, that he was a "man of the world, he was courteous and attentive and represented, for me, a peaceful home. The difference in age did not seem inconvenient to me, on the contrary something positive, as it assured me protection. I was then, don't forget, very young." Palma rather cattily claimed that Dolores's response was that such a marriage would be convenient, since Jaime was a "fine actor and has a great deal of money," though, certainly, the fact that it would be a very good match could not possibly have eluded either Lolita or her parents. In fact, her family, even though clearly of the provincial elite, was not of the social stature or wealth of the Martínez del Ríos. Palma particularly emphasized the joy of Dolores's mother at the prospect of connections with a family associated with the Spanish nobility (not to mention "extra-rich") but also noted that Jaime's mother had considerable doubts. Still, despite her

obvious jealousy of her more beautiful and more successful cousin, Palma
loyally confirmed the age that Dolores claimed, saying she was fifteen and
not seventeen at the time.[31] Yet the teenager seemed genuinely fond of her
courtly older suitor; for her it was more than a marriage of convenience.

She later remembered listening to Jaime play the piano and sing to her
for hours, whiling away the Mexico City afternoons and evenings. They
soon fell in love, he apparently with her beauty and youth, she, as she later
recalled, with "his good taste, his exquisite gentlemanly manner, his admirable way with people."[32] Much of Jaime's life had been spent in Europe,
and he had been educated at Stoneyhurst in England. He was familiar with
Europe's aristocracy and had been raised to wealth and elegance. He fascinated her with his discussions of music, painting, travel, theater, and even
the emerging cinematic field. When Jaime declared his desire to marry the
lovely teenager, both families quickly acquiesced, her parents pleased that
she had made a good match with a reliable and wealthy individual, and the
Martínez del Ríos perhaps because of the rumors circulating about Jaime's
extended bachelorhood. In any case, Dolores was a good match, Jaime was
delighted, and they made an elegant couple.

The wedding, at 2:00 P.M. on April 11, 1921, was an enormous social
event. *Excelsior* referred to Jaime as a "caballero," that is, a real gentleman,
and Dolores as a "distinguida señorita," a distinguished young lady. Streets
in front of the elegant Concepción church were "substantially obstructed,
during the religious ceremony, by the hundreds of elegant carriages and automobiles of the families who attended." Further, the newspaper continued,
"it can be said that the [wedding] was the most important event in some
time, given the [social] standing of the couple." Again, as at her christening
years before, a high ecclesiastical official, this time a bishop, presided, and
the ambassadors of Argentina and Spain, the Duchess of Regla, and members of the Braniff, Icaza, Iturbide, and Lascuraín families, the cream of the
prerevolutionary elite, attended. The witnesses for the civil ceremony, which
followed the lunch and various receptions, included three marquises. Even
an incomplete list of the guests took up almost two columns of the newspaper. The elaborate gifts included antiques, crystal and silver, and works
of art. Dolores was showered with jewelry from her parents but particularly from Jaime and his family: necklaces and brooches and pendants and
other baubles, emeralds, pearls, rubies, sapphires, and especially diamonds.[33]

High-society bride. CEHM CARSO.

Honeymoon in Europe with Jaime. CEHM CARSO.

She and Jaime honeymooned briefly at the luxurious San Angel Inn, formerly the Hacienda de los Goyocochea in which the original buildings dated from 1692. In 1921 it was a hotel and restaurant catering to the Mexican elite and well-to-do foreign visitors. Also guests at the hotel were Mercedes Martínez del Río, Jaime's sister, and her husband Javier Cervantes, who had married three days earlier. Both couples then proceeded to New York City, where they stayed briefly, and then continued on to Spain, where they met Jaime's mother and his younger brother. They visited Santiago de Compostela, the great medieval pilgrimage site, and then rented a villa at Biarritz, the fashionable French resort on the Bay of Biscay, to rest up for a quiet month. Visits to Switzerland, Vienna, and Paris followed, and Dolores shopped at the fashion houses, ordering, among other purchases, a special gown from Patou. They then returned to Madrid, where they spent the winter of 1921–22. They were presented at the court of King Alfonso XIII, and Dolores danced for Queen Victoria Eugenie in a benefit for Spanish soldiers wounded in the war in Morocco.[34] It was not Dolores's first trip to Europe; she had gone earlier with her parents. Still, it must have been fabulous and fascinating, and it may have whetted her appetite for more public performing. She later indicated that she permitted Jaime to lead her around Europe as if she were a child, choosing her new wardrobe for her because of his "excellent taste." She said that Jaime, who was rapidly going bald, laughed when people mistook him for her father; she understood the mistake, as he dressed very conservatively but insisted on light and cheerful clothes for her. Those years, according to her, were very happy for both of them.[35]

Arriving back in Mexico, things were not so fabulous. Jaime, faced with economic reverses in his family, went to manage the landholdings that the Martínez del Ríos still held in the North. The couple lived at the Hacienda de Santa Lucía, located between Torreón and the city of Durango, where Dolores had grown up. But there were still disorders related to the Revolution in the area, and Dolores was photographed wearing bandoliers across her torso, perhaps mocking the danger. She rode horseback and read extensively, and she was also reported to have practiced a little homeopathic medicine on hacienda employees who sought her help. Still, the couple was bored and probably frightened. Jaime, as it happened, had little talent and less desire to manage the properties, and flooding led to loss of the cotton crop. Dolores called it the "cotton catastrophe."[36]

Lolita mocking the very real dangers at the Hacienda de Santa Lucía.
CEHM CARSO.

Finally, a new revolutionary movement led by Angel Flores pushed them back to Mexico City. It was the second time the Revolution had significantly changed her life, and it was surely a sign that Mexico would not return Dolores and Jaime to the prerevolutionary era of easy wealth and status. She no doubt welcomed the move, however, and she and Jaime resumed their intense urban social life. Still, they were living in somewhat reduced circumstances, and no elegant trips to Europe loomed on the horizon. She continued to dance from time to time, and apparently Jaime's family was untroubled as long as she was not performing commercially. She had bought beautiful dresses in Madrid and Paris on her honeymoon, and some of them provided a wardrobe for her entertainments. Dolores later remarked that these costumes "attracted a great deal of attention."[37] Yet the couple's circumstances were reduced. Palma, as well, remembered the changes in their lives; she too had been educated in convents, in her case by Spanish and English nuns; she reported later with some satisfaction, "This education marked us permanently. But I had the advantage over my cousin in that when I went to Hollywood I already knew English."[38]

Lolita's own chance to go to Hollywood came very soon. Jaime was well connected in the artistic circles of Mexico City, and the couple regularly saw these friends socially. One of them, Best Maugard, introduced them to a veteran actor, Edwin Carewe, who had become a Hollywood producer/director. Best Maugard probably met Jaime several years earlier in Paris; he returned to Mexico in 1923, moved into the Mexico City artistic elite, and renewed the friendship with Jaime when the latter came back to the capital city in 1924. As Dolores later described the meeting with Carewe, Best Maugard invited the Martínez del Ríos to his home to meet the director; at this time, she did not speak any English at all. The next day, Carewe and Best Maugard called at the couple's home, so that, according to Lolita, "Carewe could get to know a Mexican home." Best Maugard later indicated that he checked with Jaime before he brought Carewe around, an indication that Jaime was already thinking about a future for both his wife and himself in Hollywood films. Dolores danced to the music of Spanish composers Manuel de Falla and Isaac Albéniz, all in her interpretive style, while Jaime played the piano. Despite the fact that the director was in Mexico City on his honeymoon, Carewe was immediately enchanted with her and suggested that she come to California to try an acting career. He emphasized to her that she was the "female Rudolph Valentino," Valentino having attained a huge following as a dark and handsome leading man. He insisted that if she gave it a try, he would make her into a "great star." Best Maugard had to translate his English into Spanish, while Lolita giggled. The next day Carewe sent her a huge arrangement of flowers. She claimed that she was pleased to have the attention but did not think much about it, although perhaps she was being disingenuous. Jaime, however, was openly delighted that she was being flattered in this way.[39]

Carewe continued to implore them to come to Hollywood, even after his return to California, and eventually sent her a script to consider. Not only was he captivated with Lolita, he knew that there was a large and growing market for U.S. films in Latin America, demand almost equaling that of Europe, and a beautiful Mexican woman might help the market grow. Jaime was apparently the one who made the final decision; as Dolores put it, "Jaime himself took me to Hollywood." As she described the moment, rather unfortunately, "Hollywood was just getting started, and no one had yet committed suicide." As for Jaime's attitude, she described him as a "totally European man, who looked at everything new with interest. A European would certainly permit his wife to be an actress! And so Jaime did." As for his own ambitions, "he saw the possibilities for writing scripts for the movies, writing, decorating, painting, and he became enthusiastic." He recognized the significance of Hollywood in the developing movie industry, and if Dolores's beauty was the ticket into that world, he was willing to use it. Taibo claims that Best Maugard, Carewe, and Dolores's husband had already decided on the California adventure before Carewe ever came to the couple's home. Still, the decision held consequences. According to Dolores, "Of course, the Martínez del Río family was opposed, and all of Mexican society came down on us. The best families, along with the Martínez del Ríos, heaped an avalanche of criticism on us. It wasn't very important to Jaime, but to tell the truth, it affected me. Even before we went to Hollywood, they were tearing us into pieces."[40]

Her parents, or at least her mother, supported the pair in their ambitions; Dolores later emphasized the audacity that this backing required. As she commented many years later in an interview, "My mother was a courageous woman, determined; in spite of the fact that the family thought it was a bad idea that I go into movies in Hollywood, she supported me. You had to be very courageous in those years to let the daughter of a well-to-do family go into movies. My mother and I were a family scandal." [41] Dolores always publicly deemphasized her own courage in this situation, but clearly it was not easy for a very young woman who did not really speak the language to set off for a career in a foreign country against the wishes of her husband's powerful and socially prominent family. By becoming an actress, she would be moving beyond the boundaries set for proper and prominent wives of the Mexican elite, regardless of the wishes of her husband.

Dolores years later described Carewe as a pleasant man, already advanced in years when she met him, although he had served as a leading man in a large number of films earlier in his life.[42] Her relationship with the director would be complex. Jaime, in fact, seemed at that point pleased with the man's admiration for Dolores's beauty and did not sense a potential rivalry for his wife's affections. Neither of the Martínez del Ríos completely understood that the strategy Carewe had in mind for them was both personally and professionally risky, given the ambiguous and ambivalent racial status of Mexicans in the United States. By presenting her as a romantic lead, the female counterpart to Valentino, he was pushing limits that were largely unstated but existed in a kind of subterranean connection to indigenous peoples; Mexicans of European descent were coded as white, while those with indigenous blood were considered just that, Indians. The trick would be to present her as white and make the designation stick.

Carewe himself was a native of Gainesville, Texas, and *his* birthdate is not at issue—May 5, 1883—though his name was actually Jay Fox. He was of indigenous background himself, though he had left this identity behind years before, adopting a stage name that sounded British. He was approximately twenty years Dolores's senior and an age mate of Jaime's, not quite as advanced in years as Dolores implied. He first acted in the theater and later went into the movies, directing and acting in films starting in 1912. In 1914, he had begun directing films for several studios including Metro and First National; he also had his own production company. He was familiar with Mexico from his Texas experience and had made films in which Mexico and Mexicans figured in the story, particularly *The Bad Man*, which he directed in 1923. The movie, despite a not particularly flattering view of the country and its people, was shown with some success south of the border, and Carewe had entrée in the capital city, just when many members of the Mexican cultural elite were looking at film as the great new artistic medium. Previously divorced, he had married Mary

Akin right before their trip south. They traveled with another Hollywood couple, Claire Windsor and Bert Lytell, actors recently seen in Carewe's film *A Son of the Sahara*.[43]

Although later the story ran that Dolores herself had been surprised and reluctant to make the move into a more public life, in fact painter and intellectual Best Maugard had been squiring her around Mexico City for some time, introducing her to artists and photographers who would be able to further her career through their images. Perhaps she yearned for something beyond the rather restricted life of a typical young upper-class matron in Mexico City, and as Braudy notes above, "the theater of modern fame is frequently an alternative to the more restrictive roles of the social world."[44] Among others, Best Maugard presented her to the well regarded U.S. photographer Edward Weston, who at that time was in Mexico City with his assistant/lover, the fascinating Tina Modotti. Weston noted in his *Daybooks* "Best-Maugard [sic] in today with a stunning Mexican girl, Dolores del Río, a real beauty. Suggested I photograph her, think I shall."[45] Weston and Modotti were great friends with Diego Rivera and his wife, the vivacious Guadalupe Marín, and Best Maugard escorted Dolores and her cousin María Asúnsolo to at least one gathering at Weston and Modotti's home. Rivera himself used Dolores as a model for the abstract concept "justice" for a huge mural that José Vasconcelos, the minister of education, had commissioned for the National Preparatory School. Dolores, proper upper-class young woman that she was, was fully clothed. Still, her association with the other models, who included the irrepressible Nahui Olín, the former Carmen Mondragón, as the concept "erotic poetry," and with Rivera's new art itself, caused a bit of scandal. Olín and Modotti both posed for nude photographs at about this time, and Modotti lived openly with Weston, a married man, while both women were rumored to be among Rivera's many lovers.[46] When Rivera's mural was officially inaugurated in 1923, Dolores's family did not attend, "because they were ashamed that I had been part of such nonsense." Rivera himself, recently returned from studying art in Europe, was, within the postrevolutionary climate in Mexico, the center of a group of artists and writers who simply did not observe the standards of art and conduct that prevailed within Dolores's social set before the Revolution. He had begun to establish an artistic group that would challenge Mexican society.[47] Interestingly, in his own notes about the mural, he referred to the figure of "justice" for which Lolita modeled as "Wearing white clothing, dark skin, of a completely indigenous type."[48]

Her willingness to pose, despite her position in high society, shows that Dolores herself was already moving away from a traditional role. Other women, such as the actress Lupe Marín, who married Rivera in 1922; Frida Kahlo, who at just this time suffered a horrible accident and who would later marry Rivera herself; and Concha Michel, who became a folksinger and political radical, were moving away as well.[49] All three women would become Dolores's long-term friends. These early friendships with both men and women would lead to Dolores's association with the leaders—artists, writers, filmmakers—of the Mexican high cultural scene for the rest of her life. Yet the shift from prerevolutionary social and artistic ideals, in the immediate aftermath of the Revolution, was by no means always approved of by the social class into which she was born and still less in the even higher society into which she married. Jaime initially agreed to the Hollywood plan and encouraged it because of his own ambitions to be a screenwriter and because his family's fortunes in Mexico were so negatively affected by the violence and socioeconomic turmoil of the Revolution. During the revolutionary decade, Mexico lost more than a million persons, of all social classes, to migration to the United States. Perhaps a move to Los Angeles, facilitated by the beauty of his wife, would help Martínez del Río recoup the family fortune, or at a minimum gain entrance into the artistic career he desired.

Though the planned move to Hollywood caused difficulties with the Martínez del Río family, perhaps these in-laws thought it might help with the financial situation. The Mexican movie scene was no alternative; whereas national cinema began to develop in the years before the Revolution, the violent movement nearly eliminated anything but documentary films. Although both President Alvaro Obregón and his close associate and successor as president Plutarco Elías Calles both were fascinated with film, and the former in particular did much to promote the arts during his administration, the era of government involvement in sponsoring cinematic production had not yet arrived.[50] Only a handful of Mexican fiction films would be made between the end of the Revolution and the late 1920s, when Sergei Eisenstein, the Russian filmmaker, came to Mexico to make ¡Que Viva México! But involvement in Mexican films, which largely developed out of the popular tent shows that showed one-reelers in the countryside, would no doubt have been seen as even more scandalous than going to Hollywood.[51] Yet a cousin of Dolores's from Durango, Ramón Novarro, was already making his way in the film capital, and other members of both families, including Palma, traveled north of the border and into the cinema industry.

At about the same time Dolores and Jaime were considering the move, rumors circulated that Dolores was pregnant, and shortly thereafter further rumors claimed that she had lost the child in life-threatening circumstances. These reports were greeted rather skeptically by Mexico City society, where gossip about Jaime's sexual preference for men was common. According to Dolores's later account, her physician told her she could not safely have children at that time; as she described it, "In my first years of marriage, nature prevented me from becoming a mother. I put aside that potentially traumatic circumstance by making films."[52] In fact, it is unclear whether Dolores and Jaime wanted children at that time or at all, or even that they were involved in a sexual relationship.

According to Dolores, Jaime viewed the Hollywood opportunity as a kind of a lark. "My husband seemed happy, I would even say entertained, getting ready for an adventure. He knew about film, though I didn't. . . . He and Fito [Best Maugard] spoke about films and what we would find in Hollywood; I listened amazed, with my mouth wide open." But her enthusiasm was mitigated with a nervousness about the future: "But sometimes at night, I was frightened; not because of the family criticism, but because I had never acted. My trips with Jaime . . . had removed much of my sense of provincialism and I had been in important dances and worn elegant gowns, but Hollywood. . . ." Yet, she recalled, their economic circumstances became very difficult, even to the point of selling her automobile and some of the jewelry that had been given to her—as she recalled, a pearl necklace, perhaps one received from Jaime himself at the time of their wedding, and a diadem of sapphires.[53]

In the event, it was Tina Modotti and not Edward Weston who made the publicity portraits that Dolores took with her to California. In fact, these photographs, which appeared in film magazines, would be the first that Modotti published outside Mexico, and within Mexico they appeared in *El Universal Ilustrado*. The photos showed Dolores dressed elegantly, posed gracefully, indeed a universal image of a stunningly beautiful upper-class woman in 1925 and a striking contrast to the realistic photographs of ordinary Mexicans that Modotti would become known for later.[54] Modotti herself, despite her working-class Italian background, had appeared in several Hollywood films before coming to Mexico; she was regularly cast as exotic, highly sexualized, and overly dramatic. Her roles exploited her physical appearance in ways that seem to have offended Tina's own sense of dignity, and she seems never to have been tempted to return to movies. As Weston put it after encountering one of Tina's movies showing in Mexico, "We had a good laugh over the villainous character she portrayed. The brains and imagination of our movie directors cannot picture an Italian girl except with a knife in her teeth and blood in her eye."[55] It is certainly not too much to suppose that Tina gave Dolores advice on how to survive as a beautiful foreign woman in that milieu, and her experience may have given further impetus to Jaime's later concerns that Dolores *not* be sexualized and exoticized in ways that were unbecoming to her social position. As for Modotti, she herself found Mexico a country where she, as a woman, could take a respected place within the artistic community as a photographer. She remained for several years after Weston returned to the United States, until her left-wing politics caused her expulsion from the country in 1929.[56]

Meanwhile, the controversy about the Hollywood ambitions of the young Martínez del Ríos swirled through the highest Mexican society. Jaime and Dolores sought support from others of their social set, while Edwin Carewe, back in Los Angeles, sent cablegrams imploring them to come north. Finally, he sent along the script of Dolores's first film, and this gesture finally persuaded the couple to accept. Meanwhile, Eduardo Iturbide, yet another member of the prerevolutionary elite who had served as regent of Mexico City during the presidency of Victoriano Huerta, told Dolores not to hesitate. Iturbide, noted as "the great arbiter of Mexican society at that time," and whom Dolores remembered as a dear friend, encouraged her: "Your decision is magnificent. I will give you a grand goodbye party and the most important figures in society will attend."[57] In fact, Mexico City's elite flocked to his home for the event, and the report was that invitations were in high demand. Dolores was said to be beautifully in command of the occasion, dressed to the nines. The host prognosticated to the guest of honor, "I predict your great success in Hollywood, Dolores." At the same time, he presented her with a gift from Cartier. When the couple finally departed from his home at eight o'clock in the morning, Iturbide commented "Now we will see who dares to close the doors of their homes to you." Mexico's upper class would indeed be forced to accept the choice that Dolores and Jaime had made. The couple packed their bags and left for Los Angeles.[58] Still, issues of reputation regarding various kinds of gender norms and expectations would arise persistently and negatively for some time in their Hollywood–Mexico interactions.

The train trip was a long one. Five days later, on August 25, 1925, they arrived in the city that would be so important to Dolores. Jaime spent his time on the train writing a movie script.

3 Hollywood Baby Beauty

> Dolores's triumph in Hollywood is undeniable. . . . Her image is
> to be seen everywhere; the great photographers lay siege to her
> *native beauty.*
>
> Carlos Monsiváis, "Dolores del Rio"[1]

> Advertising is the keynote of success in big business.
>
> Edwin Carewe, speech to Los Angeles
> Advertising Club[2]

THE CONVERSION OF "DOLORES DEL RIO" into a celebrity, and an upper-class celebrity at that, began immediately. An early U.S. newspaper article on Lolita, published just over a week after the Martínez del Ríos arrived in Los Angeles, reported that "Forsaking society life in Mexico City, Senora Dolores del Rio, wife of one of the richest landholders in the southern republic, has just arrived in Hollywood and will enter motion pictures." After announcing that she would be in Edwin Carewe's next film, it averred that she was "also considered one of Mexico's most beautiful women, and has had gowns named after her by Paris designers." The article then went on to detail the story of her discovery by Carewe in Mexico, emphasizing the difficulties of winning over both her own family and her husband's. Jaime was designated as a graduate of the University of Madrid and an attorney, not a prospective actor/scriptwriter, a detail that played up European as opposed to Mexican connections and underemphasized his cinematic ambitions. Dolores, not Jaime, was the obvious focus of attention. Lest the reader misunderstand her class position, she was described as moving in "the most exclusive circles in Mexican society," and the headline read "Forsakes Mexico's Elite for Films." Carewe was making sure in his publicity releases that Dolores's high status was clear from the very beginning. In a purely Hollywood touch, however, Carewe was quoted as saying that "Señora Dolores is a fine type for the screen. She is 5 feet 5 inches high and weighs 115 pounds." Very likely, this emphasis on her bodily statistics startled both Dolores and Jaime. Such a description, especially in a newspaper, would have been considered shockingly crude in their Mexican social circle. In any case, very shortly Jaime would become nervous about the focus on his wife's physical attributes. The couple, the report said, had taken up residence at the Afton Arms Apartments in Hollywood.[3] In fact, they stayed there only briefly, moving quickly into a bungalow that was somewhat more comfortable but probably a rather simple accommodation. Carewe's first contract with Dolores paid her only $250 a week, peanuts for the Martínez del Ríos. Nevertheless, it was a salary and it was hers.[4]

The photograph that was used to illustrate the September 2 story was instructive as well. Lolita was shown with her dark hair pulled away from her face, her eyes looking luminously upward. Her complexion was shown as very light, her mouth slightly less ample than it was in fact, and her rather broad nose almost entirely brushed out. Illustrations and text made her white, European, aristocratic, sophisticated. This vision would continue to be played out in her public persona, although not always on the screen, for as long as Carewe continued as her mentor. Her screen roles were somewhat more down-to-earth, and her beautiful dark skin was highlighted in screen tests, films, and personal appearances.

The couple arrived in Los Angeles on August 26, 1925, when, if we were to believe the 1906 birthdate, Dolores had just turned nineteen. In fact, she was just twenty-two days past her twenty-first birthday, but the publicity spin was already beginning, the better to extend the imagined years of her youth in which she would be able to play young heroines and romantic roles. Carewe arranged a screen test for her that was filmed just a day after she had arrived; it emphasized her exotic appearance—"exotic" being the quality he accentuated in selling her to filmmakers and to the public. For the occasion, he engaged a makeup artist and acquired several beautiful white evening gowns of classic design. These floated about her body in a sensual fashion and highlighted her beautiful skin. The filming went on for almost twenty-four hours, exhausting Lolita, who walked, posed, danced, and performed in scene after scene. When it ended, she was in a state of collapse. Still, she was unable to rest until she had seen the results. Carewe carefully edited the test itself; when it was ready, it was a success. According to one of her biographers, she was seen to be beautiful, erotic, and glamorous, a natural for the camera.[5]

Just a few days later, Edwin swept her into her first film, *Joanna*, which he himself was directing at First National. For Dolores, accustomed to dancing when she felt like it and to making up her own stories and choreography, the filming was very tense. Though she found the other cast members pleasant, they paid little attention to her, and her lack of English was a problem. A special friend, however, was the costumer, Peggy Hamilton. She invited Dolores to her parties and counseled her on her responsibilities in regard to publicity and other matters. Carewe was also constantly encouraging and insisted on her having training not only in acting but also in English (despite the fact that talking films were still three or four years away). Still, frustrated and isolated because of language problems and her feeling that it would be a humiliation to return to Mexico, she cried every night. Jaime, she said, was "as always, a little bit in the clouds. He was living in his dreams." Later, she commented that only her pride kept her from returning; that quality, she said, "is like a sword that one carries inside, like a backbone." She reflected often on Eduardo Iturbide's prophecy that she would succeed. Still, she was not entirely comfortable in her career until she had several hit movies to her credit.[6]

Carewe engaged one of the best-known publicists in Hollywood, Harry D. Wilson, to promote his protégée. Wilson, quite likely, was responsible for the article mentioned above. According to Hollywood lore, he and "Eddie," as Carewe was known to his friends, also decided on the name that Dolores would use—Dolores Del Rio—with the "d" in uppercase rather than the lowercase it would normally have taken in Spanish, and the accent over the "i" removed. The Mexican version of the story insists that her friend and promoter, painter and archaeologist Adolfo Best Maugard, was the one who chose the name. The fact that Edward Weston called her "Dolores del Rio" while she was still in Mexico City indicates that the Mexican version was correct. Yet it is indicative of Carewe's desire for influence that he claimed to have given her even her new name, complete with orthographical changes that made it inaccurate in Spanish. It symbolically separated her from Mexico, and to some degree from her husband. Later, when Dolores returned to Mexico to take up the second phase of her career, she changed the offending "d" back again and reinstated the accent.

For the time being, however, it seemed that Carewe had taken over much of her very identity, converting her into Dolores Del Rio, the Hollywood star. He would take care of everything. Quickly, his attitude began to alienate Jaime, and over a longer period of time, Lolita herself. For the time being, however, she continued being the perfect student that she had been at the convent, working hard and learning her craft, not to mention learning English.[7] Eddie, for his part, emphasized her exotic attributes, hoping to develop his young protégée in a similar manner to Valentino, who played everything from bullfighters to East Indian rajahs. Valentino's big breakthrough as a dashing romantic star came in 1921, of course, in Paramount's *The Sheik*. Interestingly, Valentino had some difficulty keeping his personal attitudes detached from those of his character and made a point of distancing himself from the anti-Arab racism in the film. He also complained about problems with the censors interfering with his steamy lovemaking.[8]

Both issues—race and sexuality—foreshadowed difficulties Dolores herself experienced in later years. Sometime in her first year in Hollywood she met "the dark lover," then at the height of his celebrity and popularity. His rise to fame had been stunning, based largely on how female audiences—and sometimes men—responded to his screen images. As one of his biographers describes it, "his capacity [was] to stir in women and men the most intimate erotic and spiritual fantasies, and to pique the possessive feelings that are usually reserved for living lovers." Surely it was the hope of Carewe that Dolores would have the same kind of appeal to the opposite sex.[9]

Lolita herself remembered Valentino as "the most beautiful man I have ever known. He would arrive at parties dressed in the best tailored garments from London . . . and all the women would faint as he passed. He had enormous charm and a certain kind of softness—almost tenderness—characteristic of the Latin man. Valentino never defrauded his public. As a living legend, he never broke the illusion that thousands of women had regarding him."[10] Elsewhere, she noted that he was charming and entertaining and had a "a marvelous intelligence." She said that he was like James Dean in his love of speed, wanting to be everywhere at once, with "a woman to conquer or a friendship to cultivate." She remembered that he collected automobiles and horses, his spectacular Great Dane always by his side.[11]

Swarms of publicity greeted Lolita's arrival in the film capital, even though she had not yet been seen on the screen. In the *Los Angeles Times* alone, photographs and stories about her were ubiquitous. In particular,

Grace Kingsley, who would cover her for some time, mentioned Dolores often in her column, referring to "that social princess from Mexico" as having "the beauty of a Madonna."[12] Publicist Wilson did his job well. She was seen in the gossip columns attending luncheons with other actresses and figures from the screen industry, such as Peggy Hamilton, mentioned above, along with the wives of producers and directors.[13] Her upper-class status and Mexican political connections were constantly emphasized by the news stories, as her public relations agent and Carewe worked hand-in-hand with the reporters who wrote the gossip columns and covered the industry. On September 15, she was positioned as about to be an "ambassadress for the films to her country through the medium of a series of articles on her experiences for the Mexican press." If this latter project came to pass, I have not encountered these writings. In the same publication, she was quoted as eager to get rid of the "prejudices created by the early producers who were in the habit of typing Mexicans as villainous in their films," a theme that she would later return to and that resonated with Valentino's concerns about racism in the movies. And she made appearances in fashion shows and benefits, emphasizing her upper-class status.[14]

Then, on September 28, 1925, just a little over a month after her arrival in Los Angeles, she was featured as one in a series of caricatures of prominent Mexicans that appeared in a large spread in the *Los Angeles Times*. They were drawn by artist Miguel Covarrubias, another Mexican who had arrived on the New York scene in 1923 at the tender age of nineteen. The artist/illustrator/caricaturist was approximately her actual if not admitted age; he was already enjoying great success working at *Vanity Fair* and had sold his work to many other U.S. publications. Dolores appeared along with six male government officials—including the president, Plutarco Elías Calles; her friends and mentors Adolfo Best Maugard and Diego Rivera, described as artists; and one other movie actor, her own cousin, Ramón Novarro. There she was, a public figure, the only woman featured among the men who were running her own country, two male artists, and the one Mexican actor who had come to the attention of the U.S. public—and she had not yet appeared in a single film.[15] She was already becoming a celebrity, the very image of a successful Mexican, through publicity alone.

In *Joanna*, she played Carlotta de Silva, a predatory female who might have been Spanish—or Brazilian—and who did her best to thwart the honest desires of the main characters. Of course, Carlotta failed, but Lolita was very beautiful as the villainess. Characteristically for the time, filming lasted only a period of weeks, ending on October 19, 1925, and she gathered a quantity of photos for her album, inscribed from her co-stars and co-workers. All were warm, with the one from Carewe full of happy auguries for her future.[16] Wilson, the publicist, continued doing his part as well. The press reported hyperbolically, and no doubt at Wilson's urging, that "Dolores Del Rio," soon to appear in *Joanna*, was the "First Lady" of Mexican society. She was presented as an heiress with $50,000 worth of shawls and combs in her collection, perhaps the wealthiest woman in Mexico given her husband's fortune and that of her parents.[17] Although these assertions were far from the truth, the publicity line had been established.

On December 6, her photograph was prominently featured in a *Los Angeles Times* spread entitled "From Sunny Southern Climes." Despite the headline, only one of the other women featured was from south of the U.S. border; the other three were European. Del Río was the only one to appear in the full-length shot, right in the center of the page, and the caption referred to her "interesting and unusual beauty." Once again, she was described as having "to desert a society career in Mexico" for her work in Carewe's film. The short blurb on the five actresses was focused on her and the "sensational interest" her discovery had created. The text closed, "The recruiting of newcomers from Mexico, notably, appears to mark a new phase." She was wrapped in a long, flower-embroidered shawl, with her hair pulled back tightly, emphasizing her eyes. Yet she was, to all physical appearances, one with the European women, though more strikingly displayed.[18] Two days later the paper announced that she was one of thirteen starlets (including Fay Wray of Canada, who would become her lifelong friend; Joan Crawford; and Mary Astor) who had been chosen to appear at the Western Association of Motion Picture Advertisers Ball as one of the Baby Stars of 1926, an important event sponsored by the screen publicists themselves.[19] Even what she wore was becoming news, with the elegance of her clothing emphasized; another society story, at about the same time, insisted that she "was like a mysterious black orchid, even at noontide, in her black velvet gown . . . the entire costume designed by Breen."[20]

Unfortunately, when *Joanna* premiered just a few days later, Dolores and her husband, her parents, and other friends and family members who attended discovered that her role had been reduced to only a few scenes and, according to Ramón, that her credit said Dorothy Del Rio, though this detail may be apocryphal and reflect a certain discomfort over the new version of her name. She glossed over her disappointment by indicating to her family that such, after all, was the way of the movies, but she was distressed at how her performance had been cut down all the same.[21] The *New York Times* review, written by Mordaunt Hall, had her name correct in the list of the characters, indicating that perhaps the credits were accurate after all, though the review itself was nothing more than a description of the plot, about a "Silly Heiress." The advertising for the film, which was showing at the Mark Strand Theater, did not mention a single actress or actor, focusing only on the Strand Symphony Orchestra, which provided the music.[22]

Dolores, now called by her nickname Lolita even by her English-speaking friends, was particularly disappointed in *Joanna* and blamed Carewe, who had led her to expect so much more. The day after the premiere, she had a long conversation with him and was assured that she was charming in the film and looked lovely, that *Joanna* was after all her first film, and that he expected her to have a long career. He himself, he insisted, had taken out all of the scenes in which she did not look her best. Though she was initially unsure about staying in Hollywood, he persuaded her that her second role, in *High Steppers*, would be better. Because it would start filming on December 23, however, she would have no time for rest during the Christmas holidays. Unsurprisingly, Jaime and Dolores celebrated with the Carewes, by which time *Joanna* was already a success in New York. On New Year's Eve, 1925, the two couples drank to her future stardom.[23]

The Mexican reception of the film was favorable, another good sign. It opened on March 6, 1926, in the then-important Salón Rojo in Mexico City, presumably with her name spelled correctly. Dolores received third place in the credits, not bad for a newcomer and a reflection of how the producer hoped to use her to appeal to a Mexican audience. A review in *Revista de Revistas*, written by Jaime Torres Bodet using his pseudonym Celuloide, indicated that perhaps Dolores was not at her best in the particular role. Cautiously, he suggested that although he was not sure she deserved something better, he *was* sure "that she deserved something else." He went on, "She's a beginner, and it is clear that she's a beginner, but haven't we seen this as well in many other actresses who are now stars?"[24] This film may have been the first to ignite Torres Bodet's interest in, and indeed fascination with, del Río; he wrote a novella a few years later in which, though disguised, she was clearly the model for his movie actress "Piedad Santelmo," the focus of obsession for his young male protagonist.[25]

Despite this apparent setback, at least in terms of her Hollywood career she remained in the public eye. In particular, her WAMPAS selection led to a series of performances and parties sponsored by the association of press agents. Indeed, such publicity seemed to be the purpose of the whole proceedings. These included a ceremony in which she and her fellow Baby Stars paraded in front of a huge audience. Her gown by Lelong was white, the color that most emphasized her dark skin and exotic appearance. When she appeared, the audience was silent, a silence that lasted for as long as she was walking across the stage. Frightened by the lack of response, she rushed backstage and was on the point of tears when a huge ovation broke out. Fay Wray pushed her back out on stage, while the audience, which was beginning to rise to its feet, continued to applaud. She paraded gracefully back and forth across the stage for an additional seven minutes until the ovation finally ended.[26] Isabel Stuyvesant's column, "Society of Cinemaland," gave Dolores by far the longest mention in her coverage of the event, reporting that "Dolores Del Rio lived up quite to the expectation of her Spanish beauty in her Mexican costume—or was it French—for Mexico City, you know, always has the latest from Paris. At any rate her skirt was so long it all but touched the floor. There was a red rose in her black sleek hair and her gown was a wonderful brocade and lovely lace."[27] Stuyvesant's report contrasted with others that claimed Dolores wore flowing chiffon, but the important issue is that her beauty had been noted and the publicity kept coming. Meanwhile Jaime, who stayed at home working on his scripts during the filming, had achieved absolutely nothing and seemed to have few possibilities, either as a writer or as an actor.

High Steppers, her next film, showcased del Río considerably more than *Joanna* had. This time she obtained the third credit even in the English version, right after co-stars Lloyd Hughes and Mary Astor. Unfortunately, the movie led to a serious disagreement between Jaime and Edwin. Lolita had already begun another film, *The Whole Town's Talking*, when in March 1926 Jaime saw the preview of *High Steppers*. Edwin had been taking up most of her time, and Jaime was no doubt feeling a little frustrated about his own lack of success and very likely jealous. Still, his difficulties with Carewe had a reasonable basis given the breaks with traditional female roles (both personal and professional) her career was requiring, and he had apparently been unable to make his wishes prevail in discussions with his wife's new mentor. This time, he decided to put his concerns in writing.

His anger was apparent from the first line, as he wrote:

My Dear Eddie: I am communicating with you by letter because I have learned by past experiences that I am incapable of coping with you in a personal conference, not only because English is not my mother tongue but also because of my deep respect and grateful affection for you personally. It becomes necessary now, however, that I insist on the rights of my wife and myself. My purpose is so decided that I do not feel like entering into an argument under the circumstances.

High Steppers obliged Jaime, he said, to face his responsibilities to his wife and her family as well as to his own "good name." Invoking Dolores's social position in Mexico and her religious convictions, he protested that some of the scenes in the film were "suggestive," to his horror even provoking laughter during the screening. He reminded Carewe that their original contract stipulated she would under no circumstances be required to perform in any way that was "obscene or lewd or which would tend to reflect upon her reputation, character, religion and social standing." His rhetoric intensified as he reached the end of the communication: "I cannot and will not brook the depicting of my wife in a character the obscenity and lewdness of which is without doubt. The releasing of the picture in its present form would do permanent harm." The film would "fatally injure her standing in her chosen profession," he protested. Nevertheless, he closed with an insistence on the esteem in which he claimed to hold Carewe.[28] But it was clear that such a closing was only a concession to Jaime's cultivated good manners. The man was incensed and humiliated.

It was no doubt a comfort to Jaime that Carl Laemmle rather than Carewe was directing his wife in her next project, the comedy *The Whole Town's Talking*. In a wonderful irony, the story cast her as Rita Renault, a Hollywood superstar/beauty married to a film director, in which she spent most of her time on screen escaping from the attentions of another ardent suitor. The focus was on the comedian Edward Everett Horton, but Dolores showed herself very good at comedic timing and playful acting in this farce. She was not only beautiful but also enticing and funny, and she did a great deal of rolling of her enormous eyes and of dashing through bedrooms. Laemmle himself, a film magnate of the silent era, had specifically requested Dolores for the role of Rita, and she was a hit, if still a minor one.[29] Her fashions, in this film, reflected a very elegant version of a style that was emerging in Mexico among young, often working women: a cloche hat with her not-yet-bobbed hair concealed in it, short skirts, very high heels.[30]

The respite from Carewe's attentions was short; unsurprisingly, even before she finished that film, he had another ready for her. It was *Pals First,* which began shooting on March 29, less than a month after he received Jaime's letter. A peculiar incident rubbed salt in Jaime's wounds. First National distributed a photograph of Dolores's disembodied face, a high Spanish-style comb in her hair. She looked exotic and beautiful, and her image was surrounded by six photographs of the male stars attached to the studio. A big question mark in the center queried who her "Great Love" actually was. Of course, her love at this time was Jaime, and it may have been merely a publicity stunt, but Jaime was desperately (though unsuccessfully) opposed to the campaign. It seemed calculated to offend and alienate him, and in fact the offense was probably deliberate. More and more, Jaime "was being converted into a kind of prince consort" and shoved into the background by Carewe and others around Dolores.[31]

Paco Ignacio Taibo relates that *Pals First* was so disappointing to First National that the studio ceased to provide Dolores with roles, although she appeared in the publicity shot for the film in the *Los Angeles Times* in a picture layout called "Girls for Any Taste." She was dressed as a lovely bride, with the caption "A new type of femininity has entered films with Dolores Del Rio. Her Mexican beauty adds an exotic note as contrast." It did not explain in contrast to what. According to Taibo, Carewe was furious with the studio's attitude and threatened to leave, taking Dolores with him. His protests were unavailing, and as a result, he did leave. A newspaper report noted his departure and the fact that Dolores, under personal contract to him, had left as well and was about to do a film, or possibly films, for Fox Studios. Whether or not the story of disagreements with First National is correct, this period seems to have been difficult and anxious for the young woman, as Taibo recounts.[32]

In a series of later interviews, Dolores reported to Taibo that in Hollywood at this time, whenever a scene was about to start, musicians would begin to play in order to drown out the noise of the cameras and to help the actors relax. She said that these moments "made me want to cry." And she did cry, though at home at night rather than on the set. The tensions between Edwin and Jaime continued to mount; her husband, after all, was himself a kind of father-figure and protector, and Edwin was usurping the role. Not only did Carewe work with her constantly, he maintained an active publicity effort on her behalf in Mexico as well as in the United States, an effort that was not always agreeable to Jaime. Attention to both sides of the border was important; everyone involved wished for Dolores to remain in good standing in her home country.

For example, a strange article appearing in the Mexico City press on September 13, 1926, reported that Dolores was *not* implicated in the rebellion of General Enrique Estrada against the government of President Plutarco Elías Calles, contrary to rumors saying she had helped in its financing. Estrada was arrested by authorities in southern California early in August when he tried to lead a group of 150 armed men across the border into Baja California. Calles himself sent her a telegram on September 14, thanking her for a message denying any connection.[33] She also reached out to the Mexican community by serving as the "Queen of the Fiesta" for a gala ball opening five days of celebration highlighted by Mexican Independence Day, September 16. Former President Alvaro Obregón was reported to be coming to town for the event, although if he did attend his visit was not as well publicized as Lolita's presence at the dance. There was a strong sense of noblesse oblige about her participation. She and Jaime were shown with other Mexican notables in the *Los Angeles Times* photograph on September 13, looking happy and vividly elegant.[34] Further, she continued to be involved principally with Hollywood's elite; almost simultaneously, Grace Kingsley again reported, she was given a "Mexican Luncheon à la Hollywood" by the wife of director Clarence Brown. Kingsley reported that Lolita looked like "the Madonna come to life," albeit in a Paris gown.[35]

Dolores's career was just about to take off, regardless of the problems between Jaime and Edwin, any difficulties with First National, and Mexican political problems. The public reception of her first three films had been strong, and she was attracting attention—particularly from male audiences, who, in a survey, indicated she was the new star they would most like to know more about. Intriguingly, in mid-1926 she was being considered as a co-star for Valentino, in a film to be based on the life of Benvenuto Cellini. The film was never made because of Valentino's untimely death on August 23, following unsuccessful surgery to correct a gastric ulcer and a case of appendicitis. Newspaper reports of his funeral—with admittance limited to those with tickets—indicated that Dolores would attend.[36]

Meanwhile, Lolita also attracted the attention of another director, Raoul Walsh, with whom she would enjoy a lifelong friendship. He had already gained fame in Hollywood and was reported to be enchanted with Mexico. Walsh had the rights to make a film, through the Fox Company, of the hit stage play by Laurence Stallings and Maxwell Anderson, *What Price Glory?* It was a World War I epic, and Walsh wanted Dolores for the female lead, the French girl Charmaine, despite some skepticism

Lolita and her co-star, Victor McLaglen, in her first big hit, *What Price Glory?* Paul Hutton Collection. Reproduced by permission.

at the studio. Edmund Lowe and Victor McLaglen would be her male co-stars, vying for her cinematic affections. There were good box office reasons for Fox's interest in casting a Mexican woman in a prominent part; Mexico, in the wake of World War I and its own revolution, was becoming reestablished as a very important market for U.S. films. Winfield Sheehan, at that time vice president of Fox, had been the head of the studio's distribution office in Mexico between 1920 and 1924, and he no doubt realized that Dolores would be very attractive to audiences south of the border. At this time, Latin America was beginning to challenge Europe as the second-largest market for Hollywood cinema. In the years 1926 to 1927, Argentina was the strongest market in Latin America and the fourth in the world; Brazil was second and sixth, respectively, and Mexico third and eighth. In the later months of 1927, Latin America overcame the European lead and gained first place. Sheehan was certainly aware of these trends, and he seems to have taken a hand in making sure that she got the role. For similar reasons, other Mexican actresses such as Lupe Vélez, Raquel Torres, and Delia Magaña would get opportunities in U.S. films, though none would achieve the luster of del Río. Lolita herself commented that she was so delighted to get the role that she was in a daze for forty-eight hours.[37]

Fox's offer to Carewe, who held her contract, was $30,000 for the film, though Carewe may have gotten part of this total. Clearly, her price had risen steeply from the $250 a week that she had gotten on arrival in California just a few months earlier. Carewe was excited about the possibilities and explained them to his young protégée. Walsh was extremely important and skilled, he said, and the actors who would play her two suitors were really excellent. She immediately began to prepare for the role. Still, she was tired, having had no time off since leaving Mexico. It was her first experience with a really expert director, and she recognized it as an opportunity to learn her craft. She was surrounded by good actors who were also good company. They worked as a team, an ensemble, and she felt both important and taken care of. As for the others, they admired her beauty as well as her discipline. She forgot about the camera and began to act. When the shooting ended, she was sad, already missing the camaraderie of the set.[38] Remarkably, however, she already had a contract with Fox for two more films, to be made "on or before January 5, 1927," one to be based on the "Grande Opera 'Carmen'" and the other on "a subject of high-class literary character."[39] Even before the shoot was finished, Fox executives were obviously anticipating her success, though neither of these movies would be completed on the schedule indicated in the contract.

Her role as "Charmaine," a French innkeeper's promiscuous daughter, must have given Jaime considerable pause, however. She flirted with the soldiers, particularly the characters played by McLaglen and Lowe, with much rolling of her eyes as she suggested that they might wish to get a closer look at the attractive coverlet on her bed. In one scene, she leaned seductively over the counter in her off-the-shoulder blouse while she smoked up a storm; in another, she permitted McLaglen to put a garter on her leg, with exhibition of much of her thigh. Still, examination of the successive stages of the script shows that her role became more sympathetic with each new rewrite, and a poignant scene of her moving through a cemetery trying to bring a mother's letter to the graveside of her son was added to the final version of the film. The question of her virtue or lack of it evolved as well; in the early synopsis, two men, Captain Flagg and Sergeant Quirt (played by McLaglen and Lowe), competed for her sexual services with no consideration of permanence; the second draft indicated that "She hopes to go to bed with the Captain—but not before he had made more open and passionate advances." This note must have made Jaime reel. In this draft, Flagg would run Quirt off after returning from the front, but would not make love to Charmaine because he was too tired. When the bugle sounded to order him once again to the front, he advised Charmaine to "marry and settle down" since he probably would not be coming back. She switched her affections to Quirt, who returned, but then he too heard the bugler and departed. The third draft has her immediately choosing to marry Quirt rather than the amorous but amoral Flagg, but with Quirt rejecting her, saying "I can't marry you tonight. I can't marry you any god-damned time at all." Yet in the fourth and filmed version, it was Charmaine/Lolita who rejected them both and hysterically refused to marry.[40] Though there is no way at this point to determine just why these changes were made, it is plausible to assume that Walsh and the scriptwriters not only were influenced by Jaime's concern with her reputation—she remains a woman (a girl, really) of easy virtue—but wished to give her a bigger and more compassionate role, not to mention making Charmaine/Lolita more of an agent of her own fate. It appears that they simply liked her, or at least felt she was more convincing in this way. Even

P. S. Harrison, of *Harrison's Reports and Film Reviews*, noticed the change. He observed, after seeing the film, that

Dolores del Rio takes the part of Charmaine, the "Sweetheart" of both Captain Flagg and Sergeant Quirt. In the play, Charmaine gets no sympathy. But it is quite different in the picture; she wins sympathy and quite a little of it. One starts sympathizing with her when she is seen as mothering the young soldier, "mama's boy," as he has been named, when he was ill with fever. The next sympathy-winning situation is where Charmaine hears of the youth's death; she is sad. She is then seen visiting the cemetery conveying the letter his mother had sent him.[41]

The filming was tough. Walsh later told the *Los Angeles Times* that the combat scenes, dazzling and realistic even though they were filmed in Beverly Hills, actually were very dangerous: "The studio had over 2,000 settlements to make for cracked plaster, broken windows and other damages to buildings in the area." At the time, explosions were detonated in "hard adobe," which would blast apart like shrapnel, and "we didn't have to tell the performers to keep their helmets on. They kept them on to save their lives. Why, we even had to put the camera into a steel cage to protect it from the flying stuff." A blasting permit had to be obtained from the city of Los Angeles; it was issued to the William Fox Vaudeville Company for use of explosives "not to exceed: 10 sticks 25% dynamite or 25 pounds black powder," which cost the company a $150 bond. Accidents happened; one bit player was injured by an explosion that was set off too early and lost an eye and had other injuries. Though Fox put him on contract for life, he died shortly thereafter. Strangely, Walsh himself lost an eye two years later while filming the first outdoor talkie in Utah, called, despite the location, *In Old Arizona*. In this case, a jackrabbit shattered the windshield of the car in which he was riding.[42]

Dolores escaped injury, but the shooting was grueling. She must have been cheered up considerably, however, by the fact that this time, in the publicity distributed by Fox, she had top billing. On the advance information sent out by the studio, her name appeared above McLaglen's, and Lowe's appeared not at all. A note at the bottom, after a synopsis of the plot, said, under the headlines "Box-Office Angle," that the film would be an "18-carat attraction," it would be "Really startling!" A later advertisement for the film at the Carthay Circle Theater announced that it was a "Twelve-Reel Film Masterpiece," which had taken "two years to complete," although, of course, Dolores was involved with it for only a fraction of the time. The ad also indicated that the film blended fiction with reality; eighteen of the forty survivors among the men who fought with the First Battalion, Fifth Marines, at the battle of Belleau Woods actually appeared in the production. Almost all of the men in the picture (85 percent) were veterans of the Allied armies who had fought overseas in World War I, and this surely heightened the viewers' sense of reality.[43]

The movie was a success. The *Fox Studio Mirror* enthusiastically proclaimed it was a "Smashing Screen Hit" and declared with typical hyperbole that the premiere was the "Biggest Event in Los Angeles Theatrical History." The writer of the score led the theater orchestra for the event, and an electrical engineer and a large staff of the studio's own electricians worked to provide brilliant lighting. Studio experts produced dazzling war effects for the "pyrotechnic display" staged outside before the doors opened. The mock battle was reported to have brought "storms of applause" from the onlookers who were awaiting the arrival of the stars. For a quarter of a mile, from Wilshire Boulevard to the entrance of the theater, batteries of studio lights shone, with every tree along the way illuminated with colored spots. Other spotlights were aimed into the sky, providing a spectacle visible all over Los Angeles. Just before the beginning of the performance, a "huge octopus bomb" exploded to reveal "a large American flag suspended on parachutes." The report indicated that "hundreds of red, white and blue rockets banked the fluttering emblem every foot of the way to the ground."[44]

The earlier New York opening was just as successful, if perhaps less warlike, and the time there for Dolores was filled with social events and happy contemplation of excellent reviews. Not only were her beauty and eroticism noted but also, finally, her acting. *Harrison's Reports* confirmed the success somewhat less hyperbolically. Its report was enthusiastic: "There are situations in which the spectator is so thrilled, so electrified, that he feels as if he ought to get up and run; where, no one, not even himself, knows—perhaps to fight." The report confirmed Sheehan's significance; he was credited with persuading Fox, formerly known for "low-priced pictures," as responsible for the high quality of *What Price Glory?*[45] Mordaunt Hall of the *New York Times* noted that del Río had "considerable talent . . . [and] gives an excellent idea of the Mademoiselle D'Armentieres type of girl." She was able to share her excitement with Covarrubias, who was in New York. Even in the United States, she was regularly in contact with the artist and other individuals important in the Mexican postrevolutionary avant-garde.[46]

The film brought Dolores undoubted stardom. It played to sold out houses in the United States, its runs were regularly extended, and it was selected by the *New York Times* as one of the ten best pictures of 1926. A story in *Film Daily Yearbook* for 1927 listed eight film critics' lists of the best films of 1926; *What Price Glory?* was in the top ten for all of them. She was the perfect foil to the rugged McLaglen and the handsome Lowe; McLaglen was so much taller than she was that she had to stand on a box for some of their scenes, and a number of publicity shots recorded the two in this fetching situation. In Mexico, as well, it seems to have been a hit, though, no doubt, an opportunity for more elite gossip.[47] Happily for Dolores, but contrary to the received wisdom, her films were immediately popular in her home country. By July 1927, the *Los Angeles Times* was reporting that 98 percent of the movies shown in Mexico were from the United States; that "Valentino was the greatest star that Mexico had ever worshipped" and after his death "his pictures were reissued and shown to capacity crowds;" and that among female stars, "[Pola] Negri and Miss Del Rio are the most popular."[48]

An article in the *New York Times* in October 1927 looked at an issue that has been intriguing academics in film studies, sociology, psychology, and even history ever since: how movie audiences identified with characters on the screen. The author, George Mitchell, used *What Price Glory?* as a case in point. After discussing how he himself had identified first with McLaglen and then with Lowe, he saw them in their struggle

not only with each other but with our inner selves, yours and mine, for supremacy all through the picture (we were first one, then the other) and it wasn't till Dolores Del Rio conclusively let Victor go that we made our final decision and faded into the man who vanquished Victor, the man who won the delightful little French girl. And who was Dolores? You needn't ask me. I know, for I could see out of the tail of my eye and could catch the glow on the face of the girl who sat in the seat beside me. Are you a young girl with a natural desire to live some of the bigger moments that life offers? If you aren't, you aren't normal.[49]

Probably, it was at about this point that she first had plastic surgery. Despite one of her websites denying to this day that she ever went under the knife, photographs make plain that she did.[50] At some point in 1926 or 1927, the upper portion of her nose was significantly narrowed, making her enormous eyes even more luminous. It may be that she had more than one operation, as publicity photos shot in 1928 for *Evangeline* show this change most clearly, and photographs over the next few years indicate further surgery. But some sort of change, though subtle, was noticeable quite early. Even by the time the stills were done for *What Price Glory?*, the upper portion of her nose looked narrower than it did in the film, although possibly shaded out in the retouching process.

Certainly, plastic surgeons at this time were involved in producing beauty according to a Caucasian, Anglo-Saxon ideal and even chose the Venus de Milo, "a classic icon of white, western beauty," as their symbol.[51] It is also possible that the particular forms of Lolita's surgeries reflect an aesthetic ideal in Hollywood at the time, or the aesthetic of a particular surgeon; it is by no means necessary to resort to a racialized explanation for these facial changes. The kind of nose that she developed through these surgeries highly resembled Greta Garbo's, her contemporary whose face and particularly whose nose changed notably during the first six months she was in Hollywood. It also resembled the nose given to Marlene Dietrich when she arrived in 1930. The women were friends and may well have patronized the same surgeon. Garbo and Dietrich, certainly, would have needed neither whitening nor racial changes, and Dietrich was already a star in Germany. It is worth noting that a doctor in Berlin, Jacques Joseph, was considered a master of the new specialty and took as apprentices a number of U.S. surgeons.[52] Yet soon after her arrival in Hollywood, Dietrich's original broad nose looked much more like Garbo's and del Río's and continued to narrow over the years.

Meanwhile, Lolita's career flourished. A new project was *Resurrection*, Leo Tolstoy's novel, in which she played the character Katusha. This project was, once again, Edwin Carewe's, through his Inspiration Pictures, to be distributed by United Artists. This latter company had been formed several years earlier by some of Hollywood's most important personalities: Mary Pickford, Douglas Fairbanks, Charles Chaplin, and D. W. Griffith. The contract was a notable improvement in terms of salary over her initial arrangement with Carewe; she was now making $1,600 a week, with six-day weeks as the norm, and all her expenses, including costuming, travel, and living on location were paid for by the producer—that is, Eddie.[53] The salary was high, but clearly Carewe and United Artists believed that Dolores's new fame was decidedly marketable. However, despite the increase in salary, the contract put her almost entirely under his control. Though it is likely the clauses in this contract were not greatly different from others of the time, the degree of his power is still striking. One completely open clause read, "Should the artist in the judgment of the Director of said motion picture prove incapable of a satisfactory portrayal of said part on the screen, the Producer shall have the right to cancel this agreement." Another clause, though probably not an unusual one, made clear the value and significance of her physical appearance:

If by reason of mental or physical disability or otherwise the artist be incapacitated from fully performing or complying with each and all of the artist's obligations hereunder, or if the artist suffer any facial or physical disfigurement materially detracting from the artist's appearance on the screen or interfering with the ability of the artist to perform properly the required services hereunder, then and thereupon this agreement shall be suspended both as to services and compensation during the period of disability or incapacity, and the producer, at its [sic] option, in the event of the continuance of such disability or incapacity for a period or aggregate of periods in excess of three (3) days during the term hereof, may cancel and terminate this employment.

An even more coercive clause was this one:

It is understood that it is of the essence of this employment that the artist shall be punctual in the matter of reporting for work and attending at the studio or on location whenever required in connection with this employment, and the artist hereby consents that a fine of $10.00 may be imposed by the Producer for the first lateness and the fine of $25.00 may be imposed by the producer for each additional lateness of which the artist shall be guilty and for which there shall be no excuse which the producer shall deem reasonable.

Yet another clause, number 11, indicated that the

rights and privileges granted to the Producer by the artist under the terms here are of a special, unique, unusual, extraordinary and intellectual character which give them a peculiar value, the loss of which cannot be reasonably or adequately compensated [by] damages in an action at law and that the breach by the artist of any of the provisions contained in this agreement will cause the Producer irreparable injury and damage. The artist hereby expressly agrees that the Producer shall be entitled to injunctive and other equitable relief to prevent the breach of this agreement by the artist.

In signing, Dolores gave Carewe the explicit basis for possible future litigation and more or less admitted culpability in advance. The provisions on health are of particular concern; perhaps Dolores's exhaustion given the intense scheduling of her films had come to concern Edwin; or perhaps such clauses were a normal part of contracts at the time. Still, they seemed strange and intimidating in a written agreement between two people who were so close yet not quite united emotionally.

Jaime still stood between. Perhaps his influence can be seen in item 7 of the contract, which read in part, "The artist agrees that the conduct of the artist will be maintained with due regard to public conventions and morals and agrees not to do or commit any act or thing that will tend to degrade the artist in society or bring the artist into public disrepute, contempt, scorn or ridicule, or that will tend to shock, insult or offend the community or public morals or decency or prejudice the producer or the motion picture industry in general."[54] Since it was far more likely that Carewe would misbehave than Dolores, or might urge her to "offend" against "decency" either on or off the screen, this clause was more of a sanction against him than her, in the reference to both film content and personal behavior. The clause itself became a major issue when Carewe negotiated with other studios for her services, and he would use it for leverage against others just as she and Jaime would use it to try to control *him*.

Nevertheless, the contract gave Carewe enormous power over Dolores, and he made the most of it. It was a very interesting instance of the extraordinary dominance that early producers in Hollywood could gain over their stars, and that older men with clout in the industry could exert over beautiful young women. In fact, as we will see later, through 1927 Carewe's negotiations with male studio moguls were far more important than her attempts to intervene on her own behalf. And in this contract, it is notable that the term *artist* was never capitalized, while *Producer* was frequently (though not always) put in uppercase.

Of course, in his own way Carewe seemed devoted to, even obsessed with, furthering Dolores's career, inasmuch as their careers were intertwined. Probably the success of *What Price Glory?* even if produced and directed by others stunned his pride, and it certainly could have readjusted the balance between Dolores and himself. He seemed to be particularly nervous about Walsh's successful direction of Lolita and his possible growing influence upon her. In fact, it is a bit surprising that she would have signed such an agreement with Carewe just at the time of the release of her first big hit, in which she had worked with another director. Perhaps she did not fully understand her new bargaining power, though Carewe did and therefore hastened to keep her under his own domination contractually. Certainly, he had strong motivation—both personal and economic—to exert whatever leverage he could over a young woman who was suddenly a bankable star and with whom he had fallen in love. In the event, the new contract kept her from becoming part of a stable of stars at a given studio, in the way that Garbo would immediately come to reign at MGM and Dietrich a few years later at Paramount. Any studio would have to deal with Eddie.

In the new production of *Resurrection*, her mentor was apparently determined to produce an epic that would compete in importance with *What Price Glory?* Perhaps it was to impress his beautiful star and recoup his position as her principal mentor. He spared no expense in putting the film together. Not only did he employ an exiled Russian general to be sure that the czarist uniforms were authentic, he also invited Tolstoy's son Ilya to serve as a technical and historical adviser. Filming took place at Inspiration's studios at 5300 Melrose. Finis Fox, a well-known screenwriter and Edwin's brother,

Dolores and Ilya Tolstoy on the set of *Resurrection*. Bibliothèque du Film.

and Ilya himself helped Carewe work the story into a script that would give Lolita an opportunity to show off her acting talents. Ilya also performed as an elder sage. Rod La Rocque, a popular leading man from the very early days of Hollywood, was selected to play opposite her, and his stature required giving him top billing in spite of the whole film being prepared as a vehicle for her. Wallace Fox, yet another brother, served as Carewe's assistant; he later directed a number of serials and westerns on his own, along with becoming a screenwriter in his own right.[55] Edwin was able to get a copy of a Russian film version of the novel from D. W. Griffith; it was claimed in Hollywood that Griffith actually used parts of it in his own movies. There had also been other U.S. cinema adaptations of the work; some were still being exhibited at the time Dolores and Edwin were filming.[56]

The shoot, spectacularly expensive, began toward the end of 1926; *Resurrection* premiered in May 1927 at the Mark Strand Theater in New York City, the same venue where Fox had opened *What Price Glory?* Advertising flyers revealed the melodramatic nature of the plot and emphasized Lolita's centrality to the production: "In the shame he had brought her, he found his Soul! He had forgotten his love. . . . She could remember nothing else! And her heart pounded with the cruel question—'Will he betray me twice?'" She was portrayed as a sexy dancer, showing her ankles. The New York critics agreed that Dolores was not only captivating but also a master of acting for the silent screen. Mordaunt Hall, in his review, indicated that the film included "several splendid character studies, notably that of Katusha Maslova by Dolores del Rio. . . . In the initial chapter, she adroitly captures the idea of the innocent girl, and when she has been betrayed by Prince Dmitry Ivanitch Nehludof she gives a vivid impression of Katusha in love." Eddie was also praised: "Mr. Carewe deserves great credit for this absorbing translation of the Tolstoy novel. Incidentally, Count Ilya Tolstoy, who lent a helping hand to Mr. Carewe in the making of this picture, is perceived in several scenes as the Old Philosopher."[57]

Mexicans were just as enthusiastic. Enrique del Llano indicated in his review in the Mexican press that he wrote to "praise and exalt the masterly work of Dolores del Río, the Mexican artist who has succeeded in commanding respect against all the low passions and all the intrigues and all the obstacles that are arraigned against those who wish to achieve glory and to wrest from the sky a star for the pride of our nationality." This review, interestingly, was a challenge to and refutation of the attitudes of the

Mexico City elite, which found her acting career unseemly, and it linked del Río's success directly with Mexico's national image. Yet another Mexican critic, Antonio Ramos Pedrueza, insisted that Dolores represented, "in her humble costume of a Russian woman, the human and universal expression of the deceived woman of any race, of any sort, of any epoch."[58]

Still, *Resurrection* did not have quite the staying power and box office appeal of *What Price Glory?* Although it enjoyed a substantial six-week run at the Criterion Theater in Los Angeles, the earlier film had shown at the Carthay from January 1 through May 7, 1927, and did not close its run at the Harris Theater in New York until May 21, making strong revenues throughout.[59]

After this somewhat more moderate success, she moved quickly into her second project with Raoul Walsh and Victor McLaglen, *The Loves of Carmen*. Taken from the mid-nineteenth-century novel by Prosper Mérimée that provided the story for Georges Bizet's opera, it had been made into several movies already, including one in which Walsh himself directed Theda Bara twelve years earlier. It was Lolita's first major role as a Spanish woman, and she was stunning in a lavish wardrobe of lace and high combs, flowers in her hair and spit curls on her cheeks. Yet once again issues of propriety and sexuality were problematic and made the relationship among Lolita, Jaime, and Edwin even worse. This little drama was played out within the context of negotiations over the filming of *Carmen*, which del Río was contractually obligated to do next for Fox. In an early communication about the role, Dolores wrote to Edwin of discussions with "Mr. Walsh," indicating that she liked the story. Yet, she noted with concern, "there are possibilities of including scenes of a lewd or vulgar nature. Before starting on the picture I want to remind you of the clause in our contract which deals with that matter and to tell you that under no circumstances will I consent to appear in any scene or costume of that nature." She indicated that Winfield Sheehan of Fox, who was instrumental in her casting in *What Price Glory?* had promised that she and Jaime could see it before release to "eliminate any objectionable scenes." She was also worried about risqué scenes in a picture called *Upstream* that seems to have already been filmed. This was almost certainly another name for the film *Jungle Rose,* which apparently was issued eventually as *Gateway to the Moon.*[60] The tone of her note was very formal; it reflected Jaime's concerns and may even have been written partially or entirely by him. Carewe forwarded her letter to

Sol Wurtzel, the Fox general manager, and then followed up with a note of his own, emphasizing that the issue was "serious" and that he and Wurtzel had already discussed the specific clause in her contract with Carewe that dealt with such matters. He closed by saying, "I hope that Miss Del Rio has been needlessly alarmed."[61]

Dolores showed up for work as scheduled. Walsh brought in several technical experts, including a bullfighter or two. Yet apparently the director was not very interested in the production, which was mounted hurriedly to take advantage of the success of their previous collaboration. Nevertheless, it permitted Lolita to develop even further the glorious sensuality that made her such a popular star and led to still more criticism among Mexican elites, especially those close to her husband's family. Carewe sent an ecstatic letter to Sheehan in May on completion of filming; he indicated that "Miss Delrio [sic] is positively splendid and Walsh has done a fine job."[62] Predictably, Jaime exploded about the final version of *Carmen*, forcing Dolores to write to Carewe asking for changes.[63] Edwin immediately contacted Sheehan, requesting the deletion of two close-ups which showed "her bare limbs, almost to her hips. . . ." He emphasized that there were still a "great many scenes which get over her sex in such a splendid way," while these particular scenes were "deplorable" and "STRIVING for sex." He also asked for a "big moment at the end of the picture so as to appease the public." This scene was the one of her death, and he suggested that she should look at leading man Victor McLaglen with a "twisted half smile," try to touch his cheek, and then let her arm fall back weakly as her life drained away. This bit of business, Carewe believed, would leave the audience with a "marked kindliness towards 'Carmen,' even though they know her life was in error."[64] These interactions also make clear how other directors and even heads of studios would have to deal with Carewe.

Dolores as well wrote to Sheehan, thanking him for his "wonderful compliments on my work," apparently referring to an earlier telephone conversation. Her requests were much clearer, asking specifically that the scene showing her trying on shoes, in which the camera was set too low, be redone to avoid a "most embarrassing exposure." She also asked for elimination of "the shot of my bare back when I am dressing" which she likewise found "very, very embarrassing." She requested the strengthening of the death scene, as had Carewe, but indicated that Walsh, not Carewe, would have ideas for improving its "intensity and feeling." Carmen, she thought,

Del Río as a sultry but relatively discreet "Carmen." CEHM CARSO.

needed something sympathetic despite being a "selfish little devil."[65] I think
it is quite likely that Sheehan responded more favorably to Dolores's letter
than to Eddie's, though we do not have the record of his replies.

Carewe and Jaime both continued to strive for sympathetic presentation
of Dolores, even as she played women of easy virtue, the issue being mentorship and control. Yet she herself was increasingly knowledgeable and self-
confident in her own behalf, as shown by her letter to Sheehan. She had some
very explicit ideas of her own, and she did not appeal to Sheehan to listen
more carefully to Carewe (which, no doubt, Carewe hoped for). Rather, she

indicated that the appropriate person to make changes would be the actual director, Raoul Walsh, in whom she reasonably had great confidence. In any event, the scenes remained in the film, and six months after the exchange of letters Carewe was still raising the issue with Fox executives in regard to her future appearances in films with the studio. He even threatened that Gunther Lessing, Dolores's attorney as well as his own, might bring legal action on her behalf. In regard to a further film with Fox, to which she was contractually obligated, Carewe again asserted *his* artistic and personal rights, as he saw them, over Dolores. He wrote: "At this time I also wish to inform you that, as Miss Del Rio's manager and personal representative, she is subject to my direction in these matters and you will please be advised that a discussion of the story and costumes with Miss Del Rio by Mr. Raoul Walsh or any other director you may designate will be without avail."[66]

Shortly after the filming, in an interview with Alma Whitaker, Dolores herself discussed the strains between the two men. Whitaker noted that del Río was in the "enviable position of having rival directors competing for her talents." She quoted Dolores, using orthography that reflected the star's slightly fractured English, as saying, "Raoul, he like to make me not very proper, what you call too much sex appeal, to do the not so lady-like things. . . . But Ed, he wished to keep me Madonna, sweet, pure girl, always very nice manners. . . ." This assessment, of course, was not entirely accurate and put a trouble-free public face on what was an increasingly difficult relationship with Eddie. The journalist went on to indicate that Dolores gazed "with appreciation toward Mr. Carewe," who obviously was attending the interview with her, perhaps to make sure she said the proper, deferential things. On the other hand, she emphasized how much fun it had been to make *Carmen* with Walsh, while making *Resurrection* with Carewe was sad and depressing. Carewe's own comment about her portrayals was, "With that face, those eyes, those lips, one doesn't have to undress Dolores to give her sex appeal; that is for beauties that only have a body. Dolores has sex charm in a thick overcoat."[67]

In fact, her appearance in *The Loves of Carmen* was exotic and dazzling, showing her as a fitting female counterpart to Valentino. In the *New York Times*, the critic commented that her acting made all previous performances seem relatively conservative. This time, she had first billing, having argued successfully that since the movie dealt with the loves of Carmen specifically, she as Carmen should appear at the top of the marquee. A high-budget film, it showed that she now had bankable status, that her appearance in a film could guarantee a substantial return.[68]

Moreover, her films were being shown worldwide, and she herself was becoming celebrated abroad. A clipping entitled "Letter to Dolores del Rio," written by Ugo Schneider Sartori, provided an Italian viewpoint on her most recent hit. Addressing her as "My distant friend," it went on, "I know that with your sizzling interpretation in the Loves of Carmen, you have chosen to give old Europe a whiff of the impetuous fragrance of the Mexican woman."[69] By then, she stood high in the opinions of Fox studio executives; soon, they called her back to finish two unreleased films, the aforementioned *Jungle Rose* and another called *My Wife's Honor*, before she started her next major project with another studio. These, it was indicated, were "made . . . some time ago."[70] Both *Gateway to the Moon* and *No Other Woman* were released in 1928; these were almost certainly the two films she had been called back to complete.

She had become a star after only two years in Hollywood, but the uncomfortable situation among Dolores, her director/manager and sometime producer Carewe, and her husband continued. An undated telegram from Carewe to Dolores indicated problems; in making a suggestion to her about a rest that might follow the Carmen role, he patronizingly wrote, "I do not want my chili peppers to get ill or run down," "chili peppers" referring to both the Martínez del Ríos but appropriating Jaime's paternal role.[71] At the same time, and probably without any of them even realizing it, she was moving into a position of power in which she would need neither of them. In fact, the conflict made it difficult for her to tolerate them. *The Loves of Carmen* opened in September 1927 in New York, and this premiere was followed quickly in March 1928 by a multiple-theater opening in Mexico City. Despite some viewing with alarm by female critics, particularly one Cube Bonifant (a pseudonym for critic Luz Alba, who was reported to have taken a particular personal dislike to Lolita) in Mexico, it was a success. Bonifant suggested that her performance would be better placed in a music hall than on the movie screen, but fans paid little attention and flocked to the theaters.[72] Her career was flourishing, her fame and popularity in the United States and in Mexico constantly growing.

4   Unwelcome Triangle

Naturally I am personally concerned in making you a United Artists
star because this is the ambition of every actress and because it
is the "highest what is" in the picture business. Just think of it,
Dolores! You are going to be a star in your own right and take your
place side by side with Chaplin, Fairbanks, Pickford, Talmadge,
Swanson and Barrymore!

Edwin Carewe to Dolores del Río[1]

It makes little difference, however, where one opens the history of
the Indians; every page in every year has its dark stain.

Helen Hunt Jackson, *A Century of Dishonor:*
A Sketch of the United States Government's Dealings
with Some of the Indian Tribes[2]

MEANWHILE, her marriage was falling apart. Nevertheless, Dolores and Jaime were still together, and
in May 1927 it was announced that she would be building a traditional,
Mexican-style home in the foothills near the Hollywood Bowl. On the
same day, the couple signed the papers to purchase property on Outpost
Drive, close to the beautiful residence Pickfair, which belonged to Mary
Pickford and Douglas Fairbanks. In fact, their own new dwelling would be
lavish, considerably more luxurious than the one they occupied before leaving Mexico City. The structure, with twenty rooms on 3-1/2 acres, was to
be Mexican in style, elaborate and beautiful. During construction, Dolores
brought workmen from Mexico to create special features such as a mosaic of
the Virgin of Guadalupe created out of Talavera tile in the entryway. These

touches helped her feel at home. Somewhat ominously, Jaime was never mentioned in the newspaper story, which included the announcement that Carewe would also be building a new house, also on a three-acre site, this one at the northern terminus of Canyon Drive. The estimated cost for the two homes was said to be $500,000.[3] Edwin, who was no doubt in charge of the press release, had once again chosen to exclude Jaime as a public factor in his wife's life and to emphasize her connection to himself, even in the announcement of the couple's construction of a residence. This time the affront was clearly deliberate, calculated to exacerbate Jaime's jealousies and doubts. And Jaime, as it happened, would never live in Dolores's new home.

Carewe and Hollywood were pushing Jaime further and further into the background. An example was a publicity photo of the Martínez del Ríos standing outside a Spanish-style home—not the one on Outpost Drive that they were building, since it was not yet completed, but perhaps one they were renting. It appeared in the *Los Angeles Times* on July 10, 1927, in a photo spread called "The Beauties of Home." They were standing side by side in front of the house, but the caption read "This Spanish Adobe with its exotic entry forms an ideal setting for the Latin loveliness of Dolores del Rio." There was no mention of her husband at all, despite his clear presence in the photograph.[4] Another story at about the same time discussed a beach party given by the "Duncan sisters," in which Dolores's form in a bathing suit was made much of; the only reference to Jaime was that, "Of course, Jaime del Rio was there with Dolores. . . ."[5]

During 1927, Dolores was establishing a fame that would eventually, though not immediately, place her beyond the control of her husband or of Carewe, even as she found them both increasingly difficult to deal with. *Photoplay* in its July issue insisted that she was "the present leader of the Latin invasion," and that "Her sudden success has been equaled only by the Scandinavian Greta Garbo and the American Clara Bow."[6] Yet she continued to let Eddie negotiate on her behalf, while making a few steps to assert her own judgment and Jaime's. During the period of time between *The Loves of Carmen* in early 1927 and *The Red Dancer* in 1928 she made no films for Fox Studios, only retakes for two earlier movies both of which they had withheld for a period of time. Apparently, Fox had to some degree backed off their interest in Dolores, probably because of the difficulties of dealing with Edwin; and after *The Loves of Carmen* they agreed to postpone any new film to complete her contract until the end of 1927.[7]

Certainly they were tiring of Carewe, who made working with Dolores more difficult with his constant interfering. The director seems to have been almost demented in his desire to make her his own, while at the same time he was vividly conscious of her value to his career and fortunes.

Carewe also had conflicts with Lolita herself. She had been approached by Metro-Goldwyn-Mayer after finishing *Carmen* to make the movie version of Robert Lee Service's novel *The Trail of '98: A Northland Romance*, and she was eager to do it. As she telegraphed Edwin, it was a "wonderful part full of dramatic possibilities and sympathy stop biggest Metro Goldwyn Mayer road show release of year will cost million and a quarter," which indeed was an extremely high budget for the studio to commit.[8] The set designer was Cedric Gibbons (a man who reappeared in her life three years later). He was acknowledged as the very best in Hollywood, and Clarence Brown, who was also highly regarded and whose wife had given a lunch in her honor a few months earlier, would be her director.[9]

Carewe, however, was distressed to be bypassed, especially by yet another powerful studio. He telegraphed her anxiously, "Querida . . . if you do Goldwyn's picture it means postponing your starring pictures and also my laying off for long period which of course will be very expensive for me you know I consider Clarence not only great director but also my friend however must consider my own plans I have advanced you to your present high position Querida and naturally am regarding your future closely. . . ." After noting that "You see Querida our little dream is coming true as I said it would and we must remember the struggle upward and not lose our heads," he grudgingly added, "I will let you decide for your self [sic]. . . ." He then communicated with Jaime, whom he addressed as "Tamalie," to the effect that "it would be bad business to let Dolores play for Goldwyn or any one [sic] else unless she receives proper billing now that our efforts have been crowned with success stop have no feeling other than best interest for Dolores. . . ."[10] Carewe's use of such a casual nickname for the elegant Jaime Martínez del Río, especially one that associated him with a humble Mexican food, and misspelled at that, shows the nature of his breezy treatment of Lolita's husband. Again, it bordered on insulting.

Dolores prevailed and was able to do the Goldwyn picture, but not without a struggle. Carewe first pressured her to accept yet another offer, for a comedy to be directed by John Considine, with Joseph Schenck's Motion Picture Enterprises. He did note that she should do it only if "physically able"—

an indication that she was beginning to have health problems. She replied heatedly, "Understood from your wire that it was definitely agreed that I should do Goldwyn picture stop have tried wardrobe for 98 and everything is set stop would have greatest disappointment of my life if obliged to give it up stop would not do Considine picture for in my opinion story is weak and my part small and uninteresting if I cannot do Goldwyn picture I will take vacation and continue my present Fox contract lots of love Dolores."[11] Such a threat must have particularly disturbed Eddie, who was increasingly viewing Raoul Walsh, her director at Fox, with alarm and jealousy.

Schenck and Considine had only recently become associated with United Artists, an organization that was more successful in terms of prestige than it was, in fact, in terms of financial success. In the years just before Dolores came to work with them, their net income was less than $300,000 after taxes for the fifteen months between May 1926 and August 1927. Schenck was brought aboard to help solve problems of distribution by developing a theater chain, which in turn led to problems of producing enough films to fill the schedule. Schenck described this time as "almost entirely a period of development." He emphasized that "the company was almost solely engaged in acquiring theaters, building some and taking partnerships in others." All in all, an investment of $3,572,134 was put into seventeen theaters.[12] Yet he also planned an enormous studio construction project, announced by Considine, "the general manager of the Schenck group," as amounting to a $2.5 million investment in "five huge stages, an administration build-ing, electrical plants, carpenter and paint shops, workgroup units and other structures."[13] Obviously, the company was now investing in facilities to ramp up movie production to fill its theaters. A contract with Dolores, a brand-new star with proven drawing power, could help them in this endeavor.

United Artists was an extremely unusual organization in that the stars themselves (along with one prominent producer) had put it together to serve their particular needs. In the early years of the industry, studios were ex-tremely resistant even to using the names of their actors and actresses on their films, believing, correctly, that public recognition of individuals might lead to a demand for larger salaries. The principals in the new company— which was set up as a distribution arm for their own independent produc-tions—were the most famous actors of the time: Pickford, Charlie Chaplin, and Fairbanks, and D. W. Griffith, the most renowned director.[14] Formed in response to attempts by First National Exhibitors Circuit in 1919 to monopolize the film business through major mergers, the company was not originally envisioned as a producer of its own films but rather as a distributor of the films of its four major investors. At this time, Pickford and Chaplin commanded million-dollar contracts with First National, but such a monopoly would put the actors' bargaining power in jeopardy. The two stars, along with Fairbanks, even hired a detective to find out what First National was up to; the story was that the company was trying to take over all film producing companies and control all exhibitors throughout the United States. After seeing the reports, Griffith became concerned as well. On January 14, 1919, Sydney Chaplin, Charlie's brother and business manager, called a meeting at his home, which included three of the eventual four partners and Pickford's mother, Charlotte, acting as her daughter's representative. A claimed eyewitness said that the discussion centered around "all the talk of combinations and mergers and controlling the stars as though we were chattels to be bought and sold. . . ." They agreed that "We are going to make pictures, and make them as we want to, without the hampering restraints of set dates of release, and we are going to put the distributing profits into the pictures where they belong." Shortly thereafter Pickford herself approved, and the four announced to the press that they were combining in one association, as soon as their existing contracts were completed.[15]

Though the effort was not greeted with much overt concern on the part of the existing studios, with one observer commenting, "So the lunatics have taken charge of the asylum," a more astute observer said, "The founders of United Artists displayed the same brand of lunacy as Rockefeller, Morgan, and DuPont."[16] Yet the firm always had difficulties making enough movies to fulfill contractual obligations to exhibitors, and by 1925 it had brought in Schenck as a professional manager to establish a more solid business foundation. Schenck then formed the Art Cinema Corporation as the production arm of the company, for which he provided much of the investment. It was to make additional films, establishing headquarters at the Pickford-Fairbanks Studio in Hollywood.

This company had only just gotten started when Pickford, Fairbanks, and Schenck himself began to think of putting other artists under contract. Gloria Swanson, yet another superstar, had joined the firm as a partner in 1925; previously, she was Paramount's biggest box office attraction.[17] Rudolph Valentino joined up, at Schenck's behest, the same year, with the *New York Times* trumpeting "Valentino with 'Big Four.'"[18]

The mogul had already noticed Dolores. Before Valentino's death on August 23, 1926, after he made *The Son of the Sheik* with Schenck's and Considine's Feature Productions, the two briefly considered starring Lolita opposite the Latin lover in his next film.[19] The deal to bring Dolores into United Artists would take a while, but throughout the next few months Carewe never ceased to push her in that direction. Evidently, he felt the new business model would give him more power than that of a more traditional studio, and a contract for Dolores would include himself as well. In this regard he was operating similarly to her husband, who was willing to ride the wave of his wife's beauty for his own career purposes. With such an association, Carewe could achieve two of the things he most wanted: the influence and financial clout of being a producer in control of a hot property (Dolores) in association with one of the most prestigious associations in Hollywood, and along with it continued personal control over his beautiful protégée. Meanwhile, Pickford herself courted the young woman, including her in various social events through 1927.[20]

In the event, she went into *The Trail of '98* with MGM in March 1927, rather than doing a film, tentatively titled *Prince Fazil*, for Fox, or Considine's production, *Two Arabian Nights*. Carewe was disappointed, since he was so eager for her to establish a relationship with United Artists. Yet the Considine piece for that studio was a silly comedy with a nonsensical plot. It featured two U.S. soldiers falling in love with a beautiful young woman on a tramp steamer and then trying to steal her from her parents' "stronghold," a description that sounded very like an assault on a harem.[21] It seemed loaded with possibilities of the kind of "lewd" scenes that Dolores (or at least Jaime) continued to try to avoid, and her comment that she did not want to do the film at all, given the weakness of the script, along with her insistence on doing the MGM movie, were entirely reasonable in this context. An undated communication from Carewe to Dolores but apparently sent about the same time sheds some light on how the negotiations were carried out. Still calling her "Querida," he emphasized to her that "our future with United Artists depends on our favoring Considine." Further, he said that Schenck himself had "phoned me from Palm Beach," perhaps to convey this particular information. Eddie reminded her that "through them we will realize profits that we can't get with any other company." The telegram also illustrated Carewe's constant concern with money and his belief that his protégée was similarly concerned.[22]

The director apparently capitulated immediately, though we do not have his reply in the archives; but she wired him later in the same day on which she left for location for *The Trail of '98*. After reassuring him that "I am so thrilled feel sure will give great performance," she signed with "love." Carewe responded yet again with a face-saving communication, indicating that he would guide "your destiny with much care so that our dream will be realized fully and bring not only happiness but much money to us both." He continued being preoccupied with billing and with his role as her mentor, patronizingly responding "just work hard on Trail 98 [sic] mia Querida study the character you will play and make it as life like [sic] as possible I know you can make a personal success Querida that will play you above the title of the picture and when I see you in Denver I will analyze and discuss everything with you lots of love Eddie."[23] The overall tone of the exchange, however, already indicated that Dolores was no longer going to accept Carewe's advice without question, despite his refusal to acknowledge that she was growing more independent and that Jaime was still a part of their ongoing negotiations.

Backing off a bit and apparently mollified by encouraging talks with United Artists, Carewe sent her a letter several days later saying he was already preparing her first starring role for them. He thought it would be *Ramona*, the Helen Hunt Jackson love story of pre-statehood California in which a woman of mixed racial descent falls in love with and marries an indigenous man. I think it is likely that Carewe had wanted to star her in this vehicle from the time he lured her to Hollywood; it was perfect for putting forward the notion that indigenous people were sufficiently white to be romantically involved with those whose whiteness was more securely established. The story is romantic and tragic: when her husband is cruelly murdered, Ramona returns to a Spanish friend of her youth, who heals her psychological wounds. The director's choice of this role was a risk (though he did not acknowledge it) because it meant focusing on the real Dolores's racial status, not to mention Carewe's own Chickasaw ancestry. In the event, production of the picture was delayed, and it was not released until late March 1928. It finally premiered in Mexico City in July of that year, and in Europe—complete with Dolores in a series of personal appearances—that fall.

Meanwhile, Carewe, wanting to conciliate Lolita and remind her of her success under his direction, reported that "every one [sic] who has seen *Resurrection* is not only delighted with the picture, but is singing your praises to the high Heavens." He added, rather petulantly, "I canceled doing the picture for Metro-Goldwyn-Mayer that they wanted me to direct, as I thought it would be best to spend the time preparing at least two stories for United Artists with you." At this time, U.A. did seem to be angling for some kind of contract that would bring all of her films under their umbrella. And she was making films fast. An indication of her intense schedule is that Carewe expected her to begin their next film only four days after completion of *The Trail of '98*. His sense of domination, or his intense desire for it, was clear when he said, "You see, Querida, I agreed to let you play for Metro Goldwyn Mayer on the strength of what you and Jaime wired me about the part, and naturally I am deeply concerned in your making a big hit in the picture as it means so much to your future with United Artists. In a way I regret having agreed to let you play the part. . . ." In fact, of course, trying to stop her would have jeopardized his own relationship with her as well as her trust in his judgment; and she, perhaps in consultation with Jaime, had made the decision. Yet he went on to emphasize that United Artists was the most prestigious in the movie business and would link her with his greatest stars, as noted in the epigram. He gushed that "surely, we have achieved great success . . ." and ended by saying, "Remember you can always talk to me just as plain and as straightforward as you like, and I will always be happy to counsel and advise you as I have in the past." He signed the letter, "Yours sincerely, Eddie," rather than his usual "Love," a stilted way of indicating his displeasure.[24]

Dolores answered by telegram almost immediately that she was pleased the arrangement with United Artists was settled. She would be happy to do *Ramona*. Still, she cautioned him that from now on she would have a hand in selecting all her projects—a reaction to his frenetic deal making and less-than-consultative management style: "As to the other stories I beg you not to agree on anything before your return because as you can well realize dear Eddie I am very much interested in discussing every detail of future stories before you accept them stop lots of love Dolores."[25] Edwin still seemed not quite to get the message, or perhaps he did not to want to hear it, as he responded, "Querida please don't worry about stories for your starring pictures of course I will gladly talk them over with you as you know your future is close to my heart and will guide your destiny with even more care than your successful past. . . . Lots of love Eddie."[26] Yet his repeated use of the term "future" in his letters and telegrams indicated concern that he continue to dominate her professional and personal life.

Edwin's own marriage had meanwhile suffered from his untoward concentration on his charming and increasingly bankable star. Rumors circulated through both Hollywood and Mexico City that there was a romantic attraction between the new star and Carewe, which just added to Jaime's distress. Edwin justified pouring fuel on the fire in order to garner publicity for Dolores's career, or so she argued to Jaime. If her account was correct, Edwin was being less than straightforward with his beautiful protégée.

The situation was complicated by her exhaustion; she collapsed on the *Trail of '98* set while involved in a romantic scene with the leading man, and the physician who was called in insisted that she needed time to rest and relax.[27]

Nevertheless, Eddie wanted to start immediately on *Ramona*. Instead, she demanded a month off, and she and Jaime left for Hawaii on the ship *City of Los Angeles* for a two-week vacation. The rumors about her relationship with Carewe, no matter how much she insisted that she felt only gratitude and admiration for the director, blazed away in the meantime. Jaime's own career as a scriptwriter had failed to take off; his most recent script, *Fires of Love*, was turned down over and over. The Martínez del Ríos described the time in the islands as a "second honeymoon," yet Jaime found himself, on return to Los Angeles, speaking to the media to defend his wife's good name. He insisted that she did not drink even wine, or spend time running around with friends of either sex; nor was she talking of divorce. The Catholic brotherhood of Los Angeles, he pointed out, had made her its corresponding secretary.[28] Yet he might not have been too pleased at the story that appeared just before Lolita left for the *Ramona* location. She reported to Grace Kingsley that she had learned to do the hula and returned with a real grass skirt, given to her by Kahali, Hawaii's foremost expert in the dance. Even worse, perhaps, she—or maybe Jaime—had invited several of the "boys" who participated in the swimming shows they had seen every night to return with them to Los Angeles. Three of them did so. According to her, they were the couple's house guests. There was no information about what role they were to play in the household, a strange omission given the rumors about Jaime's sexuality. The Hawaii trip, despite their claims on their return that all was well, did not resolve their differences.[29]

Meanwhile, Carewe was increasing the intensity of his campaign to replace not only her husband but also any other director who might have an interest in working with her. The importance of the professional connection between them was underlined in a book that appeared in late 1927, though written before they made *Ramona*. Called *Breaking into the Movies*, it was an edited volume that included pieces by both Dolores and Edwin. Del Río's was entitled "Achieving Stardom," while Carewe's was called "Directorial Training." In her article, which was certainly partly ghost-written and probably reflected Carewe's views as much as or even more than her own, she emphasized the significance of their collaboration. Almost certainly, in my judgment, it was written for her either by Carewe himself or more likely by press agent Wilson. After a silly bit of business about how lucky black cats had been for her, she talked about "the hardships, the disillusionments, and struggles" that were part of getting ahead in the film business. She credited her own success to the man she described as her "teacher and 'discoverer'—Edwin Carewe . . . Under his guidance I learned the intimate details of screen acting, from an old master hand. For months, when I was scarcely known to the public, I had the rudiments of the film art drilled into me while I was appearing in minor, inconsequential parts. These were months of painstaking, arduous work. . . ." It was a fairly accurate description of her first couple of years in Los Angeles. Her piece indicated that the greatest role of her career to date was Katusha in *Resurrection*, under the "personal guidance" of Carewe—not her first hit, *What Price Glory?* which she had done with Raoul Walsh and Fox Studios. Carewe's own article emphasized in its introduction that she would star in his next production, *Ramona*.[30] Interestingly, Dolores's article had her denying the significance of intelligence for a female actress; rather, she said (or perhaps Carewe or Wilson did) that an actress must be "gifted with emotional traits and capacities that distinguish her from other women," along with her "physical beauty." "Intellectual girls," she noted, might lack precisely the "spirit and emotion which make a good actress."[31] Not long afterward, and in some measure beyond Carewe's constant supervision, she would maintain exactly the opposite view of the importance of intellectual strength for women.

The public scrutiny of the floundering Martínez del Río marriage and the attendant three-way struggle in her personal life continued to plague Lolita. In October, shortly after their return, a sympathetic article on Jaime's situation appeared in the press. It noted: "One of the most difficult things in the picture business is for a husband to have a successful star for a wife, or a wife to have a successful star for husband. Being introduced as the husband of Miss So-and-So, famous screen celebrity, has caused more heartaches in the film colony than anything else." Jaime, it was reported, had been in that position for two years and continued to hope "to do something himself." Now, the article claimed, he had been offered a leading role in a film production that Wallace Fox, another of Edwin's brothers, was scheduled to direct. "Heretofore," the clipping went on, "Señor Del Rio has contented himself with writing."[32] Unfortunately, nothing seems to have come of the Fox project. So, in 1927, there were increasing strains in Dolores's marriage as well as in her relationship with Carewe. Still, her career was skyrocketing, though Carewe and Wilson were pushing their ideas as her own. At the same time, she was moving to embrace her Mexican identification—albeit a European-descent and white one—having taken a chance on a role, Ramona, that might call such status into question.

She later told the Argentine journalist Chas de Cruz, in regard to the struggles between Carewe and her husband and her own feelings about them:

When I first came into movies I was a modest little girl full of hope. I struggled a great deal before triumphing but I was able to open a path. And when my aspirations became reality, I fell into the claws of slander. The love of a man with whom I had never been involved romantically embittered my life permanently. Because of this love, which was completely contrary to my own feelings, I was forced to divorce my first husband, Jaime del Río. We loved each other very much, but Jaime's unjustified jealousy, a result of calumny and backbiting, destroyed our conjugal harmony. The poor man died far from me, and they say, as a consequence of our separation. He was entirely to blame, it's true, but he was good, wonderfully good.[33]

This real-life drama played itself out in late 1927 and through 1928, a hectic time for Dolores, professionally as well as personally. Eight starring films—*Resurrection, The Loves of Carmen, The Trail of '98, Ramona, No Other Woman, Gateway to the Moon, The Red Dancer,* and *Revenge*—appeared in those two years, and she began to make the transition into talkies. Two of her first big breaks, *What Price Glory?* and *The Loves of Carmen,* had come with Walsh and Fox Studios. These successes were threatening to Carewe, despite his critically well-received vehicle for her, *Resurrection,* in between those two movies. Yet the Fox films did much better at the box office than Carewe's.[34]

In late 1927, production of *Ramona* finally got under way. The filming put her, once again, in daily contact with Carewe and further from Jaime, especially when Carewe ordered the cast to Utah for location shots that

could just as easily have been made in Southern California.[35] The matter
was more serious than a simple move to location for shooting. Jaime said
later that they separated precisely at that time, September 1927, although
he did not leave California until almost three months later.[36]

In *Ramona*, she played a half-Indian, half-European (Scottish in the
book, Spanish in the film) woman raised by a Spanish family in Southern
California, who fell in love with and married an indigenous man. The film

Dolores in one of her favorite and most successful roles, as Ramona. Paul Hutton
Collection. Reproduced by permission.

had been announced in March of 1927, in a column by Grace Kingsley, long before it actually began shooting. Kingsley had become a fan of del Río's and would remain one for years; she noted that del Río was "in a fair way . . . to become the greatest actress on the screen." Later in the same column, Carewe touted Dolores's success in his film *Resurrection*, produced as he emphasized by his own Inspiration Pictures for United Artists. He reminded readers that, "Contrary to all reports, Miss Del Rio is under personal contract to me, and I shall guide her more zealously than I have guided her past."[37] This comment may have been related to a persistent rumor that her contract would pass entirely to United Artists (a notion that saw print in another of Kingsley's articles just two months later), or to her long-standing contract with Fox Studios.[38] Perhaps he should have said, "more jealously," as this seemed to be his major sentiment toward the other men in her life, whether directors or husbands. The seven-month delay was unusual, although of course she kept busy throughout that period; perhaps United Artists, or even Carewe himself, was nervous about casting Lolita as a part-indigenous woman, after the strenuous attempts made in her publicity to present her as of European descent.

The filming of *Ramona* did not go smoothly. The first problem arose immediately on their arrival in Inspiration Point, Utah; it was already occupied by a First National crew, filming under the direction of Albert Rogell. Carewe contested Rogell's right to the location, which according to the newspaper reports had "never before been caught by a cinema machine." When Carewe insisted that he had made prior arrangements and that First National should leave immediately, Rogell arranged to have a number of his company deputized and armed to resist. Then he called in Sheriff J. T. Lee of Iron County. Lee and his men went up to the location, followed by Carewe and his party, who threatened force if the location was not vacated within twelve hours. Meanwhile, both companies were quartered in the same hotel, where Rogell and Carewe had to be forcibly separated by "hotel attachés" to avoid a fistfight.[39] Carewe eventually backed down and agreed to use Zion City and then Black Mountain after Rogell's departure; Rogell's leading lady, Molly O'Day, then invited Carewe's company to a banquet to bury the hatchet, but she deliberately excluded del Río. The reason for the affront, according to O'Day, was that "I feel she urged Mr. Carewe to maintain his stand toward usurping our rights to our locations, and I consider that a most unprofessional thing to do." Rogell was also semiconciliatory, saying "I have known Edwin Carewe for years and never really believed he would shoot to gain his ends." No doubt they had been acquainted, given Carewe's long association with First National.[40]

Dolores, of course, was singled out as escalating the incident, and one can imagine that she was distressed. Adding injury to insult, she suffered an accident on the set when Vera Lewis, playing one of the character roles, slapped her so hard that her cheek was cut inside her mouth and a tooth was loosened. Despite dental injuries, she sang the title song; it played as the film was screened and became a big hit as a recording and as sheet music. It was the first time her voice was heard in connection with a film, her first tentative move in the direction of talking pictures.[41]

Other kinds of reports were not so innocent; rumors of a romance between Carewe and his leading lady, probably fueled by Carewe himself, frequently made their way back to Jaime. Headlines like the one that appeared in the *Los Angeles Times* on September 27, "Carewe's Guiding Hand Has Meant Much to Film Star," rubbed it in. It went on to say that "Each succeeding year in the films seems to have a kindler [sic] touch for Dolores Del Rio. She has been given some of the finest stories available and if Edwin Carewe's plans for her future come true, she might well consider herself a very fortunate star." The wide headlines did not even mention Dolores, much less her husband; her name first appeared three lines down.[42] Yet Carewe himself was not quite sure of his status, which perhaps led him to sponsor publicity announcements. An indication of the precarious nature of their relationship appeared in a story two days later by Grace Kingsley in the *Los Angeles Times*. It warned that Carewe and del Río had been, perhaps, close to a parting of ways in the months before shooting started.[43]

At this point, moreover, Edwin as well as his brother Finis Fox were beginning to claim that they themselves were the masterminds behind her success, as in the September 27 story. Finis, for his part, commented to the same newspaper in regard to his several scripts for her (including *Revenge*, which was still sometime in the future): "I feel that I understand Miss Del Rio better than she does herself. She has said, indeed, that she is happiest when acting in stories by me, directed by my brother. Together we contrive characterizations exactly suited to her abilities and her limitations." In an interesting aside that illustrated possible racial motivations of the Carewe-Fox tandem and the perils thereof, the story noted that Finis himself "has a little of the red man's blood in his own veins," that he was born in Oklahoma of Chickasaw descent and became a member of the legislature in the Indian Territory after he graduated from college. It also mentioned that Finis was an expert on the history of indigenous peoples. Further, it claimed that in his adaptation of the *Ramona* story he made changes only to "soften references to the social antagonism."[44]

Such care was necessary. If audiences had doubts about whether or not Dolores was of European ancestry and could be considered white, featuring her as a woman of mixed race was taking a chance. It was also, in some measure, reinforcing the idea that all Mexicans had some Indian ancestry. As Finis put it, Helen Hunt Jackson, the author of the novel, was "a woman roused by the savagery of the white man in despoiling the Indian [who] wrote a book intended as burning propaganda." But it had become, according to others, a major "a tribute to California," and "America's greatest love story." That this tale deals with a woman of mixed race and an indigenous man might have raised concerns about miscegenation, as well—yet the Jackson novel was read by millions and published in 127 editions in the decades after it originally appeared in 1884. It was recognized as picturing "the romantic and historical days of our State with . . . sincerity and vividness. . . ." According to one newspaper story, "this throbbing love tale" was carried around by tourists at the California missions much as Lord Byron's *Childe Harold* was consulted by visitors to Venice.[45] It never had the impact, though, that Jackson desired in persuading readers to fight injustice against indigenous peoples in the United States. The author envisioned it as a kind of *Uncle Tom's Cabin* for Native Americans, but the romantic love story was what took hold, while its social aspects were largely ignored.[46]

Still, it was a story that resonated with the experiences of the Carewe-Fox brothers, and they probably chose it for that reason, hoping to advance Jackson's purposes of social awareness and reform with a poignant film portrayal and a wonderfully sympathetic heroine. Dolores was enormously popular, despite the unease about Mexicans in the United States, yet here Carewe was pushing racial limits with a racially ambiguous star. He probably hoped she might break through more barriers for Native Americans, as she had easily done already for Mexicans, or at least for gorgeous Mexican women viewed as predominantly European. She had been readily accepted as a romantic partner for whites on the screen, with virtually no comment or objection from the public or film critics. Her charm and appeal might rouse audiences to new attitudes toward the indigenous as well. In fact, I

think he harbored the desire to make another film version of this story—
it had already been told in a stage play in 1905, a film version by D. W.
Griffith in 1910, and a 1916 production by Clune's Studios—from the time
he met her.[47] Yet I think it was not until 1927, when her popularity was
at its height, that he felt he could safely bring the story to the screen with
Dolores as the protagonist. Still, the film did not premiere in California
until late March 1928, several months after it was completed.

Dolores still owed Fox a film, and by now she was sufficiently popular
that studio executives Wurtzel and Sheehan were willing to deal with Carewe
again. They must have regretted this necessity. Contentious negotiations
began in mid-October 1927, just as the *Ramona* filming was beginning to
wind down. Eddie first wrote to Fox on October 18, reminding Wurtzel, the
studio head, that she would be ready to start with them in late November,
and it was therefore time to begin talking about the story.[48] Receiving no
reply, and apparently fearing that he would not be consulted in yet another
picture directed by his rival Walsh, he followed, almost a week later, with
another. What was glaringly obvious in his peremptory communication
was his desire to get free of Lolita's obligations to Fox, in addition to his
desperate jealousy of the other director. In an attempt to exert his authority, he wrote, "I must again remind you of the necessity of the discussion
of these matters with me personally before I will permit Miss Del Rio to
report to you for work." Just in case they had missed the point, he added
shrilly, ". . . she is subject to my direction in these matters and you will
please be advised that the discussion of the story and costumes with Miss
Del Rio by Mr. Raoul A. Walsh, or any other director you may designate,
will be without avail." Here, perhaps, he was trying to avoid what had happened with *The Trail of '98*, when Lolita had begun to escape his influence
by working on the film completely independently from him. Even worse, he
began to threaten legal action against Fox for "the violation of two clauses
in my contract with her by you in the making of . . . 'The Loves of Carmen.'"[49] These alleged violations concerned the literary value of the film,
along with the final product being "too far from its 'base.'"[50]

Wurtzel nevertheless wrote calmly back to Carewe that they had not
discussed scripts with him earlier because they had not yet chosen a new
property for her. Nevertheless, as of October 25, they purchased a story,
The Red Dancer of Moscow, by Eleanore Bracone and Henry Leyford Gates.[51]
Gates was a well-known scriptwriter and novelist; in fact, he wrote the novel

Joanna, on which Dolores's first movie with Carewe himself was based. She would start on December 1. The response to this letter was again peremptory: Carewe indicated almost a week later by telephone that he, del Río, and their lawyer, Gunther Lessing, would look over the story that day and then let the studio know what they thought.[52] The same day, Wurtzel, anticipating problems, sent a biographical outline of Gates's work, indicating "the high literary character of the author."[53]

Apparently Carewe was unconvinced, or perhaps he was trying to prevent her from working at Fox at all. And Fox executives were becoming testy. An unsigned letter in the archives from one of the Fox executives to Carewe—which was never sent—said again that they expected del Río to show up for work with them on December 1, and that they had chosen a new story: another work by Tolstoy, *The Kreutzer Sonata*. The unsent letter would also have warned Carewe that ". . . we will hold you responsible for any damage resulting from delay occasioned by Miss Del Rio's failure to be available."[54] On November 2, not really knowing what Fox had in mind, Carewe responded that *The Red Dancer* was *not* of "high literary value," and del Río would not do it.[55]

Wurtzel then responded that since Carewe did not like *The Red Dancer*, Fox would opt to star her in *The Kreutzer Sonata*. The novella argued for sexual abstinence and provided a frightening picture of marital violence, in which the protagonist kills his wife in a jealous fury. Having himself produced and directed another Tolstoy project, *Resurrection*, with Dolores, and having succeeded in creating a box office and critical success, Edwin voiced objections to the second project that seemed even more self-serving than his concerns about *The Red Dancer*. Yet given the explosive nature of the story, perhaps he was justified in demanding to know what the film itself would look like. Almost two weeks later, no script was available, and Gunther Lessing wrote to Carewe, obviously with the intention of this letter being conveyed to the Fox executives, that there was only "a naked, commonplace, and sordid outline of a story." Just because it was an adaptation of the Tolstoy work, he insisted, did not make it "of high literary value"—a requirement that was written into her contract with Fox. He went on, "Neither the title of the picture nor the name of an author can have a critical bearing on the finished product." He advised Carewe that he should "demand [a] treatment of whatever story" and "a proper guarantee . . . that the finished picture will be fully in accordance with the treatment submitted." Finally, he raised the propriety issue again, reminding Carewe and thus Fox that "your contract with Miss Del Rio prohibits the exploitation of her sex and body."[56] Carewe added his own note, pointing out that Dolores would start on salary with Fox two weeks after completing *Ramona*, endorsing Lessing's letter, and saying he would have to have more and better understanding of what the final script would look like: "the contract requires 'first-class *scenarios* and produced in a *high class* and *artistic manner*.'"[57] Though it was accurate that the contract read in this way, nevertheless Carewe's motives were suspect. After all, only a few months earlier, he had urged Lolita to do a very silly comedy for director John Considine because he wanted to strengthen their relationship with Schenck and United Artists.

Wurtzel's reply was firm and reflected his irritation. He indicated he wanted Lolita at Fox Studios for filming on November 28, since part of the cast had already been engaged. In a tone that made it clear that he believed Carewe was significantly out of line, he added, "It is needless for us to say that we have no intention of producing pictures which would be other than high class in literary character, nor have we any intention of violating the above provision of Miss Del Rio's contract with you." Finally, he put Carewe on notice that Fox Studios would hold him accountable if she did not appear on the specific date noted.[58] In response, Lessing wrote another letter to Carewe which he forwarded to Fox, warning that *The Loves of Carmen* had "called forth such an avalanche of adverse criticism . . ."—a hyperbolic claim at best. He argued that "another such salacious production" would "injure Miss Del Rio in motion pictures."[59] Again, the motives of Carewe and his lawyer were suspect; there had been no such outraged response, except, perhaps, on the part of Lolita's spouse.

Meanwhile, Fox Studios announced to the press that *The Red Dancer* was being prepared for her. The response from Carewe was quick. A press story on November 9, no doubt placed by Carewe and Wilson before there was a real agreement for Dolores to do either film, indicated that "There will be no vulgar touches in 'The Red Dancer of Moscow.' You can depend on that, for Dolores Del Rio put her small foot down and declined to make the picture unless it were expurgated according to her own ideas. Dolores, it seemed, felt 'The Loves of Carmen' and 'What Price Glory?' had enough vulgarity to last her the rest of her life." Walsh, again targeted as the villain, was reported to have "listened to reason" and "agreed to have some of the scenes written out." The "vulgarity," it seemed, threatened to undermine Dolores's willingness to do the role at all, or perhaps her husband's willingness to have her do it.[60] Walsh, obviously a fan of his lovely star and open to observing her wishes, had already made her role in *What Price Glory?* significantly more sympathetic, and the two enjoyed a strong and mutually appreciative working relationship. Yet it was very likely Jaime, along with Edwin pursuing his own purposes, and not Dolores, who was disturbed by the content of the new film. Carewe certainly used the issue against Fox and Walsh, once again posing as Lolita's protector. Probably Edwin and his publicist planted the story in order to distance her from a studio that had done much to advance her career and a director for whom she had done well-recognized work.

Dolores's reputation had become, for Edwin, an excuse to resist fulfilling the Fox contract and risking Walsh's becoming a further influence in his star's life. Carewe was now completely focused on working with United Artists, for whom he and Lolita had just completed *Ramona*. He continued to feel that this unusual film company would give him more control over her than more traditional studios, along with more recognition for him; his negotiations for her always included himself. The problem with *The Red Dancer*, he told Fox, involved the "literary value" of the script, which he insisted was not very good. It seems that Lessing, Dolores's lawyer, and Carewe continued to contemplate a legal suit to break the Fox contract, on the notion that *The Loves of Carmen* was not really based on the grand opera *or* on the Prosper Merimeé story, as they anticipated and as contractually agreed. In this reading of events, therefore, Fox was already in noncompliance with the agreement. Lessing, no doubt speaking for himself as well as Carewe—despite putting his argument into a letter to Edwin himself—insisted he would not put the star into a situation "where her only recourse against you would be a suit against you or others for damages." It was highly unlikely that Dolores would have sued Carewe under any circumstances, so this was basically a threat against Fox. He went on to say, "Another such salacious production would irretrievably injure Miss Del Rio in motion pictures."[61] All of this dissension was undoubtedly hard on Dolores, whose marriage during these battles was disintegrating. Carewe was obviously trying to move into what he considered a void in her life, at a time when she was vulnerable.

An example of Carewe's desperate desire for control is shown in a letter from him to Wurtzel in which he indicated that Dolores would not come in unless and until Fox abided by his contract not with *her*, but with *him*. However, at this point in the confrontation he blinked, suggesting that he and studio officials get together and talk as "our differences do not seem to be insurmountable."[62] He seemed to be reacting to a letter received on November 9, in which the studio finally made some kind of threat he found convincing. At last, on the 10th, Carewe and Wurtzel came to an agree-

A soulful Dolores on the sheet music for her big song from *The Red Dancer*.
Author's private collection.

ment. A letter almost two weeks later, from the general superintendent of Fox Film Corporation (Wurtzel) to Carewe, outlined the new terms: Dolores would report to Fox on December 5, 1927, for work on *The Red Dancer of Moscow*. Instead of $1,500 a week, she would receive $25,000 for eight weeks' work, more than double her original salary, reflecting her successes through 1927. She would get top billing, with the initial announcement reading "William Fox Presents Dolores Del Rio in *The Red Dancer.*" Fox had to some degree capitulated, a testament to Dolores's new fame and drawing power, but the capitulation was largely to Carewe. He would get a complete copy of the scenario when ready; Walsh would not be permitted to film from a synopsis. Carewe would view the final, completed film and retain the right to alter or eliminate scenes as necessary. In his communications with Wurtzel, Edwin insisted he was merely the entirely reasonable intermediary, but that "Miss Del Rio's attorney has seen fit to 'ride me.'"[63]

In fact, Lessing and Carewe were operating completely in concert, and Lessing's communications to Carewe were designed to give the latter leverage against the studio. The strategy worked to some degree. Carewe presented Dolores as difficult and recalcitrant and sought to position himself as a protector to her and as a reasonable facilitator to the studio. Whether or not she, Jaime, or Fox Studios bought this characterization, nevertheless the issues were resolved, and Dolores agreed to begin work on December 5. However, events in the star's personal life, combined with medical issues, likely a result of physical and emotional exhaustion, sent her over the edge. She was unable to report for work until late January 1928, and then continuing medical problems took her out again until February. She had been working six-day weeks almost constantly since her arrival in the United States in 1925 except for her brief Hawaiian respite with her husband, during which he acquired young male Hawaiians who became for a time their "houseguests." The intense set of negotiations between her husband and her mentor/director, in which she was caught in the middle, surely took a toll. Still, her own notions of where she needed to stand in her profession and in her personal life occasionally surfaced.

Meanwhile, in October of 1927, Carewe had also separated from his wife. Then, in December, Jaime really could not stand his domestic problems anymore. He departed for New York on the very day, December 5, on which his wife was scheduled to begin filming *The Red Dancer*. It seems likely Dolores herself had found the situation intolerable and asked him to leave. The *Los Angeles Times* reported his departure but merely indicated that his purpose was to arrange for the sale of some Mexican property and take care of negotiations over a play he had authored for a Broadway show.[64] At this point, Dolores collapsed physically and emotionally. The couple never lived together again.

5   Pushing the Envelope

[W]hatever the star attempts to hold private is subject to reckless invasion.

> Jib Fowles, *Starstruck: Celebrity Performers and the American Public*[1]

She is the Latino face of Hollywood, and this implies both devotion and sacrifice, the never-ending self-consciousness of a face forever under surveillance.

> Carlos Monsiváis, "Dolores del Río"[2]

DESPITE DOLORES'S RECENT RENOWN, the separation stayed private for a time, at least as far as press reports were concerned, but the parting was not painless. Jaime wrote her often, expressing his anguish. Addressing her with a sketch of a kitten—indicating *"mi gatita"*—he wrote her from the railroad station shortly before leaving: "I don't want to cause you the least problem, as I know you feel very badly. My darling, my head is in a terrible upheaval and I can't think, so I will let my heart speak. I am in a shameful state, as I feel the world falling in on me. It's horrible!" He went on to express his concerns for her health, which was suffering from her overwork and emotional distress, and to express his gratitude to her mother, who came to see him off. He apologized for his blunders and for adding to her problems, when, in fact, he had hoped to facilitate her happiness. His missteps were occasioned by "stupidity" rather than any desire to cause her pain. He closed by saying, "I love you and I will continue loving you all my life with all my heart and with all my soul. When you think of me, I beg you and ask you that you try to do it without harshness. Finally, I cannot tell you all that I would like to, all that I feel because in this emotional state I am really half-crazy."[3] In another letter, written the next day, he told her it he was all right "and thinking of you—all the time." He worried about her health, yet another indication that she was in trouble, and asked her when she went to bed at night to "say an 'Ave Maria' for me, I assure you that I need it, your ——— [drawing of a cat]."[4]

Jaime continued to write throughout his train journey, including during a stopover in Chicago, where he stayed at the Illinois Athletic Club. While there, he saw some of their mutual friends, including Johnny Weissmuller, who was then in his pre-Tarzan days and known best for his Olympic championships in swimming. Jaime was invited out several times by the same Duncan sisters who had entertained the Martínez del Ríos in Hollywood, though he kept insisting he did not have the heart to attend their parties. He also complained about the "bitter cold," moaning that "Only God knows how many degrees it is below zero [centigrade]." *What Price Glory?* was still showing at a theater in Chicago, and he was thinking of going; strangely, he seemed to be putting himself into the position of one of the fans who dreamed about her over her screen image. He continued to worry about her illness and urged her to "take good care of yourself, kitten." Again, he asked for her thoughts in a traditionally Catholic fashion, by asking her to light a candle for him on Sunday.[5]

Finally arriving in New York City and settling in to life there around Christmas time, he sent best wishes to Dolores's father, who had come from Mexico to be with her and her mother during this difficult transition. Dolores apparently sent Jaime a Christmas telegram, though otherwise she does not seem to have communicated, and her own Christmas cards were a simple white bordered in red, with only "Merry Christmas" and her name written in her own hand—contrasting with the more elaborate cards, some with crests of nobility, sent by her fellow stars. As for Jaime, her mother, Doña Antonia, kept in touch, letting him know that her daughter's health was better. He complained that it was terrible not to hear anything from his wife, to live in a tiny apartment in such an expensive place, to "feel so alone in a city full of people."[6] In February he wrote again, desperately, that he had sent a telegram to her father asking for news but had heard nothing. Clearly emotionally distraught, he accused, "It is not right that you all leave me in this state of anxiety and if you understood what is happening to me, you would not do it."[7]

Lolita and her mother, always together. CEHM CARSO.

Shortly after Jaime's departure, she moved into her beautiful new residence and inaugurated it with a Christmas party. She and her parents greeted the guests as they arrived through pouring rain. Grace Kingsley reported that "such is the spirit of Spanish hospitality, all three devoted themselves to the comfort and happiness of their guests." Her column noted that "Jaime del Río" was in New York, much missed by the guests and by Dolores herself, who said that it was their first Christmas apart. She was therefore "doubly happy" to have her parents with her. Kingsley's report had a slightly ominous tone, however, reflecting, perhaps, Lolita's less than cheerful mood. Speaking through her alter ego, Stella, she said, "No hostess in the world is more warmly cordial than Dolores, yet her beauty always retains its sort of spiritual, aloof character . . . as though somebody had taken the portrait of the body of the social fashion plate and had fastened it to the head of the Madonna!" Other reports claimed unrealistically that the Spanish/Californian style home, with its white walls and wide exterior arches, was a duplicate of the house in which she grew up, while Kingsley more accurately pointed out that some of the pieces of furniture were duplicates from her Mexican residence. In any case, the new house seems to have been a comfort to her and one further announcement to the Hollywood community of her elegant, upper-class roots.

At the party, she performed some Spanish numbers in the large main salon, following up on her growing reputation as a dancer and perhaps leading to some of her graceful scenes in subsequent Hollywood musicals. Though Jaime's absence was noted, there was still no indication from her that the marriage was beyond saving. Yet rumors were circulating through the Hollywood community that Jaime was homosexual and Dolores entirely too friendly with her principal director.[8] The rumors did not seem to damage her screen appeal, however; in January 1929, independent film exhibitors voted her fifth most popular in their listing of female stars, just ahead of Mary Pickford.[9]

Surprisingly for Hollywood, it took more than a month for the reasons for Jaime's move to New York to hit the newspapers. Meanwhile, Dolores and Edwin were exploring an extended contract with United Artists, the "highest what is" as Edwin called it several months earlier. She socialized with the principals, Mary Pickford and Douglas Fairbanks, for several months, at parties she described as being out of "a thousand and one nights."[10]

Her state of mind and her state of health, however, were shaky. A news story on December 6, the day after Jaime left Los Angeles, claimed she had suffered a severe case of skin poisoning when she treated a mosquito bite with iodine and bichloride of mercury. The treatment was "ultra-severe," according to a "noted physician," and caused such a bad reaction that it would prevent her entering immediately into a new production and would force her to cancel all professional and social engagements.[11] Of course, this report of illness might have served as an excuse to keep her out of the public eye in the wake of her husband's departure. According to another report, she was suffering from a bad respiratory infection—"a severe congestion of the lungs"—that would require her to leave the city for a dry climate for a period of time. Although she was already supposed to be in production with Fox, she nevertheless went to Palm Springs for a rest. On January 2, 1928, an article appeared in the press about her having been seen with United Artists president Joseph Schenck, who, the report said, did not pose for "pictures with stars unless he means business. . . ." The filming of *Ramona* had gone well, said the article, and she would go immediately into the Fox production of *The Red Dancer*. Once that film wrapped, the newspaper indicated, she would become "a full-fledged United Artists player."[12]

Eddie continued to hover close, still believing he would have the principal role in guiding her career, working with Schenck and United Artists. As a telegram from him at about this time indicated, "As Big Star Schenck agrees with me you should only appear in big emotional drama striving to make each picture a real special stop United Artists contract settled only waiting here now to agree on stories to leave Sunday love to all Eddie."[13]

Lolita was back in Los Angeles by January 20, when a notice in the paper announced that she had lost an emerald and diamond ring, worth $5,000, somewhere between Western Avenue, where the Fox Studios were located, and Fox Hills, Westwood, where she was filming. It may have been a stunt to garner favorable publicity, however; it seems that Jaime's continued absence was about to hit the press.[14] On January 20, as well, she signed an extraordinary contract with Carewe, a contract that gave him almost complete dominance over her career and private life. Given the interest expressed by United Artists, he was no doubt eager to have this control completely clarified. She agreed to do seven "photoplays" for him over three years, with the option of extension if she were ill for any of that period. It seems to have been based on Dolores's expectation that he would deliver a long-term association with that studio, but she must have been in considerable confusion and distress to have given up her own autonomy in this way. Certainly, had Jaime still been in the picture, it would have been very difficult for Eddie to persuade her to sign such a document; she still seemed to need the psychological support of an older male protector, and perhaps with Jaime's departure she rejected as well his less-than-positive judgments of Carewe. She also seems to have been ill and very likely depressed throughout January, not reporting for *The Red Dancer* until late in the month and then falling victim to "an upper respiratory" ailment almost immediately.[15]

In the crucial clauses of her new agreement with Edwin, 8 and 9, she agreed to "act, pose, and appear solely and exclusively for and as requested by Carewe in the leading female roles of such photoplays as Carewe may designate. . . ." She would also "promptly and faithfully comply with all reasonable directions, requests, rules, and regulations made by Carewe in connection herewith; and . . . she will perform and render her services . . . conscientiously and to the full limit of her ability and as instructed by Carewe, at all times and wherever required or desired by Carewe." Meanwhile, she would not act or pose or make "any public or private appearances" in any theatrical capacity without Carewe's explicit permission. In return, she would be rewarded with a salary of $6,000 a week (which seems never to have actually materialized while she was still under contract to him).[16] This agreement gave the director the stranglehold over her life and career that he had coveted from the time he met her.

The day after Dolores signed the Carewe contract, reports that Jaime had moved away from Los Angeles and was living in New York began to appear in the press. One story portrayed him as proclaiming that he would not soon return to a town that called him "Mr. Dolores Del Rio." Lolita herself made the announcement of his move, and her language was dignified and still rings true. As she put it, "He was tired of simply being my husband. He wanted to make a name for himself. He wanted to accomplish something for himself. . . . So, finally, we talked it over and decided that he should go to New York, where he would attempt something on his own account. He hopes to get a play produced there." After denying they were separating or divorcing, she closed with a further denial that either of them was involved with anyone else. About a week later, a story datelined New York indicated that Jaime had sold a play and was writing a book on crime.[17] If true, nothing came of either endeavor, and her health continued to be problematic. On February 9, she contacted Fox again to say she could not come in to work, and the studio invaded her privacy by sending representatives to her home to check on her excuse. They found her swollen "about the right eye" and, by her report, "Breaking out on her back inside." At that point, a studio conference with Walsh and others led to a decision to cancel filming on *The Red Dancer.* Yet Fox pursued the matter, checking with her physician, Dr. Samuel Ayers, the next day. He said that what he diagnosed as a poison oak reaction had almost run its course, and she would be able to return to work in about a week. Fox's representatives indicated that Dolores had agreed to a "lay-off" without pay in the meantime and set February 20 as a definite day to return to the set. The filming continued, but Fox was close to canceling, and at this time it seems that the studio preferred to deal directly with her—even to a degree invading her privacy—than with Carewe.[18]

Lolita's denials of separation or divorce, of course, were quite disingenuous. She was taking a major step in her life, watching Jaime move farther and farther away from her without making a move to bring him back. The whole set of her upper-class Mexican notions of the proper role for women were changing along with his departure. By February, Carewe was in New

York City to arrange for the East Coast premiere of *Ramona*; he indicated that the major themes of the film, as illustrated by its principal scenes, were "birth, marriage and death." Yet the work went further, in Carewe's description, to encompass "other psychological treatments" including "loss of memory, *racial prejudice* and religious fervor." The New York article also recorded the brothers' family background as Chickasaw, a background they seemed to be increasingly willing to reveal within the context of the film. As a baby, Mr. Carewe had been given the nickname "Chulla," which, according to him, meant "fox." His brother Finis had retained the Anglicized name Fox, as did his brother Wallace; he himself gave it up for "Edwin Carewe" when he became a theater actor. In the same article, Dolores was described as "a Mexican with Spanish blood in her ancestry." Ramona, he said, was "half Indian–half Spanish," although in the novel Ramona had a Scottish father and an Indian mother. The article distinguished the real Lolita from the role: "This is the first time in her brief but rapid screen career that Miss del Rio has portrayed a character at least partly parallel in heritage to her own nationality." It seems to me that Carewe, a man of indigenous heritage himself, was directly confronting the issue of race and the treatment and views of indigenous peoples, using Dolores as a highly sympathetic model to push forward a new awareness that might change attitudes. Yet once again, in the interview, he backed away from designating *her* as in any way indigenous, emphasizing "del Rio is a Mexican with Spanish blood in her ancestry."[19]

At about the same time Carewe was visiting New York, Dolores received the most important award of her young life. At the 1928 "WAMPAS frolic," she was chosen by the U.S. public, with more than 200,000 votes cast, as the *one* among all ninety-one former Baby Stars chosen since the beginning of the pageant who had made the most "progress in picture work." She had appeared in ten films, according to the report, which added that Edwin Carewe was her producer, director, and manager. A photograph showed a radiant Dolores holding "Her Coveted Cup," a huge trophy almost three feet tall.[20] It was likely the most important recognition Carewe himself had ever gotten, as well, and a good example of the kind of celebrity that could result from awards generated by the press agents themselves. She was also publicized for her connection to Mexico in the festivities planned for the April opening of a Pan-American Exposition honoring aviator Charles Lindbergh's recent tour of Latin America. The celebration was meant as a tribute as well to the 435,000 Latin Americans who were believed to be living in the Southern California area, and projections were that perhaps 20 percent of this population would attend the weeklong event. Each country was to have its own queen. Dolores served as Mexico's royalty, to reign on the final day of the show.[21] Unfortunately, if this event took place, it was not mentioned again in the *Los Angeles Times.*

And there was good news. Just a few weeks after *The Red Dancer* began to film, Carewe reported that he and Dolores had an agreement for a several-film deal with United Artists.[22] Previously, in January 1928, grieving and depressed after Jaime's departure, she had signed the contract mentioned earlier that made Carewe's control of her personal and professional life possible. It was quickly followed by this unusual arrangement with United Artists, signed February 12, 1928, obligating her directly to make seven to ten pictures for them with Edwin as director. At the same time, Carewe obtained his own contract with them with the title of "Producer-Director"; he continued to hold yet another contract with Dolores directly as her manager. The total joint returns of the series of arrangements were estimated at the astronomical level of $5 million.[23]

Her contract with Fox completed, Lolita's next project was another with Carewe and her second with United Artists, *Revenge.* It went into production quickly after the wrap of *The Red Dancer* in order to take advantage of the success of *Ramona,* occasioning postponement of her planned European tour with that production. The story, a kind of "The Taming of the Shrew" set in the Carpathian Mountains among the gypsies, featured her kidnapping by a "gypsy-bandit, the arch-enemy of her father."[24] Naturally, though she wildly resisted, a little rough treatment brought her to love her captor. It is hard not to see parallels to Edwin's views of what had happened over the last year reflected in the script, with himself as the amorous bandit and Jaime, left behind, as the father.

To cheer Dolores up, and probably with the intention of initiating a romantic relationship with her, now that both spouses were out of the picture, Edwin chartered a yacht, the "Gypsy," in March 1928. The two sailed down the Mexican coast, ostensibly to shoot the exteriors of *Revenge* in a little fishing village there. Conveniently, the passengers included Gunther Lessing, the lawyer who worked with them to straighten out the Fox contract; he would figure in the divorces of both Carewe and Lolita and would reappear dramatically and negatively in her life thereafter. A newspaper report mentioned that this visit would be del Río's first to "her native soil" since Carewe had discovered her in Mexico. The story noted that it was "Needless to remark on her meteoric rise. You all know it. Who doesn't?"[25]

Yet less than two weeks later, the couple was headed back to Los Angeles. Another press clipping indicated that "Shipwrecks don't always occur in the movies. The yacht on which Edwin Carewe, Dolores Del Rio and part of the 'Revenge' company were shooting scenes off the lower Mexican coast went aground and the company is returning by train."[26] A story two days later claimed that the party had encountered "an earthquake, a storm, a shipwreck, a battle with mosquitoes and fever. . . ."[27] It seems likely, however, that Dolores simply found being in such close quarters with Carewe

Del Río under sail on the *Gypsy* with Edwin Carewe and Finis Fox. CEHM CARSO.

a little awkward. Even so, she posed with Edwin and Finis for a cheerful photograph on board, in which she looked radiant if a little too warm in a coat with a fur collar.[28] Another more realistic shot showed Dolores in a sleeveless dress and wearing a sailor hat.[29] Reports on their precipitate return emphasized that she was coming back for the first showing of *Ramona* and for a United Artists radio broadcast, as indeed she was; no doubt she was attentive to Schenck's wishes in this regard.[30] It seems possible as well that Lolita was beginning to catch on to Carewe's less-than-disinterested designs on herself and was becoming impatient with them.

Initially, during the cruise, Lolita herself was a little worried about leaving the ship; it was her first visit to her home country since her arrival in Hollywood almost three years before. She was concerned about her reception, given her announced separation from her husband, and in fact Mexican customs authorities initially prevented her from transferring her luggage from the yacht to a train headed back to the United States. She was finally aided by two military officers who obtained the appropriate permissions. However, while she waited, she was well received in Mazatlán, walking around in sandals without stockings. In the event, it seems to have been her bare legs rather than her marital status that caused the most comment among the townsfolk, despite the heat and the fact that such garb was now in style.

On all counts, however, her success in Hollywood, her becoming a Mexican celebrity in the United States, had overshadowed any social transgressions in her private life. She went to an event at the Royal movie theater, where the crowd applauded her. She also visited the La Muralla country club and went to a dance in her honor, held by the principal families of the city, at the Hotel Belmar. On the way back by train, Mexicans hastened to the stations to greet her, bringing flowers, embroidered handkerchiefs, and specially prepared food for the star. Dolores was delighted: "Never did I experience anything like it. My people are emotional. They give everything of themselves and they wanted to show me everything they felt." At the same time, Edwin tried to take advantage of their presence in Mexico by getting Lessing to help him obtain a divorce from Mary Akin, although she had declared that she would not accept any divorce decree he might engineer south of the border. In any case, at that point the local authorities refused to grant it.[31]

Greeted by the press immediately on her arrival in Los Angeles, Dolores quickly denied that she intended to divorce her husband but admitted that there had been no "improvement in our affairs." Carewe and Lessing were reported to be trying to figure out whether or not some mail-order divorce judgment that Carewe had received from elsewhere in Mexico might actually be legal. Meanwhile, Akin announced that she herself would seek a U.S. divorce from Carewe on the basis of desertion. In another report, Dolores insisted in regard to her own spouse, "There will never be a divorce between us—it would be too terrible." Jaime, ever the gentleman, issued a statement in New York saying that "I want to be somebody in my own name, . . . and that is impossible out there [Hollywood]. But my wife and I love and understand each other and will not be broken apart by busybodies. We will manage to see each other as often as possible."[32]

Still, though Carewe and his brother were ready to take over Dolores's life and career, the results would not be quite what these new protectors anticipated. Dolores was taking further steps toward controlling her own personal and professional future. And, it seems, she was very little hindered by any problems of racial identity. Joanne Hershfield's reading claims that "feminine beauty in the United States has always been conceived as 'white' beauty," and that because Dolores was not white she would be in the same category as African American stars such as Dorothy Dandridge. Yet, in contravention to Hershfield's denial that American celebrities might rise above the color line, for Dolores her beauty and her social status—not to mention careful handling by her publicist—established her as white, leaving no color line to rise above. Mexican racial identity had never been simple, and social class was as important as skin color in determining whiteness. The celebrity text that had been established early by Carewe and Wilson, along with her own stunning personal charm and beauty, placed her beyond this kind of scrutiny, at least overtly. Dolores's early roles put her in a number of categories: French peasant (*What Price Glory?*), glamorous and villainous upper-class Latin American (*Joanna*), charming and elfin Hollywood superstar married to a movie director (*The Whole Town's Talking*), Russian peasant (*Resurrection*), and half-Indian, half-Spanish woman dramatically torn between her two heritages (*Ramona*). In this diverse collection of ethnic and racial portrayals, Lolita was running a parallel career course to that of Rudolph Valentino, who had obviously thrived from such a strategy and one, perhaps, that Carewe, deliberately emulated. She was an exciting—but acceptable—female romantic lead, a thrilling dark lover. Hershfield is certainly correct when she notes that actors of various racial and ethnic backgrounds moved back and forth in the racial categories of their roles, and Dolores was by no means unique in this regard.[33]

Del Río played roles in which her phenotype made her believable, but she herself was not categorized as "nonwhite"—exotic and foreign, yes, but not completely outside of the definition of whiteness at the time. This view, it seems to me, was one that Carewe himself sought to extend. She was not challenging the "continuing climate of cultural and legal injunctions against miscegenation," as Hershfield argues, although she was running cautiously along the edges of these laws and sentiments.[34] Rather, she herself, though constantly billed as the "perfect Latin type," was establishing a particular standard of beauty within a complex and multifaceted measure of race that included ethnicity and social class, as an upper-class, white Latina, and pushing beyond what earlier might have been acceptable in U.S. films. In so doing, it seems to me that she was actually establishing a more inclusive definition of just who might be considered white, and if so, she was fulfilling a Carewe-Fox agenda as well. Certainly, Carewe and her publicity agents emphasized her class status, rather than her ethnicity. It is correct, however, as Hershfield also argues, that she was attractive to white men, and white women and other audiences also seem to have loved her. Of course, she was also attractive to people of color and of non-U.S. nationalities. Perhaps most important, particularly for her later career, she was becoming a model of triumph—both social and professional—for Mexicans of both genders and on both sides of the border. Carewe and her publicity agents, of course, made sure that her successes—and her beautiful images—were internationally disseminated.

Other aspects of her persona, both on- and off-screen, were more complex than those involving simply race. Her husband and Carewe, struggling over her affections and over Dolores herself, still had tried to protect her reputation as a woman of "impeccable morals" within the standards of Mexican upper-class womanhood.[35] Surprisingly, given the already substantial extent of her transgressions by Mexican and to some degree U.S. standards—serving as a model for Diego Rivera, being willing to leave Mexico and star for remuneration in the cinema, separating from her husband, demanding and getting a say in her own career decisions—she was able in her early Hollywood years, and indeed throughout her career, to maintain her status as a lady, *not* a woman of questionable virtue. In this regard, she was unusual among Mexican actresses in early Hollywood, and perhaps her status had to do with the dignity she maintained in difficult personal circumstances and the personal choices she made along the way. Yet certainly through 1928, the struggle to establish some control and autonomy continued, and issues of reputation—and of being alone to face them—frightened her.

Meanwhile, the California and New York reviews of *Ramona* and of Dolores's performance were wonderful. Edwin Schallert wrote in the *Los Angeles Times* an advance review after an early showing. He insisted it was "a film with definite, though perhaps slightly restricted appeal, and will undoubtedly lend to the already keen interest in its very popular star." He discussed her mixed-race portrayal and her screen romance with her leading man, Warner Baxter, playing an Indian named Alessandro, with whom Ramona falls in love and marries when she discovers that she has Indian ancestry and will be legally able to do so. Stepping gently around issues of race and romance, Schallert indicated: "Enriching in charm are those episodes which depict the love of Alessandro and Ramona. There is reserve and gentility in the handling of this particular theme. And a note of fine sadness has been struck." When Alessandro is killed by a "vengeful rancher," Ramona is rescued by a Spanish-descent friend of her childhood, Felipe, played by Roland Drew in his first major role, and she is brought back from madness by his tender care. As for Dolores's performance, the critic noted that she was "unquestionably a talented and capable actress."[36]

Intriguingly, the United Artists organization decided to forgo "a big premiere opening." Instead, when the film, which the *Los Angeles Times* article noted had been in preparation for eight months, was finally ready, "it was determined to throw the doors open to the public, giving them an immediate opportunity of witnessing this presentation without delay."[37] Myra Nye, writing in the same newspaper after the premiere, insisted that "Dolores is more than Ramona. Ramona is she."[38]

Despite the relatively low-key introduction of the film by the studio, the presentation was designed as a spectacle to appeal to the general public. It included a musical show directed by Dr. Hugo Riesenfeld, complete with an "atmospheric prelude" of "California Memories"; a tenor singing a number from Victor Herbert's "Indian" opera *Natoma*; a woman costumed as a "Temecula maid" singing "Indian Love Call"; and six dancers presenting "brief Indian ceremonials."[39] Four days later, it was doing well at the box office.[40] When the film opened several weeks after that in New York,

Mordaunt Hall shared the views that Dolores was a fine choice for Ramona, Carewe had handled the difficult material with "admirable restraint," and the production was both "extraordinarily beautiful" and "intelligently directed." He closed the review with an assessment of Dolores's performance: "Miss Del Rio's interpretation of Ramona is an achievement. Not once does she overact, and yet she is perceived weeping and almost hysterical. She is most careful in all the moods of the character. Her beauty is another point in her favor." He was particularly taken with the scene in which Ramona discovers her Indian ancestry and is overjoyed that she can now marry Alessandro, her beloved.[41]

Finis Fox emphasized that he had written particularly cautiously to preserve the romantic aspects of the story, and Dolores's portrayal of the young woman deeply in love with a Native American man wrung the heartstrings of audiences. Certainly, both he and Carewe were careful of her treatment, and she was shown to considerable advantage. Despite her problems, she came through like a trouper and maintained her professional poise despite her distress. At the time, she described the script as a "beautiful love story—the romance of a girl, a half-Indian, who finds happiness in marriage with two men, an Indian and a Spaniard." She credited Finis with giving Ramona a "lovely, spiritual quality," along with a "depth of soul and a profound capacity for great emotion."[42] She later emphasized that the role had been very important to her in reestablishing a sense of herself and of being Mexican; in fact, she even served as a kind of expert consultant on everything having to do with costumes and sets. In the event, playing Ramona seems to have helped her get over the sorrows of the separation and her sense of loneliness and being far from home, and it certainly does not seem to have made her feel demeaned because of her race and ethnicity. She claimed that the day the script arrived she immediately felt a connection with the main character: "I was no longer a sad Russian woman, but a woman very much like myself."[43]

The advent of sound was yet another pressure at this difficult time, particularly for nonnative speakers, but also for English-speaking actors and actresses with less-than-optimal voices. United Artists and Schenck confronted the challenge directly. On March 29, 1928, the day after the Los Angeles premiere of *Ramona*, Dolores along with the other United Artists luminaries met at the Fairbanks bungalow at U.A. for a joint appearance on "The Dodge Brothers Hour" on the new National Broadcasting Company's radio network of fifty-five stations. After a discussion about talking pictures, Dolores sang the title song from *Ramona*. The important thing was to show the U.S. public that the stars of whom they dreamed possessed acceptable voices. Schenck planned the presentation to best set off his most important personalities. Pickford presented an intimate conversation for women, Swanson talked about film possibilities for young women coming to Hollywood, Norma Talmadge (Schenck's former wife) discussed fashions

Dolores's radio broadcast of the title song from *Ramona*, one of RCA Victor's first hit singles. Bibliothèque du Film.

and their role in films, and Barrymore recited the soliloquy from *Hamlet*. Estimates of the audience varied up to about fifty million people, although that seems unlikely. Still, it must have been heard by many. Carewe had encouraged Lolita to take up her singing lessons again, particularly as it seemed so clear that talking pictures were on the way. The reaction of the *Atlanta Constitution* reviewer was that her performance made them want to hear more, but as for the one song, "it wins us." Apparently her success was not just in Atlanta; the title song of *Ramona* became highly popular and one of RCA Victor's earliest hit singles despite rather tinny sound, all that the technology of the time could provide. Dolores herself said later that her singing was not particularly good and the sound, given the state of recording, was "ghastly," but the royalties continued for the rest of her life. The sheet music also sold well.[44]

Not all were convinced, however, that she could make an easy transition to talkies, despite the radio program. Elmer Douglass, writing in the *Chicago Daily Tribune*, commented rather acidly, "Dolores Del Rio [I never heard of her] followed with a Mexican song. Very passable soprano voice." Later, in the same publication, Quin A. Ryan was equally dismissive: "It is a nice treat to hear Dolores Del Rio sing 'Ramona' and elocute a bit in broken English, with a pronounced Spanish-Mexican accent, as she did . . . on a radio chain program, but we fear her speaking throughout a moving picture would be unintelligible and unhappy."[45] Perhaps Dolores was a harder sell in the center of the country than she was on the coasts; the Chicago papers rarely covered her at all. When she visited Chicago a few months later, on her way to Europe with Carewe and her mother, the *Tribune* dismissed her as a "screen actress" whom Carewe had "brought . . . to stardom from the obscurity of a Mexican village within the last two years."[46]

Less than three weeks after the Los Angeles opening of *Ramona*, she was headed back to the border to obtain the divorce she and Jaime had been denying would ever occur. In April 1928, with Jaime still in New York, she announced that they were permanently separated and that she would file for divorce, shortly after Jaime, in an interview in *Variety*, once again insisted they would "never part." He was living in an exclusive bachelor hotel, not quite the sorry circumstances he portrayed to his estranged wife, and he claimed that the dark circles under his eyes were caused by time spent observing the seamier side of the city for his crime story. He also proclaimed his "utmost regard" for Carewe and his strong support for his wife's film career, while at the same time indicating obliquely that she did not have quite the refined tastes (affection for nobility) that he himself had—that is, she did not much like Gloria Swanson's titled husband, one of Jaime's best friends in the film capital. In the same story, *Variety* reported that rumors were swirling in Hollywood that Carewe would become the dazzling Mrs. del Río's second husband, and, further, that the divorce plans were being highly criticized in Mexico City. Opinion in *that* capital, according to the report, was very much in Jaime's favor.[47]

Her announcement, made on April 19, 1928, emphasized that her separation from her husband had only made things worse and the current conditions between them more intolerable. She acknowledged extensive consultations with U.A. head Schenck before making the decision, and his advice was no doubt that the uncertainty was endangering her professionally. Edwin was pushing her in this direction as well, and it is symptomatic of her youth that she still seemed to believe he wanted what was best for her. Her traveling companions to the Mexican border town of Nogales were, predictably, her mother, her lawyer Lessing, and her press agent Wilson, the latter two Carewe's creatures. The grounds were "incompatibility." She would not remain in Mexico to await the final declaration, she declared, but would return to Los Angeles and then travel to New York, with the arrangements being handled by her Mexican lawyer, Adolfo Ybarra Seldner. Dolores indicated that Jaime agreed to end their marriage after a series of telephone conversations in which he assured her he would not oppose her wishes. She asserted strongly that she had no intention of marrying again and believed he would not marry either. As usual, she tried to spare Jaime's feelings, indicating that he was bent on a literary career and she was sure he would succeed. Her further statement was dignified: "There is nothing more to be said on the subject other than that gossip has become unbearable to us both and that we are both keenly distressed that our domestic affairs have become public property." Carewe's own divorce proceedings continued pending in Mazatlán.[48]

Jaime's statement on April 20 was equally guarded and polite, somewhat bitter yet supportive of his wife and regretful about the end of their relationship: "I shall always love her. I will no longer be a millstone about her neck. Neither will I be hampered in my own life by thinking first of her interests and sacrificing mine to them. You know, the husband of a rising star should obliterate himself"—a statement that eerily foreshadowed the tragic events to follow. He asserted his undying love and his belief that he had the same kind of love from Dolores, adding that "We will both hold the other's memory tenderly." He ended poignantly, saying that in the event she would like to retire in six or seven years, "when she is around 29 years of age" and at the "top of her career," "I should certainly wish to remarry her."[49] Nothing Jaime said was designed in any way to wound her; to the contrary. Nevertheless, given the rumors about Carewe, she seemed the villainess in the piece, and her handlers were concerned that her public acceptance might be harmed. Still, Jaime further tried to explain the issues to his friend Edgar Neville. As he described it, " . . . to the degree that [a star's] success increases, the importance of the spouse diminishes; he little by little loses all personality and is converted into a kind of a ghost. Dolores, I must say to honor the truth, did what she could on her part to preserve my self-esteem, making an effort always to give me the significance that I deserved; but the battle was lost from the beginning. I was not happy in that atmosphere and Dolores knew it."[50]

Two days later a newspaper story reported her having been marked as the victim of a $100,000 kidnapping plot devised by her former maid, Rosa Ayala, who, it was claimed, had stolen a diamond ring from her home earlier. Two men were reported as under arrest, information confirmed by Homer Cross, the LA captain of detectives. Three other men—an Italian, a Mexican, and a "half-caste Mexican," all with long police records—were being sought. The Italian, reported to be the maid's lover, was designated as the mastermind. The two men in custody included one Gustavo Carillo, who was described as "suave, well-groomed, . . . and a university graduate." Elaborate details were supplied about all the aspects of the plot, including the maid's intentions of getting into the house by bringing back del Río's fur coat. At that point, the five men were to push their way in, take Lolita, and hide her in Sonoratown. The report concluded that Lolita was under constant police protection.[51] Yet only one day later Carillo, described in the later report as a "garrulous young Mexican," collapsed in tears, denied the plot, and admitted that he had concocted the story to avoid extradition to Arizona, where he faced two felony counts. Ayala, who was also arrested, was quickly released.[52] Dolores later made statements to the police clearing the woman of any suspicion but fired her anyway.[53] It seems possible and even likely that the incident was concocted by Wilson, Dolores's press agent, in order to gain sympathy for her from the public, though her wealth and publicity made her a plausible target of such schemes. Yet Wilson may have earlier devised the story about her loss of an emerald ring for publicity purposes, and this new incident seemed to be strangely similar, even if it escalated considerably in intensity.

Another attempt to prevent her image from suffering from the divorce resulted in negotiations with Mexico's former president and once again president-elect, Alvaro Obregón. He and Dolores had met several times, as he regularly traveled in and out of Los Angeles from his home in the northwestern state of Sonora during his time out of office.[54] After the divorce was finalized, press agent Wilson went on to Mexico City to ask Obregón to name her as the ambassador of Mexican women, with the portfolio of discussing women's "emancipation," during her upcoming European tour. Whether this potential charge was more than a publicity stunt or Dolores had any part in devising it, no evidence remains. Rather, it seems to have been Wilson's notion devised to put a positive spin on her divorce. Obregón's somewhat bemused reply directly to Dolores indicated there were no precedents for the suggested nomination, but he would discuss it with the secretary of foreign relations when he arrived in Mexico City at the beginning of July. He signed as her "admirer and friend." However, Obregón's own assassination just a few weeks later eliminated any possibility of such an appointment, along with attendant public relations benefits.[55]

Meanwhile, Dolores was finally wrapping up production with Fox Studios on *The Red Dancer*. The hope, clearly, was to capitalize on the success of *Resurrection*, although in this case the story had a happier ending. Filming was delayed yet again when she went briefly to San Francisco for the premiere of *Ramona* in that city. While there, she contracted poison ivy (perhaps), spent several days in bed, and then learned, to her distress, that Jaime's projects in New York had failed and that he was going on to Europe to explore possibilities there, although in fact he did not depart for several weeks.[56] Perhaps he was still hoping for a reconciliation. Perhaps she was, too. Certainly she was still emotionally distraught over the separation, and the shooting of the film had once again put her in the middle between Carewe and Walsh, in a most uncomfortable way. One wonders, given her ongoing skin problems, if perhaps these were recurrent attacks of hives or shingles rather than poison oak or poison ivy, given the extreme stress she was under. Yet Dolores soon returned to finish *The Red Dancer*, stress or no, and it premiered on June 26, 1928, less than three weeks after *No Other*

Woman, a movie made in 1926 by Fox Films but released only after the enormous successes of *The Loves of Carmen* and *Ramona.*[57]

Meanwhile, *Revenge,* abandoned in March when Edwin and Dolores returned from Mexico, still needed to be completed. Based on a story by Konrad Bercovici, it was originally entitled "The Bear-Tamer's Daughter." This rather clunky title was changed at Dolores's request so that it would begin with the letter R, associating it with the spectacular successes of *Resurrection* and *Ramona.* United Artists wanted the filming wrapped so she could tour Europe with the latter film. These European tours had been popularized a few years earlier by her U.A. collaborators Douglas Fairbanks and Mary Pickford, when they extended their honeymoon to go to England and the continent to publicize their own movies.[58] In Europe, Dolores would speak, sing, appear publicly, become a personality. She was already known as one of the most beautiful women in the world; this trip would give her a further opportunity to be seen as more than just a screen image.[59] A report in the *Washington Post* announced that she required "two social secretaries" to deal with the "dozens of invitations from notables and society leaders of Paris, London, Vienna, Berlin and other great centers in foreign lands."[60] More important, perhaps, the tour would distract audiences from the stories about her divorce and interest them instead in her elegance; and, by presenting her as a sophisticated figure in a European setting, it would offset any questions that *Ramona* might raise about her racial background.

Just days before the divorce became final, Jaime was again reported to be about to leave for Europe, according to information gleaned from one of his friends in Hollywood. And then, in a very sympathetic story, the newspapers reported that "Del Rio" (that is, Jaime) was planning to write a play about the film colony under contract to the American Play Company, an agency that handled the work of Eugene O'Neill, Edna Ferber, and "many other reputable writers." The article went on to say that Jaime had made himself "well-beloved" in Hollywood "before the position of being Mr. Dolores became unbearable for him." He would go, it said, to his mother's hacienda in Spain to do the writing, with a representative of the agency accompanying him. An interesting closing line indicated that "the gentlemanly Jaime is to depict Hollywood in a constructive light—a fact which sets to rest whatever uneasiness besets the minds of the much maligned colony."[61]

When the divorce was granted on June 7, 1928, Dolores reported to the press that Jaime was sailing the very same day for Europe. She further emphatically denied that she would wed Carewe, declaring in regard to the difficult end of her marriage to Jaime that "I am very happy that it is over with. I am interested only in my work and do not, at this time, contemplate any other matrimonial adventures." The divorce decree indicated that she and Jaime had been separated for more than six months, since September 1927. The breach between them, it alleged, was Jaime's fault, a result of the "incompatibility of characters as well as artistic careers." Jaime did not admit guilt but did admit the separation, and the divorce was granted.[62]

Revenge was completed by August, and she could now proceed relatively unencumbered (except by Edwin, who was to accompany her) to Europe. She, of course, could claim the European experience and sophistication that Carewe lacked, and Dolores's ubiquitous mother was along. There were still strains between Carewe and Dolores, although then and later she was careful to testify to his significance in developing her screen persona. The press acknowledged her as part of Hollywood's royalty, now under exclusive contract to United Artists, and she was said to be traveling with twenty trunks full of the clothes and accessories she needed to make her queenly. Interestingly, her diamond ring, claimed stolen prior to the abduction attempt almost four months earlier, was reported found in one of her trunks.[63]

After traveling to New York by train, the party embarked for London August 18 on the *Ile de France*, one of the world's most luxurious ocean liners. On their arrival in England on August 23, the media frenzy was impressive, and the August 24 papers carried photographs of her arriving at Plymouth as well as coming into the city on the boat train.[64] The *London Daily News and the Westminster Gazette* announced that Dolores would be touring country villages and city slums, quoting her as explaining she would be "getting to know the types which on [sic] the films I myself have to represent."[65] The *London Evening Standard* reported in the subhead to their story that she hated "Society-women Parts on [sic] the Films," that she liked "Love Stories the Best," and that she felt it was "Better to be Brainy than Beautiful." Probably not even the reporter believed she actually thought that, although perhaps she meant it. In any case, it was a refutation of the story, allegedly by her, published in 1927 in which she or her ghostwriter claimed that intelligence might be a problem for actresses. A reporter, in this case, described her as "sparkling": eyes, hair, jewels. In regard to her physical endowments, she herself claimed to be unimpressed: "I do not suffer from beauty. I simply happen to be different. . . . Any pretty woman who complains of being embarrassed by her beauty is merely posing." This final comment, at least, seems reasonable. She later declared, in an interesting self-identification, that she was of the "exotic type," and that "beauty [was] a divine gift." She further said that she simply could not stand "happy endings in films." When queried if there were happy endings in her own life, she answered in a reply that must have worried Carewe, "a few, not many."[66]

Asked immediately about talkies, she responded to a *Daily Sketch* reporter that "I don't like them. . . . I think it's an awful noise," and, given the state of the technology, she was largely right. She went on to say: "Stars don't like them at all, because it's against technique and against every principle we have. . . . The theaters want them because they're making money, but I think it's only because it's a novelty, and it won't last." After mentioning that she owned six hundred perfumes, she juxtaposed the comment with another indicating how much she liked acting "in rags." According to her, "Poor people aren't taught from childhood to hide all their sentiments. They are much more free in expression, and that's what I like to interpret."[67] Again, her high-status reality was juxtaposed against the roles she played.

A *Daily Express* reporter gushed about her "cocktail of an accent—two parts American, one part Spanish, and just a squeeze of guitar music." He also exclaimed about her jewelry: "two large emeralds set in diamonds . . . on her right hand, the great diamond on her left hand, and the two diamond bracelets on her right wrist," highlighting her expensive adornments. He also reported a brief expression of defensiveness about her native land; once again she declared a concern that Mexicans were always portrayed as villainous in films, and that she intended to do something about this image: "I'll put that right good and plenty." The same article proclaimed that John Gilbert was her favorite film actor, a predilection she shared with Greta Garbo and later with Marlene Dietrich. As for love, she acknowledged its hazards, while emphasizing its Latin aspects: "I don't think the Latin girl loves more easily than the Anglo-Saxon. We just show our feelings more. They bottle theirs up. With us it is love, and then—pop!—the trouble begins." Naturally the interviewer was charmed.[68]

A *London Daily Mail* reporter, as enchanted as the one from the *Daily Express*, declared that she was "radiant as some tropical bird." He remarked on her language skills, noting "her natural choice of the right, though by no means always the expected words." As the article went on to emphasize, "Her voice, like her whole person, vibrates with energy."[69] In this way

London's newspapers predicted her success, just as silent film was on the threshold of yielding to sound. *The Daily News and the Westminster Gazette* interviewed Dolores and Edwin together. Carewe, when asked about her, said that what impressed him most was "her dynamic force." He emphasized that she was "ready to work all the time, and the result now is that, next to Charlie Chaplin, she is the biggest financial proposition in film." Though prodded, Carewe declined to put a dollar amount on that value.[70]

Interestingly, at about the same time *Cinelandia*, Mexico's leading movie magazine, speculated about the future of foreign stars in Hollywood, including Lolita, and the coming era of talkies. The story indicated that all were thinking, "Will sound film ruin us?" They named del Río and her cousin Ramón Novarro as "still questionable," while Greta Garbo, with her "detestable" Swedish accent, was singled out (quite erroneously) as a goner. The accompanying photograph of Dolores, by Chidhoff of New York, was glorious; a tight black cap contained her hair, and she wore a plain black dress, putting all the focus on her huge eyes and perfect skin. The caption read, "An interesting 'pose' of 'our' Dolores."[71]

Dolores had a fine time in London, touring everything from the National Gallery, where she spent five hours one afternoon (her favorites being da Vinci and Raphael), to an evening in the East End. The latter, unsurprisingly, she visited with a reporter. Racial issues surfaced briefly when she saw five Chinese women and three white women drinking in a public house run by a black man. "Gee, I don't like that somehow said Miss D. R.," the story reported. Of course, such a comment defined her as white and as sharing the racial attitudes of most other whites. She further commented that Limehouse was "an orderly place," "a parlour compared to some parts of Chicago," which she had visited in her U.S. *Ramona* tour a few months earlier. She claimed lugubriously that when there, Chicago's mayor took her to see the jail, where she observed "the first woman to be electrocuted . . . [and] the last man to be hanged" (both presumably still alive at that point rather than corpses) and "girl criminals of every type." She went on to say that Mexicans, like Russians, being "somewhat downtrodden . . . understand tragedy better than comedy and things that are unreal."[72]

News reports paid little attention to Carewe, although he was noted as being around from time to time. Perhaps he himself became a little impatient with his protégée's celebrity. Or perhaps the rumor that Jaime Martínez del Río had taken rooms at the Hotel Savoy, where Dolores, her mother, and Edwin were staying in London, were true. According to one biographer, Lolita invited Jaime to tea in her suite but found that although she remembered and appreciated what he had been to her, the relationship was in the past.[73]

French reporters were likewise delighted when she arrived in their country, noting that she was able to conduct her interviews in their own language. She continued her defense of silent films, objecting to talkies, insisting that movies should provide a quiet haven. She also talked about making films showing the peaceful Mexican countryside, rather than the violence, assassination, and warfare that had recently been portrayed in Hollywood productions during and in the wake of the Mexican Revolution.[74] Reporters in Paris relegated Carewe to about the same status as Lolita's mother, noting only that the two were accompanying her.[75] Almost the only major notice of Edwin came in a strange report that he and Jaime were to fight a duel in Paris over the lovely Dolores. Carewe denied the reports and insisted that he and Jaime were the best of friends. Apparently, however, Dolores saw Jaime every day during their stay there, so perhaps Carewe's jealousy was more than a figment of a reporter's imagination.[76] At about the same time, Jaime was said to be squiring Consuelo Pani, the daughter of Mexico's ambassador to France, around Paris and perhaps contemplating marriage to her. Since the well-connected Jaime was certain to know the Mexican ambassador and his family, it seems likely he was playing the gallant escort rather than the suitor.[77] Reports from the next stop, Berlin, were also focused on Dolores, and it was again claimed that she owned six hundred perfumes. A song written for her, *Der Tag der Dolores*, was popular at the time. One report headlined simply and delightedly "Dolores is here!"[78] Jaime also went on to Berlin; although it is unclear whether the now-divorced couple saw each other there, it seems likely.

Carewe's presence and stature in the film industry was finally noted when Dolores's party arrived in Italy. The short article indicated he had attended the University of Texas and the University of Missouri but never received a degree, pursuing instead a career as an actor, director, and producer.[79] Still, the heavy emphasis was on Dolores, and the two continued to be somewhat at odds as the trip wound down; whatever its nature and gravity, the tension between them was unresolved. In the event, Carewe preceded her back to the United States, claiming to the press that he needed to begin preparations for *Evangeline*, her next film, which would be shot in Louisiana.[80]

The *New York World* celebrated her own return shortly thereafter with a large photograph in its Gravure Section captioned "A Queen of Filmdom Greets New York," acknowledging her iconic, almost royal stature.[81] An interview with a Spanish-speaking reporter, Manuel Montes, in New York's *El Latino-Americano* hinted that a break with Carewe might be imminent. Despite her elegant all-black outfit from Paris with its "devilish little black hat," she was significantly more animated and informal, with her little dog and her mother both in attendance, than in her carefully scripted English and French interviews. When the reporter wondered why she had not made a film about Mexico, she said she had not encountered a good script and asked him to send along anything he came up with. When asked how she felt about being alone, she insisted, "I am not alone, I'm with my mother, and with respect to weddings, no, no, and no." When asked if she would soon travel to Mexico, she talked at length about how much she missed it but said that film contracts would keep her busy in the United States for some time. She showed the reporter a large album of Mexican and Latin American phonograph records she had been carrying in her travels to keep from getting homesick.[82] All in all, her mood seemed more cheerful and relaxed than it had been in some time, perhaps because she was speaking Spanish, or perhaps because she was beginning to resolve her ideas about her relationship with Carewe and her own divorce, though Carewe met her train when she returned to Los Angeles.[83] The press attention did not let up after her return to California; both *Screenland* and *Screen Book* featured her on the cover in November. The latter publication presented the "Complete Book-Length Novel" of *The Red Dancer*.[84]

A month later, tragedy struck. Newspapers on December 4, 1928, announced that Jaime Martínez del Río was dying in a Berlin hospital. First reports said that he had entered the hospital suffering from a boil, but that complications had resulted and he was almost moribund. Juan Sánchez Moreno, a Spanish priest who was close to the family and who had married Dolores and Jaime, was said to be hastening from Madrid to administer last rites, while Jaime was widely reported as asking his friends obsessively about Dolores. Her first comments to the press in Los Angeles indicated that she and Jaime continued to have a strong friendship, that only the week previously she had gotten a long letter from him, and that he was writing a play about Hollywood. She underlined that Jaime was in good spirits when he wrote, very happy about his new project and his plans for the future; she was therefore optimistic.

Unfortunately, new reports indicated that he was suffering from blood poisoning, had a temperature of 104 degrees, and was partially paralyzed. Rumors had circulated earlier that Jaime and Dolores saw each other when she was in Berlin during her European tour and perhaps had even remarried; Jaime's friend and collaborator Fred Stein insisted that the two had not even seen each other during her visit to Germany, but this claim is unlikely. She herself told the press that neither she nor his mother or brothers, who were in Mexico City, would go to Berlin, because the trip, which would take three weeks, would not permit them time to arrive during the crisis.[85]

The next day, reports indicated she had sent Jaime an urgent message, saying, "Fight hard, Jaime. Fight hard." At that point he had been unconscious for several days, but he briefly woke. When the message was read to him, he replied, "Tell her I'm fighting." And then, later, deliriously, "Why doesn't Dolores come upstairs? Don't let her wait down there." Dolores, meanwhile, declared to the press, I think quite genuinely, that Jaime was her best friend in the world and she refused to believe he was dying.[86] Dolores issued a statement to the press, indicating they had been in constant contact since the divorce and were writing to each other regularly. As for their contacts during her European visit, she claimed, "When I was in Paris on my tour we were together every day. There is no ill feeling whatever between us in spite of things which are said." She confirmed the report that he had contracted blood poisoning after an operation for a boil.[87] Meanwhile, she tried to stay in touch by telephone.[88]

On the 6th, she sent another cable, proclaiming her love, and a few minutes before his death, yet another arrived, saying "Keep up the courage. I don't forget you in my heart. You must get well. I love you. Dolores." Meanwhile, Dolores had contacted United Artists' representative Curtis Melnitz in Berlin, desperately asking him to keep her informed and do everything possible to help save her former husband. Melnitz did in fact see Jaime, who asked him to send word to Dolores that he was much cheered by her words and would "fight to live for her." Stein, the writing collaborator on the Hollywood story; Melnitz; and another friend, Paul Mooney, stayed with Jaime almost constantly. Stein reiterated that the dying man had repeatedly called for his wife, to whom he was totally devoted. The scene at the bedside was dramatic, with Father Sánchez Moreno, the Martínez del Río family priest, "fervently" praying, and a physician on the other side of the bed monitoring Jaime's pulse. Melnitz, Stein, and Mooney waited silently at the foot of the bed until the physician declared, "It is the end." Another report claimed that Jaime's last words had been "Dolores! Dolores!" The next morning, Dolores's mother and her secretary broke the news to her that the "handsome and talented" Martínez del Río had died. Dolores was said to be devastated and initially unbelieving. She was described in the story as a "fiery little actress," who had continued to hold strong feelings for her ex-husband.[89]

Strangely, the *Los Angeles Times* obituary indicated that the friends at Jaime's bedside could not agree on whether or not Dolores and Jaime were married at the time of his death, responding to the rumors that the couple had remarried during Dolores's European tour. Melnitz himself insisted he could not believe they were divorced, because "if there ever was a couple that loved each other, it was Dolores and Jaime. She telephoned me from Hollywood frantic with grief. Every waking moment of his illness, Jaime spoke of Dolores, kept muttering her name when he was unconscious, and died with her name on his lips."[90]

The news about Jaime's death took up seven columns on the first page of the second section of *El Universal* in Mexico City on December 9. The report dramatically stated that Dolores had sent him one last telegram saying simply, "I adore you," and that the suffering man held on for several days in the hope that his former wife would rush to his bedside. A further dramatic note indicated that Jaime's last words were "Do you think Dolores is coming?" She was said to have fainted at the news of her ex-husband's demise, after sighing in the arms of her mother, "My Jaime." At the same time, bitter assertions were recorded in print accusing Dolores's mother of forcing the couple's separation. Doña Antonia, it claimed, was looking for even more fame for her daughter and for this reason had favored Carewe over Martínez del Río.[91] Whatever the truth of the matter, it was convenient in both Mexico and United States to place the blame on her, thereby lessening the disapproval that might have fallen on the star herself. A further tragic note is added to the story when one realizes that four months after Jaime's death, a story that he had written was converted into a film starring Mary Astor. *The Woman from Hell* was produced by Fox Films, the studio where Dolores had enjoyed her first major box office successes, with a pair of screenwriters, George Scarborough and Annette West Bay Scarborough, preparing the final script for leading lady Astor.[92]

"I was a widow after Jaime's death," Dolores later said in an interview. "That's the way I felt after Jaime died." She said that she saved herself through immersion in her work. She also noted bitterly of that period that "Hollywood has no compassion."[93] Rumors that Jaime had committed suicide circulated widely, particularly in Mexico, fueled by the suddenness of his death. Whatever the circumstances, she seems finally to have acknowledged Carewe's deliberate undermining of her relationship with her former husband. Certainly Jaime had a great attachment to her (regardless of whatever the sexual relationship between them was), and the attachment was mutual. When Jaime was buried in Berlin, where his body would remain for six months until being taken to Mexico, Dolores telegraphed Melnitz, asking him, "Please purchase an abundance of flowers, including a wreath bearing the inscription, 'My beloved.'" A report of this first funeral said her flowers were the only ones on the coffin at the mass at St. Matthias Cemetery.[94]

Yet despite the continuing ties between them until Jaime's death, and Dolores's insistence that she would not marry again, she had already engaged legal representation in Europe to secure an annulment of her marriage from the Roman Catholic authorities. This representative, Dr. Emil Kammerer, proceeded to Paris to secure from Jaime certain declarations and documents for the proceedings and was there at the time of Jaime's death. It may be that his previous requests on behalf of Dolores were what precipitated Jaime's suicide, if that indeed was what it was, and his death was not caused by an infected boil. Kammerer had apparently been communicating with Jaime from Vienna and believed him to be in France, to which country Kammerer proceeded. He failed, however, to receive a reply to his requests for a firm time for a meeting and therefore, on arrival in Paris, went himself to Jaime's residence, where, to his surprise—his "great stupefaction," as he put it—he was told of the death. Therefore, obviously, the need for him to continue further had become entirely superfluous and he was abandoning the case. He twice offered Dolores his deep condolences and confirmed that despite his inability to get appropriate documentation for the ecclesiastical case from Mr. del Río, her ex-husband had always behaved as a "perfect gentleman."[95] Regardless of the ongoing annulment proceedings, I think it is possible that Dolores was beginning to fear she had made a mistake in letting Jaime go, and particularly in listening so carefully to Edwin, who, for his part, was by no means a perfect gentleman.

When Jaime's estate was settled a few months later in Mexico, Dolores made no claim on it, leaving his mother, Barbara Vinent de Martínez del Río, as his only heir.[96] Meanwhile, the rumors continuing to circulate in both

Mexico and the United States that Jaime had taken his own life on the one hand cast a certain pall of blame on the grieving Dolores, but on the other added to notions of her sexual power over the men in her life. That idea that Jaime had died for love of her gained currency, whether it had any merit or not, is symptomatic of the great power and attraction she herself was seen to have over men—so great that this particular man could not live without her.

The year therefore ended sadly for Dolores, but it seemed to mark an important turning point. She was becoming more autonomous, beginning to establish herself as separate from the older men who wished to supervise and control her private and professional existence. Despite her insecurities in speaking English, she was already making her transition into talking pictures. She was still young enough to expect several more years of roles as a romantic heroine in Hollywood. Two years of appearing in these roles led to no overt attacks on her, either racially or ethnically; and her appearance in *Ramona* highlighted issues of prejudice against indigenous people and at the same time defused them and made her an international star. A connection with one of the most important organizations in the film business, United Artists, promised a dazzling future. Despite a separation and then divorce from her socially prominent Mexican husband, followed by his sudden death, there seemed to be more public sympathy than sanction for the grieving Dolores. She made one more film with Edwin Carewe, *Evangeline*, perhaps her finest Hollywood effort and the one in which she spoke her first few halting lines of dialogue. Despite their growing differences, Carewe in the early months of 1929 directed her in one of her most poignant and sympathetic roles. It was a performance that would have made Jaime proud.

6   Fame and Its Perils

By the 1930s, Hollywood was the third-largest news story in the
country, with some 300 correspondents, including one from the
Vatican.

                    Joshua Gamson, *Claims to Fame*[1]

Modern fame is always compounded of the audience's aspirations
and its despair, its need to admire and to find a scapegoat for that
need.

                    Leo Braudy, *The Frenzy of Renown*[2]

1929 AND 1930 were years of difficult ups and downs for
Dolores, and Jaime's death brought her some sympathy—
but also perilously close to scandal. Yet the *Ramona* experiment worked;
she played the role of a mixed-race person and remained coded as white,
acceptable still as a paired romantic lead with white leading men. Her association with United Artists in two major films, *Ramona* and *Evangeline*,
brought her to the pinnacle of stardom. They were the last that she made
with Edwin Carewe. Now, finally, she made a break with him, at the behest
of her new studio, leading to personal discomfort and two lawsuits, which,
though not brought by Carewe himself, were almost certainly encouraged
by him. The suits seemed deliberately designed to destroy the reputation
she and Jaime had guarded so jealously since their arrival in Hollywood.
But her contract with United Artists and these two films gave her enormous box office power, accompanied by an association with the "highest
what is," in Hollywood studio terms, as Edwin had put it a few years earlier.
This success was entirely dependent on her remaining able to work with

her beauty unimpaired. Before the end of 1930, she remarried; her new husband was one of the most important and talented men in Hollywood. Then she was struck with a mysterious and devastating illness, and her career, always dependent on her physical well-being and beauty, took a nosedive.

The last film she made with Carewe, *Evangeline*, was a valentine to Lolita, the kind of totally sympathetic and almost saintly role Jaime Martínez del Río had unsuccessfully encouraged and demanded. The tale, based on the poignant Longfellow poem, tells the story of an ill-fated love, with sweethearts separated tragically during the forced removal of the Acadians from Nova Scotia. The film shows Evangeline (Dolores) searching for years for her lost love, spurning other suitors and going from settlement to settlement, sometimes getting close but never locating her man—not until, at last, she finds him dying at the end of the film. At this point, she speaks a few words of dialogue—the first time her voice is heard on the screen aside from her songs.

The numbers for *Evangeline* were important in her success and were carefully chosen; Carewe commissioned one of them from Al Jolson, who

Lolita on the set of *Evangeline* with director Edwin Carewe, far left, co-stars Donald Reed and Roland Drew, and her friend Ruth Tildesley. Alice J. Topjon Collection. Reproduced by permission.

by this time was the leading light of American popular song. Dolores sang in both French and English.[3] The lyrics were written by Billy Rose, and Irving Berlin, Inc., published the sheet music, which also sold well. On the back, in an early example of media synergy, appeared an advertisement for Mary Pickford's "Song Hit 'Coquette.'"[4]

Her performance was arresting and successful, perhaps because she could identify with the character who had lost her first love to separation and then death. It seems remarkable that Edwin would have chosen a role for her that emphasized loyalty to such a love, either before or after Jaime died, given how obviously he had tried to destroy the actress's attachment to her real-life husband. However, it showed her sympathetically and may have had some effect in diminishing the public's potential disapproval of her divorce and what appeared to be its drastic consequences: the tragic demise and rumored suicide of her former spouse. It may be, as well, that this role clarified her own ideas about how Carewe had pushed Jaime and herself apart, and her guilt over the devastating aftermath. One biographer has suggested it was Edwin himself who identified with Evangeline's loss of her lover, recognizing his own estrangement from Dolores; the film shows "the meeting, separation, search for, and death of the loved one."[5]

In any case, it seems clear that as the filming began Edwin still had hopes that they would marry; instead, it pushed them further away from each other. Not only did these last few months of collaboration make it clear to Dolores that he had played a major role in the disintegration of her marriage and had inflicted humiliation after humiliation on Jaime; she began to resent his heavy-handed attempts to dominate her. He had helped to make her a great star. Now, however, she possessed the power of stardom as well as of her personal friendships with the Hollywood elite, which would make it possible for her to break off their connections. She was eager to be free of the male domination experienced from the time of her engagement, only weeks after leaving the convent as a teenager. Tellingly, in February 1929, she asked Gunther Lessing, her attorney, to change her name, cutting out both Asúnsolo and Martínez, leaving her officially with Del Rio. The press noticed that this operation resulted in "slenderizing her nomenclature and rendering it more in harmony with her sylph-like figure, which is one of her chief assets in the films."[6] It also brought her legal name into compliance with English orthography, rather than Spanish, and she continued to use the spelling publicly until her return to Mexico in the early 1940s.

Dolores was now very popular, and that popularity extended beyond the United States, though *Revenge* and *Ramona* were not the box office hits that some of her Fox movies, particularly *What Price Glory?*, had been.[7] But the *Ramona* tour in Europe was successful, and during the filming of *Evangeline* she tied in the London voting (250,000 total ballots cast) for favorite actress with Betty Balfour, followed by Clara Bow, Vilma Banky, Florence Vidor, and Mary Pickford. (The previous year, only Balfour and Pickford were in the top six, with Balfour number one and Pickford number five.) The British actor Ronald Colman, also a United Artists star, topped the list of men, which included both Sydney and Charlie Chaplin. The same poll discovered that talkies had not yet won British hearts; 70 percent of the women and 50 percent of the men voted against them. Astonishingly, 60 percent of the voters were reported as attending motion pictures twice a week or more.[8]

Evangeline wrapped on April 28, 1929, ending the shoot on the seventeenth anniversary of Carewe's debut as a director.[9] Despite his already planning her next film—a potboiler featuring her as a courtesan, princess, and warrior—to be shot in India, *Evangeline* would be their last work together.[10] The film premiered in New Orleans, appropriately for its historic association with the removal of the Acadians from Nova Scotia to Louisiana, and Dolores traveled there with her retinue: journalists, her mother, her private secretary, and, of course, her publicity agent. Fans poured out to see her. A telegram from Carewe in June on the day *Evangeline* opened in New Orleans showed he had not yet given up on maintaining his influence over her and her career. Congratulating her for the enthusiastic reception on arrival in town, he informed her what the next three stops on the tour would be and that he was arranging the others. Now, however, he allied himself with her boss at United Artists as he indicated, "Mr. Schenck and I [are] exercising our careful judgment regarding your next picture . . . and want to be positive your first talking picture is 100%." (*Evangeline*, with its few spoken words, apparently did not count as a talkie.) He was finally acknowledging Schenck's preeminent importance to her future, and he had dropped his cheerful and affectionate "Querida" for "My dear Dolores."[11]

Her tour took her to New Orleans to Baltimore to Pittsburgh to Detroit—singing the title song, which, like the song from *Ramona*, became a hit recording from RCA Victor.[12] At this moment, Dolores, in a physical declaration of independence, decided to change her appearance. She had been very proud of her long hair, although it was usually tied back elegantly.

Now, suddenly, she decided to cut it. Her decision was made just before the first showing of *Evangeline* in New York City; Schenck himself was her escort for that spectacular event, and he approved of her new look.[13] The contrast between her role and her new appearance caused a sensation. Her reputation as a modern woman, cut off from the traditions of her class in Mexico, opened up not only a new professional world but also a private one. Her travels included a visit to the president of the United States, Herbert Hoover, at the White House, though her appointment was delayed because she arrived without a diplomatic representative of her country. She contacted the Mexican Embassy, which solved the problem by sending First Secretary Pablo Campos Ortíz to escort her. The *Washington Post* announced it was a big day for Hoover, as he was visited by "three women internationally famed for their pulchritude": Dolores, the Viscountess de Sibour, and "Miss Brazil," who had recently represented her country at a beauty pageant in Galveston, Texas.[14] Lolita also attended a diplomatic ceremony to honor the memory of the nineteenth-century Mexican President Benito Juárez at the Pan American Union building. Again, her presence produced a commotion, and even the guides were reported to have forgotten their usual formal manner in straining to get a glimpse of the beautiful star.

Meanwhile, the Mexico City newspapers covered her successes with pride.[15] Several days later, she came back to Washington to appear on stage with showings of *Ramona*; a reporter noted that she was "a young woman of admirable qualities whose taste run [sic] more to the wholesome things of life than to the artificiality so often looked upon as inseparable from the theater." He noted that she wanted to be close to recreational facilities such as tennis courts and swimming pools, and that she prioritized her availability to the public over her meeting with the president.[16]

Valentine or no, *Evangeline* was not a big box office success. The review in *Variety* lauded the production: "Pictorially it's a smash; romantically it's a rave; but as entertainment it's very mild indeed." There was a further comment: "Doubtful if even the special following of Miss Del Rio will go wild about it. The paprika Latin girl has some good emotional sequences but somehow she doesn't seem to fit with the role of the saint-like maid. . . ." It noted that there was "no talk except one brief line at the finish, spoken by the heroine as her long search for her lover ends with his death in her arms. But it has three or four admirable song numbers, two by Miss Del Rio and one by Roland Drew, the hero. Singers are shown in closeups and impressions they are actually doing the songs is convincing in all cases."[17] The *Film Daily* critic concurred; the subhead noted that it was a "dignified, sympathetic version of Longfellow's classic poem. A photographic delight." Dolores was singled out for praise: "Miss Del Rio gives an interesting and nicely sustained performance and stands out easily from her supporting cast. She sings the theme song and, while her voice is small, it is charming."[18]

A beautiful photograph of Dolores by Edward Steichen published in September 1929 called into question in its caption the appropriateness of her appearance in the role. Pointing out that *Evangeline* had become an "American tradition" and the "idealization of the Nordic heroine, the fair flower of Puritanism," it noted, "To the children of today *Evangeline* will mean not the classic, if somewhat sentimental, Longfellow muse, but Dolores Del Rio, classic in her beauty, certainly, but as far from Nordic as Salem is from Mexico City." It went on to say that "Her début in the motion picture version of *What Price Glory?* established her immediately as one of the most glamorous figures on the screen. Subsequently in *Resurrection* she proved that she was also an actress of tragic intensity. Now she is embarking on a very different role—and a hazardous one—for *Evangeline* is an American tradition."[19]

Carewe hovered close to her during the filming, and yet when it was over she moved away from him quickly. She had ceased to believe he was a real protector. Soon she discovered that he would attack with ferocity what he no doubt viewed as her disloyalty, and what she felt was her escape. Meanwhile, whatever feelings existed against Dolores in her native country as a result of her engaging in a movie career were vanishing. Others of her class continued to become involved in the film business, either in Mexico or in Hollywood. The shift is reflected in a letter she received from her compatriot, the Marques of Guadalupe, during the filming of *Evangeline* in March 1929. The marques wrote to her from Mexico City with some pride, and perhaps a whiff of embarrassment, that he had just participated as an actor in a film known as *La boda de Rosario* (*The Marriage of Rosario*). This film, he claimed, would enhance the worldwide vision of the Mexican charro, the dashing horseman of the Mexican countryside. The plot, as described by the marques, was a fairly melodramatic story of unrequited love and death, with the heroine taking refuge in a convent after her hacienda-owner fiancé killed her true sweetheart in cold blood. He announced that he was sending Dolores some photographs for her entertainment.[20] Why the marques thought this film would improve anyone's view of Mexico is a little hard to discern. Yet the letter shows that people of her own social class had not only come to accept her celebrity, despite her divorce and its unpleasant consequences, but were also participating in films themselves.

Others with their own kinds of cinematic ambition were contacting her from the homeland as well. One of these was Federico Gamboa, the novelist whose works were beginning to be used in Mexico as a base for films and who hoped for more of an international audience. The social connection here is indicated in Gamboa's reminder that he had met her on the eve of her wedding to Jaime Martínez del Río at the home of her uncle, José María Luján, whom he claimed as his close friend. Further, he announced that he admired her cinematic work, particularly *Resurrection*. A friend and contact at UCLA had urged him to get in touch with her, seeking, if possible, to get United Artists to produce one of his novels with her as the star. With that in mind, he enclosed three of his books—*Suprema Ley*, *Metamorfosis*, and *Santa*—for her consideration. Perhaps, he said, United Artists would be interested in producing one of them, resulting in "a new triumph for you and your ascending trajectory as a star, a delight for Mexico, and a benefit for me." He indicated that he would be ready to move to Hollywood, at studio expense, if it seemed desirable. Even at this early date, he was already a little concerned about possible censorship in reference to *Santa*, the story of a prostitute: "If the hypocrisy of those people causes them to mount objections to *Santa*, let them modify it to your tastes, as long as they don't destroy it and change it into something different."[21] The letter was written almost simultaneously with the announcement that she was about to be married for the second time, and so she may not have paid much attention to it then. But she must have answered, because correspondence between them continued.

Another document in her archive shows it was not only Mexicans who were hoping for her help but also other Latin Americans as far away as Argentina, a country just beginning to develop its own film industry. In this case, the writer was seeking advice, and perhaps somewhat more direct help. Gregorio Martínez Sierra, the director of an acting company in that country, wrote her in the hope that she would counsel him about working in Hollywood in producing Spanish versions of English-language films. He said a number of representatives of U.S. companies had approached him with the idea of using his actors in this way, but he was concerned that these firms might not be entirely reliable. He worried that the market for Spanish-speaking films would never be sufficient to justify giving up the theatrical business in which he and his company specialized, a concern that was much mistaken. On the other hand, he was willing to consider the prospect, in the event she thought there might be an opportunity for him to do the actual writing of the Spanish dialogue. He told her he was planning a visit to California to investigate the possibilities, if she thought it was worth the trouble. We have no record of her reply, but it is indicative of the way in which she was becoming an important contact for Latin Americans hoping to get a foothold in Hollywood.[22]

At the same time, many Mexicans were crossing the border and some of them were coming to Los Angeles, looking for work. Dolores was not the only one who succeeded, but she was the most visible in 1929 and 1930. Many of her compatriots actually tried to make contact at her home, leading her to take measures to isolate herself a bit. These efforts gave rise to the idea that she was eager to distance herself from Mexico. At the same time, Dolores was beginning to take on a more elegant and more universal persona, even in her appearance.[23] Her contacts in Mexico, as in the United States, were largely with people of her own class, especially the artistic and intellectual elite.

Carewe's communications with her were now rather frosty and formal, indicating that he recognized her efforts to escape his control. A May 1929 letter to her about the tour with *Evangeline*, indicating that Art Cinema had made the arrangements in accordance with "our contractual agreements with them," was a case in point. In a sentence in which he made clear his former and now waning influence in a major aspect of her life, he indicated he would "purchase and pay for your appearance wardrobe, which is now being made under your supervision, as per your order." Before, even her clothing had been subject to his approval. In an ominous indication that her health continued to be fragile, he closed by saying, "I am happy to learn you have fully recovered from your recent illness, and I wish to complement you upon your splendid work in our recent picture of EVANGELINE."[24] By June, however, he was friendlier, apparently still believing he would be working with Schenck in directing her career.[25]

When she returned to Los Angeles in September after her tour with the film, she discovered that Carewe had remarried his former wife. This news was likely a huge relief to her, and yet another release from personal obligations and responsibilities.[26] Apparently, at about the same time Schenck told her he and Considine had decided to buy out Carewe's interest in her contract and that Schenck himself would be directing her career in the future—news that she certainly welcomed.[27] In an interview at about this time with journalist Adela Rogers St. Johns, Lolita emphasized that she was, for the first time, able to do what she herself wanted, after having been under the control of others from the time she left the convent. She declared she was ready for romance, laughter, and silliness, to make up for lost time.[28] However, there was a disturbing note in the contract she signed on October 18, 1929, directly with Feature Productions, a wholly owned subsidiary of United Artists run by Schenck and Considine and the production arm of Art Cinema Corporation. It went on at length about cancellation of her contract should she become ill and unable to report for work. It may be that her health problems, which almost derailed the filming of *The Red Dancer*, were becoming a major concern for her new employer.[29]

On October 31, Carewe sold del Río's contract to Schenck and Considine's Feature Productions. The cost was reported to amount to more than $500,000, an astronomical sum in 1929. He was represented at the conferences by the personal lawyer he had earlier shared with del Río, Gunther Lessing. Lessing's involvement distressed her, and so she decided to dismiss him as her attorney in future matters.[30] Dolores was now, in a certain measure, liberated. Her decision to move on from her association with Edwin, along with Jaime's death, freed her from older male protection and patronage and her sense of obligation to a set of difficult relationships, and she seemed to be sheltered by a contract that would pay her an enormous salary. Carewe was furious and demanded damages directly from her for breaking her contract with him, and at the advice of the lawyers at United Artists she settled her part of the case for about $100,000, a serious personal expense. According to one of her biographers, United Artists, in order to make the blow a little softer for Carewe, gave him exclusive control over future productions starring Lillian Gish, who had been active in pictures since 1912 and was one of the largest female draws in the business.[31] Even if this were true, however, Gish was at this point already thirty-two years old, approximately seven years older than Dolores, and in Hollywood terms facing a much shorter future career. Even with this sop to his pride and the substantial cash payoff, Carewe was wounded and furious.

At that very moment, the world around her was shifting. Black Tuesday, October 29, 1929, saw the abrupt collapse of the stock market and destruction of great fortunes all around her—just two days after United Artists bought her out of Carewe's contract. Dolores herself had put almost all her money into real estate, so her financial well-being was relatively unaffected, but her fortune made her a target. An immediate and very unpleasant incident followed the crash, when in December Gunther Lessing sued her for $31,000. Lessing, of course, was much closer to Carewe than he was to her. Edwin, having agreed to a financial settlement with Lolita that precluded further legal proceedings in his own behalf, almost certainly urged him on. According to the *Los Angeles Times*, the film colony was shocked by the suit, as it was "the first intimation that he [Lessing] and Miss del Río had broken business relations of several years standing." The lawyer noted that he was filing because of the "lack of gratitude and appreciation" she had shown him. It seems more likely that he was really bitter because of the break between Carewe, for whom he continued to work, and del Río, and the loss of control over her that both men had suffered.[32]

In bringing the suit, he claimed that she had sought his services after the armed movement against Mexican President Plutarco Elías Calles, led by the former revolutionary general Enrique Estrada in 1926, collapsed. According to him, she had taken an active part in the rebellion and sought his help after its defeat to avoid her own deportation. Estrada, an associate of Calles and his predecessor, Alvaro Obregón, when the three fought together in the Mexican Revolution, had revolted first against Obregón and Calles in late 1924. The second rebellion, in which Lessing claimed that Dolores participated, took place in late 1925 and early 1926 and never really got off the ground. Estrada was eventually convicted of violating U.S. neutrality laws in 1927, the proof being his extensive purchases of instruments of war, from machine guns to airplanes. He spent several months in prison; Lessing's claims seem to have confused the dates of the court proceedings against Estrada and his "army" with the purported rebellion itself. Dolores would have been just moving to Los Angeles at the time that Estrada was engaged in gathering supplies and getting ready to invade Mexico, and it is extremely unlikely she was involved in any revolutionary conspiracy. Certainly her name never came up during Estrada's trial. In making such claims against del Río, the lawyer was deliberately putting her position in Mexico—as well as in the United States—in peril. Not only was her image as an innocent young woman in jeopardy, but perhaps also her immigration status: involvement in Mexico's internal problems could be grounds for ejecting her from the United States.

Dolores told a different story. She attributed the lawsuit to her break with Carewe, who, she claimed, had made her professional life impossible, trying to prevent her from obtaining new roles, new contracts, new directors. At that time, she decided that Lessing, given his direct relationship with Carewe, was no longer an appropriate legal representative. She had dismissed him, paying him a large sum for legal services already rendered. She denied any involvement in any plot against the Mexican government, insisting that her Hollywood career had kept her busy "24 hours a day" in recent years. Her new lawyer presented the court with a complete schedule of her activities, showing it was impossible for her to have taken part in any such scheme. And yet far from discouraging Lessing, the lawyer continued pressing his case for more than two years, adding charges that del Río influenced his wife against him, leading her to sue for divorce in early 1930; that the star had almost been named as co-respondent in the divorce complaint that Carewe's wife took out against Edwin in 1928; and, in general, trying his best to besmirch the reputation that Jaime *and then Carewe* had been so zealous to protect during her early years in Hollywood.[33] Though Lolita fought the charges, as we will discuss below, it seems reasonable to believe that she would have been frightened and feeling very much alone, and yet to some degree liberated.

In still another interview, this one with Gladys Hall, probably given on December 23, 1929, she said quite directly:

I find that I am born again. I have never been myself. Never, in my life. I have never been free. I have never been happy. I have bowed to conditions, circumstances, to the dict[ates] of other people. . . . I have been suppressed and repressed all of my life. Repressed [in] my work, repressed in my personal life. I am not, by nature, melancholy, weepy, sorrowful, languishing, sweet. I am not patient. I am not conventional. I am not a Ramona [or an] Evangeline. More, I am the girl of *What Price Glory?* There for a bit, I could show my real self. I am, by nature, tempestuous, fiery, stormy, eager. I have never had a chance to express the sex that is in me. I am going to begin now. I am going to be free.

It was an interesting declaration of independence, one not free of bitterness. In a reprise of her life to date, she said, ". . . I have been maid and wife, divorcee and widow and actress. I have made money and I have known success. I have lived in a dream and I have worked long hours on end. I have known the greatest grief of my life—the death of Jaime. Death had never come near to me before. I had never experienced it. I shall never recover from that scar. It is one of the scars that has made me a woman." Still, in an interesting and telling reference to the circumstances of her marriage and possibly to Jaime's homosexuality, she called Jaime "a stranger" and insisted that her marriage to him was like living with "another kind friend who told me what to do and how to do it. I loved him as a child loves an older man who is kind to her, who takes her places and gives her things, who knows more than she does. *My husband loved me as a man loves a child. He did not love me as a man loves a woman.*" Insisting that she regretted nothing, *"Nothing,"* she nevertheless said, in a probable reference to Carewe, "I have learned ugly things about people. *I do not believe in anyone.* I know that there is no loyalty in man or woman. . . . I am going to take advice from no one, counsel from no one, persuasions from no one."

In a further declaration of independence, this time from her birth family (though not, presumably, from her beloved and supportive mother), she confessed: "When I was a child I was repressed because of family traditions. Because my people were conservative and old-fashioned, I couldn't do this or say that or go there because of how it might 'look.'" In a disclaimer of class, she asserted that "I have become democratic. America has taught me democracy. Hollywood has taught me. When I came here I believed in class distinctions. I felt that I could not know this one or that one, could not go into this or that group. I have no more of that feeling. I understand better. We are all akin." In closing, she announced, "I want freedom. I am going to get down to life, whatever it may be."[34]

Yet despite her declarations of independence and whether or not she felt strongly about acquiring a new male protector, her mother was very concerned that she marry again as quickly as possible. A good new marriage would furnish her both private and professional shelter.[35] In the meantime, she continued her professional career. In the first few months of 1930, she made *The Bad One*, produced by Schenck and Considine. Originally, Carewe was slated to direct her, but the relationship between them had grown so difficult that it led to the huge settlement between him and the studio mentioned earlier. He was replaced by George Fitzmaurice, an experienced director who had worked with luminaries such as Pola Negri and U.A. stars Valentino, Colman, and Banky.[36] During this time, Lolita was very much distracted by the problems with Lessing and Carewe. The lawsuit showed that neither of them had accepted, much less forgiven, her defiance, and Lessing's legal action seemed designed to destroy her.

In fact, what seems to have ensued was a kind of older man, younger woman gender war, played out very publicly in the press, a reverse campaign from the one carried out in the first three years that del Río was in Hollywood. In July 1930, Lessing claimed that Dolores had engaged in a deliberate campaign to get his wife to leave him, calling him "an ugly older man," reminding Mrs. Lessing that she was "a young and beautiful girl," inviting her to stay at her own home and even permitting her to wear her own jewels, "humiliating" him. Although Mrs. Lessing promised her husband she would not see Dolores again, the promise was not kept, according to the complainant. Del Río promised his wife employment in the film industry and "cast aspersions and slurs upon the integrity of Attorney Lessing." He further claimed that his wife continued to see del Río, despite the fact that she knew her "to be a personal and violent enemy" of her husband's. Mrs. Lessing denied the charges, calling them "unfounded and approaching the ridiculous," though she did not deny their friendship. Dolores's lawyer called the accusations "preposterous and unfounded." Del Río herself immediately refuted Lessing's accusations, saying these claims were "false and malicious and are made in an attempt to embarrass me. . . . There is absolutely no foundation for his ridiculous statements. They are made of whole cloth and are falsehoods." Mrs. Lessing's counterclaim against her husband accused him of dragging her around by the hair at a Hollywood party and throwing water in her face, as well as having had two or perhaps more extramarital affairs. There were also intriguing Mexico connections. Lessing and his wife had married years earlier in Mexico City, where the lawyer was the judge advocate of the U.S. Army in that country. Mrs. Lessing had a child by a former marriage, whom Gunther Lessing adopted. The legal status of this child, John Carter Lessing, was also in dispute, as both parties to the divorce sought to obtain custody.[37] Doña Antonia, Dolores's mother, was even called to the stand, where she admitted that Dolores helped Mrs. Lessing after she left her husband, particularly since Lessing was only giving the woman $40 a month, an inadequate sum for her and a child to live on.[38]

Dolores, still grieving after Jaime's death, was discovering that Carewe and his crowd were much harder to shed than her gentle and gentlemanly former husband. Meanwhile, her new film, *The Bad One*, despite Schenck's and Fitzmaurice's supervision, was not as successful or flattering to her as were the movies under Carewe's and Walsh's direction. The story told of a young woman who worked in a bordello in Marseilles but struggled to preserve her virginity for the man she would marry. Despite the dramatic theme, it was a musical, and Irving Berlin—perhaps the best known U.S. composer of popular tunes—was engaged to write her songs. She danced the tango and sang, and this time she could choose her own costumes. In one scene, she wore a heavily fringed dress, cut low at the back, with a flower on her hip. Conveying a sensuality that would have distressed Jaime but would become her trademark through the next decade, she broke away from the *charming, innocent young woman* role in which she was being type-cast. Yet even though the film made clear that she could be convincing in English dialogue, with an acceptable accent that was certainly less problematic than that of another major female star, the Swedish Greta Garbo, the problems of interacting with the microphone—which might be hidden almost anywhere on the set and was only unidirectional, dictating where the actors would stand and in what direction their voices would project—made the new production tense and difficult. The film was not a success, except insofar as it showed Dolores's ability to transition to sound.[39]

Life on her own was not working out well. Then, suddenly, romance and marriage put her once again under the protection of a powerful male. Cedric Gibbons (best remembered, perhaps, for his design of the Oscar statuette in 1928) was the artistic director at Metro-Goldwyn-Mayer. Despite this slightly innocuous title, he was one of the most powerful men at the studio, and indeed in all of Hollywood, setting the style for MGM and supervising sets for more than a thousand films over a period of thirty-two years. The story of his creation of the Oscar gives a sense of his significance in early Hollywood: he designed it on a sketchpad at a founders' meeting of the Academy of Motion Picture Arts, and it was sculpted by an artist named George Stanley. Cedric was born in Dublin in 1893 (though accounts of his birthdate differ, as do those of Dolores, and some reports say he was born in Brooklyn), the son of a family of architects. As a teenager, he spent time in Europe, developing an appreciation for art that would lead him later to develop an impressive collection of books on art and architecture. Lacking an aptitude for mathematics, he studied painting at the Art Students League in New York City, and was working in the film industry at Edison by 1915. He was one of the first designers to insist on three dimensions for his sets, rather than filming against flat painted backgrounds. His style was simple, yet elegant and lavish; Billy Wilder, the director, called Gibbons's signature style "white satin decor." It was a design motif into which Dolores, with her dark beauty, fit perfectly.[40]

Gibbons had the elegance that Carewe lacked, and the success in the film industry that Jaime never achieved. Classically tall, dark, and handsome, strikingly similar in appearance to her first husband, he towered over the petite Dolores. He knew how to dress, arriving at work every day in a three-piece suit of excellent cut, his outfit completed by gloves and a gray homburg. His vehicle was a Duesenberg. Yet he was no temperamental genius, despite the "cult of personality" that developed around him; art director Preston Ames later commented, "You never worked for this man. . . . You always worked with him." Although he himself did few of the actual designs (with the exception, of course, of the Oscar), he supervised his department carefully and worked closely with the plans that came to him from others. Access to him, however, was limited; operating from above, he did not interact much with those down the line among his enormous staff. According to Ames, however, "nothing, absolutely nothing, went through unless Gibbons had okayed it." He was exceptionally well organized and a good judge of talent, choosing outstanding individuals to manage the subdepartments where the actual sets were produced. He disliked cluttered rooms, preferring white walls and sets that were highly lit. In his own home, he opted for simplicity and light. Although Ames was not referring to Dolores when he commented that "Cedric Gibbons believed that the case had to be worthy of the jewel," the house Gibbons eventually designed for Dolores would fit into his aesthetic, known as the BWS: the Big White Set.[41]

Dolores was a jewel indeed, despite her troubles. At about this time, journalist Julia Lang Hunt described her arrival at a party for two hundred guests at the home of Fredric March. She came dressed in white, her face like "a madonna of Leonardo da Vinci" and her body that of a "Greek statue, a goddess." For a moment or two, all conversation stopped. Then the man standing next to Lang Hunt declared to her that the woman who had just entered was the most beautiful woman he had ever seen in his life. When Lang Hunt asked if he wished an introduction, he declined, claiming that he would not know what to do, that it would be like meeting an object of art. Another actress, standing nearby, declared that seeing Dolores always spoiled her day and made her want to run for a beauty parlor.[42]

Although accounts differ, it is probable that Dolores met Cedric in 1928, when he was overseeing the design of the sets for *The Trail of '98*, the movie that led to her early defiance of Carewe. She had also been at the Hollywood studios of MGM for costume fittings and other matters related to the film and may have met him there.[43] In 1928, of course, Dolores was still torn between her husband and Carewe. But in July 1930, she was on her own and under attack, vulnerable yet as lovely and charming as ever.

At this same time, another Mexican actress with quite a different background was developing a "Mexican spitfire" image that was far from ladylike and would end in tragedy and suicide. Lupe Vélez, also associated with United Artists, had played a "wild mountain girl" in Douglas Fairbanks's film *The Gaucho*. She received a five-year contract from the company, playing mostly "half-caste" women. In 1929, just as Dolores was suffering through the effects of her divorce, Jaime's death, and her difficulties with Carewe, Vélez was engaged in a public and flamboyant love affair with Gary Cooper, her co-star in *Wolf Song*. During the affair, she gave an ill-advised interview to *La Opinión* in Mexico City, declaring that women in Mexico were being lied to and controlled, unable to "laugh, speak, say what [they] think. . . . Here [in the United States] I laugh and do what I want, because the American boys understand well." The interview led to outrage in Mexico, and Vélez apologized in the same publication a week later and blamed the quotes on bad translations.[44] As the flap around Lupe became more and more condemnatory, Dolores no doubt felt herself threatened as well. Vélez never had the kind of family support and social standing that del Río did, and the especially precarious nature of her position was clear even in the period when Dolores herself was at risk.

Perhaps, then, when Cedric and Dolores met again in July 1930, she might have been open to accepting the protection of a new, elegant, and cultured man—this one, however, highly successful. An article in the *New York Times* a year later suggested he had "probably ordered the artistic destinies of more pictures than any other art director in the industry." He had come to Metro-Goldwyn-Mayer with Samuel Goldwyn after a merger between studios, and he directly controlled six unit directors, twenty draftsmen, and about a dozen more staff; indirectly, his office "sets in motion the hands of some two thousand other artisans within the studio." He had already won an Oscar

(1929) from the Academy before he and Dolores met for the second time; he would go on to win ten more, and would be nominated twenty-seven times.[45]

Gibbons saw her on the screen, and possibly in person when she was preparing *The Trail of '98* at MGM. After her divorce, he asked two friends of hers, actress Marion Davies and newspaper magnate William Randolph Hearst, for an introduction. Cedric and Dolores finally met at a weekend party at San Simeon, the couple's elaborate southern California estate. Cedric's reaction to her film images was not unusual in her romantic alliances; after all, both Jaime and Eddie had seen her dance as a teenager and were enchanted. Later romantic entanglements involved similar circumstances: males would see her on screen and yearn for personal encounters, and some of these fantasies would be realized during her lifetime. Happily Cedric was not trying to use her to advance his own career; nor did he want to be a kind of Svengali controlling her performances.

Along with Pickford and Fairbanks, Davies and Hearst were among the most powerful couples in Hollywood. Prevented from marrying by Hearst's inability to get a divorce from his wife, they openly and lavishly lived together for years, throwing some of the film colony's most elaborate parties. The estate was in fact a series of palaces and pavilions, and it is still a tourist attraction.

On this occasion, the guests came by private train on Friday, leaving in the late afternoon from Glendale, dining lavishly on board, and arriving in the wee hours at San Luis Obispo, where a bevy of chauffeur-driven cars waited to convey them to the estate. Davies and Hearst greeted their guests the following day at lunch; in this particular gathering, the two guests who were seated in places of honor were Dolores herself and Gibbons.[46] At opposite ends of the table, each was queried by the respective host or hostess what he or she thought of the other; both of them expressed interest. After lunch, Gibbons asked her whether or not she liked animals, and receiving an affirmative he invited her to see the Hearst zoo, among the best in the country. The two spent the afternoon walking through the grounds of the estate. Discovering their mutual interest in art, he showed her some of the fabulous paintings and sculptures Hearst and Davies had acquired to adorn the various buildings. They were seated together at dinner, and their hosts were pleased to see that their two guests seemed to be getting along. When they returned by train to Los Angeles, Cedric's Duesenberg was waiting at the station, and he gave her a ride home. By the time they arrived, they had already made a date for lunch at MGM.

Within days they were acknowledged as the most exciting new couple around town, dining together in such star-studded venues as the Cocoanut Grove. One such occasion was a discreet dinner party that her old friend Eduardo Iturbide, who encouraged her in 1925 to go to Hollywood, gave at the Blossom Room of the Roosevelt Hotel, though Myra Nye's newspaper account listed both of them as guests but did not indicate that they were together.[47] Iturbide must have approved of the match. Cedric proposed to her on the last day of July, after just a few days of lavish parties, dinners, and constant conversations. She accepted.[48]

The wedding proceeded with suspicious haste. The first announcement seems to have come from friends, with the report in the *New York Times* datelined July 30. On July 31, she herself confirmed the engagement, which, tellingly, followed Gunther Lessing's filing of the suit blaming her for his marital problems by only a week. Headlines on that occasion trumpeted "Star Accused of Breaking Up Marriage," as Lessing charged that Dolores had used "Gifts, Promises of Film Work and Parties" to "Lure" his wife away. He claimed that the course she followed was deliberately designed to alienate his wife's affections. Regardless of the truth of the matter, both women were clearly defying gender norms of the time and place, and the headlines were damaging. Even in some of the reports of Dolores's upcoming nuptials, the Lessing charges were mentioned as a part of the story, with reminders that Jaime Martínez del Río had died only a few months before. The *Los Angeles Times*, for example, noted Dolores's rise "to screen fame almost overnight after being brought here by Edwin Carewe" and went on to mention that "only last week Miss Del Rio's name was mentioned in a divorce suit." The announcement of the engagement startled the press, and the newspapers reported that although she and Gibbons were seen together, she had also been dating a number of other men. The Mexican reporter covering Los Angeles at the time, Rafael Ibarra, was a little behind the curve, as he reported bemusedly that "nothing had been known about this relationship."[49] On August 4, the *Los Angeles Times* cheerfully headlined a story with a photograph of Dolores looking soulfully at Cedric, "Here Comes the Bride."[50]

The ceremony took place on August 6, just a few days after what she claimed to be her twenty-fourth birthday but was actually her twenty-sixth. The site was the Santa Barbara Mission, her gown that of a "Spanish señorita," according to one fanciful journalist. In fact, it was a simple and elegant pale gray dress, covered in her wedding pictures by a wrap coat with heavy fur collar and cuffs, and a cloche hat, all in a pale color. Dolores's mother's outfit was almost identical to her own. Cedric was dapper, as he always was in public, in an elegant suit and his signature gray fedora hat. Despite published reports that Father Augustine of the mission would refuse to perform the ceremony, Dolores received official permission from her home parish to remarry since Jaime's death had freed her to re-wed. The investigation centered, therefore, on Gibbons, and the authorities found that his previous marriage did not conform to church laws and therefore presented no impediment. Newspaper coverage quickly shifted from the harsh headlines generated by the Lessing suit to the wedding, which took place just at the beginning of the annual Santa Barbara Fiesta. A perhaps not quite accurate report claimed that del Río's "eyes were big and wide with excitement and she clung to the arm of Gibbon [sic] who, to tell the truth, was as white as a sheet and scared to the point of collapse." Photographs, however, do not bear out this latter assessment; Gibbons looked proud and pleased, and Dolores thrilled.[51]

Quickly, she went into a new film for United Artists. Unfortunately, before the month was out, she was ill again. *The Dove*, in common with many films that starred del Río and other Mexican stars, was to be made simultaneously in Spanish and in English, in the hope that it would get good Latin American distribution. Yet it would be some time before it was made, and then not by United Artists. According to news stories, at a dinner toward the end of her honeymoon she became ill, possibly from ptomaine poisoning. Then she collapsed on the set of the film; her physician ordered her to bed. Another report in September claimed she had been ill for more than a month, and this one hinted at the seriousness of her illness. Indications were that she would not be able to return to work for two months, or perhaps more, while United Artists was reported to have spent $100,000 in preparations for the filming. Studio executives, of course, registered their concern but were hesitant to make a statement about the delay. Current speculation about her malady was that it was a serious kidney infection, causing dangerously high temperatures.

Nevertheless, between the glamorous marriage and falling sick, Dolores had begun to turn around the bad publicity relating to her divorce, Jaime's death, the relationship—whatever it was—with Carewe, and Lessing's lawsuits. A September article made this plain: "Her illness, following so closely on her marriage to Cedric Gibbons, has the sympathy of all Hollywood."[52] This serious affliction, which seemed to be a relapse of the pelvic problems that had plagued her earlier, was extremely problematic for both her career and her marriage. Later, she commented that she had had "a delicate illness" during the years of her marriage; Cedric, she said, behaved as a perfect husband throughout these ordeals. These hints suggest that her poor health interfered with her sexual availability, and it is even possible that it arose from an abortion that had become septic. One of Greta Garbo's biographers suggests that Garbo and other actresses, in these years before reliable contraceptive devices were available, had access to abortions performed by a doctor who was engaged by the studios "on a shared-cost basis," and that after a couple of these procedures Garbo might have been terrified of sex. If that had been the case with Dolores, the social stigma would have made it an even more frightening experience than if it were, indeed, a kidney infection. In any case, an illness that likely could have been easily cured with antibiotics got badly out of control.[53]

No doubt her general level of exhaustion and stress contributed to her collapse as well. At the end of November, she was still ailing and submitted to what was described as "minor" surgery at the Good Samaritan Hospital. Her physicians said at that time that she would be able to return home in two weeks, and indeed she seemed finally to get better.[54] Only one letter from Cedric to Dolores is available in her archive, though he must have sent her many. It is undated, but it is clearly from the period of time when she was ill in the earliest days after their marriage, and it makes clear how sincere and deep his feelings for her were. Addressing her as "Darling," he wrote:

It seems strange to be writing you; it makes me feel you're far away somewhere and this [is] the poor substitute for speech. And it is the first time of many times to come I write you the words I love you darling and I am completely happy at the thought of your love for me. I feel so certain that there is such great happiness in store for us and it is all just beginning. I am the most fortunate man with the most beautiful woman in the world for my wife.

He went on to discuss the changes he was making in the house that they would occupy, and commented that he would go by on his way home to give the builder some instructions on the painting. He closed: "My dear little angel who's going to get well so quickly now. I send this with James. Please consider yourself completely kissed. I love you, Cedric."[55]

But Carewe had not given up, though he was now replaced in every aspect of del Río's life, and the lawsuit resumed despite her illness. In May 1931, the Lessings announced publicly that they had reconciled. This action forestalled further discussion, in court at least, of del Río's involvement in their breakup. Four months later, in yet another skirmish in the case, Lessing again brought up the fact that Lolita had almost been named co-respondent in the divorce case brought by Mary Akin against Edwin Carewe. The "association" (i.e., sexual relationship) was said to have occurred in 1928 while Carewe was directing del Río in a motion picture. Dolores herself admitted that Akin had threatened to bring suit for alienation of affection against her, and that Carewe gave Akin a great deal of money to drop the action. Dolores was quoted as replying, "Say, they sure had me scared of that for a little while. . . . Nothing happened . . . because Mr. Carewe gave some money to Mary Aiken [sic], and it was settled right here in this office." Lessing further accused del Río of owing him money for consultations with her own family during her problems with Jaime, for suppressing unpleasant publicity, and finally for going to Mexico to help her with divorce proceedings there. In addition, Lessing claimed to have advised her about possible actions regarding "libelous articles" that appeared about her in film magazines. Other services were noted: he had aided Chala Brown, del Río's secretary, when she was threatened with deportation, and advised del Río and negotiated with her employers when she objected to particular "salacious scenes" in her productions.[56]

The first of these allegations posed a veiled threat against del Río, because the loss of her own visa would have meant an end to her Hollywood career. Further, his charges constantly reminded the court that she was Mexican and violating gender norms. He seems to have hoped that casting doubt on her sexual reputation might lead to a questioning of her upper-class Spanish-descent Mexican identity. A scandal could bring her closer to the Mexican/Indian designation for less-respected persons of her nationality. In this way, he might damage her and avenge the challenge to his male dominance, and maybe her rejection of Edwin in the process.

A peculiar further development in the long-lasting suit was the soap episode, which illustrates not only the pressures brought by powerful men, even outside of the film industry, against young female stars but also the early commodification of film celebrity. Lessing claimed that del Río was approached by a soap company in search of her endorsement, but he advised her against the contract because he felt it would be "not . . . very dignified." The same company, obviously one with significant funds to spend on advertisements, persuaded a film magazine to publish an unpleasant article about del Río and then threaten to bar her name from any of its issues. Lessing claimed he had managed to prevent that from happening. Though we have no further evidence for the allegations, Lessing's testimony was taken seriously by the court. It is an interesting example of how stars, commodities, advertising, and editorial content in fan magazines were connected and of how celebrities were pressured into actions of which they may or may not have approved. Still another claim Lessing made was that he had obtained a $25,000 bonus for her for *The Red Dancer*, even before she was in what he referred to as the "big money." In fact, this money was a flat fee for the film, but he was eager to take credit for it. The conflation of legal consultation and friendship brought a brief rebuke from Judge Minor Moore, who pointed out, "Examination of a lengthy contract, of course, comes under the head of legal service, but the reading of a beautiful story—a scenario, perhaps—or conversing with a beautiful screen star, even frequently, might not be such hard work."[57]

The next day, there was even more damaging testimony from Lessing, who insisted he had handled the divorce between Jaime and Dolores with great care because of the possibility for scandal. He also mentioned that she received a number of letters threatening her life, from a former employee, and that he (Lessing) found it necessary to hire a Hollywood police officer as a private guard. "Because of the quietness and lack of scandal" (one that he clearly was now trying to foment), Lessing believed he should receive $10,000 for this incident alone. Detailing his duties, he claimed he took care of twenty interviews or more with reporters and dispatched forty-two letters and telegrams to Jaime, telling him what he should be saying publicly and what he should not. Although Lessing repeatedly tried to enter details of the divorce charges into the record, del Río's attorneys were sustained in their objections.[58]

Dolores herself testified a few days later. Described as "ravishing in an ultra-smart costume of black, its severity relieved only by the scarlet of her lips and sharply-pointed and hennaed fingernails," she was accompanied by Gibbons. The reporter noted that she would speak to her husband animatedly, though in whispers, whenever Lessing would take the stand. Occasionally she could be overheard, particularly when she objected to

Lessing's claim that he had helped her mother with an immigration matter, "Eet ees not true!" The orthography used was typical of the way in which her accent was recorded in news stories.

The following day, Loula Lessing appeared for her husband, claiming she heard del Río employ him for a particular task. On this occasion, the newspaper focused on the contrast between the women's clothing: Mrs. Lessing was in a "luxurious coat of beige hued beaver fur with darker brown collar and a demure little brown hat, with its brief brim only slightly shading her large blue eyes," whereas del Río again wore black. Mrs. Lessing's testimony shed light on what del Río had been expecting from United Artists and Joseph Schenck. The *Los Angeles Times* headline trumpeted, "Miss Del Río's Hope Revealed: Ex-Counsel's Wife Asserts Actress Elated at Deal; Schenck's Name Linked to Dinner-Table Talk; Talmadge Called Model for Career." The witness added that "she [Dolores] told me that Joseph Schenck was going to present her just like Norma Talmadge. . . ." Significantly, Talmadge was Schenck's former wife.[59] This reference may have been an indication that Schenck expected sexual favors from Dolores; minimally, it spoke to her high ambitions, and not in a particularly favorable way.

Dolores, testifying on the same day, was bitter. She emphasized that she believed Lessing had gone over to Carewe's side in her difficulties with her former director and mentor, and she must have resented the fact that the woman she had tried to help was now giving evidence against her. She obviously felt that Edwin had become an enemy, and she spoke about her happiness when Joseph Schenck and United Artists bought out Carewe's contract with her. She then understood from Lessing that he would continue to work for Carewe as well and dismissed the lawyer because she quite reasonably felt that this dual representation would jeopardize her own legal situation. Dolores's testimony was apparently teary and emotional, as she admitted having to forgo a year of salary to get out of her legal agreements with the director. Yet it was worth it, as she described her unhappiness working with her former mentor. In this case "unhappy" was written as "onhappee."[60] Even her accent was grist for the media mill, and it was an issue that went beyond the current case to her ability to fit into talking pictures.

Another report on the same day of testimony, though it did not make fun of her pronunciations, gave a complete and striking quote of her description of the moment when Lessing revealed his clear conflict of interest: "And when he called me on the telephone . . . and told me that he wanted also to represent Mr. Carewe, my worst enemy, regarding the cancellation of our contract and the drafting of the direct contract between United Artists and myself, I was shocked—I cried." The newspaper account did, however, report with surprise that she spoke five hundred words of "perfect English," except for her "broad accentuation of all vowels." The case rested after her heavily accented testimony. Earlier, however, Lessing had called several attorneys to the stand to estimate the value of his services to her; they testified that the proper amount might be anywhere from $27,000 to $43,000.[61]

A few days later, Judge Moore entered a more moderate $20,000 judgment against her in behalf of Lessing, with $16,000 left to pay. The judge's earlier sympathy with del Río seems to have eroded significantly, however. In regard to Lessing representing both Carewe and herself in the renegotiation of the agreement between them, he astonishingly claimed that ". . . the discharge was unjustifiable . . . in view of the long period of faithful service and of the fact that there could have been no conflict of interests of Carewe and Miss Del Rio in the proposed negotiations." He commented that she was "a young woman of more than average intelligence, . . . but temperamental and not especially crafty in the fine art of business." He also went on at length about her "phenomenal" success and the fact that "her services were readily in demand by the most prodigal [sic] of producers." [62] The judge does not seem to have been particularly clear in his wording; specifically, what he might have meant by or instead of "prodigal" is a mystery. But it *was* clear that he found both her success and her "temperamental" nature offensive, "temperamental" in this context perhaps being a code for Latin and female assertiveness. Though he cut Lessing's claims by $12,000, the judgment was still costly in 1931 dollars, and she had already paid Carewe a great deal of money. She cannot have enjoyed having to pay off her former director and her former lawyer in this way. It was several years before she again found a lawyer whom she trusted, and when she did, his association with her would last until his death.

Yet the verbal slap probably worried Dolores more than the money; she already had a great deal of it, and Cedric likely had more. Certainly those who worked with him believed him to be wealthy. Through her marriage, she became allied not only with a man whom one historian calls "the most powerful arbiter of style" at MGM but with someone who was very successful financially as well. He was respected throughout the film industry. His support for her and his willingness to take her seriously must have been very reassuring at this time, when her public break with Carewe and Lessing was being exposed in an ugly court case. Without Gibbons, it is likely that her career would have been over. With Gibbons, she was able to make a successful defense of herself against Carewe, who wished to dominate her and had done everything he could to ruin her first marriage. But in so doing, she risked the loss of whatever power and autonomy she had so far gained.

She survived the first major challenges of her film career; her charm and beauty, which led to the marriage to Gibbons, once again gave her a powerful male in her corner. However, Gibbons's support was much different from Carewe's. The latter crassly tried to dominate her and alienate her from others who loved her, and even worse, he worked her far beyond her physical capacity in order to make himself as rich and famous as possible. He even tried sexual conquest and then moved on to character assassination when his attempts to persuade her to marry him were unsuccessful. Her marriage to Gibbons would be quite different, as was his protection and perhaps mentorship. Her failure to do any significant work for MGM, the studio where he was so powerful, indicates to me that they were both eager to keep this marriage separate from their careers.

She was not entirely undamaged. Lessing's charges hurt del Río, not only privately but also publicly. At the same time, the sweet young thing of *Evangeline* was getting a little older, and perhaps her innocence was not quite as believable as a few years earlier. The marriage to Gibbons, with the security it provided, came at an opportune time.

7 Second Chance

[T]he reality of comeback attempts is grim, and the prospects for
retrieving success are bleak . . . some comeback attempts prove to be
successful . . . often a successful comeback entails a slight change of
persona, so that the public is shown a new facet of the performer.

Jib Fowles, *Starstruck*[1]

A second chance at love, a second chance at marriage, a second
chance at work, even a second chance as a personality.

Gladys Hall, "Second Chance"[2]

DOLORES HAD MUCH TO DEAL WITH during her first
year and a half of marriage to Cedric: the two major
lawsuits brought by Gunther Lessing, a devastating illness, a canceled contract, the prospect that her career might be over. By June 1931, however,
even before the lawsuits were settled, much of her bad luck was beginning
to turn around. By that time, her health was better, so much better that
she was about to start back to films. Her marriage seemed secure; Cedric
was attentive throughout her illness; and her great regard for him would
continue lifelong. Many of these themes appear in a second interview she
gave to Gladys Hall in that month. Titled "Second Chance," it furnished
interesting insights into del Río's thoughts and preoccupations at the time.[3]

Hall described del Río's situation as one of second chances—in love,
marriage, career. Hyperbolically, the author insisted that she had "remade
herself," that she was "a new personality." Hall had not forgotten the interview two years earlier in which Dolores declared she would be free and
would not remarry for years, regretting that "She had never in her life

been really free, free to come and go, to speak, to think as she pleased. She met Cedric Gibbons and the cry of freedom gave way to the gentle chorus of love."[4]

In a story that would be reprised often with other men in her life, Cedric fell in love, according to Hall's romantic but not implausible account, despite never having met the object of his affection. Rather, he "had been in love with the lovely Dolores since her first shadow had appeared upon the screen." She might have met her future husband briefly when she went to MGM's studios to try on the costumes she would use for *Trail of '98*, the film done in 1928 with director Clarence Brown. If so, the two did not get to know one another at this time. According to Hall, Brown told Gibbons that del Río was not his type; unfortunately, he maintained that she was "cold and lifeless and dull," that she probably would merely say hello and "walk away." Of course, the truth was that she was unhappy, struggling with Carewe and with Jaime, overworked and still uncomfortable in a new country with a language she had not yet completely mastered. So, instead, Gibbons went to the set to watch her act, went to parties in the hope that she might attend, and finally asked Marion Davies for an introduction that led to the famous day when they both attended the weekend party at San Simeon. Struck by her beauty, he proposed and she quickly accepted, but only after they agreed they would always be careful of one another, tolerant, and "civilized." They would try marriage once again and if "a break should come they knew that they could discuss even the break understandingly."[5]

The similarities in manner, appearance, and even age between Cedric and Jaime struck the interviewer, yet Dolores objected. As the journalist described it, Dolores animatedly pointed out the differences between them: "There is no similarity between my first and second marriage save only one—both times I married a gentleman. That is the *only* likeness. Jaime was jealous of my shadow on the wall, he was jealous of the clothes I wore, the chairs I sat in; he was jealous of my friends, my directors, the men I played [acted] with, my girlfriends, my dogs and cats and birds. He was frantic with jealousy." Then in a revealing passage that made quite clear what the major problems between them were: "He couldn't stand my success though it was he who brought me here, thought it would be fun. It wasn't fun—for him. And so it wasn't fun for me. He didn't like the people I liked, he didn't like the things I liked to do, he didn't want to go anywhere, he didn't want to entertain. He was ashamed of the things I was doing. *Our sympathies were divorced long before we were."* Cedric, on the contrary, had

no jealousy *because he has confidence.* He likes people to admire me, men as well as women. He is proud of me and he likes to take me out, to entertain, to display me. He loves my work. He is more ambitious for me than I am for myself, if that is possible. We laugh together, we have fun together, we discuss everything under the sun and moon together. Our one and only thought right now is for me to *come back on the screen.* To be where I was, to be more than I was if possible.[6]

She was not completely optimistic, however; she told Hall she would probably be in films for only three more years, if she could succeed in "coming back at all," and she was wary that she should "not make a fool of myself when I reach the end of the movie rope."[7] In fact, her career would continue almost until her death more than fifty years later. Though the idea that she was on "display" may grate a little with twenty-first-century sensibilities, display was, of course, a major part of her public as well as her personal life. While she was with Gibbons and then throughout her life, she would be highly visible in professional and social settings.

In the interview, del Río was very forthcoming about the nature of the problems in her first marriage. Even so, now she seemed to have found the perfect man, and indeed for a decade to outside appearances they were content together. Years later, in another interview, she insisted that

he was an educated man who treated me in a paternal manner, taking care of me. The two of us had each had a great love which ended sadly. Very sadly. At Metro, he was an institution, all the workers admired him. I believe that his most visible characteristics were his elegance, his perfect manners, and his excellent education. He always knew what he wanted, and he was always capable of putting across his artistic point of view to stars that most people considered impossible to deal with. He didn't let me see the house in which we were going to live until it was done. Then he took me in his arms and carried me in. I had said that I adored the rain; he put me down in an armchair and went to press some buttons. In back of the panes of the large windows, I began to see the rain falling. He had devised a mechanism so that I could have rain whenever I wanted it.[8]

She remembered evenings with the Hollywood elite, including Charlie Chaplin, who was briefly her colleague at United Artists and whom Cedric liked very much. Charlie, according to Dolores, had suffered through a very poor childhood, but he educated himself very well, and even he complained of loneliness and isolation in Hollywood. He and Cedric liked to talk about art—always a huge enthusiasm for Cedric, the former art student—and Dolores claimed she learned a great deal from the two of them. Perhaps these conversations contributed to her appreciation for the Mexican artists who were her friends and whose talents she fostered over the years. Though she claimed to be unaware of the scandalous parties that were supposed to be occurring in Hollywood at the time, the couple were frequently photographed among the major stars at the best places. She did admit to going out dining and dancing, even to teaching Errol Flynn the conga.[9] The couple's social life was often reported in the press; soon they were seen out and about even with her former associates at United Artists, Pickford, Fairbanks, and Schenck.[10]

During this same period, del Río became extremely friendly with two other actresses, Marlene Dietrich and Greta Garbo, the other acknowledged great beauties of the time. It is unsurprising that she would find much in common with these two. The circumstances of their arrivals in Hollywood were similar, they fought prejudices against foreign actresses, they had to work through problems of language and accent as they made films in English, and they all had cosmetic surgery. Del Río and Garbo reached Hollywood within months of each other, Dolores in August 1925 and Greta in September. They both arrived with powerful directors as their sponsors: Greta's was Mauritz Stiller, the great Swedish director, and of course Dolores's was Edwin Carewe. Yet Stiller, who was gay, was not pushing a sexual relationship onto his protégée, while Carewe certainly was. On the other hand, Stiller as a foreigner with no particular clout in Hollywood was not in a position to put Greta immediately into films, although she had had previous success in Europe.

Despite the luminous appearance that enthralled European audiences, the nineteen-year-old Garbo was perceived on arrival in the United States as too fat and her nose too large. Louis B. Mayer, the head of MGM, who invited Stiller and Garbo to come to the United States, warned Stiller before she and the director left Europe that "in America, men don't like fat women." She did not appear in a film for six months after her arrival, and then not with Stiller as her director. Meanwhile, she submitted to a diet and exercise plan that had her working with (if the publicity stills are to be believed) Jannes Andersson, the athletic trainer at the University of Southern California. She also had cosmetic surgery to create a nose that was narrower at the bridge, making her eyes appear larger and even more luminous, and dental work to make her two front teeth symmetrical. Her cheeks also became more sunken, possibly a result of weight loss but very likely as well from the common practice of pulling molars to permit the fashionable sunken look which emphasized her eyes even more.

Stiller worked with her on only one film, her second, *Torrent*, and then only for a few days before he was removed. He never completed a Hollywood film and died in November 1928, at the age of forty-five, a rumored suicide though his death certificate indicated water in the lungs. Concern for Stiller had occupied Garbo from the time he quit *Torrent* until he died, and his treatment by the film industry wounded her greatly.[11] Yet the Hollywood failures of the two paternal figures who came to the United States with those two stars, Stiller and Jaime Martínez del Río, and their distresses and anxieties about their deaths may have brought Greta and Lolita together.

Garbo also had the early advantage along with Dolores of not having to speak English in her first films, which were, of course, silents. Nevertheless, she made embarrassing mistakes that distressed her and made her even shyer than she was by nature. In a telling incident, she announced to cameraman William Daniels one day that, "I'm important." When he replied that she was the most important person on the set, she then said "Important Garbo—important sardines—just the same." What she was trying to say was "imported." Later she confessed she had not learned English quickly, as *Cinelandia* so cattily noted, and that her original vocabulary was mostly slang. Though she had an interpreter on the set, she felt isolated and embarrassed by her mistakes and would respond brusquely if misunderstandings occurred. One day, when she was standing on the MGM lot, she picked a fig off a tree despite a sign warning against doing so; when chastised by a studio guard, she replied, "Beat it!"[12]

Dolores, on the other hand, was judged slim enough and had sufficiently lovely facial features on arrival that she went immediately into a film, working with Carewe, and continued to work with him for some time. Yet she too felt great anxiety about her English and feared the transition into talkies. She too underwent plastic surgery, and, it seems, of almost exactly the same kind, since she soon appeared with a narrower nose and more sunken cheeks. She too eventually had a painful break with her mentor, although it came later rather than sooner and through her own initiative. Dolores, early on, had Jaime as a support to help her make the transition. Still, she lost him to divorce and death, possibly suicide, the rumors surrounding his death reprising those that had circulated about Stiller. Both women also saw the men who had accompanied them to Hollywood and whom they regarded highly end up defeated by the Hollywood system and dying in humiliation. But later, Dolores had Cedric to support her resistance to powerful, dominant, and insistent Hollywood males, while Garbo was left largely undefended despite her great fame.

Both women had to contend with a kind of nervous xenophobia that pervaded Hollywood at the time, one that would persist until they abandoned it in the 1940s. At about the time that the two women originally arrived in the United States, *Photoplay* magazine ran a story about foreigners in the industry, calling them a "menace": "Foreigners are going through the studios with the speed of mumps through a day nursery."[13] A more favorable assessment of del Río and Garbo and three other foreign female stars in the *Los Angeles Times* called them "Victorious Invaders" and asserted "They have conquered."[14]

Garbo, however, was less protected than Dolores although she was more immediately successful; in the long run, however, her already shy and retiring personality did not serve her well and made her isolated in a way that Dolores never had to suffer. Further, it is quite likely Dolores found people around her who spoke Spanish; even Carewe spoke his own (albeit demeaning) version of her native language, and there were hundreds of Mexicans working in Los Angeles at the time, in films and out of them. There were very few Swedes. And although Dolores was sometimes seen as standoffish, particularly in her early years in Hollywood, she immediately had a platform for entertaining and making friends with a loving and socially accomplished husband, her own charm and naturally outgoing nature, and Carewe's efforts to put her forward in the best society in order to reinforce public perception of her high social standing. Both Dolores and Greta were very young, Dolores billed as nineteen but actually twenty-one, and Garbo about nineteen; a major difference was that Garbo came with film experience and was treated as a star in her publicity, whereas Dolores initially was inexperienced and had to make her own way (except for Carewe's not-always-benign help). Still, quickly, both became very big box-office draws; in early 1929 the *Exhibitors' Herald and Moving-Picture World* named them as number five (del Río) and number twelve (Garbo) among the most popular female stars in Hollywood. The following year, Garbo was number five and del Río number ten.[15]

Marlene Dietrich, who became Dolores's other good friend during the 1930s, also came with a major sponsor—Josef von Sternberg—who already had Hollywood experience but who found her and worked with her first in Germany on a dual German-English production of the even now iconic film *The Blue Angel*. She was older than the others, having been born in 1901, and had performed extensively in Europe both on the stage and in film. One author claims Dietrich knew Garbo from this earlier time and had played a small role in *The Joyless Street (Die freudlose Gasse)*, which had been a starring vehicle for Garbo in Germany in 1925.[16] When Dietrich arrived in February 1930, she was already experienced in talkies; though the English version of *The Blue Angel* had not been particularly taxing in terms of dialogue, nevertheless she did not have to suffer through the nervous worry of whether or not she would be able to make the transition. She already had. And as one biographer points out, "Lola Lola [sic] was the first character Marlene played on the screen who was what she was, a stage performer who sang, who knew how to use voice and body to insinuate, provoke, charm, and excite. The microphone merged the sound of her to the look of her." *The Blue Angel* was a huge hit, combining her appearance and her voice, surprising both German and U.S. film executives with how "that look and that voice, joined and amplified and more than life-size, would not merely connect, but overwhelm."[17]

Von Sternberg was not quite the same kind of mentor as Stiller, nor the same kind of protector as Jaime Martínez del Río, and Dietrich was not in love with him; nor did he harbor many illusions that she would be. Still, he imagined that she was Trilby to his Svengali, a hope that Stiller, Carewe, and even Jaime Martínez del Río surely shared in the cases of Greta and Dolores. Von Sternberg asserted after her triumph that he had completely dominated her performance, had "put her into the crucible of my conception, blended her image to correspond with mine, and pour[ed] lights on her until the alchemy was complete," so that she would "externalize an idea of mine, not an idea of [hers]."[18] Again, we have the case of a man who was hoping to use a beautiful woman to bring his own ambitions in the film world to realization, but in this case perhaps even more of an egomaniac than the others. Still, it was the woman, not the sponsor, who triumphed, though von Sternberg (the "von" had been added by him to give himself a little more cachet) would work with Dietrich again, notably in *The Devil Is a Woman*, their most notorious film together, in 1934 and 1935. One biographer claims that, knowing Dietrich was slipping away from him, von Sternberg turned it into an unflattering portrait. Nonetheless Marlene knew her role in his films: "an image of desire, longing, erotic attraction, and frustration."[19]

Though the portrait was unflattering, it was convincing. It therefore had trouble with the Breen Office, Hollywood's self-appointed moral guide; one of her songs was cut as too masochistic, and the film offended censors, audiences, and reviewers—and even Spain, where the film was supposed to have been set. Finally, the Spanish government (in a country that was headed for civil war) demanded withdrawal of the film and prohibited showings within its borders. So Marlene had the same experience that Dolores would with *Bird of Paradise* and later *Madame DuBarry* in the mid-1930s, causing an uproar with their transgressive and assertive film performances, though finally Dolores's films were distributed after major changes were made. *The Devil Is a Woman* was Dietrich's favorite performance, the one in which she felt she looked the most beautiful, one it must have grieved her to see withdrawn from public view.[20] Dolores lost only certain scenes from *Bird of Paradise*; Dietrich lost the entire film. Garbo also had encounters with the censors that were problematic, and occasionally frightening.

Del Río discussed these two figures in an interview with Elena Poniatowska in 1964. Garbo, she said, was "the most fabulous figure in film, exceptionally intelligent and full of complexes. She was frightened of people. This was no pose or publicity stunt, she simply did not like people to come close to her because it made her panicky. She is dominated by fear. . . . She is frightened of disappointing herself."[21] In another interview, she said she found Garbo "the most extraordinary woman—in art—that I have encountered in my life." Finding her a rare combination of beauty and kindness, she went on, "It was as if she had diamonds in her bones and her interior light struggled to come out through the pores of her skin." She was also aware of Garbo's "terrible childhood." Greta, she said, "had suffered . . . much cold in her body and her soul and that had created for her an enormous quantity of timidity and complexes. . . . Someone had injured her, and you can't put a torn petal back on a rose," indicating, probably, that she had been sexually abused or exploited.[22] Of Dietrich, she said that she was "the opposite of Greta. Extroverted, she loved parties, publicity, being seen, great romances, and having everyone know everything about her. The most unlikely thing for a woman is to have gorgeous knees, and Marlene in addition had beautiful and famous legs, with such beautiful knees you can't even imagine it. Fantastic!"[23]

Del Río and Garbo had met by 1928, though there is no evidence they were friends before her marriage to Gibbons.[24] During the 1930s, however, the women became close, introduced again by Gibbons himself. He was the artistic director of Garbo's films at MGM, where she was under contract and for most of this time the great diva, as Dietrich would be at Paramount. They enjoyed swimming in one another's pools and playing tennis together at their various courts. Del Río and Gibbons often socialized, far more, of course, than the reclusive Garbo, and Marlene and Dolores became good friends. Often photographed together at dinners and parties, they were attractive as the great public beauties of their times, the blonde and the brunette spectacular together. Their friendship was intense. Del Río was the one who introduced Dietrich to John Gilbert, one of her great loves and Garbo's greatest, and when he died in 1935 Dolores and Cedric attended the funeral with the distraught Marlene.[25]

Like Garbo and del Río, Dietrich also underwent physical changes; she was put on a diet, her face and legs became more striking, and her nose de-

Cedric Gibbons with two beauties: Dolores and Marlene Dietrich. CEHM CARSO.

creased visibly in width as well. Perhaps the three women went to the same surgeon; certainly the changes in their faces were similar, though the results were not and they never looked alike, despite comparisons between Garbo and Dietrich that grieved Dietrich. And Dietrich hated her nose, which grew visibly narrower over the years, in precisely the spots where such reduction made her eyes seem larger.[26] Dietrich, however, came to Hollywood on the strength of an enormous U.S. and European success, *The Blue Angel*, with a director who was determined to make her the biggest star of her time. Though it is difficult to tell whether or not Garbo really sought or enjoyed film success, and though Dolores enjoyed the success but was always uncomfortable about the public scrutiny that it brought to her personal life, Dietrich reveled in the filmatic and public attention that her open sexuality attracted. It may be that Lolita's close friendship with Dietrich in the decade after the latter's arrival in Hollywood made her more willing to take chances in her personal life and make changes in her professional one.

Despite new friendships and a new security with Cedric, things were not so cheerful for Dolores. She did not made a film for almost a year after her marriage. When she was unable to complete *The Dove*, United Artists canceled her contract in what must have been a very serious blow to her hopes. It may be that Joseph Schenck was not particularly patient, given that Dolores was now not personally available to him. He was known as a great womanizer, he had been married to screen beauty Norma Talmadge earlier, and years later he would suggest to the not-yet-famous Marilyn Monroe that he would marry her and keep her, though she was still grieving for a dead lover.[27] Though he had not spent much time with Dolores, it may have been that he desired her as well and lost interest when she remarried. Or perhaps the studio could no longer afford her or the production, given the collapse of the stock market in 1929. It does seem that Schenck himself may temporarily have been in professional and financial difficulties. In November 1930, Samuel Goldwyn was brought in as head of the Art Cinema Corporation, the production arm of United Artists. Schenck, the *New York Times* announced, would "devote himself to theatre and distribution activities." Interestingly, two months after her firing, del Río was still listed in the same article as part of the United Artists star stable.[28]

Regardless of the circumstances, in the case of Dolores, Schenck acted swiftly. Dated September 30, 1930, less than two months after her marriage to Gibbons, the notice arrived at her home on Outpost Drive, where she and Cedric were living during her illness. It canceled her contract of employment of October 18, 1929, and cited her "illness and incapacity for a period exceeding thirty (30) days during the photoplay 'The Dove,'" as the reason for exercising Paragraph 3 of said contract permitting cancellation and termination.[29] Then, in February 1931, Edwin Carewe was reported to be about to start filming a new version of *Resurrection*, the big hit he had made with Dolores just a few years earlier, this time starring Lupe Vélez, with whom she had at best a seriously cold relationship.[30] It seemed a deliberate affront, a sorry attempt at revenge in response to her rejection of him, and of a piece with his earlier ugly treatment of Jaime.

Dolores was exhausted and distressed, whatever the specific nature of her illness was. One of her biographers believed that in addition to her physical problems she also suffered a "nervous collapse" and a generalized weakened condition resulting from the intense work schedule she had kept since her arrival in Hollywood six years earlier. During the worst part of her illness, she was kept in the hospital under constant observation. Her fevers gave her nightmares and perhaps even waking horrors: visions of her first husband, angry and hateful, of Carewe following her, of scandalous headlines. But eventually she began to get better, and those around her did what they could to get her to rest. Gibbons built and decorated a cottage in Malibu for her to spend her leisure hours, and in her honor he named it *Ramona.* He also, as mentioned earlier, had his home in Santa Monica on Kingman Avenue redecorated, making it into a kind of stage set on which to perform their marriage. In November 1980, twenty years after Gibbons's death, architectural critic Paul Goldberger wrote in the *New York Times* that "if this tucked-away house had gotten the attention it deserves, Gibbons, who died in 1960, would have been known as one of Los Angeles's finest architectural designers—for this is one of the most exciting modern houses on the West Coast."[31] Another discussion, in *Architectural Digest* of April 1992, ranks it with houses designed by well-known architects Richard Neutra and Rudolf Schindler, who were working at the same time. The author, Brendan Gill, emphasized that "Every inch of the interior strikes a visitor as having been intended by Gibbons to serve as an act of homage to his flawless bride."[32]

The house was a striking background on which to display one of the most physically exquisite women in the world. A lived-in version of the Big White Set, it overlooked Santa Monica Canyon and off toward the Pacific

Palisades. Cedric was already living there when they married, around the corner from Louis B. Mayer, the head of MGM, whose home he had designed and constructed on the Pacific Coast Highway. Mayer's home was Spanish-style with a red tile roof and a beautiful ocean view; Mayer's closest associate at the studio, Irving Thalberg, lived close by, on the Pacific Coast Highway as well, though the two men rarely socialized.

By relocating to Santa Monica from her home in Hollywood, Dolores moved away from the stars, acquaintances she was familiar with, and into the midst of the production people (albeit magnates) that her husband worked with every day.[33] This move was accompanied by a style change from her carefully designed and crafted dwelling with its Mexican decorations to a simpler locale, from traditional to Art Moderne, from color to black and white.

Meanwhile, her mother set about selling her home in Hollywood, using the proceeds to buy new properties that would prove good investments for her daughter. Dolores moved into a different social set, and unquestionably a different cultural milieu, in which her friends and her physical surroundings were very much influenced by her new husband. Probably this tendency to let Cedric design their existence was heavily influenced by her illness. She could not work for almost a year, and her doctors insisted that what she needed for recovery was absolute rest.[34] Therefore, much of the decision making was left to him, and he set the style, as he was accustomed to doing. Still, he insisted on her comfort, putting together lovely spaces for her, even if the taste was more his than hers. They also agreed, given her health and their desire to have time together, that she make only one film a year.[35]

The house had white walls throughout, the better to set off her dark beauty. Cedric included a dressing room for Dolores that was almost entirely mirrors; even the plates for the light switches were mirrored. The master suite was upstairs, next to the living room where they entertained. In simple but elegant Hollywood style, which Gibbons was so much responsible for developing, there was a staircase that swept down to the entrance hall where she could descend to meet her guests. Her dressing table, as described in Gill's *Architectural Digest* article, was "not unlike an altar raised to honor some primordial pagan goddess."[36] In a 1986 *New York Times* story on vanities (i.e., dressing tables), Joseph Giovannini discussed the one Cedric had created for Dolores, especially its "sleek, Moderne" lines. At the time of the article, it was still in the home, and, as the author described it, "it is beautifully detailed, elegant and impeccably organized: he even planned for drawers so that the left-handed Mexican beauty could, as she looked in the mirror, reach for cosmetics without breaking her concentration."[37] Gibbons, much influenced by his 1925 visit to the Paris Exposition des Arts Décoratifs, carried that sensibility into films such as *Grand Hotel* and into his own home: black floors, white walls with straight or arched setbacks in strategic places, decorations simple to the point of spare, a good setting for Dolores and his accumulating Oscars.[38]

Dolores, however, would not be satisfied to serve as a decoration for very long. Extended absence from the screen often led the public to forget an actor or actress, and certainly the loss of her United Artists contract made many wonder about her future prospects. To bring her back slowly, Gibbons suggested she get a drama coach and recommended his friend Oliver Hindsell from MGM to work with her on acting and diction. Naturally, Oliver fell in love with her beauty and charm in the same way others had, but he also appreciated her dedication and discipline. They became great friends and even confidantes. She later credited Hindsell with working with her for two years to correct her "horrible" English; then, she said, she was "able to get by" in sound films. And Dolores had not been forgotten by the public or the studios. As her health improved, Paramount inquired about her availability for their film *Rose of the Ranch* and began to do preproduction on the assumption that she would be the star. Yet she demurred.[39]

Still, Dolores also maintained her contacts with Mexicans and other Latin Americans, helping to provide a connection to Hollywood and to films in general. In February 1931, as she was thinking again about acting projects, she received another letter from novelist Federico Gamboa. Addressed to "My beautiful friend," it began with the usual concern for her health. However, the major issue was the novels he had sent her at about the time she became ill, and she responded in January that she indeed had an interest in filming one of them, *Santa*. Gamboa was already in communication, he said, with producers in the United States, especially Columbia Pictures of New York. They were interested in the novel, in spite of "the recent crisis over films in Spanish," and had arranged for Carlos Noriega Hope to write the screenplay based on the novel. Gamboa told her that he always envisioned her in the title role, and he urged that she communicate directly with Columbia to discuss the possibility. He said he believed the person she should contact would be "Míster [sic] Harry, Kahn or Cohn."

Harry Cohn, his brother Jack, and Joe Brandt had founded the predecessor of Columbia Pictures, CBC Film Sales, in 1919. In the early 1930s,
the studio was upgrading its production significantly, particularly after the
arrival of director Frank Capra, and was also making Spanish-language
films. Gamboa closed by saying she should do as she wished, but the out-
come should be that "Dolores del Río, and only Dolores del Río, whose
feet I kiss and whose complete health I desire very cordially," should play
the lead.[40] *Santa* had already been produced in Mexico in the 1910s, along
with Gamboa's work *La llaga* (*The Wound*). Gamboa was eager to move his
work into the international arena, and Dolores would have been a wonderful intermediary in that process. Though del Río did not make the project,
because she was not yet interested in working in films entirely in Spanish,
it was eventually produced in Mexico, using Noriega Hope's screenplay.
She remained lifelong friends with Gamboa.[41] Carlos Monsiváis, the great
Mexican critic, pointed out that this second version of the story created a
new symbol, "a woman who stands for hunger and misery redeemed and
consumed by love, . . . the essence of a fundamental character: 'suffering
Mexican woman.'"[42] Dolores would later play her share of those.

By February 1931, Dolores felt well enough to hire a new manager,
Phil Berg, and she began to explore Hollywood employment possibilities,
calling on old friends. Raoul Walsh, who directed her five years earlier
in her first big hit, *What Price Glory?* responded to her disappointment at
one unrealized project by saying he too was "sorry," and he would "keep a
look out for a good story for you and when we find one, you will not get
first billing but all of it."[43] They too remained lifelong friends, now without Carewe to interfere.[44]

The Hollywood project she wanted came along soon. By the time of
her interview with Gladys Hall in June 1931, she was already planning to
do *Bird of Paradise* for RKO Pictures. RKO was founded in 1928, when the
Radio Corporation of America, a company with great interest in talkies
that had developed much of the new technology that made them possible,
merged with the exhibition chain Keith Orpheum. The new company needed
stars, and they offered Dolores approximately $8,500 a week for two films
and the option to renew. Perhaps because of her health, she made another
film for them in Hollywood before *Bird of Paradise*, which was to be shot
on location in Hawaii. They prepared a beautiful bungalow in their studios,
which were located on Gower Street, and obtained the rights to *The Dove*,

which had been canceled at United Artists, to try to please her and clear any remaining obligations to her former studio.[45]

They began preproduction immediately on *The Girl of the Rio*, the new title of the film. A version of *The Dove* had been filmed only four years before with Norma Talmadge (then married to Schenck) and Gilbert Roland; Dolores's co-star in the new version was Norman Foster, a young actor then married to Claudette Colbert, with Leo Carrillo as the villain. Happily, now that her health was improved, she was able to come to the set regularly. [46] Her energy, which Carewe had earlier remarked on in one of the London interviews and so heavily exploited, was depleted, but not her sense of professionalism. Production reports confirm that rehearsals began September 28, 1931, filming on October 5. The movie wrapped on November 2, just four weeks after the shoot began. Dolores worked hard, as usual, often arriving early and staying until the early evening. It is clear that despite weakness from her illness, she was determined to maintain thoroughly professional work habits.[47]

Dolores played a Mexican woman working in a cantina on the border; it was a melodrama in which a rich landowner tried to seduce her, while she struggled to stay true to her real love, not so incidentally an American (Foster). It opened in New York in early 1932. As described by the *New York Times* film critic, it was "groaning under the impact of words that alternately sigh and leer with a heavy Spanish accent. Dolores, the spotless dancer of the Blue Pigeon, proffers her all to save the life of her Americano, and Don Jose Maria Lopez y Tostado, the bes' caballero in all Mejico, sneers thickly through an evil little mustache." The critic found the performances better than the story, with Leo making "the villain a man of moods and interesting humors," and Dolores providing "an attractive performance" although he noted her return to movies after a "fairly lengthy absence" from the screen. Summing up, he found it "an unconvincing spectacle of a determined woman not getting her man."[48] The next day, a large photograph of Dolores in her new film appeared above a review of another film about espionage; though the stars of that work had their own publicity shot, she dominated the page.[49] Regardless of the quality of the movie, it was clear, her face still sold newspapers. At the same time, Cedric—not Dolores—received an interesting offer for her from an unexpected source. Burlesque magnate Florenz Ziegfeld wrote to her husband, offering her a part in his next production for his New York theater; Bert Lahr was to appear as the comedian. Ziegfeld urged them to think it over, as "it is an ideal part for her." She, not Cedric, declined with thanks, indicating that her commitment to filming *Bird of Paradise* made that impossible.[50]

Unfortunately, del Río's new film increased the attacks on her in the Mexican press, though it is not clear that they affected her popularity with the Mexican public much. The script of *The Girl of the Rio* did not portray Mexico in a particularly attractive light; Dolores's character (named Dolores) was pursued by a villainous landowner, played by the excellent (and for Mexican tastes too convincing) Leo Carrillo, and when she and her American lover tried to flee, they were captured and put in jail on a charge that the landowner trumped up. Sentenced to death, the pair were about to die nobly when Carrillo's character relented and spared them. The vision of Mexico's postrevolutionary judicial system and thus the government was obviously not very favorable. Although clearly set in Mexico, the producers initially thought of pretending that the story took place in some Mediterranean country, but no one in del Río's homeland would have taken such a subterfuge seriously, and probably no one anywhere else either. It did not help that in Mexico the original name, *La paloma*, was kept, making it clear that it was a remake of the Norma Talmadge film.

Lolita was pegged by some as a sellout, representing this false and even ugly vision of Mexico. The *New York Times* reported on May 9, 1932, that "certain members of the National Revolutionary party [sic] intend to stone the theatre and that tomorrow a delegation probably will call on President Ortíz Rubio to request immediate suspension of the film," though it is likely that the government fomented any demonstration rather than succumbing to one.

Predictably, the film was judged by the authorities to be denigrating to the dignity of the country, and it was closed in Mexico City the next day. Dolores's character was quite sympathetic, but according to the news reports antagonism toward the film became antagonism toward her, though the evidence is slim. Interestingly, Norman Foster later fell in love with Mexico—and, one might speculate, with Dolores—and he spent considerable time in that country and directed films there.[51]

By early 1932, Dolores was in Hawaii filming *Bird of Paradise*, while Cedric remained in Hollywood working on *Grand Hotel* and other projects.[52] Though both were busy during the filming of *Girl of the Rio*, this separation was the first of many caused by their work. And, it seemed, Dolores was not a has-been after all.[53] She had feared films with sound, as she confessed to

Gladys Hall, insisting then that "If I can't do it, if the talkies defeat me, I shall try the stage . . ." but despite the *New York Times*'s critic and his assessment of the "heavy Spanish accent" of *The Girl of the Rio*, the talkies would not defeat her. *Bird of Paradise* was the film that completely reestablished her as a major star, and it was not really necessary for her to use English at all, simply twittering away, making sounds, not truly words. This time she resurged as a sex symbol, through only movements and actions, her dialogue being noise rather than meaning. Jaime Martínez del Río would have been chagrined at her giving in completely to her own sexualization, despite the film's significance for her continuing popularity. Still, she must have been relieved to be part of a hit movie again.[54]

Her enemies of the previous year soon suffered their comeuppances, as well. Loula Lessing filed again for divorce from her husband in March 1932; just two weeks later, Edwin Carewe was arrested as a tax evader. A secret indictment had been entered against him for withholding more than $100,000 in income tax. At the same time, in Hawaii, three teams of a man and a woman each were working frantically to produce a feather wardrobe for Dolores for her *Bird of Paradise* close-ups.[55]

Further, the international news gave a hint of things to come. The Mexican president decreed a tax on foreign films in order to give its own "infant industry" a better opportunity to compete.[56] The Mexican film business was beginning to pick up, which in the future would lead to new opportunities for del Río. However, despite significant advances in terms of technology and the number of films being produced south of the border, no great filmmakers had yet emerged; according to Carl Mora, "producers were often businessmen out to make a profit who had little interest in building a solidly based production company."[57] Although this situation was changing through the decade, and stars such as Mario Moreno (Cantinflas) began to emerge in Mexican films, for as long as Dolores's career was reasonably strong in Hollywood she did not return. Part of the reason, of course, was that salaries were frighteningly low; in 1933, Mora estimated that the total cost of making a film in that country ranged between 20,000 and 30,000 pesos (U.S. $5,700 and $8,500), less than Dolores often made in a week for her film work in the United States.[58] For *The Girl of the Rio*, she received a flat fee of $30,000.

Bird of Paradise caused an even greater scandal than *The Girl of the Rio*. It had come about because David O. Selznick, then head of RKO, called King Vidor, a director who had long admired Dolores, and said that he wanted a movie starring Joel McCrea and del Río. It did not matter to him what the details were, but it would be named *Bird of Paradise*, it must have three big love scenes between the principals, it was to take place on a tropical island, and it had to feature Lolita jumping into the crater of a volcano at the end. Selznick later claimed it as one of the films he produced "personally."[59] Indeed, it did feature love scenes, her steamiest to hit the screen up to that time. The publicity itself led to a sexualization of Dolores of the most extreme kind; even before the film was made, the studio released the news that she was sunbathing nude in the garden of her home, getting ready for the filming. Immediately, according to one biographer, the story created an air traffic jam, as private planes tried to fly over the residence. A local paper even published a caricature of Gibbons trying to shoo the planes away.[60]

The filming in Hawaii led her to spend hours a day in the water, and she had her hair curled to imitate what Hollywood thought a Tahitian princess should look like, a beautiful princess who would fall in love with a handsome white man weary of "civilization." She spoke in an unintelligible twitter, sounding almost more like a bird than a human, perhaps reflecting the title of the film or the nervousness of the director about her Mexican accent. Most likely, there was just no zeal for trying to use an actual Polynesian (or any other) language. Her leading man, McCrea, was handsome and blonde, a beautiful contrast to the lovely brunette; immediately there were rumors of a real romance between them. McCrea in a 1971 interview reminisced that the film "was the first big thing that I did." His comment about Dolores was that "Del Rio of course was beautiful and still is very beautiful, lovely woman," and that "She was really wonderful in that."[61]

Other reporters preferred to imagine that she was involved with Selznick himself. Selznick was a man of enormous success and power, a man who might have been expected to have his pick of Hollywood lovelies, but who was at that time engaged to be married to Irene Mayer, the not-quite-so-lovely daughter of the head of MGM. Only shortly thereafter Selznick made history when he produced one of the legendary films of Hollywood history, *Gone with the Wind*. Intriguingly, in 1931 Irene showed up at a Hollywood costume party dressed as Dolores in *Bird of Paradise*, with Selznick himself costumed as Ed Wynn, the comedian, though Irene wore more above the waist than Dolores had in the film.[62]

Dolores would later comment that the film business in the United States was filled with gossip and jealousies, and that the necessary separations and rumors occasionally made her life with Cedric difficult. As Dolores said later, "The movie world is very hard, it is filled with intrigues and slander; Cedric seemed to be immune to all these difficult things. Yet marriage between two movie people isn't easy. Cedric was surrounded by beautiful women and I by handsome men; it was unavoidable that jealousies would appear from time to time."[63]

It may be that in the case of *Bird of Paradise* the rumors were started, as they were while she was working with Carewe, by the publicity people on the film. Certainly, the movie was designed to highlight the sexual charge between male and female, light and dark, civilized and savage, and the idea that there was an attraction between McCrea and del Río was believable, given the love scenes that Selznick demanded. To keep her connections with Cedric clear, del Río telephoned her husband every night while she was away, but the shoot itself was plagued with difficulties. Most days were so rainy that only an hour or two of filming was possible, and even that required booster lights. Soon rain and wind knocked down the palm trees where they had hoped to film, forcing a return to Los Angeles and ending the couple's separation.[64] The movie was finally completed in California,

Dolores in a revealing shot with co-star Joel McCrea in *Bird of Paradise.*
Bibliothèque du Film.

although at great cost, and the shoot took much longer than planned. Both del Río and McCrea suffered illnesses, and filming was not entirely finished until May 16, 1932.[65] According to the *New York Times*, though it was unlikely to make a profit, "try-out showings in several Southern California towns" indicated it would be a great hit with the public.[66]

The electric charge between romantic leads was evident from the earliest moments of the film. The love scenes were as steamy as Selznick could have desired: one took place amidst the usual tropical vegetation, but the other two were even more controversial. Two years later, after the Breen Office was established to more rigorously censor sexual content and language in Hollywood films, it is unlikely that these could have been shown. The first showed Lolita and McCrea characters cavorting in an underwater scene, apparently in the nude. Although comment about the circumstances of filming has always assumed that it was actually the two actors who appeared unclothed, this scene is very filmy and veiled by the water; the bodies are, suspiciously, uniformly white; and particularly del Río, or perhaps a double, seems to be wearing a flesh colored bathing suit. Nevertheless, it was a highly sexualized scene that particularly appealed to male fantasies, perhaps even Selznick's and Vidor's. Importantly if not entirely felicitously for Dolores's future, it was seen and remembered vividly by an adolescent Orson Welles. He, like Gibbons earlier, fell in love with her image. An even more sexually heated scene, however, came close to the end of the film, though it did not involve nudity. In that one, del Río, as the savage island princess, was taking care of her injured lover on the boat that would return him—but not her—to civilization. When he asked her desperately for water, she went to the galley to find something for him to drink, but, in the role of a woman designated primitive and therefore ignorant but resourceful, did not recognize glasses or water faucets. She therefore took a piece of fruit back to where he was lying, bit off chunks of it and extracted the juice in her own mouth, and then, in what amounted to extraordinarily deep kisses, transferred the liquid to him.[67]

Despite the production problems, the movie, though very silly, was eventually packaged into a polished entertainment. An import from the New York theater, Busby Berkeley, directed the complicated dance and ritual scenes in this, his first film with Dolores. It was also the first film in which she had long dance sequences. She later described Berkeley as a "genius," as "strong, dark, concentrated." He was meticulous in his execution, she added, and some objected to his moving the dancers around like "chess pieces." In an interview in 1971, Berkeley commented that he actually began to design the numbers when he had everyone assembled on the set, and never had to shoot more than one take. He, like Dolores, was not formally trained, but, as he commented, "I found out I could create." Dolores definitely became one of his fans, and he contributed significantly to her enormous success in the 1930s as a dancer. Berkeley, she later reminisced, worked quite independently of the director of a given film and did his scenes in his own way, "like a movie within a movie." She went on, "He would take a group of male and female dancers and convert them into pieces of an extravaganza, each taking part in an immense game."[68]

When the film was finally reviewed in the New York press, the *Herald Tribune* lauded her dark loveliness—if not her acting—as lending the film a beauty that was not provided by the director or cinematographer, despite the reported cost of $1 million. The *New York Times* critic, however, noted its "many beautifully photographed scenes," though he indicated that the film was often "unconsciously humorous." The latter comment was possibly directed to its over-the-top, old-style dangers: the hero threatened by sharks, earthquakes, lava flows, and angry islanders, the heroine eventually thrown into a volcano. There was little notice of Dolores, though a slightly ominous note was sounded by the reviewer in his comment that "There are one or two glimpses toward the end that might better be excluded, but the flashes of the dances and the fighting are well directed and moderately interesting,"—a positive if hedged nod toward Berkeley's choreography.[69] The "glimpses toward the end" probably indicated the sexy feeding—or rather drinking—scene between del Río and McCrea, and indicated a new reticence toward films that ultimately led to stricter controls.

But such reticence was not visible in the publicity handouts for the film. Rather, Dolores and McCrea were shown in a torrid embrace, and she was naked from the waist up except for a lei of flowers barely covering her breasts. McCrea appeared to be completely nude, with her body covering his genital region. The message in the handout emphasized the unrestrained, almost savage, nature of the encounter: "Its vivid romance is lived by primitive children of nature unfettered by the chains of civilization." [70]

Selznick himself had been instrumental in setting up a system of film industry self-censorship that he was now subverting in *Bird of Paradise*. In the early 1920s, he and other studio heads contacted Will H. Hays, an

Indiana politician/publicity man who was President Warren Harding's postmaster general. Hays's task would be to "sell the legend of a cleaner Hollywood, . . . head off the censorship legislation, . . . [and] stop the agitation against movies," in the wake of the fallout from a number of Hollywood scandals. After some hesitation, Hays accepted the task in 1922. The Hays Office had a number of duties in addition to monitoring Hollywood morals, both in behavior and production, but this monitoring was certainly one of its most important and best remembered functions. The first written rules were produced in 1927, and then recast in 1930 into a Production Code known colloquially as the "Twelve Commandments." Among these prohibitions were explicit presentations of crimes, sexual acts, vulgarity, obscenity, profanity, nudity and indecent exposure, lewd dances, offenses against national feelings (presumably U.S. and otherwise, given the need to preserve markets abroad), and repellent and disgusting subjects. When, in the early 1930s, Hollywood producers tried to lure Depression-era viewers back into the theaters, much of this self-conscious restraint fell away. Dolores was not the major target of the public backlash in the United States—that honor probably belonged to Mae West—but nude swimming scenes certainly did not help as protests from public and private groups reached a crescendo in 1933. The response by the Hays organization was to put a $25,000 fine into place to threaten errant or audacious filmmakers, and Joseph Breen was appointed to head the office that would enforce the Production Code more stringently. Known from its establishment in July 1934 as the Breen Office, it began to enforce the production code more stringently and made a major difference in filmmaking for the next several decades. West herself, and some of the film magazines, fought the censorship, and rather successfully; West's colorful comment, as quoted in the *Los Angeles Times*, was "If you can't go straight, you've got to go around." Yet the controversy died down, despite struggles with Breen and even with state governments over West's films, and government censorship was not forthcoming.[71]

Marlene Dietrich, who was friends with Dolores and with Mae as well, rather peevishly commented, "I like Mae, but it is all her fault that we have the Hays Office and this childish censorship. So American—to see sex everywhere and then try to hide it."[72] In fact, the focus on West may have drawn attention away from other films and actors and actresses, as Breen seemed to be almost obsessed with overseeing West's productions, while her studio pushed forward and her films drew an enormous public.[73] *Bird of Paradise*, fortunately for the producers, preceded the second crackdown, and it successfully established Lolita as a highly sexualized fantasy for the public. Selznick himself put together a gimmick to reinforce her glamour, when he got RKO to put together a "nationwide poll" to choose the thirteen most alluring women in the country. Garbo, Dietrich, and del Río were all among the chosen.[74] The Midwest was finally warming up to her as well. Chicago film critic Mae Tinée exulted about the "ecstatic, appealing, starry-eyed radiance of her . . . ," and the *Chicago Daily Tribune* ran its own poll later in the month in search of the "First Lady of the Movies," with Lolita's photograph right above the ballot.[75]

Whether or not the supposedly nude scenes in *Bird of Paradise* caused much problem in Hollywood or in the rest of the United States, they did lead to negative publicity for del Río in Mexico. Opening on November 10, 1932, in Mexico City, the film apparently did not include the swimming sequence, yet according to one biographer "Dolores's very fragile social prestige in Mexico was destroyed by the story of the swim in the southern islands, above all, because the popular imagination exaggerated the nudity and the amorous incidents involved."[76] Even before the film was released, RKO was concerned about del Río's supposedly waning popularity in her home country, and rumors circulated that her contract would not be renewed, though in fact she signed a new contract for two films in April 1933.[77] Social prestige or no, both Mexicans and Americans, as well as substantial audiences in other countries, went to her films. One of the most intriguing of her fan letters for *Bird of Paradise*—and one she saved for the rest of her life—was from India. Princess Sushila of Kapurthala wrote that, "I thought you were wonderful," and "that part suited you to perfection." She urged Dolores to make a film with Ramón Novarro, her "favorite actor," and, predictably, asked her for an autographed photograph.[78]

Meanwhile, RKO had decided to put her into a new comedy (albeit one with no nude scenes) that featured Dave Gould instead of Busby Berkeley as choreographer.[79] This film, *Flying Down to Rio*, though as silly as *Bird of Paradise* in its premise and its execution, was a huge success and introduced the dancing partnership of Fred Astaire and Ginger Rogers. A wonderful fantasy with which to forget Depression-era troubles, it featured Dolores as a languid, lovely, and impeccably clad upper-class Brazilian. Sex was diminished to a few teasing scenes, including one in which she was isolated with the romantic hero—played by a blond Gene Raymond—after a plane crash, in which no untoward injuries were incurred. She appeared well clothed throughout the film, though occasionally in elegant but not filmy lingerie; reviewers were again lyrical about her beauty.[80] The vision of Brazil was not particularly flattering, making fun of everything from politics to dance, but it made the country look like it would be pretty entertaining. Perhaps it helped tourism, although few U.S. viewers in the 1930s had the money for such a trip.

Dolores as a well-dressed, upper-class Brazilian, with Fred Astaire in *Flying Down to Rio*. Bibliothèque du Film.

Probably the most ridiculous scene was one in which chorus girls carried out their dance routines on the wings of aircraft in flight, thus leading somehow to a successful political coup against the government. Still, Dolores, Fred, and Ginger made it a huge hit, complete with lavishly beautiful costumes and sets and wonderful dances. It was perfect escape fare, and the public responded. Yet despite the fact that by this time she had top billing, the reviews featured Fred and Ginger, with Dolores relegated to the status of "beautiful girl" even as she aged.[81] Her salary reflected the studio's waning interest; she received $10,000, just a third of what she had received for *The Girl of the Rio* and $1,000 more than relative newcomer Astaire.[82] The film was one of RKO's biggest hits of the year, but Dolores's contract was not renewed, as the studio decided to save money by not keeping stars on exclusive contract. Moreover, Selznick had departed and was beginning to operate as an independent producer. He immediately offered her a role in a film about Pancho Villa, but given the early reaction to *The Girl of the Rio* she turned it down as potentially damaging to her Mexican reputation and demeaning to her native country.[83] Selznick himself seems to have decided two years earlier that Dolores was useful only for certain kinds of roles, meaning exotic and foreign, and did not offer her more work.[84] In fact, the way in which he framed *Bird of Paradise*, with its doomed love affair between a white civilized man and a darker primitive woman, seemed to indicate his own racialized view of del Río, not to mention his intrigue with love affairs on the dangerous edge of race. In the next film that Selznick and Vidor made together, *Duel in the Sun*, the new set of "racially crossed" lovers *both* died.[85]

Selznick notwithstanding, del Río's career continued, featuring in particular the dancing that she began in *Flying Down to Rio*. She made two more films with elaborate dance numbers in the next two years: *Wonder Bar* and *In Caliente*, both for Warner Brothers. *In Caliente* was filmed in the great pleasure dome and gambling resort of Agua Caliente in Tijuana, Mexico (a prototype for the later development of Las Vegas, Nevada), a fabulous backdrop for these numbers. The received wisdom is that del Río wore the first two-piece bathing suit on the screen in this lightweight but entertaining feature. Meanwhile, her old friend Joseph Schenck had become "Hollywood's biggest investor" in the resort. In *Wonder Bar*, which starred Al Jolson, Busby Berkeley came back to work on the dance scenes, and they were even more elaborate than those in *Bird of Paradise*. Jack Warner, head of Warner Brothers, had met del Río at a party, was charmed, and decided to star her with Jolson; Kay Francis had the romantic female lead. Yet Dolores and the well-known Jolson hit it off so well that they, with the collaboration of Berkeley, stole the show. Dolores's role grew constantly while that of Francis diminished, with her regularly threatening to walk off the set but ultimately sticking around. In one of her numbers, a tango, Dolores murdered her dance partner, the villain of the film, and, given the sensual nature of the choreography and its stunning climax, reemphasized her stature as a "maximum sexual symbol," and a lethal one at that.[86] The reviews,

In Caliente. Bibliothèque du Film.

however, largely focused on Jolson, though Mordaunt Hall, the *New York Times* critic, mentioned del Río's dancing. However, he said nothing about the quality of her acting.[87] Still, her films were making money. In the first six months of 1934, *Wonder Bar* ranked third in total grosses at the box office; *Flying Down to Rio* ranked eighth.[88]

Despite these relative successes, Dolores was conscious that she would have to make changes as she aged. Given her discomfort in Hollywood, it is unsurprising that she would think of a possible return to Mexico, a return she had been contemplating since the advent of talking films. And in March 1933, she received a very interesting communication from one of Mexico's leading intellectuals and the current ambassador to Brazil, Alfonso Reyes. The son of General Bernardo Reyes of Nuevo León, who came to political prominence during the presidency of Porfirio Díaz in the years before the revolution and died in a rebellion against revolutionary President Francisco Madero, Reyes had nevertheless established himself very securely as one of the leading intellectual lights and major writers of Mexico in the 1920s and 1930s. His letter, which arrived out of the blue, was as courtly as its author. He began by indicating that he wished to remind her of a past era, one she had long ago "transcended with your life and your glorious career." He wrote that before the European War, that is, World War I, while he was serving with the Mexican legation in Paris, he had met her one summer at the resort of St.-Jean-de-Luz, an encounter so short that no doubt she did not remember it. He also mentioned there had been some minor conflicts between himself and the family of her first husband, at a time when the latter was thinking of entering politics—a pursuit that, Reyes made clear, was one in which he himself had no interest. Yet for years he had remembered her well and followed her career attentively, tempted, from time to time, to send her a letter expressing "my admiration and regard," but fearful of being lost among her "millions of admirers."

Now based in Río de Janeiro, he put aside his reticence and decided that it didn't really matter if she considered him only "one more annoyance." He was writing, he said, to ask her to send him her picture with his name inscribed above her signature, "if it is not too much to ask." A handwritten note at the bottom of the document showed that she had responded by sending a large photograph.[89] This letter, arriving as it did at a time when newspaper reports led her to believe that many considered her a disgrace to her country, must have been very reassuring and even disarming. Later, she and Reyes, at least fifteen years her senior and more of Jaime Martínez del Río's generation than her own, would be strong friends.

So despite the critical and sometimes moral attacks in the press, she may have felt that Mexico might not be as unwelcoming as some of the press might suggest. Though the film critic Luz de Alba, who was powerful at that time in Mexico, was particularly unimpressed with del Río as an actress and willing to say so, Dolores had appeared regularly in the Mexican publication *Cinelandia*, the Mexican version of James R. Quirk's *Photoplay*. Del Río's popularity in the two countries led both publications to feature her constantly. Of course, her films were shown in Mexico in their Spanish versions and were certainly popular. Though criticized, she was never the public embarrassment that Lupe Vélez sometimes was. Thus when she announced in 1934 that she would visit her homeland, there was enormous enthusiasm among the Mexican public. Great crowds greeted her as she stopped in several Mexican cities, Hermosillo, Manzanillo, and León, on her flight from Los Angeles to the capital. She arrived in Mexico City on the seventh of August, a woman who now professed to be twenty-eight years of age but was two years older. Mexican crowds responded with joy to this "immeasurably beautiful, famous, rich, triumphant, glamorous, woman with a handsome, refined man on her arm—a magnate of Hollywood."[90] Celebrity trumped Mexican upper-class gendered notions of passive, male-dominated womanhood; Mexicans gloried in the north-of-the-border success of one of their own.

The major event of her visit was the long-postponed inauguration of the Palacio de Bellas Artes, the Palace of Fine Arts, in construction alongside the Alameda, the beautiful Plaza in downtown Mexico City, since the time of Porfirio Díaz. The event took place on September 29, 1934, with President Abelardo Rodríguez heading the ceremonies. Dolores not only attended with Gibbons but also arranged for her friends Mary Pickford and Douglas Fairbanks, along with United Artists head Joseph Schenck, to be there as well. Del Río and Schenck, and perhaps the others, no doubt met Rodríguez during the filming of *In Caliente*, as he had been a major protector of the Agua Caliente resort while governor of Sonora and continued to look out for its interests.[91] Apparently Dolores forgave the shock of her firing from United Artists a few years earlier in return for the friendship and prestige that this group of former collaborators brought her and her native country at these and other events.

In another box, her cousin Ramón Novarro watched the festivities; close by, her early sponsor, Adolfo Best Maugard, sat with Roberto Montenegro, yet another well-known artist who had painted her portrait. During the time she was in Mexico, she was in constant contact with the country's two most notable artists, José Clemente Orozco and Diego Rivera. She visited Orozco several times at the Palacio while he executed his murals there; she and Gibbons went to Cuernavaca with Rivera, his wife Frida Kahlo, and the U.S. ambassador to Mexico. Gibbons, himself an excellent photographer, recorded all these events with his own camera.[92]

Dolores gave a number of interviews explaining how thrilled she was to be back in Mexico and how much she appreciated her wonderful reception. Although there had been occasional problems with the press of her native country in the past, now the reporting was almost ecstatic. On the 25th of September, 1934, the magazine *Todo* exulted in her return and urged that her triumph abroad be considered in the same light as those of "men of science, writers, artists, military men" who brought luster to their native land. The story went on with the reasons she should be lauded: "Because she is a genuine Mexican woman, representative of our race, with undeniable artistic gifts that are internationally recognized. Because her triumph is that of beauty, of grace, and of feminine enchantments, in short, perfumed and splendorous. Because she has not needed to injure anyone. Her rapid and graceful rise to the heights has resulted in providing hours of dreams for unimaginable multitudes." The story concluded that her screen acting provided "the dynamic and plastic expression of the ideal woman."[93] So much for the concern that her somewhat unorthodox private life and daring film costumes (or the lack of them) might negatively affect the Mexican public. The visit showed that neither the public nor the Mexican artistic and political elite regarded her as an affront to Mexican identity and nationality. Rather, she was becoming an icon of that very nationality to Mexicans themselves, a beautiful compatriot who had conquered the United States. The next year, she made four films in Hollywood.[94]

This success occurred despite the shift to talkies, despite the aging process, despite the Breen Office, despite a sense of isolation from her native country. Though she suffered through what seems to have been a long period of depression—brought on by Jaime's death, her own illness, the problems of criticism of her lifestyle and performances in Mexico—Dolores continued to work steadily through the 1930s, making fifteen films, ignoring her agreement with Cedric to limit her film production to one a year.[95] Though none were particularly notable, and her billing began to slip, she was still regarded as beautiful and continued to be cast in Hollywood. She made new friends, including Garbo and Dietrich, who, along with del Río herself, were among the most famous stars of their generation, and she became an important fixture among the Hollywood elite. She developed her talents as a dancer and worked with Busby Berkeley, whom she greatly admired. At the same time, she renewed and cemented her ties to her own country through contacts with artists and writers and through increasingly frequent visits. These new associations and friendships were a draw back to Mexico.

8   Affair

Every woman owes it to herself never to fall out of love. . . . The
woman, if lucky, will keep on seeking a beloved. If one love finishes,
pursue another. . . .

> Dolores del Río, press release by Alice Tildesley[1]

For Dolores, life with Orson was entertaining, extravagant, and
different, a whirlwind.

> David Ramón, *Historia de un rostro*[2]

SEVERAL PROBLEMS were converging in del Río's personal and professional life in the late 1930s. Her depression
had not yielded to her clear position as one of Hollywood's social elite, and
neither did her career completely recover to its heights of the late 1920s.
She, like Garbo and Dietrich, was suffering from the double bind of being
cast as a sexual fantasy, and finding popularity, admiration, and even ado-
ration there, while at the same time struggling against the moral strictures
of some sectors of the U.S. public and of the Breen Office, which worked
against exactly such representations. Worse, feelings toward actors from
other countries were less and less sympathetic as the situation in Europe
became clouded with Adolf Hitler's increasing power in Germany and
threats against other countries. The possibility of war led increasingly to
feelings against del Río, Garbo and Dietrich, along with a growing perception of them as too sexual to be good. And all were growing older. Although
Dolores was at the height of her beauty, it may be that race or the perception of it made the situation worse; her dark loveliness versus the lighter
Garbo and Dietrich made her seem alien, and as she aged her early sweet

vulnerability no longer mitigated her difference. Available roles began to be slanted toward the ever more exotic and the slightly or very dangerous, in both sexual and national terms. Still, the careers of del Río and Dietrich survived the challenges of the 1940s; Garbo made her last film in 1941.

For Dolores, the last years of the 1930s in Hollywood were difficult, with problems in her marriage and a marked decline in her popularity. An early Gallup poll in 1940 did not even list her among the top ten most beautiful women stars, though Hedy Lamarr (a del Río look-alike) was ranked number one; nor was she among the top forty-nine Hollywood actresses. However, the "new Dolores del Río," Mexican Rita Hayworth, was listed as one of the actors and actresses who had gained most in marquee value that year.[3] The end of the decade of the 1930s saw Lolita begin a flaming love affair that held both personal and professional consequences. In 1942, she returned to Mexico and retained it as a base for the rest of her life, although she maintained residences in the United States and continued to travel extensively.

Unquestionably, the roles she was getting in the late 1930s and through 1942 made a difference in her decision. The highly sexualized parts she played in early 1930s films such as *Bird of Paradise, Flying Down to Río, Wonder Bar,* and *In Caliente,* though not providing much challenge for her dramatically, paid reasonably well and featured her high on the credits. They also gave rise to a number of still photographs that showed her as stunningly lovely. In these films, she was clearly a female lead. But in the late 1930s, she was cast more often as an alien and suspicious European in films such as *Lancer Spy* and *International Settlement.* Her last film before her return to Mexico, *Journey into Fear,* another in the same genre, was developed for her by her then lover, Orson Welles, but the project dissolved into chaos and mediocrity as their own relationship collapsed.

Hollywood, during World War II, was not interested in exotic foreign stars, especially aging ones such as del Río and her great friends Dietrich and Garbo, with attention turning to All-American girls. In 1937, as storm clouds gathered in Europe, Dietrich and Garbo—but not yet del Río— were declared "Box Office Poison" by the Independent Theater Owners of America. Garbo, who would prove them wrong with her late-1939 success in *Ninotchka,* was shocked two years later by the reaction to her film *Two-Faced Woman,* which opened three weeks after the Japanese attack on Pearl Harbor. The Breen Office required significant changes in the film before it was permitted to screen publicly, changes focused on Garbo's own sexuality, and reviews of the completed film in the same moralistic tone humiliated her personally. She, like del Río, had been popular in Hollywood for more than a decade, and her film career ended as "Wartime audiences needed Betty Grable's great legs more than Greta Garbo's great art."[4] The same could be said for Dolores's beautiful eyes, now more perilously than innocently come-hither.

Dietrich's contract with Paramount Studios was canceled. Still, she recovered after becoming a U.S. citizen, an affront to the Nazis that led to calumny from the political rulers of Germany. After a short hiatus in Europe, and rejecting overtures for a glittering future in German films from Hitler's culture czar Joseph Goebbels, she returned to the United States. She escaped the continent just as Germany's Panzers crossed the Polish border. She then made *Destry Rides Again*, though her compensation dropped from $250,000 at its height to $50,000. It was a low-budget film that became a huge hit, making a star out of the not-previously-famous Jimmy Stewart. This boost made it possible for her to resume her U.S. career, and her political allegiances were clear. She made several more feature films between 1939 and 1944, three of them with a new young star, John Wayne, in a combination that was sexually explosive, on and off the screen.[5] But Marlene was the exception. The period's bias against foreign stars noted for their sexual attractiveness extended to Dolores's cousin, Ramón Novarro, who had succeeded Rudolph Valentino as the reigning Latin lover in Hollywood. He did not appear in a film between 1940 and 1942, when he returned to the screen in a Mexican project about the Virgin of Guadalupe. Unfortunately, Mexico did not receive him with much enthusiasm. Unlike Dolores, but like Greta, by 1943 his career as a leading actor in the United States was over, though he made a handful of movie appearances and some television shows (including an episode of *Rawhide*) before his death in 1968.[6]

Del Río's trajectory in the mid-1930s was illustrated by the problems she encountered in a film she did for Warner Brothers, *Madame DuBarry*.[7] A remake of a highly regarded Pola Negri film directed by the legendary Ernst Lubitsch, it portrayed the mistress of Louis XV. DuBarry was a tragic figure who died by stoning during the French Revolution, but the initial framing of the film was as a risqué comedy. The Breen Office hated the script from the beginning, writing to Jack Warner that it was so "filled with vulgarity, obscenity and blatant adultery" that it was "dangerous from the standpoint of industry policy" and would "involve the industry in a serious controversy with France." Though the production boss, Hal Wallis, tried to challenge Breen, eventually Warner caved. Even with changes in the script, the final film was rejected by Breen. Local boards were concerned; the New York censorship board called it "indecent, obscene, and immoral," with the Ohio board threatening to prevent its showing as well.[8]

Eventually, it was completely remade without the intervention of the original director, the German William Dieterle. He maintained throughout his life that in this film del Río exhibited an enormous talent for comedy, all of which was lost in the remake. The original was shown years later at a retrospective of Dieterle's work and was considered by many critics to be a wonderful entertainment with a wonderful star, but the bowdlerized version that came out in 1936 was not a success. She looked lovely in her period costumes, and the film included a scene of a courtier kissing her bare foot as she stuck it out from within the bed curtains. Sadly, not even her longtime lucky charm of featuring her bare feet in every film would save her this time. Dolores had great hopes for the film; it was a switch from her recent musical roles and gave her an opportunity to move into a different kind of performance. Unfortunately, though Dolores's loveliness was again noted by the critics, along with the sumptuousness of Orry Kelly's costumes, it did not attract the public.[9]

After *Madame DuBarry*, Dolores traveled to England to make *Accused* with Douglas Fairbanks, Jr., the son of Douglas Fairbanks, her longtime friend and the co-founder of United Artists. She had continued to be popular in Europe, and even some of her Hollywood films were released there first. The negotiations were handled directly between Fairbanks and her agent.[10] It was a one-picture deal, but very much to her taste. Her devoted coach Oliver Hindsell prepared her carefully, going over the script with her and discussing questions of accents and intonation. He wrote to her when she left, reassuring her that even with script changes, she was ready for any situation she might face. He included a little pencil for her to keep at hand for marking the script, in the hopes that she would think of him and be assured of her success with every mark she made. He also included a list of words and their British pronunciations, just in case.[11]

She was paid $36,000 for approximately eight weeks' work, along with travel expenses, and she received star billing. The studio was Criterion

Films, where, Fairbanks Jr.'s lawyer assured her, she would find it very pleasant to work with Marcel Hellman, the managing director, and with Mr. Fairbanks himself. The terms of her contract permitted her fourteen hours of rest every night, which she continued to insist upon because of her physical collapse at the beginning of the decade.[12] Shooting in London gave her a chance to travel a bit. She went immediately to Paris before filming began, arriving a little late on the set with the permission of Hellman. He nevertheless emphasized in his communications that they would need her, perhaps, for an extra week of shooting at the end.[13]

Del Río enjoyed being away from Hollywood, apparently, and the courtliness of Hellman and Fairbanks Jr. made the filming pleasant. It may be that this experience made her think even more seriously about a return to films in Mexico, or at any rate not in Hollywood. Fairbanks had extensive contacts within British society, including with royalty, some of whom Dolores herself had met back when she was married to Jaime Martínez del Río; London treated her like the great star and well-connected upper-class woman she was. She went often to the theater and loved what she saw. Once again, she commented to Cedric about the possibility of doing theater herself. According to David Ramón, on her return from England she began to focus more directly, during her elegant parties, on "intelligent and cultivated persons." Ramón insists that she continued to be the "Queen of Hollywood," but unfortunately, if this were so, she held this title only socially and no longer professionally.[14] In Europe and in Mexico, perhaps age would be less of a handicap to her continuing career.

The trip to England may have come at an opportune moment. Regardless of Gibbons's still being consulted by her agent about the Columbia contract, the marriage was less than stable, and the two seem to have parted for a short period of time. They may, in fact, have looked at her trip as an unannounced separation. When she returned to Los Angeles from England, she requested that the Beverly Hills Hotel reserve a "small suite" for her, suggesting that she did not move back immediately into the house she shared with Cedric.[15] She also spent time in Mexico. A letter from Jack Gordean of Famous Artist Corporation was directed to her in Mexico City in December 1937, discussing an offer from Fox Films for $40,000 for seven weeks' work, a chance to return to the studio where she had been so successful in the previous decade. She would also receive first-class round-trip transportation and $200 a week living expenses while in Hollywood.[16] Obviously, this compensation would not have been needed if she had still been living with Gibbons in Santa Monica.

Even as early as 1931, when she was visited by the Mexican journalist Chas de Cruz, she told him that "a great shame keeps me from being happy." The shame, of course, was the death of her first husband and the rumors that had been circulating ever since. She did not blame Cedric for her sadness, she said, insisting that he was a "tender and respectful companion." She went on, according to Cruz: "God knows, Cedric is not at fault, and has done everything possible to help me forget my sorrow. When I am at his side, I am a constant annoyance to him, because of my intense despair." At the time of the interview, Cedric was waiting to play tennis with his wife and was apparently quite ungracious at the delay. Cruz found del Río "ethereal" rather than "erotic." During the 1930s many people found her so—distant and a little sad, rarely smiling.[17] The columnist Fred Othman, noted for his willingness to offend the famous, commented that she scratched her back with the wings of a butterfly and she was so ethereal that she slept floating in the air. He further commented that she ate orchid omelettes as appetizers.[18] Whether or not she was really as distant as all that, her illness, followed by her profound sadness, cannot have made her marriage to Gibbons particularly easy for either of them.

Throughout this period of time, Dolores faced growing difficulties in arranging for new roles, and she never had a long-term Hollywood contract such as the one that Garbo had at MGM and Dietrich enjoyed at Paramount. Yet as she was leaving for England, Columbia Pictures approached her agent, Phil Berg, about a multipicture deal. She hesitated, although the contract would have been for five years; in the first year she would do two pictures for $20,000 each, much less than she had earned a few years earlier, but double what she received for *Flying Down to Rio*. Though in the fifth year she was to receive $50,000 for each of two films, it was by no means certain she would actually get to that point with Columbia retaining her contract. It may have been that Cedric raised objections because Columbia was not yet a major studio; the last letter on the matter to Dolores from her agent revealed that her husband had doubts. Dolores did make one film for the studio, however, but no more. *The Devil's Playground* was yet another in a series of melodramas in which she played a bad woman, this one torn between two men. It was unsuccessful, and she probably did it only to keep working.[19]

Her next two films were with Twentieth Century-Fox, which was willing to pay her more than Columbia initially, in the neighborhood of $40,000 a film. First, however, in early 1937 she made *Ali Baba Goes to Town*, a silly production in which practically everyone working as an actor around Fox appeared in one cameo or another.[20] This distinct slip downward in the size of her role and in billing was significant and must have caused her some considerable anxiety. The two major films she did for Fox at this time were *Lancer Spy* (1937) and *International Settlement* (1938), both co-starring George Sanders, both involving stories of intrigue in an international setting. Sanders was a sophisticated European, a little younger than Dolores, born in Russia of British parents. He had arrived in Hollywood in 1937, so *Lancer Spy* was one of his first films there. Another actor in this movie was Peter Lorre, who had fled Germany in 1933, moving first to Paris, then to London, and finally to Hollywood as Nazism surged.[21] So Dolores was well aware of events in Europe, from her own stay in London and from her co-stars in these two projects. She was radiant in *Lancer Spy*, as stunningly beautiful as ever, playing a cabaret dancer who, as a Nazi agent, tries to seduce Sanders as a British officer impersonating a wounded German. Sanders escapes, but predictably she is tragically executed for helping him do so, and Sanders visits her grave years later, as the movie ends.[22]

Although she was able to keep working, it became harder and harder to get any roles, let alone good ones. She went rapidly through a number of agents between 1937 and 1939. Phil Berg soon left, then M. C. Levee, and finally John Hyde of the William Morris Agency, all of whom insisted they had expended their best efforts in her behalf; and, for a time as noted, she worked with Jack Gordean. She continued to think about doing films in Spanish and explored those possibilities; Berg, in one of his late 1937 communications, said he did not want a commission on her upcoming Spanish language film but offered his help if she needed it.[23] The project did not materialize. Her on-screen billing was also an issue. In negotiations with Fox in December 1937, probably in regard to *International Settlement*, Gordean informed her that although she would receive a high salary and her listing for Latin American countries would be in a position as co-star, in the rest of the world she would receive only first feature billing.[24] This change mattered, and it makes any claims to Hollywood queenship suspect at best. Further, if her marriage were as shaky as it seems to have been, her ties to Los Angeles were becoming attenuated.

At this time, she was also thinking about age, appearance, and love. In a May 1937 press release written by Alice Tildesley, a socialite and journalist she had known and been friendly with since the late 1920s, she declared:

An older woman is often stunning looking. I have seen women who are much better looking as they take on years. Think of all the lovely snowwhite heads at any important international affair—not only the debutantes are attractive. If a woman is beloved, it helps her to be beautiful, so it is up to us to keep love and cherish it. No woman should spend hours before a mirror carefully inspecting herself for the first wrinkle, the earliest gray hair, and shedding tears as her years begin to tell. Age overtakes us all, and the one triumphant woman is she who rises above it, who has something to offer that years cannot dim.

It is not clear why this press release was issued at this time. Dolores was now undeniably into her thirties, and perhaps her publicity people felt it was best to confront the issue head on. Certainly she was still beautiful. But the release did not deal only with appearance and age; it dealt with love. And in a strange foreshadowing of the next phase of her life, she insisted every woman should continue to seek love, and that if one love ended, she should move on, "seeking a beloved." Stunningly, given what would follow shortly in her life, she asserted: "A woman may walk out of her house one fine morning and meet some one [sic] who will overwhelm her heart. Whether or not he is free, a brave woman will not let that person get away from her."[25]

We know that del Río's course changed radically three years later, much affected by the problems and disappointments of her marriage to Cedric and by her sudden, intense, and relatively brief love affair with Orson Welles. In March 1940, Dolores announced that she and Cedric were separating; her statement to the press was direct: "Both Cedric and I have decided it is best to part. We are parting the best of friends, and I think Cedric feels as badly as I that we were not able to settle our differences. . . . We simply decided that our marriage had become impossible." She insisted, however, that they were not divorcing and would not do so; they had appeared regularly at public functions together throughout 1939 and into early 1940. The separation announcement came just six days after a report in the press that she was already planning for "her yearly pilgrimage to the Santa Barbara Mission on the sixth of August," which would have been their tenth anniversary. They had made several visits to the mission on August 6 to renew their vows in previous years. Gibbons, apparently dismayed and possibly

As her U.S. career waned, del Río took pleasure in her champion bull terriers, though they gave her an occasional anxious moment. Alice J. Topjon Collection. Reproduced by permission.

surprised that the break was finally occurring, commented to the press only that "I guess I have nothing to say."[26]

By the end of 1939, she and Welles were involved in a romantic relationship, of which Cedric must have been aware. Orson arrived in Hollywood in July of that year, a twenty-four-year-old prodigy who had made his acting debut on Broadway five years earlier in 1934, playing Mercurio in *Romeo and Juliet.* By age nineteen, he had married Virginia Nicholson, from Chicago's highest society, an eighteen-year-old who shared his acting ambitions; made a movie short in which only he and his wife appeared as actors; and made his first appearance on the radio.[27] In 1938 he frightened the public with his radio broadcast of *The War of the Worlds,* the H. G. Wells work, which many people actually believed announced the invasion of the planet by spacemen. In 1939 he came to Hollywood with a contract for one picture a year from RKO, for whom Dolores herself had been working fairly regularly in the 1930s; his reputation as a theatrical genius preceded him. He moved into a house formerly owned by Mary Pickford, next door to Greta Garbo on one side and Shirley Temple on the other, and by midyear he was appearing regularly in the gossip columns.[28] Dolores by this time was great friends with Garbo and socialized with her regularly.

Orson was a colorful figure. As one interviewer described him, "He is young and inexperienced in movies; but he is far from being inexperienced in showmanship. It is not impossible that he may give the movies something they have needed for a while—a sense of the zest and life and color that should accompany entertainment. No one has yet ventured to say that Mr. Welles is not entertaining."[29] And Dolores, in her not-quite-happy marriage, seems to have needed entertaining.

It is unclear exactly when Dolores met Orson, and he later claimed that she left Gibbons before they began to see each other, a claim that might be correct if the couple had begun to live apart some time before she announced their separation. Certainly she and Orson were involved by December 1939, well before the official announcement. On Christmas Day of that year, the *Los Angeles Times* ran a picture of her sitting next to Welles at a party, the headline reading "Film Notables Forget Their Troubles in Festive Party for Hollywood Guild." The others at the table were Canadian actress Fay Wray, one of Lolita's closest confidantes since the WAMPAS Baby Stars days, and Cary Grant; Gibbons was conspicuous by his absence. Wray was aware of the affair with Welles from the beginning. The *Los Angeles Times* on Christmas Day 1939 mentioned that Cedric and Dolores were among those invited to a party given by the Basil Rathbones, yet no reports confirmed that Gibbons himself was actually there. Rather, celebrity columnist Ed Sullivan noted in his column for the *Chicago Daily Tribune* that "Orson Wells pointed his whiskers, setter fashion, at Dolores Del Rio as they unhinged a rhumba."[30] In mid-January 1940, Dolores and Orson were photographed again at a Hollywood party, this time in intense conversation, the picture making it seem that it was more than just a casual social encounter.[31] Still, she and Cedric continued to be seen together through February 1940, appearing at the Santa Anita racetrack and at a party for pianist Artur Rubinstein, and even after she announced the split she and Cedric were reported by Louella Parsons to be talking about a reconciliation.[32] Nothing came of this effort, and it is not clear that even Gibbons wanted the marriage to continue.

By mid-1940, the affair with Welles was public; Diego Rivera, writing her from San Francisco in June, was his usual flirty self, addressing her as "Marvellous Lolita." He averred that he was writing to say hello to "the most precious girl that I have seen in my life and that is you," but also to greet her mother and father, both now living in Los Angeles, and Orson Welles, "the luckiest man in the world."[33] Elsewhere, he referred to Orson as the "happiest of radio stars envied by all the artists in the world," and noted that Dolores herself was "the most beautiful, most delightful in the west and the east and the north and the south." Further, he claimed that he himself was "totally in love with her just like forty million Mexicans and one hundred and twenty million Americans who couldn't be wrong."[34]

Orson claimed later that they met at a big party given by Jack Warner, for whom she had worked at various times during the previous decade. He recalled that the guests moved along to Darryl Zanuck's ranch later in the day, and that he and Dolores went swimming together in the evening. As he recounted it, "Oh, she swam beautifully!" He, of course, had seen her several years earlier in *Bird of Paradise*, and subsequently fantasized about the fact that she was, as he put it, "maddeningly beautiful." "That's when I fell in love with her," he later asserted. "It changed my life."[35]

Shortly after she began to see him, on January 22, 1940, she received the unfortunate news that Edwin Carewe had committed suicide, though the death was reported in the *Los Angeles Times* as a heart attack. The obituary was entitled lugubriously, "Carewe Gets Death Call." It noted in the first line, bestowing pride of place as his major accomplishment, that he was the "Discoverer of Dolores Del Rio and many other famous stars of the screen." Mary Akin was listed as his widow, and he was reported as leaving behind four children, though it was not clear from the article just who the mothers of the individual children were. He seemed to be living alone at the time of his death, though his nephew resided nearby and was the one who discovered the body. The story noted that he had been married four times, twice to Akin, and that he "lost much of his fortune in a Texas garbage disposal deal."[36] In fact, his movie career had almost collapsed after his public disagreements with del Río a decade earlier, as did that of his brother, Finis Fox. Carewe's directorial career took an immediate nosedive after United Artists bought out his contract with del Río, and Finis's screenwriting opportunities vanished as well. Carewe directed *The Spoilers* for Paramount in 1930, and he and Finis collaborated on a new version of *Resurrection* in 1931, with no major projects following for either man. Only their brother Wallace, whose career had never been tied to del Río, was able to continue in films, directing westerns for the big and the small screen for several decades thereafter.[37]

In the report of the funeral, Dolores figured prominently, along with what the *Los Angeles Times* called "Hollywood notables." But she was really the only "notable" to appear, with the exception of her already (though not publicly) estranged husband, who was sitting behind her. Dolores sobbed throughout. The others in attendance were largely the technicians whom Carewe hired during his directorial years.[38]

It must have been difficult for Gibbons, who rescued her years earlier from the attempts by Carewe and lawyer Gunther Lessing to ruin her reputation, to witness this grief. Yet Carewe had launched her on her path to fame, and perhaps the loss of his support and friendship years earlier was what now grieved her. Ramón reports that after hearing of the death Dolores pulled an album out of her library in which he had written to her after her first film, *Joanna*: "You are much too beautiful, clever and sincere to fail. Nevertheless in your future I wish you all happiness and success."[39] Because Jaime Martínez del Río's death was long rumored to be a suicide, for which she felt responsible, this new tragedy must have been a severe blow. Whether or not Jaime died by his own hand, it is likely that Carewe's taking of his own life made her feel doubly guilty and doubly cursed.

Then, in July, she was struck by another tragedy: the loss of her father. He succumbed at his home at 739 Kingman Boulevard in Santa Monica, near the house she had shared with Cedric. Described in the press as a retired banker, he was to be buried in the family plot in Mexico City after a memorial service in Los Angeles.[40] The demise of so many people important to her may have made her sensitive to her own mortality, and perhaps she felt that what there was of life was passing her by. She had been married for almost ten years to yet another man, Cedric Gibbons, whose sexuality was questionable and who furnished protection but very little passion. Welles was a different story. As Ramón put it, "The almost animal, magnetic force that Orson projected seduced the very proper lady who for the very first time in her life found herself in the arms of a man who was not her husband."[41]

It may be, or not, that the encounter with Welles was her first extramarital affair. Still, the connection with Orson was serious from the beginning. She seemed not to consider the possibility of a simple, clandestine relationship. Rather, she believed she must divorce Gibbons in order to be involved with Welles. According to Wray, "she apparently didn't consider having an affair with Orson, but thought she must leave Cedric, get a divorce. She seemed herself a lady of purity." She told Wray that, "If I don't, I might do something I'll be sorry for."[42] She moved into a luxurious residence that her mother found for her in Bel Air, joining Orson as supporter, adviser, and lover during what would become one of the great film projects of the first half of the twentieth century, *Citizen Kane*. She filed for divorce on December 18, 1940, the *Herald* noting that "Until a few months before the separation, the couple's marriage of nearly 10 years had been looked upon as one of the film capital's most nearly successful," an interesting indication of how few Hollywood marriages were actually happy. The charge was "mental cruelty," a relatively new legal formula and one that did not unduly embarrass either of the principals, and the suit contained no elaboration.[43] Meanwhile, her own career came to a complete standstill. She made no films for two years.

The March separation announcement claimed that neither she nor Cedric had other romantic involvements, but Orson was already clearly in the picture despite her denials.[44] He terminated his own marriage in February 1940. Rumors about their involvement and possible future marriage—not just photographs of them at the same social and professional events— were reported in Ed Sullivan's *Chicago Daily Tribune* column on March 25, though the Los Angeles papers seem to have suppressed what was common knowledge at that time.[45] At the court hearing in January 1941, she was a bit more forthcoming about what caused the difficulties with Gibbons. When asked by her attorney, "Was he cold and indifferent, did he refuse to take you to parties and to see friends?" she responded, "Oh, yes." Fay Wray also testified that Gibbons was inattentive, and that the strains between them made Dolores "quiet and sad," "unhappy to the point of becoming ill." When Dolores was asked about her vow, made at the time of the initial separation, that she would never divorce Gibbons, she said that she had "just changed her mind."[46] Interviewed on the same day she was testifying in court, Welles insisted that he had thought for many years that "she was the most beautiful woman in the world," and still thought so. He continued to insist that they had not met until after she was separated from Gibbons.[47] Hearst's *Los Angeles Examiner* announced in its report on her divorce filing that Welles was a "massive theatrical jack of all trades, whom she is expected to marry as soon as she is legally free to do so."[48] Although Cedric was reported to be devastated by her abandonment, he did not oppose her wish for a divorce, which was granted—with a one-year waiting period before it became final—on February 27, 1941.[49]

At about the same time she met Welles, other things were going a bit better for Lolita. At the end of 1939, she began making *The Man from Dakota*; no del Río movie had appeared during that year. This film was the only one she made at MGM during her marriage to Gibbons and for which he served as art director. By this time, however, they were in fact separated, despite attending a number of social engagements together. It is unlikely that Cedric spent much time anywhere near the set. The scriptwriter was Laurence Stallings, who had written *What Price Glory?* and who admired Dolores from that time forward. The director was British, Leslie Fenton, and her two co-stars were Wallace Beery and John Howard. Again, she felt she was among friends, and Oliver Hindsell communicated with her to let her know that those involved with the shooting were happy with her performance. Only one scene showed her in elegant clothes; for the rest of the film she was dressed simply, engaged in adventure. Ray June's cinematography was stunning, providing a tense contrast between the blacks and whites that accented both her beauty and that of the scenery. The film was released quickly, and publicity photos show her looking luminous between Beery and Howard. Yet in the hinterland, announcements of showings sometimes left her out entirely. The film did not do well.[50]

Pulls back to Mexico continued. Frida Kahlo and Diego Rivera communicated with her regularly, together or separately, depending on the state of their marriage, as did José Clemente Orozco. Both Rivera and Orozco expressed their interest in painting her portrait, and about 1937 Rivera, having returned for the moment to easel painting, did so. It was a lovely canvas, immortalizing her as "the most exquisitely beautiful Mexican woman imaginable . . . the ideal of Indian or mestiza beauty." She loved it. Before the divorce, it hung above the fireplace in the Gibbons's elegant Santa Monica home.[51]

Frida, also a wonderful artist, sent her an amazing painting at the end of 1939. It showed two women at the edge of a tropical forest, nude. The dark one is seated, the second a luminous contrast lying with her head on the other's lap. The picture is clearly amorous, as the one caresses the other. Dolores herself later commented, "the indigenous nude is solacing the white nude. The dark one is stronger." Yet the painting is also a celebration of homoerotic love and one of the sources for the long-standing rumor that Kahlo and del Río had a homosexual affair. It surely expressed Kahlo's longing for the beautiful Dolores. Kahlo's biographer, however, suggests that "Frida's most passionate love affair was with herself," and that the two female figures in the work may actually be a doubling of the artist. This interpretation seems a little strained, particularly since the painting was intended for Dolores. Frida, of course, preferred men to women, if the former were available; yet she was a master of manipulation and deeply anxious for attention. At this time her marriage with Rivera was shaky, and she had several heterosexual love affairs that went wrong. Perhaps her loneliness accentuated her desire for del Río, who became a close friend and often visited Frida's home when she was in Mexico.[52]

It seems likely to me that the painting contained a direct erotic and financial plea from Frida, whose physical and emotional and monetary needs were enormous. Whatever the explanation, the painting was intimate. That Kahlo, even though she herself noted her audacity, felt she could approach Dolores in this way implies a significant level of friendship, sexually intimate or not. The painting was followed by a request for a loan of $250, and perhaps the motivation for the gift was financial. At this point in her life Dolores was becoming a great patroness of the arts, and she was a wealthy one. Yet the affective connection between the two was based on more than money, reflecting a real link of caring along with Kahlo's needs. At about this time, Kahlo and Rivera decided to divorce, accentuating Frida's difficulties. In March 1940, Frida wrote Lolita that she would try to pay her back as soon as she could, but her eagerness to be completely free of Diego's help had left her without funds. She begged her "not to think for even one moment that it is an abuse on my part not to return your money" and to write her if she was not too busy, "don't be mean, girl." And she implored

Dolores to return to Mexico: "Tell me pretty thing how you are, and if you think of coming to Mexico soon. All of us miss you terribly." She went on to say that Diego was behaving like a spoiled baby, although she "still love[d] him more than my life."[53] Personal relationships—of one degree of intimacy or another—were pulling del Río to return and assuring her of a warm welcome.

But it was the erotic appeal from Welles, not from Kahlo, that led Dolores away from a marriage she was finding problematic and into a sexual relationship that threatened her reputation as a great lady and left her shaken. One of Welles's biographers notes that Dolores was the "first in a succession of iconically beautiful consorts who were always to be found at his side for the rest of his life." In fact, he was overwhelmed by her loveliness and thrilled by her stardom; later, he told several stories about just when he became enamored of her, one of which proclaimed that the infatuation started when he was eleven years old. It seems more likely he had actually noticed her when he was seventeen and watching *Bird of Paradise*, as discussed earlier. There are further stories that while he was in New York he occasionally followed her on the street, hoping to attract her glance.[54] Regardless of when his obsession began, it was clear that Welles had been fixated on her as an image of fantasy for years.

The affair with Welles gave one of Hollywood's most poisonous journalists, Hedda Hopper, the opportunity to turn her ire on Dolores. When, in mid-June 1940, Jimmie Fiddler, another of the *Los Angeles Times* columnists, pointed out that Welles and del Río, who heretofore confined their dating to out-of-the-way spots, were now appearing in public, Hopper followed that up with the first of several mocking attacks. On June 27, 1940, she wrote, "You would have howled at Paulette Goddard, Marlene Dietrich, and Dolores Del Rio, all dressed up and bejeweled, with Charlie Chaplin, Diego Rivera, Orson Welles, and Erich Remarque, going to look at the Eddie Robinsons' [actor Edward G. Robinson] paintings. The men went into a huddle on world politics, war, art, music, drama, what have you, and the girls—poor darlings—were left to talk to each other."[55] It must have been a fascinating gathering—Rivera was one of Mexico's leading artists; Chaplin, her former colleague at United Artists, and Welles were two of the geniuses of Hollywood film; and Remarque was one of the leading popular novelists of his day and at that time Dietrich's lover—yet Hopper chose to pretend that the women were dumb decorations accompanying these famous and intelligent men. Rivera was quite intrigued with Welles; Ramón has noted that the bombastic, genial, "explosive" Mexican artist was a perfect mirror for Orson.[56]

Citizen Kane began being shown almost simultaneously with the divorce decree, though it was not released by RKO for several months after completion. Based on the life of William Randolph Hearst—at whose estate Dolores met Cedric Gibbons more than a decade earlier—it was to be Welles's most acclaimed and innovative film. When he began in June 1940 to shoot the earliest scenes, using a cast drawn largely from his theater company in New York with himself as the star, Dolores was by his side at RKO. There she was greeted as the superstar and film luminary that he imagined her to be. Sometimes he wanted her close, sometimes not, and she remained attentive to his desires, ready to come at a moment's notice. Given to rages, he would bang his head on the wall, while Dolores tried to comfort him.

Yet despite the problems of the relationship, when *Citizen Kane* appeared, to the enormous acclaim of the film community, Orson in gratitude gave many of the telegrams he received to Dolores, and they remain in her archive. One interesting communication, from actor Tim Durant, read "Saw your picture with Chaplin last night thought it brilliant and thrilling Charley said picture moved him more than any he had ever seen this is no exaggeration congratulations and best of luck with it regards." Chaplin, of course, had long been a friend of Lolita's and was very close to the couple from the time Orson came into her life, but this was still high praise from a master. King Vidor, who directed del Río in *Bird of Paradise*, saw it in February and acknowledged Dolores's contributions by congratulating them both. In March Frank Capra shared the praise and added an ominous note, "If it is not released it will be a most terrific loss to pictures," a concern that did not come to pass, despite Hearst's attempt to suppress the film. Noel Coward, who viewed it in April before release, enthused "Thought Citizen Kane absolutely magnificent from every point of view stop it seemed to me flawless stop apart from its technical originality photography conception imagination and performance its utter artistic integrity is beyond praise stop all my profound congratulations and gratitude they will never pull you down regardless how hard they try." Novelist Sinclair Lewis was likewise impressed when he saw it after the release in May: "I don't suppose there is such a thing as 'the one greatest film ever produced'—how could one compare a farce with a serious dramatic effort—but if such a thing were possible I think it would be 'Citizen Kane' which I saw last night and which kept me awake for hours afterward."[57]

The film premiered in New York on May 1, 1941. Radio City Music Hall refused to show it, so the premiere was at the second choice, the Palace Theater. Arnold Weissberger, Welles's lawyer and good friend, went to Los Angeles to bring Dolores and Fay Wray to New York City for the opening. A number of advance reviews had already praised the picture, so Welles was relatively unconcerned about the critical reception; still, movies needed a mass audience, and that assessment would take much longer. The second opening, which Orson was extremely concerned about, took place in Chicago on May 6, his twenty-sixth birthday. When he and Dolores entered the theater that evening, they discovered a birthday cake with twenty-six candles along with a radio commentator ready to report on the party. What they did not find were very many people; the audience was embarrassingly small.[58] Chicago was always a hard sell for her, and this skepticism seemed to apply to Welles as well. The *Chicago Daily Tribune* critic was unimpressed overall. He praised Welles himself in the title role, along with the work of the Mercury Players, his New York theater company brought almost intact to Hollywood; the latter actually formed most of the cast. The report commented about the film itself, "It's interesting. It's different. In fact, it's bizarre enough to become a museum piece. But its sacrifice of simplicity to eccentricity robs it of distinction and general entertainment value." At the end of the review, the intention to smear Hearst was obliquely noted: "The usual foreword disclaiming intentional identification of the picture characters with persons living or dead is conspicuous by its absence."[59] Clearly Chicago critics were not quite ready for Orson's kind of innovation, just as they had not been a few years earlier to acknowledge Dolores herself as a star.

Finally, however, it was the Los Angeles premiere on May 8 that glittered. A number of dinner parties around town preceded the showing at the El Capitan Theater, converted from a venue specializing in stage dramas for the occasion. Marlene Dietrich, Howard Hughes, Edgar Bergen, Charles Chaplin, Edward G. Robinson, Darryl Zanuck, Milton Berle, Fred Astaire, Joan Crawford, and even Gunther Lessing attended. A number of pre-premiere parties gathered Hollywood's elite; among others, Lucille Ball and Desi Arnaz gave a dinner of *arroz con pollo* for their guests before the film. The opening was headline news for the several days preceding it, and a photograph of Dolores and Orson with John Barrymore and *Kane* leading lady Dorothy Comingore entering the theater was displayed prominently next to the write-up of the social event the next day in the *Los Angeles Times*. The film colony was striking in its support, defying Hearst and his power in order to honor a film that, they had already heard, broke new cinematographic ground.[60]

Orson's achievement was clearly extraordinary, and Dolores was attracted by his genius and by what both regarded as their mutual success. That she was completely serious about the relationship is evidenced by her changing her will only five weeks after the divorce became final to make Orson her executor. This extraordinary act indicates her total involvement with him, and not incidentally her suspension of good judgment, as Orson's inability to manage money was already becoming legendary. Virtually all of her estate would go to her mother under this document, but complete control, including the right to sell any and all properties, was given to him. The document was drawn up by Weissberger, Orson's longtime lawyer, who had gone to Los Angeles earlier to bring Lolita to New York for the East Coast premiere; in this regard her choice was a good one, and Weissberger remained her lawyer until his death many years later.[61]

Some non-Hollywood people believed Orson and Lolita to be married already; Jerome Zerbe, a longtime celebrity photographer who worked regularly at El Morocco in Manhattan commented in an interview in 1979 that the two had come to the restaurant often when they were "married," and that he thought Lolita was "a marvelously beautiful woman," certainly in the top ten ever, and "most charming, most charming." All those years later, he said, he found it difficult to think of Orson as "the slim young man that I knew when he was married to Dolores."[62] Hollywood, of course, believed they had not yet tied the knot, but certainly in public they seemed securely partnered.

In the meantime, the couple took part in a collaboration that was a good deal more frivolous than any of those discussed above. In mid-1941, with Dolores as his assistant, Welles debuted as the star of a magic show presented in Sacramento at the California State Fair.[63] It was a kind of silliness in which she had rarely engaged, and they both apparently enjoyed it. Welles himself had long been fascinated with magic shows and loved doing them himself, even appearing as a magician in a short play he did in 1939 called *The Green Goddess*.[64] Later, after his affair with Dolores ended, he tried to persuade the Mexican woman whom he did marry—Rita Hayworth—to resurrect the show he and Dolores had done, now called *The Mercury Wonder Show*, for presentation to GIs during World War II. Rita's studio did not permit her to perform regularly, but Dietrich was willing, and they presented it for servicemen for a couple of months. They also did a short bit in which Orson sawed Marlene in half in the film they did together called *Follow the Boys*. This little scene was quite effective, with Orson "droll" and charming, Dietrich funny and beautiful.[65]

But in 1941, for both Orson and Dolores, *Citizen Kane* was by no means an unmixed triumph, and the strains of waiting for its release had been intense. During the filming, rumors leaked out that it was based on Hearst's life, and his battle to suppress it took a toll. It is strange that Dolores would be so supportive of a project clearly aimed at her erstwhile friends; it may reflect resentment of the kind of power, not to mention hypocrisy, that Hearst and his mistress represented. In the case of Orson, there were connections to Hearst and especially to Marion Davies; his first wife, Virginia, had married Davies's much-loved nephew, screenwriter Charles Lederer, after their divorce; the film seems to have been partly designed by Orson to wound Virginia and her family. Orson was familiar with some of the most intimate details of the Hearst-Davies relationship, and there were hidden references to them in the movie.[66] Although there is no doubt that *Citizen Kane* was an amazing and pathbreaking film, it was also very likely a personally motivated attack. Welles threatened to sue RKO and then Hearst himself if it did not appear. He railed, "How can you copyright an enterprise, a profession? I must be free to film a story of a newspaper publisher. If I am restrained, it will force us all to go back and take our characters, say, from Greek mythology." Of course, it was definitely about Hearst, as Orson had confessed to Lolita months before. For a time, he claimed to be considering the possibility of buying the film from RKO in order to release it himself, though this was likely a ruse agreed on by Orson and the studio head to spring it loose. The veteran Hollywood reporter Herb Drake commented on Welles's press conference by saying, "Welles will show the picture and show it in tents, if necessary. He will probably open it at Soldiers' Field and saw Dolores in half at each intermission."[67]

Dolores certainly felt that Welles was an amazing artist and talent, "second to none, not even Shakespeare," as she later remarked, and she believed he appreciated her talents as well.[68] Despite her intelligence and taste, she was at this time apparently a little in awe of her wunderkind lover. Welles and del Río talked a great deal during this time about her future prospects. Though her career was in decline, they both viewed Welles as a kind of White Knight who would use his extraordinary talents to resurrect her professional life and guide it in a more dignified fashion.

They began discussing her recent career setbacks in the earliest days of their relationship, and in 1940 and 1941 they worked on two projects. One was a new film version of *Santa*, the Federico Gamboa novel of a woman who is seduced, falls into prostitution and illness, and is finally redeemed by death. As noted earlier, del Río had wanted to do one of Gamboa's works for some time. There were two previous movies based on the book, one made in 1918 in Mexico during the silent era, and another, the first sound film produced in Mexico, from 1931. Dolores considered the story carefully, finding the character of Santa herself intriguing and challenging. In Mexico the subject matter would not suffer from the problems with the Breen Office that she was experiencing in Hollywood. Orson quickly produced a film treatment of forty-seven scenes that "avoided melodrama and consisted of a real lesson in the production of a cinematographic script and the visual translation of a literary work to film." It clearly was designed to show off the female protagonist. But the Mexican film company that was interested was unable to come up with a suitable remuneration for Dolores, and the project never got off the ground. Nevertheless, for a while she had even considered starring for a very reduced salary, 30,000 pesos, and 10 percent of the profits. The attempt illustrates her interest in returning to Mexico and her continuing ties to her home country's literary and artistic community.[69]

A second possibility was developed by the two early in their relationship and later resurrected during the filming of *Citizen Kane*. A movie version of *The Way to Santiago* by Calder Marshall, the basic script seems to have been worked out by Welles and annotated extensively by Dolores. Again, the ties back to Mexico were apparent. The female lead, to be played, of course, by Dolores, was repeatedly referred to in the script as "the most beautiful girl in the world." Orson would have a role as well, "a person without a name," who was portrayed waking up as an amnesiac in Mexico City. In a complicated script full of conspiracies and dangers, the del Río character saves the amnesiac from a small-town lynching; of course, they fall in love. Finally, they frustrate a Nazi plot to take over the country, and the fade out, in the script, shows Orson and Dolores in a romantic clench.[70] This story as well was never filmed, since Orson planned to make it entirely in Mexico and would thus need permission from the government of that country to shoot there. Although Dolores would probably have been able to obtain it, nevertheless such permission would have required time.

They therefore moved on to other potential projects, among them an adaptation of *Cyrano de Bergerac*, but finally began to look at a novel by Eric Ambler, *Journey into Fear*. It is possible that one of the inspirations for Dolores and Welles in developing scripts that would put the Nazis in a bad light was their connection with Nelson Rockefeller, which later resulted in a filmmaking project for Orson in Brazil. Rockefeller, as head of the Office of the Coordinator of Inter-American Affairs, was charged with supervising economic and cultural ties to Latin America during the war. At the same time, cameras and all kinds of film and equipment were in short supply. Meanwhile, throughout Latin America and in some areas of the United States there was a significant demand for movies in Spanish. Mexican producers wanted to be able to fill the soaring demand, but equipment and film were difficult for them to obtain.

Rockefeller went to Mexico at the behest of President Franklin Roosevelt, to talk to movie producers there about helping them out with the shortages, the hope being that Mexico would produce anti-Axis films favorable to the United States; his ability to speak Spanish was extremely helpful in these meetings. Eventually, of course, when Mexico declared war in support of the United States, that nation stood high in the estimation of the Roosevelt administration. The OCIAA gave the Mexican movie industry a huge boost by providing 45 million feet of virgin film at a time when celluloid was a strategic material and movie film a product almost completely monopolized, in terms of distribution to Latin America, by the United States. Brazil, also considered an ally, received 12 million feet with the excuse that the Portuguese-speaking audience was much smaller; Argentina, seen as a supporter of the Axis and particularly Nazi Germany, received none. Rockefeller was clear about the power of the screen and was eager that Latin Americans be propagandized in this fashion—using Mexican filmmakers and, secondarily, Brazilian—to provide pro-U.S. views in their work.[71] This assistance was one of the most important factors permitting development of what came to be known as "the Golden Age" of Mexican cinema, and Dolores would soon be a direct beneficiary of this influx of film and equipment.

Before starting *Journey into Fear* with Lolita, Orson began filming *The Magnificent Ambersons*. He did, however, and with Dolores in attendance, start to work on the script for the Ambler novel. Unfortunately, his penchant for multitasking overloaded him, and he was completely manic in his multiple activities. Lolita and her film took a backseat to *Ambersons*, which he considered his more important and more artistic film. *Journey* started shooting, with the script still incomplete, on January 6, 1942, before Orson completed the *Ambersons* project. His involvement in the latter movie finished on January 31, and on February 2 Orson terminated his own scenes in *Journey*, after working on it for less than a month. Meanwhile, Norman Foster was in Mexico directing a film called *Bonito the Bull*, for RKO and Welles's Mercury Players, and in theory Welles was supervising that project as well. Orson had begun taking Dexedrine, which very likely added to the crazy way in which he was behaving. His performance was over the top as a Turkish secret service officer, complete with wiggling eyebrows and sly smiles. As his biographer Simon Callow has noted, "it was just the sort of part that Welles was drawn to and which he should have resisted at all costs." What Welles created, Callow says, was "a mountain eagle crossed with Count Dracula." Callow further reminds us that it "was only his second excursion into the medium [of film], and he is cruelly exposed in a way that he was not, paradoxically, in the much larger role of Kane."[72] His acting was perhaps influenced, and not for the better, by the silly magic skit he and Dolores had initiated a few months earlier.

Besides overwork and drugs, not to mention an announcement that he would be marrying Dolores, something else happened to derail him, along with the rest of the country. On December 7, 1941, the ghastly news of the bombing of Pearl Harbor was broadcast to the American people. On December 10, he completed a letter to his good friend Norman Foster in Mexico that he had begun writing on the set of *Ambersons* three days before, when he got the news. Welles admitted to his distress and confusion: "What did I want to tell you? I can't really think. War has broken out and I have broken down."[73] According to one biographer, "For three days Welles directed as in a dream, unable to concentrate on the rushes from Mexico or to deal with the problems of rain and mud and red tape."[74]

By December 11, the following day, he had made an arrangement with Nelson Rockefeller to go to Brazil to cover Carnival. He planned to add episodes to *Bonito the Bull* to put together *It's All True*, a composite film of stories and travelogues favorable to Latin America. He was also to act as a kind of cultural/goodwill ambassador. This arrangement, not incidentally, would put him out of the reach of military service.[75] Welles left immediately for New York to prepare the final cut of *Ambersons*, which he did not finish and left under the control of a subordinate. None of his projects were really complete, but he seemed frantic to depart for Brazil. He apparently did not consider taking Dolores, despite the fact that they were still supposed to be getting married almost immediately and that the Brazilians expressed more interest in her than in him. She was, in any case, finishing up *Journey into Fear* and was too professional to depart before the project was completed, unlike her agitated fiancé. The responsibilities of marriage, possible military service, finishing up two difficult films, and coping with the United States at war seemed to be just too much for him. Soon, RKO went through major leadership changes. The studio gave up on both *Ambersons* and *Journey* as good box office material and then proceeded to cut and reframe both films, though *Journey* did rather well for a time after its release.[76] Meanwhile, the draft board exempted Orson from military service on health grounds, and as one biographer put it, "Welles had to make an effort to pretend he was sorry."[77]

Predictably, things did not work out well with either film once he left California. When *Ambersons* opened, audiences hated it; forty-five minutes were cut without Welles's permission, and new scenes added. Even though David O. Selznick wanted the original kept in the Museum of Modern Art, no one paid any attention. Welles became a kind of persona non grata in Hollywood; his great protector at RKO, George Schaefer, resigned the presidency of the studio in June 1942, and Dolores herself heard little from him. He had lost control of himself in Brazil, on the one hand trying to make a film and on the other hand throwing himself first into Carnival and promiscuity, and then staying on for some time, accumulating expenses and doing little shooting. Meanwhile, *Journey into Fear* looked good in the rushes, with Dolores beautiful as ever and Welles's framing of the scenes successful cinematographically. Herb Drake wrote him that the movie was "100% natural and Dolores is marvelous, which I may as well confess is a surprise to me. . . . I think you will be proud of Norman's work. Altogether, everything looks successful, elegant, and happy." Yet without Welles to produce the final cut or to film new scenes, the story made no sense at all. When it was shown to the trade press in New York City, reaction to it was sharply divided.[78]

A group of documents describing successive versions of the trailer for the movie in RKO's production files for *Journey* make clear the studio's changing attitudes toward Welles. In the first, the trailer began with a shot of Welles himself as Colonel Haki, and the text across the screen would read "The Man Whose Famous Radio Broadcast Scared All America," followed by "Brings His First Great Movie Thriller to the Screen." The next shot would show Dolores as Josette sitting in a café, and the text would read "The Picture That Brings Orson Welles and Dolores Del Rio Together." A succession of shots of Joseph Cotten would follow, but at the end the viewer would see Dolores as Josette walking through the rain and the text would read, "Orson Welles Himself Returns to the Screen As His Camera Captures the Magnificent Suspense of Eric Ambler's Thrilling Novel!" Although there is no date on this first continuity, another simpler one dated June 30, 1942, five months after Welles left Hollywood, still acknowledged that *Journey* was "A Mercury Production by Orson Welles" and that the screenplay was by Welles and Cotten, though Orson's credit was far less prominent than in the earlier version. Another continuity, from January 1943, still noted that it was a Mercury Production and that Cotten had produced the screenplay, but Welles was left out entirely except to indicate that he had a role in the film, his credit appearing at the end of a list of the other actors.[79]

The *New York Times* noted that the confusion in *Journey* was "entirely normal procedure for just about anything Mr. Welles does." Those who had disliked *Ambersons*, the column claimed, saw *Journey* as "a simple melodrama of no particular distinction." Those better disposed saw it as "a masterpiece of its kind, comparable only to 'M,' the early pictures of Josef von Sternberg, and perhaps the best of Hitchcock."[80] Meanwhile, in July, Orson's Mercury Productions was completely removed from the RKO lot, while at the same time the studio angled to get whatever film of *It's All True* actually existed under their own control.[81] Welles's irresponsibility sank his own company, three films (though all were eventually produced, with mixed—mostly bad—results), and Dolores was permanently alienated.

Journey into Fear was generally panned. Mae Tinée, reviewing it in the *Chicago Daily Tribune* in February 1943, found it "funereally photographed" and "neither the story nor Mr. Cotten very believable," yet "was delighted at the chance to see Dolores Del Rio in action again." Tinée added, "She is a lovely creature."[82] Though Orson tried to salvage the film when he returned from Brazil, it remained incomprehensible to the viewer.

The magnitude of the failure was shocking. The movie itself, the portrayal of Dolores, and Welles's own performance, complete with wiggling eyebrows, lead the viewer to question his emotional stability at the time of the filming. Cotten, who ultimately received credit for the script along with Orson, played an engineer traveling in the Near East during the run-up to World War II who is dragged off into a suspicious encounter in a Turkish bar and then goes on the run in a tramp steamer. Lolita (her athletic dancing role requiring a double) appeared in tiger skins and headgear complete with little tiger ears and a partner dressed as Tarzan. Of course, she winds up on the same boat as Cotten, and they enjoy a few photogenic scenes looking at the water. If she had been looking for a more dignified role requiring better acting, this one was not it. Her part as Mam'selle Josette was sexualized and absurd. [83] She did not see the final cut until it opened later in Mexico, and she was mortified by the result.[84]

Orson himself was embarrassed by the failure, especially his own performance, and years later denied he had ever intended to direct it. He claimed that the cutting was to blame for the "horrible" result; that the script had been good, as well as the cast; and that it should have been a subtle film of "antiaction, antiheroics. . . ." He further praised the "brilliant character performances which all got chopped out and thrown away," and admitted his own acting had verged on parody. The character, he said, "was supposed to be a cynical sort, and that's the way I played it—but I think it missed."[85] His judgment, this time, was accurate.

Dolores was not Orson's only friend to be dismayed by his behavior. Foster, who was recalled from Mexico to take over as director for both *Journey* and *Ambersons* when Orson was eager to leave for Brazil, was, according to one of Welles's biographers, "angered, shocked, and maddened by this disastrous mistake to the day he died." The film he abandoned was well along, and he felt it would have been a fine one, a potential masterpiece, an achievement discarded by Welles in his haste to escape what was now an uncomfortable Hollywood environment. *Bonito* was reduced to the status of an episode in the confused production *It's All True*. Although Dolores was quiet about her own possible feelings of abandonment, Cotten later confirmed that Orson's departure was a disaster for *Journey*.[86]

Welles, meanwhile, apparently influenced by his guardian, who disdained del Río's ethnic background and her age, was having second thoughts about the marriage. These doubts may have hastened his departure and increased his confusion. His later behavior in Brazil continued to be frantic and was now both irresponsible and personally promiscuous.[87] Dolores's lover, despite his genius, did not seem able or willing to lend his talents to her career, or even to maintain his personal loyalties to her. For a time, Dolores gamely tried to maintain that all was well. In March 1942, once her divorce from Gibbons was final, she revealed to the press that she would join Orson somewhere between Rio and Mexico City. But their wedding plans, announced only the previous November, were now in tatters. In another part of the same statement—this time more accurately—she noted she was finishing a film at RKO (*Journey into Fear*) and would soon leave Hollywood to make another in her home country.[88] Then, in April, Dolores told the press she and Welles would not marry, though the decision was not yet final.[89] By May, Welles informed his guardian they had ceased to communicate after she sent him a cablegram breaking off their engagement, a message he never returned.[90]

As she said later, she was newly divorced, her father had recently died, and she was ready to "leave stardom to convert myself into an actress and I could only do that in Mexico. I wanted to return to Mexico, a country that was mine and that I did not know. I felt the necessity of returning to my country." Despite the pleas of many of Welles's friends, she decided

Lolita with Diego Rivera, Frida Kahlo, and the out-of-favor Orson. CEHM CARSO.

to break her engagement with him as well. By the time of her thirty-eighth birthday, August 3, 1942, she was back in Mexico; on that date she gave herself a huge party attended by, among the Mexican intellectual and artistic establishment, the artists José Clemente Orozco and Diego Rivera, novelist Salvador Novo, composer Carlos Chávez, and her old friend the caricaturist Miguel Covarrubias with his wife Rosa, along with Chilean poet Pablo Neruda. Also honoring her birthday were Mexico's social elite and a number of foreign ambassadors.[91] Though a contrite Orson arrived in Mexico shortly before the party, probably to importune her to marry him anyway, and attended the party as a surprise guest, she had made up her mind. Soon she announced to the press again that they would not wed. She went back with her mother to Los Angeles to wrap up her affairs and sell her properties and then returned, as she had said she would, to her country.[92]

Welles never got over her completely, and off and on he went to Mexico in usually fruitless attempts to see her, or sent his children, whom she did receive. He married Rita Hayworth, another Mexican crossover star and "the new Dolores del Río," and he shopped for beautiful underwear for her at the Juel Parks lingerie store, where Dolores had been a regular customer. The marriage ended badly, with Orson continuing to engage in promiscuous sexual behavior that led to Hayworth's "nightly crying fits and recriminations."[93] He took Dolores look-alikes as his third wife and as his final lover. But another man who had long been infatuated with del Río, this time Mexican, would be the one who found her the roles that led to her comeback as an actress and directed some of her finest films.

9   Return

What could be better for the national film industry than the return
of Dolores in 1943? Del Río: the artistic guarantee of excellence,
the center of all social life, the *de luxe* hostess.

Carlos Monsiváis, "Dolores del Río"[1]

Del Rio's wartime return to Mexico represented not only the *push*
of a US industry that had type-cast her as the exotic "other" but
also the *pull* of the developing Mexican industry that offered an
opportunity to apply her Hollywood-training to better roles in first-
rate films that played internationally to Latin American audiences.

Seth Fein, "Hollywood and United States–Mexico
Relations in the Golden Age of Mexican Cinema"[2]

D EL RÍO RETURNED TO MEXICO with no promises of
work, but she quickly established herself as the cen-
ter of a social and intellectual group reflected in the invitation list to her
birthday party in 1942. Emilio "El Indio" Fernández, who directed her first
pictures after her return, called her "an overwhelming figure, the most important in Mexican cinema," and cinematographer Gabriel Figueroa commented reverently, "[Dolores] instilled in all of us a kind of mysticism."[3]
Dolores herself emphasized in her conversations that *Mexico*'s cinema
should become *Mexican* cinema, a stance in which she was reinforced by
longtime friend Diego Rivera, and it should have an artistic dimension in
line with the intellectual/artistic renaissance that had been going on in
Mexico since the end of the Revolution. Fernández directed two films that
reestablished her as a *Mexican* star, films whose themes emphasized the

developing nationalist vision of the Revolution, and later he directed her in six more, one of them in conjunction with John Ford; they were some of her finest productions.

She was in and out of Mexico in 1941, renewing ties as she was deciding whether to return. Frida Kahlo wrote to her with another appeal for money in October, sending a messenger to her house from her own home in Coyoacán with a note asking her for the 10,000 pesos she had "promised" for a painting—probably the one of the two women discussed previously. Frida relayed that although her health was better, she was suffering from terrible concern about a child that both knew, who had fallen ill and was in a coma, and as Diego was away in Patzcuaro, she had no money for medicine, "for the child or for me." The letter was written in an uncontrolled handwriting, tilted upward from the left side of the page to the right, indicating perhaps Frida's anxiety or pain, or drug use, or need for drugs. Another letter, the same day, was written in Frida's up-and-down, controlled handwriting and was poignant in its message, both for what it shows us about Frida's relationship with Dolores and for the relationship between Diego and Frida themselves. It also probably reflects, in the quality of the handwriting and the stilted language, that Frida was now properly medicated and carefully controlling herself. Rather than being addressed to "Marvelous Dolores," as the previous communication had been, it opened simply and formally "Dolores:" and noted briefly, "When Diego came home, he was very angry because I had written you in the terms that I did, as everything he earns with his work he gives to me and I don't lack anything. He's still angry. Thank you so much for your kindness. Frida." Diego had added a note addressed to "Lolita:" in his characteristic hand. It read, "I am still indignant that Fridita received the thousand pesos that you sent for 'the sick child,' that she should have returned to you immediately, which I am doing with the attached check . . . please excuse the sick woman and receive the most attentive greetings of your attentive Diego Rivera."[4] These communications clearly reflect the intimacy and poignancy of the connection between del Río and both artists.

José Clemente Orozco painted Lolita in late 1941, although he was busy with other projects and occasionally had to cancel sittings with his famous model. His communications also furnish evidence that Orson accompanied her to Mexico at the end of 1941; she stopped by Orozco's studio with her then fiancé in November of that year, but the artist was away. Orozco expressed his disappointment that he had missed the visit but hoped it would not be Welles's "last trip to Mexico." It was not, though Orson's trip at the time of her birthday in August 1942 was a less happy occasion. Orozco's communications also offer evidence of who *was* at her side most of the time: her mother, whom he found "truly agreeable and charming." And Orozco told her of his future artistic projects; he would be starting a new mural project in the "ex-temple of Jesus," which he believed would become a museum. Indeed, Orozco painted a mural there, known as "The Shy Devil" ("El diablo atado").[5]

The Mexico City that she returned to was larger, more sophisticated, and more stable than the one she left in 1925. Increasingly prospering during the years following the Revolution, the arts flourished along with the urbanization and cosmopolitanization of the city. Dolores and her mother first found a place to live in the Colonia Condesa, on Calle Amsterdam, a two-story residence that was not nearly big enough for her voluminous possessions and those of her mother. She began to renew and strengthen the friendships within the artistic and intellectual community that had helped lure her back to her homeland. Significantly, she resumed writing her name in the Mexican way, no longer "Del Rio," in the American fashion, but "del Río," following the proper Spanish orthography.

She and her mother and many friends were often guests at the restaurant Ciro's, where she liked to entertain and where she eventually celebrated her thirty-ninth birthday. One of the investors in the restaurant, Archibaldo Burns, a young man-about-town, took an interest in her and managed to get an introduction, which led to a relatively short flirtation. Burns was similar to her first husband, Jaime Martínez del Río, in that he was an elegant connoisseur of the arts who had studied in England, though the age difference was reversed. She found him an attractive and interesting companion; his mother, one of the great ladies of Mexican society, enjoyed Dolores as well and made no objections despite her being significantly his senior. Archibaldo began to have illusions that he could be the director who would bring her back to prominence. He wanted to do a story about the Mexican Revolution that would feature a female character, to be played by Dolores herself. However, on one of their dates, he criticized her manner of looking into the camera, which he claimed resembled her peering into a mirror. Dolores took exception, protesting that not a single director, from Raoul Walsh to William Dieterle, had ever told her anything of the sort, and presumably she did not want to hear it from an inexperienced kid, romantic interest or not. The potential collaboration was off.[6]

Still, he helped her search for a new house, which she finally found in the tranquil suburban neighborhood of Coyoacán, where Hernán Cortes had lived with his native mistress and translator centuries earlier. She purchased a small estate composed of two houses, a larger one for herself and a smaller one for her mother, at 37 Santa Rosalia Street. Called "La Escondida" ("The Hidden" or "The Secluded"), it was next door to that of the noted intellectual Salvador Novo. Novo, a poet, playwright, and historical chronicler of Mexico City, was closely connected to the Mexican government, and held several official posts in the cultural field, despite his overt homosexuality.[7] Lolita had brought Novo to Hollywood two years earlier to talk to Orson about the possibility of doing a script on the conquest of Mexico; nothing came of the project but Novo continued to be a friend.[8] His proximity illustrates her interest in and access to Mexico's cultural elite.

Dolores's homes were remodeled extensively, under the watchful eye of Doña Antonia, and adorned with del Río's growing art collection. Included was the painting that Orozco had done, apparently paid for by Welles, in 1941. It showed her as anguished and aging; Orozco was beginning to lose his vision during the sittings, and Dolores later commented that he had "painted his tragedy in my face." She was not fond of the painting but nevertheless displayed it prominently in her home for a while. The decoration of the residence was simple, in relatively neutral colors—though not as stark as those with which Gibbons had surrounded her—but softened, to some extent, by her flourishing collection of pre-Columbian art.[9]

The three major figures who would contribute to her enormous success and that of Mexican films more generally were El Indio himself, Gabriel Figueroa, a cinematographer of enormous talent, and Pedro Armendáriz, who would become her almost-constant co-star. Fernández was a fascinating figure, far more dynamic and visceral than her two husbands and more like Orson; yet he was not a cultured figure, and his ideas and images came more from experience than from any cultivated knowledge. He was born in Hondo, Coahuila, in 1903 or 1904 (again the dates differ, though not as much as those for del Río), and was her near age-mate. His early experiences in Mexico, however, were far different from her own. He was probably illegitimate, his mother a Kickapoo Indian from the area around Sabinas, his father "of Spanish stock." Though he was too young to be involved in the fighting during the early part of the Mexican Revolution (1910–1917), he joined the forces of disappointed presidential hopeful Adolfo de la Huerta when he rebelled against the government of Alvaro Obregón in 1923. The uprising failed, and Fernández was sentenced to twenty years in prison. Escaping to the United States, he followed the now exiled de la Huerta, who settled in San Diego.

El Indio remained in Southern California for a number of years, working around Hollywood as an extra and a bit-part player. Most of his roles were in westerns such as *Oklahoma Cyclone* and *Sunrise Trail*, which he did for Monogram's Joseph P. McCarthy. He also admired Dolores, his successful compatriot, from afar. A peculiar rumor, and a particularly persistent one, is that Dolores brought him to Cedric Gibbons's attention when Gibbons was designing the Oscar statuette, and that Fernández had posed for it.[10] The statuette was designed before Gibbons knew Dolores, however, let alone Fernández, and it is unlikely that she herself had yet met El Indio. It is possible that Fernández himself was the source for the rumor; it fits with his self-aggrandizing personality along with his rather extravagant sense of humor.

El Indio later claimed that it was de la Huerta, now living in San Diego, who encouraged him in his ambitions to make films. According to the director, Don Adolfo told him that "'Mexico does not want nor does it need more revolutions. Emilio, you are in the mecca of films, and the cinema is the most effective instrument that man has invented to express himself. Learn to make movies and come back to our country with that knowledge. . . . No other kind of message will be more widely diffused.'"[11] Fernández returned to Mexico in 1934, when President Lázaro Cárdenas issued an amnesty to the de la Huertistas; de la Huerta himself was pardoned, brought into the government, and served in a number of relatively insignificant government posts.

El Indio, on the other hand, began to work as a screenwriter and an actor, on films in which the stories were often based on the Mexican Revolution itself. Before working with Dolores, he had directed only one film, *La isla de la pasión (Island of Passion)* but performed in fifteen others, sometimes collaborating on the screenplays. Though he was rarely featured, he worked with many of the Mexican movie greats such as Jorge Negrete, Pedro Armendáriz, Arturo de Córdova, and Lucha Reyes. His directorial debut was based on a script that he had carried around for six years while in Hollywood, while he slept in his car because he had no rent money. It told the story of a Mexican military detachment abandoned on an island during the Revolution. That film was well received, and then he was called on to direct Dolores in what would become *Flor Silvestre*. Agustín J. Fink of Films Mundiales was the one who initially contacted her and who put the production together, using Fernández and Mauricio Magdaleno to adapt the script from a novel by Fernando Robles, *Sucedió Ayer* (*It Happened Yesterday*). Fink initially wanted to get Fernando de Fuentes, then Mexico's most prominent director, but he was otherwise engaged. Fink therefore decided to give Fernández a chance.[12] El Indio later credited Dolores with smoothing the connection between the displaced members of prerevolutionary high society and the new cultural elite emerging in the arts despite the initial reluctance of the former. As he stated, " . . . a moment came in which these people needed to open contact and, through Dolores, and through film and through the painters they found a place."[13]

Gabriel Figueroa was selected for the camerawork, unsurprisingly, as he was one of the principals who had put together Films Mundiales and was quickly becoming Mexico's leading cinematographer. His background was different from those of Fernández and del Río; he was from the culturally aware upper-middle class oriented to the arts but had to make support himself starting as a teenager. Difficult family circumstances forced him to give up his early musical goals and fulfill his artistic interests and ambitions while making his own way. Figueroa's mother died at his birth in 1907, the deaths of his older brother and father followed shortly thereafter, and he and another brother were raised by relatives in Mexico City during the last troubled years of the Porfirian regime and through the Revolution. His childhood was filled with elaborate puppet shows that the siblings put on for their own amusement. He loved going to movies at a nearby theater, where friends permitted him to enter free to see U.S. comedies starring Buster Keaton, Harold Lloyd, and Charlie Chaplin as well as Italian and French productions. Although he studied violin at Mexico's National Conservatory, financial problems led him as a teenager to make his hobby of still photography into a paying business. He began to take stills on movie sets and then moved into filming itself. He went to Hollywood in 1936 with the assistance of friends in the United States, and there he met Gregg Toland, a cameraman who later worked with Orson Welles. Toland remained a lifetime friend, and they communicated regularly, as he did with other international cinematographers and filmmakers.

Although it is unclear just when he met Lolita, it is possible they encountered each other first on the U.S. side of the border through the mutual connection to Welles. On his return to Mexico, Figueroa became friends with Diego Rivera and Pascual Orozco, whose work he studied, seeking relationships between their use of light and perspective and his own film-work, and it may also be that his first encounter with del Río came through these two artists.[14]

He began his involvement in film with Mexico's first sound production, Gamboa's *Santa*, in 1931, for which Alex Phillips was the cinematographer. Phillips invited him to help him develop and retouch the photographs of the stars and then brought him into the filming itself. His first major job behind the camera came in 1936, with *Allá en el Rancho Grande*, for which he immediately won both a national and an international award, in Mexico from the Periodistas Cinematográficas in 1936 and in Italy at La Mostra Internazionale d'Arte Cinematografica di Venezia in 1938. At the time he began working on del Río's first Mexican film, he was thirty-five years old and had already done distinguished work on *La mujer del puerto* (*The Woman of the Port*), and *Vamanos con Pancho Villa* (*Let's Go with Pancho Villa*).[15] He was so successful by the time Dolores returned to Mexico that he and others, including Chano Urueta and Arturo de Córdova, persuaded Mexican investors to help them form a filmmaking cooperative that they named Films Mundiales. Agustín J. Fink was brought in to head the new business.[16] It was Fink himself, working with this organization, who put together the team of Fernández, del Río, Figueroa, and Armendáriz, the collaboration that most clearly characterized the Golden Age of Mexican filmmaking in the 1940s.

For Figueroa, the return of del Río was encouraging almost to the point of cosmic; Her determination to use Mexican themes in the films she made in her homeland was an inspiration. According to Figueroa, Dolores showed them that "it was up to us to leave our mark on Mexican film."[17] The artistic group that surrounded Films Mundiales at the time of Dolores's first movies there was filled with artists and writers devoted to provid-ing a distinctively Mexican atmosphere. According to Figueroa, Mauricio Magdaleno, who collaborated with Fernández in the writing of her first two scripts in Mexico, was one of those. And del Río, when she came back, "also knew how to create a very Mexican atmosphere. She had a collection of shawls, of embroidered blouses, of Tehuana costumes, pre-Cortesian jew-elry that she began to use for parties."[18] In these fashion choices, Dolores was much like Frida Kahlo, another urban, sophisticated Mexican woman who had also started to use more traditional Mexican clothing, particularly during her earlier stays in the United States and afterward when she herself returned to Mexico.

In so doing, they combined to create a permissible and sought-after fashion. Perhaps del Río was emphasizing her Mexican roots, making up for her years of absence, looking for another kind of authenticity, one beyond that afforded by her upper-class background. Yet there was certainly a sense that she was playing a role, because she was assuredly *not* of peasant background, though it was a role she quickly moved onto the screen. It was as if a Mexican peasant persona was a new version of the exotic, a role she had been playing since her earliest days in Hollywood, but a new exotic that she and others were in the process of creating, and not only in the process of performing. Moreover, it was an exotic that was substantially shorn of the heavy sexuality with which some of her performances in Hollywood had been laden. She was still appealing and even, sometimes, sensual in these early Mexican films, but not usually dangerous nor come-hither.

Her co-star, Pedro Armendáriz, had a cross-border background that was resonant with but very different from her own. Born in 1912 in Churubusco, a suburb of Mexico City and the later site of the most important movie studio in Mexico, he was several years Dolores's junior. His mother was an American, Della Hastings, and his father, Pedro Armendáriz García Conde, came from a Mexican family of some social standing. The family left the disorder of Mexico in 1918, following the most violent years of the Revolution, and settled in San Antonio, Texas, which provided a refuge not only to the Armendárizes but also to many Mexicans seeking safety in the United States.[19] He attended California Polytechnic Institute at San Luis Obispo, receiving an engineering degree despite his early interest in amateur theater, and then returned to a more peaceful Mexico. Extraordinarily handsome, he soon attracted the attention of Mexican filmmakers, and at the age of twenty-three he appeared in his first film, *Rosario*. His bilingualism, familiarity with the United States, and quickly accelerating career (twenty-eight films in eight years, albeit entirely in Mexico), gave him much in common with his glamorous co-star. He appeared in Fernández's first directorial project, *Isla de la pasión*, and was an obvious choice to star with del Río.[20]

The first film for the team, *Flor Silvestre*, was the story of a peasant/ indigenous woman who marries the landlord's son and sees the family torn apart by divisions over the Revolution. Del Río was paid 30,000 pesos for her

role, peanuts compared to her Hollywood salaries but a significant amount
for Mexico.[21] Shooting began on January 11, 1943, and was completed five
weeks later. Magdaleno described the writing of the script as a little tense;
Fernández was "temperamental" and both were nervous about working
with Lolita, who was returning from Hollywood with "great fame and star
status." Soon, however, according to him, Fernández and the leading lady
became involved romantically, which temporarily made everything easier.[22]

The story recounts the divisions of the Revolution itself. The father
supports the Porfirian dictatorship and the son the opposing revolutionary
forces. Armendáriz played del Río's sweetheart and then husband, the son of
the wealthy hacendado. The Armendáriz character is eventually executed,
Dolores crying piteously behind him as he stoically accepts his fate. Yet
he leaves behind a son, raised by his mother (del Río). This child becomes
the embodiment of the merging of classes in the revolutionary process.
The film is designed with Dolores's character as the narrator, telling the
story of the Revolution and the family to that child, now an adult and an
officer in the postrevolutionary Mexican army. [23] It included in the cast as
del Río's mother-in-law Mimi Derba, a popular actress who had been appearing in Mexican films for years, and this association was very pleasing
to both of the actresses. In an emotional scene together, the two dramatically reached out to one another; at the time of the filming, the crew broke
into applause. At some point during the shoot, Lolita and El Indio became
lovers. Yet despite the relationship between them, at one point he lost control of his temper and almost struck her. She pulled out of the project and
came back only out of a sense of friendship and professionalism when others in the film begged her to do so. Fernández later said that even though
all films were a collaboration, a movie shoot should be almost "military,
with all the soldiers and officers and chiefs moving under one authority,
and he is the one who decides what is going to happen, no?"[24] Perhaps this
conflict was about who should be the "one authority," as illustrated by his
own view of what the director (himself) should be doing, and he needed to
bring Dolores, with all her prestige, under his control.

Still, she was the star. Her presence in Mexico helped the film industry there gain some recognition from the United States; in March 1943,
two months before the premiere of *Flor Silvestre*, a long piece entitled "The
Film Scene Down Mexico Way," by Leah Brenner, appeared in the *New
York Times*, pointing out that "national products have assumed new impor-

tance since this country's [Mexico's] declaration of war." She credited new laws requiring theaters in the country to show a certain number of films made in Mexico, along with dropping production in Hollywood; the growing Latin American market for films in Spanish; and Mexico's proximity to the center of filmmaking in Los Angeles, which had made it possible for Mexicans in the business to gain technical expertise. These factors all contributed to the fact that "Mexican movie production has reached a high mark unequaled in its history." Films Mundiales and Agustín J. Fink were pointed out, along with Clasa Films, as making huge strides technically, building new studios, and providing enhanced excellence in stories and productions. The article highlighted del Río's return to her home country and the fact that she was currently starring in one production for the first of these companies and had another planned.

Brenner pointed out another important factor in the market for films in Spanish. "The Mexican masses," she stated, would rather go to films in which the dialogue was in their native language, as the widespread illiteracy still common in the country made it impossible for them to read the subtitles of U.S. productions, and the same would hold, of course, for much of Spanish-speaking Latin America. She emphasized too that "American slapstick comedies and Hollywood escapist films also fail to thrill them because of the deep gulf between Mexican and American psychology."[25]

After the film was complete, success was not immediate. At first, the Mexican army objected to it being shown without changes and tried to get it suppressed, a strange stance since the film reflected the notion of class leveling, in the army and elsewhere, which many in the Mexican government wanted to promote.[26] The movie premiered on April 24, 1943, the day before Easter Sunday, at the enormous Palacio Chino. Fernández described the premiere as "a bath of cold water . . . more like an art show than a film showing," with almost all of the handful of people in the audience being painters: José Clemente Orozco, David Siquieros, Roberto Montenegro, Rivera and Kahlo, Miguel and Rosa Covarrubias, and María Izquierdo among them. Almost all of them had, at one time or another, painted Lolita. She, according to most accounts, was devastated, remembering the opening of her first film, *Joanna*, many years earlier in similar circumstances. Fernández later claimed the issue was that Dolores was not well liked in Mexico, although subsequent events make such a judgment questionable; it may have been one of his ways of cutting his star down to size, or his taking more credit for her subsequent success than perhaps he should have.[27] Diego Rivera's take at the time was supportive if not necessarily reassuring: "Shake it off, Lolita, the deal is that the public doesn't like us because we are communists, which we can't control." Later, after the dinner party for her friends that she gave following the premiere, she talked the situation over with her mother. Dolores decided that despite the setback she would persevere.[28]

Despite her initial disappointment in *Flor Silvestre*, her friend and constant supporter Eduardo Iturbide, who saw it on that first day, wrote to her with praise. As he noted in his letter, he had often been at her side during her "great crises" and tried to give her good advice at these times. Indeed, he was one of the few individuals among her family's upper-class friends who initially suggested that she go to Hollywood. In this letter he recalled having taken satisfaction over the years in usually being right about what she should do, but recently, he admitted, he had been dead wrong. He reminded her that when she returned to Mexico, he entirely approved of her investing in Mexican films but thought it a bad idea that she should actually appear on screen. He felt that "having acted in a better situation, with all the resources [necessary] and truly well directed," she would have little chance of success in this new situation. He had not wanted her to suffer a public "failure."

Yet when he saw the film, on the "Saturday of Glory," a reference both to the day of vigil before Easter and to her own success, he was overwhelmed. It was her second "Resurrection," he said, a reference to her early hit film with Carewe and to her emergence from her moribund Hollywood career into a new artistic existence in Mexico. He was particularly impressed that she could shift from her well-known public persona and her "well-deserved vanity as a chic and beautiful international woman" to emerge onscreen as entirely Mexican, and, furthermore, as a *campesina*, a woman of the countryside. He closed, "Dolores, you have come back to being Mexican, the best Mexican woman, and you have known how to demonstrate it in front of the whole of Mexico."[29]

Soon the reviews began to appear, for the most part strongly positive. After a short lapse, the film was brought back to the Palacio Chino for several weeks, with great success. The critics liked it; the film was clearly Mexican; Dolores let herself be directed rather than playing the grande dame; and the public soon came. The studio immediately began blanketing radio stations with announcements about the film and cultivated the press. Quickly it was playing to sold-out houses.[30] Moreover, in the final analysis and despite the objections of the army, it suited the developing ideology of the post-1940 Mexican state, which promoted the story of reconciliation of classes and races in the wake of the revolutionary sacrifice of blood and life, just as those historical memories were becoming less painful. In the meantime, in an interesting new career adventure, she took a job singing at Ciro's, which she and the public both enjoyed.[31] It was the first time in years that she had appeared before a live audience, and it may be that this small success led her to a continuing interest in doing something on the stage. Public honors began to come her way as well. On June 10, 1943, the Mexico City press gave a function in honor of her return and her role in *Flor Silvestre*, presenting her with a medal. It was the first of many honors in her home country, and as she left the event the public gathered in enthusiastic support to cheer her.[32]

Neither was she forgotten in the United States; she still had Spanish-speaking fans north of the border who would happily go to her films and, perhaps, non-Spanish-speakers who still just liked to look at her. Moreover, Hollywood columnists, particularly Hedda Hopper, now a fan, kept Dolores's name in the U.S. press. After the release of her first Mexican film, Hopper noted regretfully that del Río had informed her of her intention to live in Mexico permanently; further, she would not do the story (probably *Santa*) that Orson Welles had written for her.[33] And despite *Flor Silvestre* being at this point in time neither dubbed nor subtitled, it was soon shown in Los Angeles at the California and Mason Theaters, which apparently catered to Spanish-speaking audiences. The reviewer (who was probably another longtime supporter, Grace Kingsley, but who signed only as G. K.) noted that "She is an impressively skillful, even at times inspired actress in her first story filmed down there. Not even in Tolstoy's 'Resurrection' did she do as notable work as she does in the Mexican film." Yet it closed by noting that despite her fine performance, "she looks far more the aristocrat than the supposed aristocrats!" Still, this was high praise in a newspaper that had noted her appearance in *Journey into Fear* just seven months earlier with one sentence: "Miss Del Rio emerges from the shadows now and then to lend a pictorial moment." Armendáriz was likewise singled out for praise, and the reviewer noted that "the other actors live their characters in vivid Mexican fashion."[34]

Fernández, by now deeply involved with Lolita, was concerned with the social differences between them. The romance did not make the papers, perhaps because of respect for the principals. Still, it was a serious relationship, sanctioned by her mother, though Fernández did not visit La Escondida a great deal. Instead, he built a house nearby. De los Reyes points out that a line spoken by Armendáriz in *Flor Silvestre* might well be taken from the relationship between star and director. As he says, "Social differences are not erased by good intentions," and the real-life relationship between the son of a Kickapoo mother and the daughter of the upper class was complicated. It is interesting that El Indio wanted her to continue to play "women of the people," that is, women of a lower social category than that of her birth, perhaps because it made her more accessible to him and the relationship between them more acceptable.[35] Fernández later said to an interviewer that del Río was "skilled . . . but she was also enormously lovely, the most beautiful woman and besides she spoke in a most charming way. She was very disciplined, very dedicated, and she concentrated on her work. She had a technique of maintaining silence, very exaggerated, very theatrical."[36] Perhaps this observation was not just a reaction to her acting and came from their private relationship as well as from their professional one.

The second film they made together originated out of a birthday present from Emilio to Lolita, a gesture of both love and respect. As he recounted the story, the film was "a logical result of *Flor Silvestre.* It was a completely Mexican film, conceived and made for Dolores del Río who had all at once taken her place as our country's distinctive woman. At that time I would have proclaimed her 'the fairest flower of the *ejido'*" (Mexico's historical indigenous communal landholding, reinvigorated and legalized in the land reform program that followed the Mexican Revolution). He went on to explain that he had written the script on thirteen napkins at a restaurant and sent it to the star on her saint's day, "because I had no money to buy her flowers."[37] In fact, the gift was more dramatic; the day before *Flor Silvestre* premiered, Good Friday of 1943, Lolita and her mother gave a big saint's day party at their new home, La Escondida. Again, it was attended by Mexico's artistic community, from next door neighbor Salvador Novo to the usual artists, Julio Bracho (who was beginning to make his name as a film director and who was yet another of Dolores's relatives), composers and musicians, and even Concha Michel,

Mexico's bad girl intellectual. Michel sang a song composed in Lolita's honor, recounting her history from her birth in Durango, her triumph in Carewe's *Resurrection*, President Obregón's friendship, her beauty, and her return to Mexico to lead the artistic revolution: "And now you've returned to Mexico, with sincere enthusiasm, to develop our art, which costs and makes money."[38] Her position at the center of the artistic and literary scene could not have been clearer.

At this point, it was Fernández's turn, and he brought the napkins to her, threw them at her feet, and announced dramatically, "Here is your saint's day present, a film story. Let's see if you like it, it is your next film, and it is called *Xochimilco*. It's yours, it's your property, if someone wants to buy it they have to buy it from you."[39] Fernández had taken the plot from the Mexican film in which he himself first starred, *Janitzio*, and changed the venue from the island in Lake Patzcuaro to the indigenous community near Mexico City, noted for its enormous production of flowers on the *chinampas*, floating gardens that were the product of an agricultural practice surviving from the pre-Columbian past.

The story is set in 1909, the period just before the onset of the Revolution. It furnishes a picture and an interpretation of the indigenous communities of that time, suffering from ignorance on the one hand and repression by mestizo middlemen on the other. Interestingly, the prerevolutionary government of Porfirio Díaz is portrayed as relatively benevolent, providing medicines for the population, which the wicked mestizo shopkeeper, Don Damian, withholds at his pleasure. María Candelaria, the title character played by Dolores, is the daughter of a prostitute, an outcast from the community, and she herself is an outcast as well. Her protective sweetheart and fiancé is played by Armendáriz. The narrator is a U.S. artist, who tells the story as a tragedy of misunderstanding; at the end, María Candelaria is stoned to death for a supposed violation of the moral standards of the native community, after he paints a nude picture using her face and another woman's body. The picture of the Indians is a mixed one, mirroring the schizophrenic view of the indigenous population, referred to earlier, that emerged from the Revolution. The native community is ignorant and brutal; María Candelaria is pure and beautiful, a throwback to the glories of the pre-Columbian past, as scenes in which the artist compares her to ancient artifacts make clear. A glorious past, a degraded present: these characterized the view of indigenous people held by the Mexican state and the men who had formed Mexico's policy toward the indigenous for more than twenty-five years.[40]

The film was meant to show the bad old days, emphasizing by contrast postrevolutionary improvements. The contradiction in the supposed positive view of the indigenous in El Indio's representation has been pointed out by Fernández's biographer, Paco Ignacio Taibo: ". . . it is the Indian community itself that kills the young woman and destroys all possibility of a happy life between the couple; the only manifestations of honest, peaceful, and innocent behavior, are seen in the two principal figures, and the rest of the town's behavior is as a degraded and uncultured group." Taibo himself believed that the film presented Mexico "in a new way, with beautiful human beings and a singular lyrical charge," while, according to him, Mexican viewers may have been a little too familiar with the reality of Xochimilco to see it in quite such idealized terms.[41]

The shoot began less than two weeks after her birthday in 1943 and, along with *Flor Silvestre*, reestablished her solidly in the film world and in the affections of her own country. Dolores found El Indio hard to work with, even worse than during the production of *Flor Silvestre*. The script called for her to carry around a little pig, which she hated but was supposed to love and protect. The scenes were strangely resonant with Christian images of the Mother and Child, Dolores as Mary, and the piglet as the Christ Child. In the story, the pig is killed by the wicked mestizo, Don Damian, and María Candelaria grieves over its dead body in a kind of Mexican pietà. During the filming, Fernández himself killed the piglet, not wanting to use a fake. The little corpse attracted bugs, which also began to attack del Río, but the director continued to order take after take, until her body as well was a "living wound." Dolores was stoic and professional, unprotesting. Fortunately, lunchtime finally came around, and Matilde Landeta (in this film the script girl and later a distinguished screenwriter and director in her own right) and makeup artist Anita Guerrero took Dolores back to her dressing room to patch her up. Landeta later remarked that Fernandez's dictatorial way of running a film shoot led her to start directing on her own. She commented years later in an interview with Susan Dever: "There he was, high and dry, shouting orders like some Revolutionary general, and there was I, the muck sucking up my shoes, trying to do my duty and keep my mouth shut. I knew I couldn't last long as the camp-follower kind of *soldadera*; I had to direct."[42]

It may be that Dolores was equally resentful, though she put up with El Indio's abuse for the time being. Rain made it impossible to continue later in the afternoon, and she was able to rest since her contract made it clear that from the end of the day until beginning work the next, she was to have twelve hours of rest. Still, throughout the shoot, El Indio continued to film her constantly in the mud and water of the chinampa, scenes that did not appear in the final cut and seemed, perhaps, intended to illustrate his dominance over his more prominent star. Finally, after another outburst in which Fernández struck both Dolores and her mother, del Río walked off the set. When she did not return, the management of Films Mundiales became concerned and forced the director to apologize; he did so in a meeting of cast and crew, climbing onto a chair to proclaim that he apologized "to the actress, but not to the woman." In the midst of these trials with her new director and lover, she received word from Welles that he and Rita Hayworth had just been married. This news was another blow, perhaps a petulant act of revenge on Orson's part, as Hayworth was being touted in Hollywood as the new Dolores del Río.[43]

The film wrapped, probably to her relief, on October 14, five weeks after she received the news of Orson's marriage. She nevertheless took time to return to Xochimilco, dressed in a glamorous formal gown, for the baptism of a child belonging to an agricultural family of the community; of course, the baby was given the name María Candelaria.[44] And, in the meantime, she continued to be noticed by the U.S. press; Leonard Lyons, reporting from Mexico in the *Washington Post*, pointed out just a month after she finished shooting *María Candelaria* that she was now enjoying "a new and more successful career here."[45]

Both actress and director were concerned about the reception of the film; clearly focused on the indigenous population, it was disdained by some who felt there was not much to celebrate in that subject. Further, the film was tragic. As El Indio described it, "A few good people couldn't go along with the film. It sounded strange to them. It seemed to them— imagine!—exotic and also depressing. They were scandalized and ousted me from the production company . . . because I had made 'such shit about Indians.' I had to resolve to starve to death."[46] Although it seems likely the director's bad behavior was more of a problem than was the subject of the film, there were some concerns about the theme, and the premiere was put off until January. Even within the company, people were nervous. Magdaleno, who worked on the script with Fernández, later commented that ". . . I was not as enthusiastic as he was. I thought that the story of *María Candelaria* was phony. I modified it where I could, many times against the wishes of Emilio. What most bothered me about *María Candelaria* was its folkloric aspect." Emilio Azcárraga, who controlled a number of movie theaters, was opposed to the film, and seems to have influenced some other owners to boycott it, but a strike in the industry limited the number of films available and the head of the studio, Agustín Fink, rented the Teatro Palacio for the premiere. When it was shown, not only were the artistic and film crowds in attendance but also a number of residents of Xochimilco, who were enthusiastic and made a point of shutting up those in the audience who were vocally expressing their displeasure. Fernández characterized the attitude of the latter, whom he believed to be other film professionals, as jealousy.[47]

Again, early disdain, which Fernández may have exaggerated, turned to success and praise, and it was not just luck that made it so. The combination of story, photography, and acting made a huge impression on Mexican audiences, and the critic Efraín Huerta, writing in *Esto*, opined that "Dolores

Pedro Armendáriz grieving over Dolores as the dying or dead María Candelaria.
Bibliothèque du Film.

del Río reaches her dramatic heights, her consecration as a powerful dramatic actress. She . . . never loses the somber air of a persecuted woman." Telegrams of congratulation poured in, from the premier Mexican director Fernando de Fuentes, who characterized her performance as "masterful"; from the former president of Mexico Emilio Portes Gil, who concurred with the director and the designation "masterful" and sent congratulations as well to the entire cast; from the Mexican intellectual and longtime correspondent Alfonso Reyes, who said it was the best Mexican film he had ever seen and her best performance ever and that he was "moved and—I don't know why—proud"; from U.S. novelist John Steinbeck, who called the film "magnificent."[48] Here, another of Lolita's performances was changing U.S. and international attitudes toward Mexicans in racial terms, but the shift in vision was becoming cultural as well.

A particularly moving tribute came to her several months after the initial opening from composer and conductor Leopold Stokowski, whom she had known in Hollywood and who wrote her in June 1944 that he was "in such a daze" after seeing the film that "I do not know what I said to you." However, thinking about it he now realized that it was a "*great film.*" He was especially struck by how the images carried the story, "almost completely without dialogue," and the beauty of the photography. He pointed to Figueroa's craft, saying that he "knows well how to light your face so that all its beauty is expressed on the screen." That the two, Stokowski and del Río, were close friends is made obvious by the intimate nature of the communication, and he averred that "I am happy for you and Emilio that you have achieved it." Stokowski seems also to have fallen under the del Río spell, and confided that he would "look forward to the time when we have our three-person rancho together. I know we shall be happy there. We can sometimes invite friends we like the most to be with us there for a time."[49]

Also shown at the California and Mason theaters in Los Angeles, the U.S. title was *Xochimilco, the Story of María Candelaria*. The *Los Angeles Times* reviewed it on September 27, 1944, nine months after the Mexican opening, saying that despite the lack of translation "the meaning of its more emotional scenes is unmistakable" and del Río's "work as the poor Indian peasant girl measures up to all the terrific requirements of her role. In fact, no one can gainsay that Miss Del Rio has become a great actress, with all the old posing and artificiality gone, giving place to a genuine power that is at times almost startling. Her grace remains, but as servant to her emotional power." With some surprise, the reviewer, again probably Grace Kingsley, noted that in "no place . . . does she attempt, in emotional crises, to look beautiful."[50] This effect was no doubt due in large part to Fernández's punishing direction.

The success led a few months later to its purchase and dubbing for general U.S. release by MGM, which also pushed for a nomination for an Academy Award. It was released with subtitles and another new title, *Portrait of María*. A review by critic Edwin Schallert praised it highly, saying that for those who wanted to get away from the typical Hollywood picture "it was a deeply moving study of two people harassed by poverty, and putting up a hopeless fight for happiness. . . . The scenic backgrounds would, indeed, lift it far out of the ordinary realm. They are a magnificent, almost unearthly setting of splendor for the stark grim realism of the narrative of Maria Candelaria and Lorenzo Rafael." The review reflected favorably on Figueroa's stunning cinematography, the fine acting of both Dolores and Armendáriz, and El Indio's direction.[51] The film does not seem to have been honored by the Academy, but a few months later, no doubt still promoted by MGM, it was named one of twelve winners of the Golden Palm, the grand prize at the first Cannes Film Festival held after the end of World War II. Figueroa won the sole first prize for cinematography.[52] Even if it is frequently reported inaccurately that *María Candelaria* was the *only* winner of the top prize, the award mattered.[53] It brought great prestige to the Mexican film industry and to all of the principals involved. A year later, it also won awards, especially for Figueroa's cinematography, at the Locarno film festival in Switzerland.[54] Even in 2007,, among the ten or twelve images that flashed onto the home page of the Locarno festival website at that time, there was one of Dolores.[55]

Del Río always considered the two first films that she made with Fernández and Figueroa the best of all of her work, and they clearly established her as a great Mexican star. The second film was conceived and written by El Indio specifically for her, in a loving effort to place her in a totally Mexican context that would endear her to the audiences of her country, and ultimately he succeeded. Fernández and his cinematographer, Figueroa, saw themselves very much within the developing "Mexican aesthetic" characterized by Dolores's friends Orozco and Rivera. As Figueroa explained it, "Diego Rivera . . . classified my work saying that I was 'the moving muralist' . . . So it was that there was a mystique [of the Mexican] to pursue."

Figueroa saw this aesthetic not only in terms of painting and cinema but also in music, including the compositions of Silvestre Revueltas, who collaborated as well with Mexican cinema. He also brought other Mexican artists into the productions. For example, Leopoldo Méndez, famous for his work in the Taller de Gráfica Popular, did the titles for *María Candelaria* and became better known outside Mexico. Figueroa proudly declared later that "I got him into cinema."[56]

Del Río, pleased with the final realization of her hopes to be a fine actress and her desire to make significant films, continued to work for some time with various members of the team, despite her difficulties and humiliations at the hands of Fernández. The personal relationship, however, soon faded away. Figueroa himself indicated the difficulties of being friends with El Indio. Although he acknowledged that they formed a real team, with an important understanding about the use of film images, he was reluctant to spend very much time with him. Figueroa's daughter later said that Figueroa would not invite him to their home, since when El Indio had a little too much to drink, "he was scary with his pistol."[57]

If this violence was disturbing to Figueroa, it was very likely even worse for Dolores, as she tried to maintain an intimate personal relationship with a director of undisciplined personal habits who thought about filming in terms of military dominance. She was hard-working and professional, as all attested, and she brought great prestige to those who worked with her. Recognizing El Indio's talent, she continued to let herself be directed. Still, this kind of submission, with its personal as well as professional aspects, surely rankled. Eventually, even this professional relationship became difficult as Fernández grew more and more erratic. Her later comment in relation to El Indio was that

he didn't know when to get out of making Mexican cinema. We should have left a space for the young people to make innovations. We can't repeat over and over again to the point of overkill what we did well once. We did it very well! Wonderful! It doesn't make sense to go back and do it again. The Golden Age of Mexican cinema of the "indigenous or Mexicanist," if you want to call it that, is past. Now we should go on to another stage that can be equally good, but different.[58]

Though she made more films with Fernández, her cinematic vision by now surpassed Emilio's. However, her friendship with Figueroa would be lifelong, as would her friendships with Armendáriz and others on these films. She later said of the cinematographer, recognizing him as the extraordinary talent that he was: "I have immense respect for the human virtues of the artist Gabriel Figueroa. He has great honesty in his work and in his person. He never makes a false move."[59] Collaboration with Fernández and Figueroa and of course Armendáriz established Dolores as one of the two great female faces (the other was María Félix) of the new aesthetic vision of Mexico that was emerging in painting, music, and film.

10   Resurrection

[R]arely is it that a single break makes a star. . . . Rather than one
break, the star-to-be normally receives a series of breaks.
> Jib Fowles, *Starstruck: Celebrity Performers and the*
> *American Public*[1]

In her best moments (La Otra, Doña Perfecta), Dolores is
commanding, cruel, not the humiliated but the humiliator, the
inverted apology of *machismo*, the woman whose fancy takes her in
the opposite direction to traditional femininity.
> Carlos Monsiváis, "Dolores del Río"[2]

THE ENORMOUS SUCCESS of her first two films after her
return securely reestablished her claim to a Mexican
identity and made it clear that she still had an admiring and paying public
in her home country, in the United States, and in Europe and Latin America
as well. Del Río's film career continued to thrive for seventeen more years.
From 1944 through 1960, she made sixteen Mexican films, one Mexican-
Spanish co-production, and two U.S. productions, though one of these was
actually filmed in Mexico. In many ways, for her, these years may have been
the most satisfying in terms of pace, quality, and her own control over her
artistic production. Certainly, considering critical reception, awards, and
honors, this creative period was extraordinary. At the same time, she continued the interest in the arts and literature that characterized her return
to Mexico from its earliest days. She felt a real responsibility along with
a strong interest in developing these aspects of national culture, both in
tandem with her own career and separated from it.

Important in this success was her stardom in Hollywood, which afforded her high status in the Spanish-speaking world. Her celebrity north of the border made possible inclusion among those other national superstars in Mexican films: Pedro Armendáriz, María Félix, Jorge Negrete, and, emerging at about the same time that she began making movies in Mexico, Pedro Infante, who was already a radio star renowned for his singing and a national icon on his own.[3] Moreover, the subject matter, filming, symbols, subjects, and landscapes of her first two films, along with representations of rural Mexico and peasants and Indians, distinguished the team of del Río, Fernández, Figueroa, and Armendáriz as exemplary of what was seen as a new "Mexican school of film." These two films became "a luxury article for export of what was considered representative of Mexican culture." In these films, rural Mexico was shown as being converted by the Revolution from ignorant and backward, as seen in *María Candelaria*, to representative of the very nation itself in *Flor Silvestre*. It was the exaggerated and idealized presentation of the Mexican countryside in these two films that some in the Mexican urban classes found unacceptable. But the international honors that *María Candelaria* received in 1946 and 1947—along with a possibly related increase in tourism—made these representations more palatable in retrospect and Dolores's own contributions to them more admirable. The indigenous peoples themselves, whether pre- or postrevolution, became "noble savages."[4] In the meantime, however, the Mexican viewing public needed something a little different.

The next two of del Río's films, *Las abandonadas* (Abandoned Women) and *Bugambilia* (Bougainvillea), were again collaborations with Fernández directing and writing aided by Magdaleno, Figueroa as cinematographer, and Armendáriz as leading man. Films Mundiales, with Don Agustín now replaced by Felipe Subervielle, produced. These films were not nearly so political as the first two; nor was she a peasant woman. In fact, in *Las abandonadas*, Dolores got to wear some beautiful costumes and make her way down a staircase or two, as she had in some of her Hollywood films and in the house that Cedric Gibbons designed to showcase her. In her role as a woman abandoned by her bigamous husband, Dolores as Margarita (and later Margó) becomes successful as a prostitute and later winds up destitute on the Mexico City streets. But the major and most poignant theme of the film is motherhood.

Although *Flor Silvestre* and *Maria Candelaria* have received more critical attention, *Las abandonadas* was one of the best films Dolores ever made in

terms of her performance, full of social content and Mexican revolutionary history. Margarita is a woman of the provincial middle class who is seduced after a false marriage to an upper-class and conspicuously blond man
from Mexico City and, returning pregnant to her home, is thrown out by
her angry father. Del Río had the opportunity to display her acting talents
in a role that aged her from a very young woman to a worn-out drudge
dying of poverty. Struggling, she works as a laundress, but after her baby
is born she begins to work as a dance hall girl and then later moves into
a high-class house of prostitution, leaving the child behind in an orphanage. In a dramatic scene, she appears at the top of the staircase (albeit not
a particularly long one), in a dazzling, formfitting gown and with feathers
in her hair, just as Armendáriz as General Juan Gómez enters the house
with his men. The putative general is stunned by her beauty. As his men
roughly shout out their desire for her, he fires a shot into the air, quieting
them all, and carries her off to the best hotel in town. There he gallantly
and gently leaves her, to her surprise, without demanding sex. That scene
comes after a romance and after he has bought her a mansion "where the
wealthy live" ("*donde viven los ricos*"). They cohabit happily and luxuriously
for a while, her only sorrows being the secrets of her past and her separation from her son. When Gómez/Armendáriz discovers the existence of
the child, he asks her to marry him and promises to care for both of them
and to make the son a "great man" ("*un gran hombre*").

Despite their momentary happiness, things fall apart quickly. As they
celebrate their engagement at a local club, the police arrive. The man
Dolores/Margó knows and loves as Gómez is arrested as a bandit who
has assumed the identity of the deceased General Gómez. He has used his
important position in keeping order in Mexico City in the years immediately after the Revolution to perpetrate a series of robberies and attacks on
the wealthy. The glorious jewels he has been bringing Margó are stolen.
Knowing himself guilty, he is able to get hold of his own pistol and shoot
himself before his apprehenders are able to take him to jail. The scene is
a stunning and unfortunate precursor to Armendáriz's own death in the
UCLA Hospital in Los Angeles, when, in 1963, he shot himself on discovering that he had incurable cancer.[5] His fictional character leaves Margó
alone to face the charges in regard to the false Gómez's crimes, even though
she is completely innocent. After eight years in prison, she returns to the
orphanage where she has left her son Margarito. Realizing, on arrival,

that the head of the orphanage has taken him under his wing and will see to his education, she pretends to be a friend of his mother's and tells him that his mother has died. For years, she sends money to the orphanage to pay for his lessons and later for his legal training. She watches him from afar as he develops into a prominent lawyer.

In the last few scenes, she watches from the gallery as he dramatically defends a woman accused of killing her husband, making claims that motherhood is close to God and that the woman is a victim of the unjust social system and prejudices that exist in Mexico. The crowd leaps to its feet, clapping and cheering, and the jury exonerates his client. Margarita, emotional and proud, leaves the courtroom but is pushed down by the enthusiastic crowd clamoring to get to her son. He leans down and tenderly helps her, despite her disheveled and dirty appearance, and, mistaking her for a beggar, gives her money. Then he is borne away on the shoulders of his supporters. In the last scene, we see her watching his retreating figure and kissing the coin, announcing that he is indeed a "great man."[6] Ramón reports that the scene was greeted by an "uncontainable wail" when it was premiered in May 1945 at the Cine Chapultepec.[7]

Many of the bits of business in the film are recapitulations of well-known scenes in her earlier work. Her bare feet appear early, as she leaves her hometown in an oxcart; Fernández's predilection for having her walk around in the mud—this time after her fall from grace—leads to scenes showing her trudging through Mexico City in the rain and the dirt. Screenwriter Magdaleno later reported that much of the script was borrowed by Emilio from films he had seen in the United States, along with a heavy appropriation from Mexican history and film.[8] Among others, it bears a resemblance to *Santa*, the Gamboa novel that Orson Welles thought to develop for Dolores years earlier. Norman Foster had produced *Santa* again in Mexico in 1943, with great success but without Dolores.[9] Del Río did not have to carry around a little pig in *Las abandonadas*; real children this time played the object of her motherly love. But her beautiful hands were again displayed as she caressed her son, even as he aged through five young actors. Indeed, her mother's tenderness was emphasized by shots of her hands as she put letters and financial contributions into mailboxes while she was separated, first by her relationship with Gómez and later by her pretense that she was dead, from the object of her caring. Much of the dialogue was disturbingly stilted, but despite the material Dolores excelled.

Even as she played an aging prostitute, now ragged and dirty, her importuning of a possible client recalled her scenes in *What Price Glory?* in which, for financial benefit, the young Dolores as Charmaine tried to tempt U.S. soldiers into her bedroom. Yet here, a scene that had once been comic becomes tragic, as her desperation to support her son despite her aging and despite her lack of options shines from the screen. Although Figueroa's cinematography remains stunning, in this film Dolores herself is the center of attention throughout, and her acting maintains the flow of the story and keeps it centered and believable.

Some of the most successful scenes involved staircases. When Margarita first goes to Mexico City to begin work as a laundress, that phase of her life is introduced in a scene in which women dressed in peasant clothing walk down a staircase carrying baskets full of dirty clothes. The scene is filmed by Figueroa against the clear Mexican sky, and the conical shapes of the baskets contrast with the vertical of the staircase and the horizontal of the platform above as the women approach and descend. The scene is stunning to look at and stunning in its representation of social class. The next scene using stairs is the one in which Dolores appears elegantly posed—as on a stage—while Armendáriz below falls instantly in love with her and claims her as his own. Fernández later explained to Julia Tuñon Pablos that "my staircases have a very important dramatic function, in order to present characters, in order to see them for the first time, thus, coming down. . . ." In this particular case, although Dolores's entrance is not the first in the film, it presents her in her new persona. She is no longer the struggling young woman but the mature, self-confident beauty whose power stems from her sexuality. If drama was what El Indio was aiming for, in this scene he certainly achieved it, because the instant attraction of Gómez to the vision of Dolores above him is obvious and, indeed, almost certainly shared by many of the viewers. Further, stairs presented differences in levels, symbolically and visually, and the representations of these differences appealed to him greatly.[10] He would use them again, on even greater scale, in the next film they did together.

Las abandonadas, called *Abandoned* in U.S. distribution, also showed to crowds at the California and Mason theaters in Los Angeles. The first editorial notice of its appearance pointed out that del Río's role was "controversial" and had "caused some excitement among film censors."[11] The showing was delayed because of some disquiet among the military, particularly the portrayal by Armendáriz of a general—even an imposter—involved in crime and corruption and in love with a prostitute. The delay was not long, however, as the script was approved by the government, "scene by scene," including retakes. The film was shown, despite the "excitement" noted above, indicating that Dolores and filmmakers in general had more latitude south of the border than she experienced during her last years in Hollywood.[12]

Once again, the film was shown in Los Angeles. The *Los Angeles Times* critic, again probably Grace Kingsley, loved Lolita's scene just after her illegitimate child's birth, when she turns away from him initially and then takes him in her arms. The critic, though, disliked what she or he saw as the stagey "theatricalism" of the staircase appearance in which Armendáriz as Gómez first falls for her. Apparently the critic liked her vulnerable better than self-confident.[13]

Bugambilia was a period piece, with Dolores wearing exquisite costumes designed by Louis Royer, who had come from Hollywood for the occasion. It was Fernández's answer to *Gone with the Wind*, complete with hoop skirts, other period costumes, and luxurious sets on a grand scale. Del Río herself worked with Royer to select the exquisite fabrics, and they used jewelry and furs valued by the insurance company at a quarter of a million pesos. Finally, she was emerging out of the mire to which El Indio's writing and direction had earlier consigned her. Nevertheless the story ended tragically for the character played by Dolores (as did all of her other films with El Indio).

Some of the filming was in the picturesque colonial town of Guanajuato, though the Guanajuatenses, who were unaccustomed to having films made in their city, often delayed shooting as they crowded around and made noise. Finally, some scenes had to be made in the CLASA Studios in Mexico City. The glorious sets were by Mauricio Fontanals, and they were regarded by the professionals involved as true works of art. The production cost more than a million pesos, making this one of the most expensive films to date in Mexico, and with the ending of World War II and the advantages it had provided to Mexican filmmakers in the absence of European pictures, the producers were nervous.[14] El Indio, in this film, abandoned—for a while—the peasant/indigenous vision of Mexico that he had pushed in *María Candelaria* and *Flor Silvestre* and the poverty-to-wealth-to-poverty scenario of *Las abandonadas*, for a sweeping epic that was far more like Hollywood films than the Mexican productions with which he had previously been involved. According to de los Reyes, Fernández was "expressing in images the vision that he had of Dolores," and this vision "contradicted the purpose of the film, which was to show the repressed life of a young girl, daughter of a miner, who lived in a small provincial house."[15] Rather, it was *one* of Fernández's visions of Lolita, and these visions varied depending on his mood, the state of their relationship, and the requirements of the script. Toward the end of the filming, he offended Roberto Montenegro, a distinguished artist and longtime friend of Lolita, by having him paint her picture in nineteenth-century style for one of the sets, and then having the portrait retouched by another artist. He treated the extras with disdain, and on the last day of the Guanajuato shoot, he offended Lolita so badly that she stopped speaking to him for other than professional reasons.[16]

Bugambilia was also shown in Spanish in the United States and received good reviews. At the same time, the U.S. press began to point out that with the end of World War II, films from other countries would give

A spectacular scene in *Bugambilia*, Fernández's Mexican answer to *Gone with the Wind*, on yet another staircase. Bibliothèque du Film.

Hollywood a run for its money. It was suggested that Mexican films would be among the top competition, with Dolores herself aiding that effort. On January 2, 1946, a photograph of Dolores and her hoop skirts—unsurprisingly standing at the bottom of a magnificent staircase—was captioned, "Mexican Perspicacity—Republic to the south rediscovered the talents of Dolores del Río, who reigns anew in popularity." The story itself noted that "the gates are open once again for a worldwide competition in the films." It went on to say that Europe and Latin America "know the power of pictures from a financial standpoint," and that Hollywood would "continually have to look to its laurels." Alongside, another photograph illustrating the story showed Vivien Leigh and Claude Rains in the British production *Caesar and Cleopatra.*[17]

Mexican producers were not as optimistic. Ominously, the filming of *Bugambilia* ran significantly long, with Lolita having to take some time off because of an attack of bronchitis. Criticisms began to circulate of what were perceived to be the huge salaries that stars such as del Río were making. Worse, the idea that she was box office poison, despite her enormous successes, surfaced again.[18] At the same time, rumors that del Río would appear in various projects—both U.S. and international—ran constantly in the press. When *Bugambilia* opened in Los Angeles in September 1946, the praise from *Los Angeles Times* critic G. K. was all for Dolores. This time, the review insisted that Armendáriz was "out of place," and was "cast in the shade by that lady's [Dolores's] charms." Further, "As for beauty, it flashes in Miss Del Río's grace and 1860 costumes. . . ."[19]

Meanwhile Films Mundiales was taken over by a businessman, Carlos Carrido Galván, the ever-supportive Agustín Fink having died in mid-1944. While Dolores had been making these first films in Mexico, there were increasing challenges from a number of Hollywood studios. These enterprises wanted to dominate the Mexican market and were even interested in producing entirely in Mexico. For a time, the war and the help from Nelson Rockefeller's OCIAA had given Mexican films an advantage, particularly in the Spanish-speaking world, and because Hollywood's own production had dropped. Unsurprisingly, the U.S. studios viewed the possibilities somewhat differently than did official Washington. Rockefeller and the OCIAA were helping the Mexican movie industry develop through technical assistance and by providing huge amounts of film, but Hollywood studios were doing their best to expand into and even take over the Mexican market. Columbia Pictures, which as we have seen had been interested for some years in producing Spanish-language films, bought into one Mexican production company, while RKO invested in the two major studios, CLASA and Azteca. In 1943 Twentieth Century-Fox contacted President Manuel Avila Camacho in the hope of making an arrangement to produce Spanish-language features in Mexico. By this time, however, Mexican cinema was operating very nicely with the support of its own government as well as the OCIAA, and their query was not answered.[20]

Competition in regard to films was not the only threat from the North just before the end of the war. Hollywood also tried to take over the Mexican film distribution system but was met by a government effort to found its own new and extensive chain of theaters. In addition, the Avila Camacho administration was planning to impose a minimum quota on the number of national productions to be exhibited in the country's theaters, an obvious threat to U.S. distribution south of the border. Finally, in February 1944 a chain of two hundred movie theaters was purchased by a Mexican consortium including private and government investors. A new Operadora de Cines was formed; the capital of two million pesos was supplied by a group of four Mexican banks, with CLASA and Films Mundiales as part owners. CLASA would use its system of distribution outside the country for the productions made by Films Mundiales, and in return that organization made its Mexican movie houses available to CLASA. This threat to exhibition of non-Mexican films led U.S. producers to put pressure on the Department of State. These problems led to an investigation by the OCIAA into the circumstances of the establishment of the theater chain and of the new government regulations. The Mexicans explained that, more than any other factor, explorations by a group of U.S. exhibitors, who had sent agents to try to acquire Mexico's major movie theaters, alerted them to issues of control and spurred the founding of the new consortium and adoption of new legal protections for their own national industry.[21]

At the time this new theater chain was inaugurated, the completed movies from CLASA and Films Mundiales and from other Mexican producers without distribution outlets were few. Films that took a long time to produce and cost a great deal, such as the last two Dolores had made with El Indio, were now impractical.[22] So it seemed, in any case, to the new head of the organization, Carrido Galván, who dismissed the team that had brought it to prominence—Dolores, Emilio, Gabriel, and Pedro—with the slighting comment that "I don't want geniuses." He decided that instead of continuing with the enormously successful del Río-Fernández-Figueroa-Armendáriz combination, which he viewed as too arty and too expensive, he would let them all go.[23] He needed to make money quickly; now, in 1944, it seemed that World War II might be coming to an end, and Mexico would soon lose the advantages that the war had provided, despite the contrary anxiety that was circulating among U.S. filmmakers.[24] Reduced exports from Hollywood, almost total stoppage in European production, and the drop especially in Argentina—which had been deemed unworthy of receiving film stock from the United States, given the predilection of its leaders for the Nazis—left the Spanish-speaking field open to the Mexicans. Now, as the world situation changed, all was uncertain, and Films Mundiales began to focus on quick and cheap commercial production.[25]

The setback for the foursome was brief, though they initially went their separate ways. Emilio immediately directed two films, the first one with almost an entirely new set of collaborators. Lolita was not among them. By this time her relationship with Fernández was no longer intimate, and their professional association was even more difficult. Nor did Figueroa or Armendáriz stay with El Indio initially. Many of Fernández's new team were brought from Hollywood, including Ricardo Montalbán, yet another Mexican who was already becoming famous in the United States, and, once again, cinematographer Alex Phillips. Armendáriz was whisked away to Hollywood by Dolores's friend Mary Pickford, much as Dolores herself had been whisked away by Edwin Carewe twenty years earlier. Dolores was not particularly pleased by Pedro's move to Los Angeles, and she warned him that he might wind up settling for inferior roles in the United States.[26] Still, Armendáriz went for a while, and then off and on for the rest of his career. He was careful, however, to cement his own professional connections with Fernández when he, about to head for the United States, complained publicly that Mexican directors were terrible and that "Only Emilio has new ideas."[27] Pedro returned soon to act in *La perla*, a John Steinbeck story, with Emilio directing. Figueroa also came back to work with Emilio on Steinbeck's story, producing one of his cinematographic masterpieces. It would take Dolores a little longer before she worked with El Indio again, even though news reports in the United States initially suggested she would star in the film.[28] Perhaps del Río's fame was still being exploited to gain attention outside of Mexico, even though she and Fernández had come to a break.

And once again, Orson Welles showed up in Mexico, this time with his bride, Rita Hayworth, in tow. Since Lolita did not respond to his attempts to contact her by telephone, he tracked down her next-door neighbor, Salvador Novo, who a few years earlier had been approached by Orson and Dolores to do a screenplay of the conquest of Mexico, featuring Orson as Cortés and Dolores, of course, as La Malinche, his indigenous lover. Welles appeared at Novo's home without Hayworth. Although Novo deliberately did not mention his beautiful neighbor, Welles asked him to call her before Rita showed up, saying he wanted to say hello to her before leaving Mexico. He had seen her first two Mexican films, he said, and found them very beautiful. Novo declined to call Dolores, however, understanding the tensions between the former lovers. Welles finally telephoned Hayworth to summon her from the hotel to join them. As they waited, they chatted about possible scripts on various historical subjects having to do with Mexico. It was, of course, an interest that Dolores had sparked in Orson, as Novo commented. It was also a poignant reminder of the circumstances that brought del Río back to Mexico, but in fact she was the one who continued to triumph, while Welles's career never quite recovered from his Brazilian escapades. One of the more extraordinary things that Novo and Welles discussed was the possibility of a film on the life of the president's controversial brother, Maximino, recently defunct, who struck Novo as a worthy subject to follow the portrayal of William Randolph Hearst as *Citizen Kane*.[29]

Dolores did not lack for offers, however, and when the script for *La selva de fuego* (*Jungle of Fire*) arrived at her home from CLASA, she loved it. But it had come to her by mistake; it was supposed to go to María Félix, while another script was actually supposed to come to her. She liked the idea of playing a shady adventuress in the hot and steamy jungle among the rough crowd on a chicle plantation, where men without women collected the substance from which chewing gum was made for American consumers. By the time studio executives realized their error, she had already decided she would do the role and refused to consider another, though they thought it better suited her younger rival.

Finally they conceded, and this time she worked with Fernando de Fuentes, who was still considered Mexico's premier director. Her lover, this time, was played by the extremely successful actor and co-founder of Films Mundiales, Arturo de Córdova. Lolita threw herself into her role, beginning filming in July 1945. At the same time, rumors circulated in Mexico

City that she was about to marry a bullfighter. The rumors were false, but she was now completely over her passion for Orson. He returned again to Mexico in December 1945, Rita now having filed for divorce, but it is not clear that he and Lolita saw each other on this later occasion.[30]

Dolores was not particularly convincing in *Selva*, always looking just a little too beautifully turned out for a woman who had struggled in through the jungle. Still, she and de Córdova made a beautiful pair, hating each other at first, according to the script, but later falling in love. Dolores's character never sweats or gets dirty, despite wearing white clothing throughout the film; she never gets hysterical, even when she defends herself by shooting and killing the man who has brought her into the camp. Of course, she dies at the end, avoiding by death a fate worse than death at the hands of threatening *chicleros*.[31] Startlingly, Jimmie Fidler's column in August 1945 depicted her role in the film as being one of an "irresistible siren who is passionately loved by 40 men." The columnist also indicated that Dolores had recently turned down three "comeback offers" from major Hollywood studios. "What actress" he asked, "would give up roles like that for the paltry rewards offered by Hollywood?"[32] In fact, her salary initially had fallen significantly under what she had been making in the United States. By the time she made *Las Abandonadas* and *Bugambilia*, her salary had risen to about 65,000 pesos a film, around $5,700 each. Her first film away from Films Mundiales, *Selva de fuego*, brought her 100,000 pesos, about $12,500, and shortly thereafter when she made another U.S. movie, *The Fugitive*, which was filmed entirely in Mexico, her salary went up to 175,000 pesos, more than $20,000.[33]

Hedda Hopper inaccurately noted at about this time that Lolita had "been offered more coin to remain" in Mexico than she would have gotten in Los Angeles.[34] Still, she was doing very well. These figures make Carrido Galván's concerns that she might not be a good box office draw seem specious at best. She was still very, very popular, and the Mexican public went to see her movies, as reflected in her rapidly ascending salary. These films were being shown in the United States as well. Hopper noted just a few days after the report mentioned earlier that Dolores was "finally doing the kind of pictures we wouldn't let her do here, and making more money than she ever did . . . ," and her source was almost certainly del Río herself.[35] Clearly, del Río was putting the best possible public face on the changes in her professional life and keeping herself before the U.S. reading and viewing public by cultivating the cultivable Hedda. Just two months later, in January 1945, *Flor Silvestre* was subtitled and noted as showing in "midtown theatres" in Manhattan.[36]

In January 1946, *Bugambilia* and *La selva de fuego* were playing at the same time in Mexico City, showing that the latter movie had been made quickly. The former film led playwright Rodolfo Usigli to send her a poem of the same title, in which he identified Lolita with the flower. The last stanza read, "No more will I reconcile your beauty with my fortune/You are my adornment and my death/bougainvillea flower!"[37] Also, in January 1946, a major story in the *Christian Science Monitor* discussed a new program put together by Arthur M. Loew, president of MGM International Films Corporation, to bring excellent foreign films to U.S. viewing audiences with the spoken dialogue in English. One of the first of these was to be *María Candelaria*, now presented as *Portrait of Maria*. The technical issues were presented as tricky but well worth the effort, and the actors who provided the new voices were said to watch projection of their individual roles as many as forty times before beginning the dubbing process.[38] The new version began showing about six months later in Los Angeles, and critic Edwin Schallert praised it as being very unlike Hollywood productions: ". . . its simplicity is so strong, so noteworthy that it is uniquely admirable. Even such a technical handicap as dubbed dialogue cannot diminish its underlying intensity of emotion. It is a tonic of its kind."[39]

Dolores in the meantime moved on to a project with director Roberto Gavaldón. He also had Hollywood experience, working as an actor starting in 1933 and serving as an assistant to a number of U.S. directors. He had directed only one film before he worked with Dolores on *La otra* (*The Other One*). The story had originally been developed by Warner's as a vehicle for Joan Crawford, but the Mexicans bought it away. Gavaldón himself and José Revueltas wrote the screenplay. Again Dolores was surrounded by intellectuals and artists; the set design was by artist Gunther Gerszo, and the script was written by the already well-known writer José Revueltas, with the director's collaboration. This film was also successful, and again Dolores did very well, playing the roles of a wealthy widow and her plainer, poorer sister. As usual, the film ended unhappily for her characters, with one sister dead and the other serving a prison sentence for a murder that the deceased sister had committed. Her shifts back and forth between the two characters were beautifully done and showed the range of her acting skill far better than the unrealistic *Selva*. Gavaldón was success-ful in creating an eerie, Hitchcock-like atmosphere of danger and intrigue, something perhaps Welles had thought to achieve and failed at in the ill-begotten *Journey into Fear*. Gavaldón enjoyed working with Lolita, noting that she was "very disciplined, very professional . . ." and submitting easily to his direction.[40] Dolores was helping to create and sustain an industry that provided employment to people of talent and, sometimes, experience, and with whom she enjoyed working.

When the film played in Los Angeles the following year, once again at the California and Mason theaters but now also at the Roosevelt, G. K. was particularly admiring, recognizing that the "fine performance by Dolores Del Rio and superb directorial touches by Roberto Gavaldón" almost brought it to the "stature of a great picture." This praise was not without caveats, however: "If ever Miss Del Rio can forget about wrinkles, and will occasionally let the strain of emotional experiences . . . show in the lines of her face, she will prob-ably become one of the world's greatest film actresses. . . ."[41] In fact, however, Lolita had permitted herself to look quite plain as the less glamorous sister.

DOLORES DEL RIO

DOUBLE DESTINÉE

Réalisation de ROBERTO GAVALDON — Production MERCURIO

Dolores in trouble in *La otra*, entitled *Double Destinée* in this French publicity photo.
Bibliothèque du Film.

Throughout 1946, reports that Dolores would star in one or another project appeared constantly in the press, both in the United States and in Mexico. On September 26, 1946, Hedda Hopper—now Lolita's loyal fan—reported that "John Ford has got Dolores del Rio for 'The Power and the Glory' and hopes Pedro Armendariz will play opposite her."[42] These hopes were soon realized.

Ford had been a prominent director in Hollywood for many years and was best known for his very popular westerns starring actors such as John Wayne, who had not gone to war, and Henry Fonda, who had. His most recent project was *My Darling Clementine*, filmed in Monument Valley as many of his movies were, with Fonda as Wyatt Earp. Ford served in World War II as well, attached to the navy as chief of the Field Photographic Branch of the Office of Strategic Services, which later became the CIA. As he described the function of his office, "Our job was to photograph both for the records and for our intelligence assessment, the work of guerrillas, saboteurs, Resistance outfits," and the group had undertaken a monumental documentary project.[43]

In *The Fugitive*, he surrounded himself with ex-servicemen such as Fonda, who served in the Pacific. The director particularly liked working with Fonda, whose face was expressive even when his body was immobile so that he could leave the camera on him and let the audience react to him directly without further explanation. In this film, according to Ford biographer Ronald L. Davis, Fonda as Earp "rescued civilization from primitive forces through superior frontier skills, aided by Doc Holliday, a renegade from culture with a death wish."

It was almost inevitable that Ford would cast Fonda in the film he was putting together from *The Power and the Glory*, Graham Greene's novel about a priest caught in the turmoil and anticlericalism of postrevolutionary Mexico. Ford intended to shoot it sparely, with little dialogue, and Fonda had the face and body—and perhaps at the moment the psyche—to portray the man's suffering between his priestly duties and his longing to flee in the face of violence. Yet Fonda was initially skeptical about the role, suggesting another actor, only at length to agree to do it himself.[44]

Hoping for a really strong critical success, Ford decided to make the film in Mexico, reuniting Dolores with Fernández, Figueroa, and Armendáriz. That he would reassemble this particular team was a tribute to the success of their film *María Candelaria*, only recently honored at Cannes. His choice of the story of the persecuted priest reflected his religious concerns, shared by many Catholics in the United States, about what they saw as the persecution of the church by Mexican governments emerging out of the Revolution. The novel was quite obviously set in the Mexican state of Tabasco under radical Governor Tomás Garrido Canabal, who had undertaken a major anticlerical campaign in the 1920s. To avoid Mexican government censorship, the new setting was to be in some imaginary Latin American country.[45] No one, of course, was fooled; viewers in both countries realized that the tale of "an indifferent priest who lost his life, but found his soul through persecution in a country where anti-religious feeling was fostered by the Government" was set in postrevolutionary Mexico.[46] That the big four agreed to do it, given its antirevolutionary theme and the potentially bad reaction within Mexico itself, is, I think, a credit to Ford's own eminence and their desires to work with one of the most respected and successful U.S. directors. Hedda Hopper was now optimistic about Dolores's prospects; in a story about "has-beens," she noted in regard to del Río that "I have a hunch she's in for a great comeback."[47] For del Río, it was a new approach to a film of the Revolution, focused on the losses, not the gains.

Ford's own relationship with the big Hollywood studios was changing at precisely the same time. At the close of World War II, the U.S. movie business was becoming more commercial, more dominated by studios with corporate mentalities focused on profits. Ford, along with other directors of talent, was eager to establish a structure in which he could work more autonomously. Shortly before the War began, he discussed just such a possibility with Merian C. Cooper of RKO, who had produced *Flying Down to Rio* in the 1930s with Dolores and tried to find more good properties for her.[48] In April 1946, Ford created Argosy Pictures to provide himself with more independence. Cooper became his partner, taking over as president with Ford as chairman of the board. Though there were occasional tensions between them, Ford admired Cooper, who was David O. Selznick's executive assistant at Paramount for a while and had a glamorous and adventurous background as a World War I pilot and explorer, as a writer, and even as a documentary filmmaker. One observer indicated, "I think Ford envied Coop his incredible military record . . . .Here was a man who had lived the John Wayne life, and here was a man who was directing the John Wayne life."[49] It is a little surprising, under the circumstances, that Ford would launch the company with a film so unlike most of those that had led to his

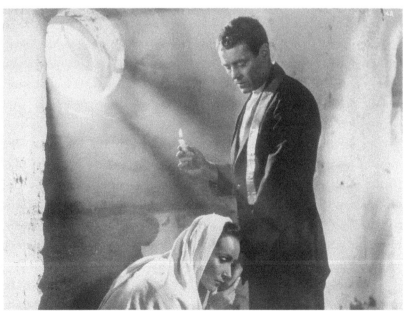

Resonant Catholic imagery in *The Fugitive*, featuring del Río and Fonda.
Bibliothèque du Film.

particular successes. Yet he seems to have been thinking of the project for a while, though unable to do anything of the sort because of the lack of studio support. Dudley Nichols, who wrote the script, related that he and Ford "had talked about this project for years, but no studio would back it."[50]

Ford was by no means the only U.S. Catholic who was concerned about the postrevolutionary regime in Mexico. Certainly Greene's powerful novel in the form of a movie would highlight and perhaps even protect the Catholic Church in Mexico, which was faced with an unfriendly national government. Strangely but deliberately, the film that Ford actually produced was very low on story and very high on cinematography; Figueroa's camera work again generated dazzling landscapes, along with equally dazzling close-ups of Dolores lasting so long that the film had the pace of a silent movie. Moreover, the use of light emphasized Catholic symbolism, particularly in Fonda's scenes, to such a degree that even the actor became a little uncomfortable. Fonda later said, "I didn't like *The Fugitive.*" The images, he said, were put in by Ford and took the film in the direction of an art movie, and the director was not interested in hearing any dissenting voices. Ford finally agreed to film one particular scene both his way and the way Fonda wanted it; naturally, they did it the way Ford wanted it first, and then the director just walked away without trying it the way his male lead had suggested. J. Carrol Naish, who played Fonda's nemesis, a strange and twisted indigenous figure who seemed to stand for the Devil, felt frustration because Ford refused to discuss his character's motivation. In my opinion, this hesitance was because the figure was not truly human and did not have intelligible human motivations—rather, he was the personification of evil.

Despite the discomfort of Ford's cast—at least the U.S. members—the director believed he was making "great progress" and the story was fine. He did admit, however, that filming had not been entirely easy, in what he described as "the wilds of Mexico"; rather, ". . . it has been very very difficult."[51] However, many of the cast and crew were accustomed to the conditions, and when they were in Mexico City Dolores was the perfect hostess, throwing the occasional magnificent party for them at La Escondida.[52]

The Mexicans seem to have been less discomfited by the style of the movie and by the difficulties of the shoot than the Americans. Certainly, Figueroa had done a great deal of filming in which the cinematography was as important as the story. Dolores was used to being shot with the camera lingering on her lovingly, which was the case here, and she apparently enjoyed working with Ford—despite his reputation for being hard on his actresses. Although she ran across rocky ground barefoot, she did not have to trudge through the mud. Ford was delighted with her professionalism, crediting her as the "spark plug for Mexican pictures," as he told Hedda Hopper, and said that the whole crew "adored" her.[53] Yet there was a struggle between the photography and the story, a story that particularly pleased Ford as it turned into, according to Nichols, "an allegory of the Passion Play in modern terms." It seems reasonable to suppose that Ford got the photography he wanted. It was less pleasing to others, particularly Fonda, who wound up as a not-very-well-disguised "Christ figure, with Ford concentrating on the mystical aspects of the story," as Davis has so accurately pointed out.[54] As the filming continued, Naish enjoyed working with Lolita so much that he contemplated directing a film, *The Green Dove*, at the new state of the art studio at Churubusco, with her as the star.[55] Another rumor had her in a stage play to be directed by Mel Ferrer; still another said that Pennant Films had engaged her for *West Winds*, with George Raft as a potential male lead.[56] She did not, however, return to U.S. films for some time.

Although El Indio appeared as co-director with Ford on the credits, it is hard to know just what part he played in the filming. Certainly, the result was more like his own *María Candelaria* than like Ford's westerns. It was languorous, lingering on landscape, permitting Figueroa much cinematographic scope. The Mexicans found Fonda, who had just come back from the war, "taciturn and irritable."[57] However, these qualities were not out of place in this particular film and enhanced the tortured quality of his struggle not only for deliverance from his persecutors but also to follow his conscience in spite of the dangers involved. Nichols, who authored the script, reported that when Fonda returned from Mexico he was "unhappy and perplexed. He said he didn't know what had happened to Ford down there." However, in this case, the script was not driving Ford *or* the picture. As Nichols remarked, "To me, he [Ford] seemed to throw away the script."[58]

In a sense, Ford had done just that, and he was not unhappy with the results. Fonda himself, despite his misgivings, gave a brilliant performance. It seems to have been Ford rather than Fernández who determined the pace of the film and the sparse dialogue. In fact, Ford admitted early on that he was looking back at the "silents" in *The Fugitive*, "making a picture which . . . has less dialogue than any movie made since sound became a part of films."[59] For the observer watching *The Fugitive* today, this intention seems to have been completely realized. He understood from the beginning that the film was probably not going to be a major commercial success, but as he admitted to one former collaborator, "my heart and my faith compel me to do it." Significantly, he was doing it his way.[60]

Whatever nervousness Ford may have felt about filming in Mexico, ultimately he was delighted with the equipment at Churubusco Studios, much of which was quite new and very up to date. The studio itself was almost brand new as well, Rockefeller having helped in its development. Ford was also pleased, once the picture was in the editing process, to acknowledge the efficiency of his Mexican crew, who, despite the fact that the Mexican film industry was heavily unionized, pitched in where needed rather than insisting on dividing tasks along craft lines as they did in Hollywood. The location shooting, which he had suggested earlier was so arduous, actually finished in eleven days instead of the planned twenty-five, and the film wrapped early and under budget.[61]

Yet there were tensions among the Mexicans themselves. El Indio stayed out of trouble during the filming, but Armendáriz, who always carried a gun, was involved in a very unpleasant incident at the closing party on February 4, 1947. Fonda, del Río, and Ford had already left the party, but the drinking continued. The story that appeared in the U.S. press almost two months later was that the girlfriend of one of the secondary actors had been giving Armendáriz the eye, when her man objected and slugged him. Pedro retaliated, knocking him down, and the shooting began. When it was over, two men—not including either of the principals—were in the hospital, and another was released for a minor gunshot wound. No charges were filed and no arrests made.[62] Ford made no further films in Mexico to my knowledge; perhaps the gunplay made things just a little too real.

Certainly, *The Fugitive* did not make the money that might have been hoped for as the first production from Argosy Pictures, but critical reception was strong when it finally opened at the end of 1947. Symbolically, it was first shown on Christmas day. The film critic of the *New York Times*, Bosley Crowther, was fascinated with it, calling it "strange and haunting," focused on "a terrifying struggle between strength and weakness in a man's soul, a thundering modern parable on the indestructibility of faith, a tense and significant conflict between freedom and brute authority." He indicated that it was "a true companion piece to 'The Informer,'" a film that Ford made to considerable acclaim in 1935, which earned him both an Academy Award and a New York Film Critics Award. For this earlier film as well, he worked for several years to interest a studio and get backing; Merian Cooper, then at RKO, was the one who let it go forward. Therefore, this new critical triumph resonated with excellent previous work by the director. That earlier film was also full of symbols and images—in this case Irish—rather than dialogue. Clearly, what this critic saw as the strengths of *The Fugitive* had little to do with the original story, or even the script by Nichols, which the review called "a workmanlike blueprint for action."[63]

As for the Catholic response, even before the film opened in New York City *The Sign*, the national Catholic monthly, presented Ford with an award for production and direction of the movie as "the outstanding motion picture of the year."[64] Crowther acknowledged that all of the performances were extremely good, including that of Dolores, described as providing "a warm glow of devotion as an Indian Magdalene," and Armendáriz, who "burns with a scorching passion as a chief of military police."[65] Two days later, Crowther selected *The Fugitive* as one of the ten best films of the year, along with several classics that have survived well into the twenty-first century: *The Yearling, Great Expectations, Miracle on 34th Street, Life with Father*, and *Gentleman's Agreement*. Crowther this time called it "a cinema of lasting distinction, a symphonic directorial job," and said that "Henry Fonda gives an agonized performance as a desperately bewildered priest."[66]

The *Los Angeles Times* reviewer, Philip K. Scheuer, however, was not quite so ecstatic: ". . . as drama I found this one intermittently faltering and diffuse." He described Fonda's performance as "like a man who walks in a dream," and he found the dialogue "inadequate." In short, it was a "Passion Play without passion."[67] The European reception was more like New York. The French critic Louis Chavet acknowledged in his *Le Figaro* review of *Dieu est mort* (*God Is Dead*), the French title, that the languor of the film, which he called "an often perilous slowness," made it possible for the film to "equal those works that ensnare certain exceptional qualities into memory."[68]

As for Dolores, her assessment was clear. When asked, fourteen years later, who was the best director with whom she had worked, her reply was direct and simple, "John Ford. He's marvelous."[69] As for Ford, his sentiments were equally positive. In a letter from him to Dolores that was apparently written close in time to the filming, although it is not dated, he said "I ran 'the Fugitive' last night and darling!—you are wonderful! It is still my favorite picture. *You* were divine!" He closed by sending his "respects to Madame su Mamacita + of course Sopey Figueroa—my bridge partner," and added a postscript, "When are we doing 'Carlotta?'"[70] Apparently he and del Río had discussed the possibility of filming the tragic story of the nineteenth-century French intervention in Mexico that imposed European monarchs Maximilian of Austria and his wife Charlotte (Carlotta) as emperor and empress. Del Río's role would be Charlotte, who lost her reason after her husband was executed by Mexican Republican forces. His letter also suggests the ubiquitous presence of Dolores's mother at her side, along with her secretary (Figueroa), and many nights of socializing during the filming.

Only three months after the initial unfavorable review in the *Los Angeles Times* by Scheuer, Edwin Schallert wrote in the same newspaper that the film had won eleven U.S. awards and been voted the best film of the decade in Belgium. As *The Fugitive* continued to rack up awards, Cooper and Ford thought about doing something similar starring del Río and Armendáriz. The idea was to get Graham Greene, who had written the novel on which *The Fugitive* was based, to do the new script.[71]

Unfortunately, the project never came to fruition, and Dolores did not work with Ford again for almost twenty years, though they remained friends and corresponded from time to time. To give Ford credit, he did not lose his commercial sense. Much as he had enjoyed making *The Fugitive*, his next Argosy feature was *Fort Apache*, a rock 'em, sock 'em Western in which Armendáriz worked with him once more.[72]

There were criticisms within Mexico about the vision of the anticlerical campaign critiqued in the film, which led to a polemic between Santiago Reachi, producer of the popular Cantinflas comedies, and Fernández himself. Reachi had made fun of El Indio's filmmaking, which he acknowledged as "luminous" but so noncommercial that he left "many producers broke." Fernández responded with an interview in which he strongly declared, "It is always important to keep in mind that the film industry is the only one that gives the people of the country and outside it a permanent and significant vision of what Mexico is." He went on to discuss the importance of his art in social and educational terms: "My films are result of patriotism and ambition, because I come from below. I was a little boy when I entered the Revolution. In my family, my father was the only one who went on to a better life and a natural death. And this, despite carrying around in his body thirty or more pieces of lead [bullets]. You have to understand why I can't make films that are sterile or effeminate. I don't feel them! I don't feel them!" He went on, "Mexico is a child that has to be taught, using films, what its errors are, and underlining its virtues."[73] Ford's respect for his co-director and his cinematographer led him to think about future projects in which the three could work together; unfortunately, though he tried to put together a project called *The Family*, it was never made. However, in *The Searchers* (1956), arguably Ford's finest Western, he included a gentlemanly Mexican—played by Antonio Moreno—whom he called Emilio Gabriel Figueroa y Fernández.[74]

At the same time, more acknowledgments that Dolores's career had taken off once again began to appear in the U.S. press. In March 1947, Edwin Schallert interviewed her by telephone for a piece that appeared in the *Los Angeles Times*. It was headlined "Dolores del Rio Achieves 'Miracle' in New Career." Pointing out that she had made five films in Spanish in the past four years and one film in English (*The Fugitive*, of course), Schallert acknowledged that she had become very active in her own career, founding her own organization with one of Mexico's "most prominent producers," Mauricio de la Serna. According to Schallert, this new company, named Mercurio, produced her very successful, and perhaps best, film, *La otra*. When Schallert pointed out to her that the name "Mercurio" was very similar to that of Orson Welles's production company—the Mercury—Dolores claimed that de la Serna had named it, perhaps with "a touch of ironic humor." Schallert went on to explain the joke: that Welles, before marrying Hayworth, had been "very devoted" to del Río. She denied to her interviewer that she was currently in love, insisting (inaccurately as it turned out) that "I am through with love after my last experience," apparently talking about Welles rather than Fernández. She indicated that she was enjoying the more languid pace of her life in Mexico: "You know, things move more slowly; we can really enjoy ourselves." But as Schallert noted, " . . . in the case of Dolores del Rio it is a busy enjoying indeed."[75]

A few weeks later, the *New York Times* reported that del Río was in the Big Apple for her "first vacation in years." The article noted her constant appearances in Mexican films and her recent work with Ford in *The Fugitive*, and mentioned that she was looking at possibilities for pictures in Argentina, France, and possibly Spain. She talked about the production company she had founded with de la Serna and shared that they were planning an adaptation of Marcel Pagnol's French film *Fanny*, though in fact this film was never made. She insisted that it was easily possible to make a profit in

Mexican films; each cost about 250,000 pesos and the return was two to three times that. The problem, she said, was story material, which was not abundant in Mexico given the lack of theater or much in the way of novels that could be adapted. Because U.S. stories were so expensive, they were out of the question. She also noted that as a Mexican it was a "great satisfaction" to appear in a film like *Maria Candelaria*, which had won awards and presented "the best face of my country to the rest of the world."[76]

What she did not say was that she had any interest in returning to Hollywood. She made a number of films over more than a decade and a half in the United States, and only the first few had much artistic merit. Now that she had been back in Mexico for five years, she participated in one film that won an international award and others in which she had far more scope to display her acting skills than in the United States. In Mexico, she had control over what she would do, and she could focus on and even develop vehicles for her own performances. In the United States, she was almost entirely dependent on powerful men who succumbed to her charms but cast her, often, in their own fantasies (heavily edited, of course). In terms of quality, *The Fugitive* was an exception; but, made in her own country with her own team, Ford had helped bring their talents to a peak, imposing more of his own ideas on the American actors while cooperating, apparently, more completely with the Mexicans.

In the event, her next film was made in Argentina, *Historia de una mala mujer* (*Story of a Bad Woman*), an adaptation of Oscar Wilde's play *Lady Windermere's Fan*, a role she would later rework as a theater piece and perform extensively on the stage. She was delighted with the opportunity to work in the southernmost Latin American country at a time of considerable political innovation. President Juan Perón's wife Evita was a former actress, engaged in political and social work with the poor of her country, already gaining a status of sanctity among the working classes if not much recognition for her previous acting career. One day, after having been invited to tea with Argentina's first lady, Dolores was invited to accompany her to speak to a group of women from one of the labor unions with which Evita was working. According to Ramón, on this day Evita would take Dolores "like a trophy" to show the women that she, herself the daughter of a poor family, was a great friend of this "fabulous and mythical" woman. Evita spoke first, and afterward Dolores gave a short speech, both to tremendous ovations from the women workers.[77]

Del Río was fascinated with Argentina and loved working with the Argentine director Luís Saslavsky and the excellent cast. She appreciated the adulation she got from the film community, including actor Fernando Lamas, and from the public in that country, which was very familiar with her earlier movies. She stayed over for some time, which caused her to miss the opening of *The Fugitive*, but also missing some objections, though apparently not from Catholics, to the film. Both del Río and Armendáriz were attacked for having taken part in what was being called a "communist" project—a strange notion given its heavily pro-Catholic message. Again, however, the attacks seemed to come almost exclusively from Mexican critics, rather than from the public.[78] As for Argentina, Hedda Hopper reported from Hollywood that Dolores found it "beautiful, progressive, civilized, and rich," and that "President and Madame Perón gave a dinner for her at the White House," though she meant the Casa Rosada, Argentina's presidential residence. In her conversation with Hopper, Lolita claimed to be unconcerned about the controversy surrounding *The Fugitive*. Hopper claimed that "left-wingers got the film officially banned" in Mexico, but that President Miguel Alemán permitted it to open nevertheless. According to Hopper, "Dolores said the controversy added millions of pesos to the profit of the picture."[79] Lolita's friend Salvador Novo had a somewhat different take. He found nothing in it that was "demeaning" to Mexico but rather saw it as a biblical allegory of the "persecution of the just and the abuse of force." He went on to say that films were "the most typical medium and the least suitable for either learning history or documenting facts."[80]

In stark contrast to Ford's film, *Story of a Bad Woman* opened in Argentina to enormous acclaim and huge box office receipts. Having forgone a salary and taken instead a percentage, Dolores was pleased to see that her earnings on the film were substantial, larger even than the good salary she got from Ford. According to a letter that del Río sent to Atilio Mentasti of Sono Film, the producer, the film played to full houses in Buenos Aires at least through the fifth week. She was pleased to have arranged for it to be distributed in Mexico by David O. Selznick and asked Mentasti to send along a print of the movie immediately since they were pushing her hard to get it to them. She was particularly glad that the Selznick organization agreed to handle it; she felt such an arrangement "guarantees me wonderful promotion and distribution for the film," indicating her personal interest in doing these tasks as well and as quickly as possible. She further asked him for the rights not only to New Zealand but also for the Philippines, enabling her to make a package deal with the same company for a little more money. Then she begged him to send her all the newspaper clippings and publicity and announcements that he could gather together since she was eager to see them.[81] When the Argentine film opened in Mexico on June 20, 1948, it was an immediate hit. Though the Mexican critics did not like the film much, certainly not as much as the Argentine ones, it was a box office success in Mexico, and only a few days after its Mexican premiere, in August 1948, Dolores was fêted when she received the Ariel, the Mexican Oscar, for *Las abandonadas*.[82]

Her next film, *Malquerida (The Unloved)* was again with the old gang: Fernández and Magdaleno, Figueroa, Armendáriz, and even Subervielle and Fontanals. But things were not the same. In his private life, Fernández had moved on to a younger actress, Columba Domínguez, who was also in the film, and his relationship with Dolores was tense. She did not like Columba much either—and really did not like playing her mother. At one point she had to slap her younger replacement, and in this case she did it so well that fortunately for Domínguez they were able to use the first take.[83]

After the film wrapped, she went almost immediately into another: *La casa chica (The Little House)*, the Spanish term for the house of a mistress. The director was, again, Roberto Gavaldón. She played a professional woman who becomes involved with a married man and is forced to live out a life in the shadows. It finished filming on August 21, 1949, with scenes in the Palace of Fine Arts where a Diego Rivera retrospective was showing; in this way, they were able to take advantage of his magnificent art in one of the scenes.[84] Lolita remained good friends with Rivera and a great admirer of his work; a note from him inviting her to an art opening the previous year had begged her to come in order to "bring us good luck—and give us all, especially myself, the pleasure of seeing you as beautifully lovely as always." He addressed it to his "respectfully adored friend."[85] The appearance of his paintings in her film would be yet another boost to his already substantial international reputation, and it is one more example of how her own art in the making of films intertwined with and enhanced that of other artists.

Dolores had returned to Mexico, appeared in Mexican and U.S. and Argentine films, worked with excellent directors, won awards both for herself and for her films, and generally added substantially to her reputation as an actress and to Mexico's reputation as a booming center for the arts. She had an affair with the first director she worked with in Mexico, but that ended badly, though the professional collaboration continued. All this notwithstanding, one of the world's most beautiful women, the object of fantasy for men all over the globe, was still alone.

11   Diva

[S]he is exceptional in every respect: she survived her epoch, her
contemporaries, the temptation to stop—just for one moment—
that work of art renovated daily: the face, figure and behaviour of
Dolores del Río.

> Carlos Monsiváis, "Dolores del Río"[1]

Growing up, I used to say that I descended from Moctezuma,
Hernando Cortes, Maria Felix, and Dolores del Rio. They were my
ancestors.

> Carlos Fuentes, Interview with Arthur Holmberg[2]

A U.S. OBSERVER IN 1956 commented that Dolores
del Río "is a woman who has bewitched time."[3] Yet
time and age made a difference, and in the 1950s she had to find a way
to continue her acting—so central to her existence and her happiness—
as available roles for women became less suitable. At the same time, the
Mexican film industry was beginning to suffer structural problems that
led to a move away from the beautiful films of Mexico's Golden Age. In
her personal life, the beginning of the decade brought enormous changes
that would give her a stability she had not previously known. Her transition to a different kind of life and career took some time, and the process
was not always smooth. With an occasional misstep, she nevertheless successfully negotiated the move from young, romantic roles to those more
suitable for her (always beautiful) maturity. Fame and recognition, despite
disappointments, in her career and reasonable contentment in her personal
life characterized the decade.

In 1947, she acquired a new escort, Alvaro Gálvez y Fuentes, a radio host known to his friends as "El Bachiller," "The Big Talker." He moved as easily in the world of art and culture as she did, but it was not yet love. Nevertheless, he became part of her entourage, which also included Adolfo "Fito" Best Maugard, who had years before introduced her to Edwin Carewe, Diego Rivera, and Salvador Novo. Often she went to the theater and other social and cultural events with two or more escorts.[4] She became a major player in the cultural scene in Mexico City, not only because of her own achievements and ability but also because she constantly attended openings of plays and art shows and other events, inspiring public interest. She also spent a great deal of time in Acapulco, attracted by her love of the ocean and the beauty of the developing region. After the searing disappointments of her relationship with Orson Welles and the violence—both public and private—of her affair with El Indio Fernández, she found safety in numbers, as well as distance and independence.

At some point, during the last months of 1949, she became reacquainted with the man who would finally become her great love: Lewis Riley.[5] Though it is not clear precisely when and where they began to see each other, the romance seems to have flowered toward the end of 1949, when, needing a period of recovery after a bout with appendicitis, she went to Acapulco. Nevertheless, it was several years before they began to be linked publicly.

Lew came from money, one of the two heirs of a well-to-do Pennsylvania businessman who had made his fortune with Union Carbide. Born in 1914, he was almost exactly ten years younger than Dolores herself. Before arriving south of the border he spent time in Santa Fe, New Mexico, where he moved with his father and brother after the death of his mother. When he was about eighteen, he went on to Mexico, spending time in both Mexico City and Acapulco, still a fairly sleepy fishing town in the 1930s. His brother Miles Beach Riley (always known as Beach) joined him there in 1934, after Lew founded the Club de Yates, the Yacht Club. The brothers continued to travel between the coast and the capital city, where they moved among the intellectual elite and the best society. Lew's romantic background was not promising; according to Ramón he married Peggy Rosenbaum, a woman who moved easily in these circles in Mexico, shortly after he first arrived. He then married a somewhat mysterious "aristocratic" woman named Yvonne, who left him for Malcolm Lowry, the author of *Under the Volcano*. Several years later, this particular ex-wife was mentioned in the *Los*

Angeles Times as marrying Sir Charles Mendl, an octogenarian reported to have been "extremely lonesome since the death" of his wife.

These may not have been Lew's only marriages. In April 1983, just after Dolores's death, art historian Rosamond Bernier claimed she had married him when she was nineteen and moved with him to Mexico. Bernier reported that connections through her father, who was the vice president of the Philadelphia Orchestra, gained them an introduction to Carlos Chávez, a major figure in the Mexican music world. Through Chávez, they met Mexican artists Orozco and Rivera, both good friends of del Río's. Lew seems to have been fascinated with Hollywood as well, and to have gone back and forth from Mexico to Los Angeles. There, in the early 1940s, he volunteered with the Hollywood Canteen, a service group that was working to connect the movie industry with the war effort. Rumor had it at the time that he carried on a passionate romance with Bette Davis; he was clearly not intimidated by famous and powerful women.[6]

In 1949, just before he and Dolores became frequent companions, Lew spent a great deal of time in Los Angeles and was becoming a bit of a society figure there. In March, Hedda Hopper reported dining with him at Romanoff's; in November, the *Los Angeles Times* mentioned his having placed highly in a number of yacht races.[7]

It seems likely that the soon-to-be couple were acquaintances before this time, since they had many friends in common in Mexico and California. Dolores, however, would almost certainly have been aware of his previous involvements, and given her recent bad luck with unfaithful and even abusive men, she may have been put off by his well-deserved reputation as a playboy. She was forty-five; he was thirty-five. Though age never seemed to matter to her, she did grow cautious about romantic involvements. Over Christmas of 1949–50 they began to see each other, but ten years would pass before they tied the knot. She had, after all, twice suffered the consequences of a precipitate marriage. Still, Dolores and Lew spent a great deal of time together—if not exclusively—and he supported her professionally and emotionally in a steady way that seemed free of the constant jealousies Jaime Martínez del Rio had suffered, the inconstancy she endured from Orson Welles, and the need to dominate her artistically and physically and even violently that El Indio displayed. Closer in temperament to Cedric Gibbons than the others, perhaps, he came to Dolores at a better time. The wounds of Jaime's death and Edwin Carewe's betrayals were far in the past. Though her health was still fragile, she was not desperately ill as during the first year of her marriage to Gibbons. With Lew, she shared many of the things she loved most: art, film, and theater, the sea, and especially Acapulco. Even so, she was wary.

When she returned to Mexico City in January 1950, Lew came with her, and from then on he often accompanied her on travels and even on the sets of her films in and out of Mexico City. Lolita's film career in Mexico was still in full bloom; in 1947, 1948, and 1949 she made four films, including John Ford's *The Fugitive*. Between 1950 and the end of 1953, she made four more and moved into television as well, first in the United States in 1951 in a live appearance of a short play, "Trio by Lamplight," by Paul Tripp, and then in Spanish in 1952 in a barnburner of a *novela* (soap opera), filmed at Emilio Azcárraga's XEW studios in Mexico City. This latter, "El derecho de nacer" ("The Right to Be Born"), had been produced a number of times in other Latin American countries; a real tear-jerker, it was based on a novel by Cuban writer Félix B. Caignet. Shooting on the latter lasted for two months, and she enjoyed working with Manolo Fábregas, a Spaniard active in Mexican films and theater productions since the 1930s.[8]

Lolita had no problems about appearing on the small screen, which at that time was considered by some Hollywood actors and actresses as a step down in status from movies. Further, her success on live television in the United States may have indicated to her that she was ready to go on to theater performances. While she was engaged in all this professional activity, she was still seeing Lew regularly, though she also went to plays and social events of various kinds with other men. A first discreet mention of the relationship in the U.S. papers came, predictably, in Hedda Hopper's column. On December 6, 1952, she mentioned in a piece about her trip to Mexico City that she had had dinner with Dolores; Gary Cooper; a woman who seems to have been his flame at the time, Loraine Chanel; and others including, finally, Lew Riley. The couple's names were placed discreetly at the beginning and end of the list of guests. Hopper noted that Lew had been a production assistant on a film called *The Young Lovers*, before moving on to producing television shows in Mexico.[9] Not until 1954 were Lew and Lolita linked publicly by Salvador Novo, the chronicler of Mexico City social and cultural life in his regular column in the publication *Hoy*. By then the couple were living together at La Escondida. Only in 1955 did the U.S. press pick up on what Walter Winchell called her "long-time secret."[10]

Not only was Lolita busy professionally and personally, she was garnering awards for her acting in film. *Doña Perfecta* brought her a second Ariel in the 1951 awards, and two of her collaborators on the film, actor Carlos Navarro and screenwriter Alejandro Galindo, were also honored. Carlos Jiménez Mabarak was recognized at the same time for his score on her film *Deseada*, yet another collaboration with director Roberto Gavaldón.[11] Lolita continued to attract attention to her collaborators and to herself. Yet despite her shared fame along with María Félix as the two first ladies of Mexican film, her bid for office in the screen actors union, the Asociación Nacional de Actores (ANDA), failed in 1953, as she lost to male matinee idol Jorge Negrete. No sore loser, she took part in the film *Reportaje* shortly thereafter, made under union auspices for the benefit of workers in the film industry and journalists covering it. Emilio Fernández was once again the director, and he and Mauricio Magdaleno produced the script. The plot featured the offer of a 10,000 peso award by a press mogul to the journalist who could find the best news for the New Year. Interestingly, it was produced by Miguel Alemán Velasco, the son of Miguel Alemán Valdés, who had left office as Mexican president in 1952. Alemán Velasco was becoming a media mogul himself, involved in Rómulo O'Farril's *Novedades* press empire and, in 1955, partnering with O'Farril and Emilio Azcárraga Vidaurreta of radio XEW and XEWTV in founding Mexico's major television network, Televisa.[12]

Del Río soon received a third Ariel for her 1953 film *El niño y la niebla* (*The Child and the Fog*); her life was good in all its aspects, and Lew Riley continued to be her constant companion.[13] Her continuing success as an actress was not unnoticed in Hollywood. Suddenly, in late 1953 or early 1954, Twentieth Century Fox, the studio that had been most supportive of her over time and was the scene of her first film triumph, *What Price Glory?*, offered her an opportunity to return to the United States for *Broken Lance*. Her co-star was set to be Spencer Tracy, her role that of the indigenous wife of a "domineering white father," i.e., Tracy, in a film about racial prejudice.[14] The start date was initially projected for mid-February, though it was later pushed back a couple of weeks. Lolita must have been enormously pleased; it was thirteen years since she had made a Hollywood movie, with the exception of *The Fugitive*, which was as much a Mexican as a U.S. project. Her last, *Journey into Fear*, was the ill-fated project Orson Welles began for her and then abandoned for his wild months in Brazil. Yet she was not forgotten in the United States, by any means, as her Spanish-language movies continued to be shown north of the border both with and without English subtitles or dubbing.[15]

She was so secure about the contract that she could negotiate over billing. Though she was willing to relinquish her demands in this regard for U.S. distribution to the United States, she insisted that for Europe and Latin America she be granted fourth billing "above the title."[16] By January 28, she had a long, detailed letter that served for a contract and offered her an astonishing $40,000 for her acting services.[17] The *Los Angeles Times*, in its February 24 edition, announced she would be returning to Hollywood. On February 25, 1954, her old friend Hedda Hopper reported, falsely as it turned out, that "Dolores del Rio arrived here yesterday for her first picture in many years. . . ."[18]

Her expectations came crashing to a halt in mid-February when her U.S. visa application was denied. Nothing of the sort had ever happened to her before, and she had traveled regularly to the United States for many years with no problems. Her agent, Jack Gordean, alerted her to the difficulty; although Twentieth Century-Fox had requested the visa itself, the "Washington State Department [was] holding [it] up for reasons unknown." He urged her to communicate with his agency's attorney, Harry Sokolov, who was at that moment in Mexico City, and to give him any information possible so that he could help straighten things out.[19] Three draft letters to the U.S. Embassy in her archive, annotated in her own hand, reflect her shocked surprise. In her own words, which appear in all three drafts, "I have to confess that this determination has stunned me." We do not know if any of the drafts were actually sent, but all three expressed her affection for and gratitude to the people of the United States, to whom, she said, "I owe, in large part, the development that I have achieved in the cinematographic art." She went on to declare in the two earliest drafts that she had just been granted a special ceremony in her honor at the U.S. Embassy in Mexico City itself, although this circumstance was omitted in the last version. But she did declare strongly in all three drafts that she had "nothing to reproach myself for. I am a Christian woman [corrected in her hand to "Catholic" in drafts two and three] who has only aspired to live in peace with God and man." In the final draft, this statement was moved from the middle of the document to provide a dramatic ending to her protest.[20]

A clue to the problem can be found toward the end of her first draft in a sentence that she changed later. It read, "On some occasions, at the request of my fellow Mexicans, I have offered my solidarity with humanitarian and patriotic acts of aid to the weak and the persecuted, with exclusively humanitarian intentions, as I have never engaged actively in politics."[21] The final version, instead, insisted that "I have never belonged to any political party, and when I have provided my modest collaboration to alleviate suffering in its multiple manifestations, I have done so always with neither sectarian nor political goals but rather with the intention of serving either my country or humanity."[22]

Del Río had run directly into Cold War McCarthyism, and she was accused of being at the least a communist sympathizer, if not actually a communist herself. Despite her previous acceptance and even honoring by the U.S. Embassy, the issue was so explosive that the ambassador refused to see her to resolve the matter. Dolores, as always the perfect lady, telegraphed him:

Am so sorry you have not had the time in the last three days to receive me stop if my visa is not granted in the immediate future 20th Century Fox will be obliged to contract other actress and this delay will cause me to lose my employment in this very important picture I respectfully request my visa be granted in time to avoid this loss to me or that I be given some explanation for being denied visa.[23]

Though no explanation seems to have been forthcoming at this time, the apparent cause of the visa denial was that she had earlier signed the Stockholm Peace Appeal, a statement issued in March 1950 from a meeting of the Permanent Committee of the Partisans of Peace, an organization whose membership included a large number of European communists. It asked for "the unconditional prohibition of atomic weapons" and "strict international control" of such weapons and warned that the first government to use them would be branded as a "war criminal." It urged "all people of good-will" to sign the document. The problem, of course, was that the Peace Partisans, even though not completely controlled by the Soviet Union, nevertheless, according to some U.S. observers, were serving Joseph Stalin's purposes by targeting the United States as a perpetrator of crimes against humanity. It tapped into European terrors of a war that might bring use of nuclear weapons to their own continent with the same kind of ghastly destruction they had caused in Japan. Many noncommunists did sign the declaration. Estimates claimed that fourteen million signatures were gathered in France, and nearly seventeen million in Italy.[24] The moral appeal of such a condemnation of atomic weapons was widespread, of course, and important well beyond the reach of the Soviet Union. The International Committee of the Red Cross, less than two months after the Stockholm Appeal was formulated, issued a similar declaration and called for all governments that had signed the Geneva Conventions to move forward on "an agreement on the prohibition of atomic weapons."[25]

At this time, Senator Joseph McCarthy was at the height of his power. He had been holding hearings to root out U.S. communists or Soviet sympathizers in many areas of American life through his chairmanship of the Senate Committee on Government Operations, at the same time as the investigations in the House Un-American Activities Committee (HUAC). He had a 50 percent approval rating among the American public, and was given a seat on the Senate Rules Committee. Attacks on the entertainment industry had been going on for some time and were highly publicized: two years earlier, Lolita's dear friend and sometime colleague Charlie Chaplin, who was born in London, was not permitted to return to the United States after he and his family went to England to promote his film *Limelight*. His response was to settle permanently in Switzerland. The State Department's visa issuing authority was being used in the anti-Communist crusade, preventing Americans such as playwright Arthur Miller (temporarily) from traveling abroad and suspect foreigners from coming into the country.[26] Newsman Edward R. Murrow's *See It Now* programs attacking McCarthy did not begin until March 1954, and the Army hearings that would ultimately bring McCarthy down and lead to his condemnation in December of that year were also still in the future.

Ramón claims that in March 1950 Dolores's cousin, María Asúnsolo, brought her a document supporting a "peace conference," and this signature was the source of her problems, but he seems to have confused it with the Stockholm Appeal.[27] It may be that María was influential in her cousin's decision to sign this particular text, but it is also likely that Lolita herself was horrified by the destruction of World War II. The widespread signing of the Stockholm Appeal in Europe, and especially in France, the country she loved so well, may have been factors in her decision to add her name to the document. Quite possibly, the devastation of her own country that she experienced as a child during the Mexican Revolution and later on her husband's holdings in northern Mexico during the continuing violence of the 1920s, led her to abhor war. Further, a Red Cross document, which was very similar, may have misled her as to the more pro-Soviet uses to which the Stockholm Appeal was being put.

Whatever the circumstances of her signing, her efforts to gain help from her friends on her visa problems were unavailing. By March 1, she wrote to her friend and sometime assistant Veada Cleaveland in Los Angeles that she would be unable to do the picture. Still, efforts on her behalf were continuing through the Mexican official establishment and the National Association of Actors (Asociación Nacional de Actores). The latter protested on that same day to the Mexican Secretariat of Foreign Relations that there were "absurd rumors" of the American Embassy refusing her visa on "absurd extra-official pretexts that cannot be accepted by our association nor by our compatriot Dolores del Río who is dedicated only and exclusively to artistic labors." The following sentences noted that Mexico had always been open to North American cinema and theater, and they further contained an implied threat at retaliation by closing the country to those productions.[28]

It was already too late for her to arrive in time for *Broken Lance*, as Dolores herself acknowledged. Devastated, she withdrew to Cuernavaca, where she remained incommunicado for a few days. In the United States, the *New York Times* on March 2 reported that the news had "aroused indignation among Mexican movie people and hence [talk] of reprisals." Meanwhile, her spokesperson, Francisco Cabrera, directly confronted the issue of her potentially anti-American or communist political alliances: "This is absolutely not true. Dolores comes from a very good family. Her mother is very rich and spends half the day in church. Neither Dolores nor anyone in the family has anything to do with communists."[29] This statement, of course, was not strictly true, given del Río's close involvement with the artistic, intellectual, and film community of Mexico, a number of whom—such as Kahlo, Rivera, and Figueroa—belonged or had previously belonged to the Communist Party. Those associations were not important to Fox, but the filming schedule was. The final word came on March 4, with a letter canceling the agreement because of her "failure" to make herself available on that day.[30] But she still had her fans in the United States; on March 7, 1954, Drew Pearson's radio broadcast noted that she, one of the "great idols of the Mexican public,"

has had her passport visa held up by the State Department on the grounds that she once signed a peace petition—which later turned out to have been circulated by communists. This is not going to help our relations with Mexico—already

badly sagging. Delores [sic] Del Rio happens to be one of the most popular figures in Mexico and the Mexican people know that Lucille Ball of "I Love Lucy"
was not only a registered communist, but a member of the executive committee
of the Communist Party in California. Yet she's still on television; while Delores
Del Rio who merely signed a peace petition was stopped from leaving Mexico for
Hollywood just as she was to begin a new picture.[31]

On March 9, 1954, the same lawyer from Gordean's office to whom she
had appealed in Mexico City, Harry Sokolov, confirmed that the Fox deal
was off. Her U.S. lawyer, Arnold Weissberger, wrote her on March 11 that
the problem was she had signed "the Stockholm peace petition," and that
French star Maurice Chevalier's entrance into the United States had been
prevented on the same grounds. As he noted, before ending with his love, "It
is just too absurd, but it is very much America's loss."[32] Among the letters of
regret that she received from the United States was a gracious one from the
man who would have been her co-star, Spencer Tracy, reading as follows,
"Dear Miss Del Rio: May I express to you not only my sincere regret for
your personal feelings, but a deep sorrow because of my loss in not working with you to which I have so looked forward. My deepest good wishes."[33]

Her sometime friend Hedda Hopper, however, piled on with a reference
in her column to Dolores's problems, indicating that the answer might be
found in the book by FBI agent Guenter Reinhardt, *Crime Without Punishment*, in the chapter "The Little Comintern." Reinhardt had met del Río at
a U.S. embassy cocktail party, where her beauty and charm delighted him
despite "the fact that she was known to support various Communist-backed
Spanish refugee organizations" and was a "front-woman" for an organization that ran an orphanage for Spanish Civil War orphans, a number of
whom had been accepted into Mexico. Still, the worst that Reinhardt said
of her was that she was "an altogether attractive dupe." It seems possible
that his accusations were based on her rejection of his romantic intentions
toward her, which he readily admitted, or perhaps reflected his pique at an
incident at the orphanage when a child asked Dolores if Reinhardt was "an
American fascist."[34]

Fellow Mexican actress Katy Jurado replaced her, a change not calculated to make Dolores feel any better. Hopper was again delighted to herald
this change, indicating that "Katy is quite a gal. She writes for magazines
and newspapers, and has a radio show in Mexico." Yet Hedda's scalpel was

still out, as she wrapped up, "For her articles, she uses an assumed name, and always writes glowingly about—Katy Jurado."[35]

Yet del Río's work and name were still before the international public. Only two weeks after the announcement about her replacement in *Broken Lance*, Dolores's film *The Child and the Fog* was showing at the Cannes Film Festival.[36] Her supposed communist connections did not discourage Colgate-Palmolive of Mexico from renewing her contract to endorse Colgate soap for the next two years.[37]

The visa situation was still not resolved in June 1954, when she received word from a friend in the Mexican diplomatic service that, after constant inquiries, he had ascertained that the Stockholm Appeal was indeed the issue. What she needed to do, he advised, was to present evidence to the Visa Department in the U.S. Embassy in Mexico that she had not taken part in communist activities during the last five years.[38] Apparently she did so, as eventually the problem was resolved.

Her difficulties in finding suitable movie work even in Mexico continued. The problem had little to do with Dolores. The period of the early 1940s through 1952 is generally acknowledged as Mexico's Golden Age of Film, an artistic fluorescence aided by the general economic prosperity of the country during the administration of President Miguel Alemán Valdés (1946–1952), but there were significant structural problems within the industry. These would soon lead to increasing commercialization and fewer of the high-quality, beautifully photographed and unusually well-written films in which del Río had become accustomed to participating and that she herself had done so much to make possible.

Distribution within the country fell largely into the hands of William O. Jenkins, former U.S. vice-consul in Puebla, a controversial figure involved as the supposed victim in a political kidnapping in 1919 who had later made a somewhat shady living—and fortune—dealing in medicines and alcoholic beverages. Jenkins and his Mexican partner began with ownership of a group of theaters in Puebla. Jenkins consolidated his power there during the presidency of Manuel Avila Camacho (1940–1946), with the financial aid of the president's brother Maximino, who was the governor of the state. Jenkins and his consortium quickly took over theaters throughout the country, and despite the attempts of the next president, Alemán Valdés, to counter his influence and aid the Mexican movie industry, by the early 1950s Jenkins had locked up a major portion of the country's distribution system.

The scarcity of theaters led to *"enlatamiento"* (literally, "canning"), which meant withholding a new film until space could be found to show it, leading to delays for moviemakers in recouping their investments. Meanwhile, many films were being imported from the United States and a lesser number from other countries. These productions were also using up the available screens. The problem was particularly acute in 1954, during which only 22 Mexican films and 251 U.S. films were shown; the previous year, in marked contrast, 87 Mexican films and 226 U.S. films were exhibited. In the latter year, even the number of French (33) and Italian (28) films in Mexico's movie houses exceeded the number of Mexican offerings.[39] The number of Mexican films was back up to 85 in 1955, but these movies had more to do with formula than with art and were mostly silly comedies, weepy melodramas, U.S.-style westerns and more Mexican *comedias rancheras*, dance features, and hero-style adventures about cowboys (and even wrestlers) as the principal productions. None of these low-quality possibilities were likely to interest del Río; nor would she fit with the purposes of the producers of such fare.[40] And, of course, television was beginning to provide serious competition to movies.

Nevertheless, despite the problems of the Mexican industry and of her own visa difficulties, another project, this one in Europe, came along quickly. *Señora Ama* (roughly translated as "Boss Lady"), to be filmed in Spain with her cousin Julio Bracho directing, might have been an antidote to her distress over denial of her U.S. visa. The contract was a generous one, involving a co-production between Diana Films of Mexico and Union Films of Madrid. Her salary was 100,000 Mexican pesos, and she would receive 1,000 pesos a day for expenses while in Spain. Bracho himself would work on the screenplay with Enrique Llovet.[41]

However, the Mexico City papers reflected the unfortunate tenor of the times. They were filled with Cold War rhetoric (and U.S. sponsored disinformation) related to the military revolt that had just deposed the progressive and U.S. denominated "Communist" president of Guatemala, Jacobo Arbenz. *Excelsior* trumpeted that the world had been saved from the "red terror" in the country on Mexico's southern border, and it announced the discovery of (completely fictional) mass graves of anti-Communists.[42] As Guatemala's prisons were reported to be filled with the arrested and the embassies with refugees, the papers reported other ominous notes for the Mexican film industry that had direct implications for Dolores. A full-page discussion of the new television industry appeared during the same week, as did coverage of the shrinking U.S. market for Mexican movies because of competition from the new medium. According to the article, Mexican families owned more than 250,000 television sets in the Los Angeles area alone, cutting significantly into the market for Spanish-language films on the big screen.[43] Very shortly thereafter, Dolores suffered another, more personal, blow when her dear friend Frida Kahlo, long in terrible health, died in mid-July after attending a rally to protest the U.S. intervention in Arbenz's overthrow.[44]

Franco's Spain was not particularly welcoming, either, resulting in another disappointment for Lolita. The script was based on a story by the well-known Spanish author Jacinto Benavente, and the Spanish seemed to resent Mexican involvement in the filming.[45] The plot involved a complicated love triangle squared, in which Dolores's role was of a betrayed wife, with her husband falling in love with her younger sister, who then married the husband's brother.[46] Del Río was at this point fifty years old, and it showed. Her film rival was an evident thirty years younger, and unfortunately the actor playing Lolita's husband was obviously much younger than she as well. The directing was poor, with Bracho highlighting Dolores as John Ford and other directors had been doing for years, bringing her continually to the front of the scene. Even if featuring her in this way pleased the Mexicans, it interfered significantly with her depiction of the character and the flow of the film. It also irritated their Spanish collaborators. Bracho later noted the nasty atmosphere and resentment toward both Dolores and himself. The shooting was prolonged, perhaps by the hostility between the Mexicans and the Spanish, and the film fell into delays and financial difficulties.

Finally, the local producer ran out of money and the Mexican producer, Fernando de Fuentes, Jr., gave up. Bracho and del Río then gave up as well and left postproduction, including cutting and editing, to the Spanish crew. According to Bracho, he told Dolores that the wonderful Mexican hospitality that was supposed to come from their Spanish background actually must have come from indigenous Mexicans, since their Spanish collaborators did not even invite them to dinner. Bracho also felt the picture "had been torn apart in the cutting." Despite high hopes, the film that resulted was stagy and unconvincing and ran into difficulties in recuperating its cost.[47]

Thus 1954 was a discouraging year, despite receiving her third Ariel for *The Child and the Fog*, given the rejection of her U.S. visa early on and then with the bad results of the Spanish adventure to which she had so much looked forward. Dolores was not offered a suitable film for the following year, although her visa problems were corrected, finally, in the spring, leading a *Daily Variety* columnist to coo nastily, "Dolores Del Rio has a date in Washington in October to find out who tried to put the Commie-tint on her and kept her out of 20th's *Broken Lance*. Del Río received a visa to return to the United States three months ago." But revenge was not really del Río's style. She returned to the United States in August, where she celebrated her birthday with old friends, Mexican and American: Marion Davies (reconciled despite the flap more than a decade earlier surrounding the release of *Citizen Kane*), Carmen Figueroa, and Alfredo Vega.[48] If she were to continue to act, she would have to take on a more active role in developing her further acting opportunities. Unsurprisingly, she did.

The vehicle would be theater. What was a surprise was that she decided to try it first in the United States, not in Mexico. Perhaps she was unwilling to risk a failure in her own home territory, where, whether she worked or not, she had established a reputation for excellence in all her endeavors. In any case, in order to keep her career going, she was willing to appear before live audiences in a language that had given her so much agony thirty years earlier in Hollywood. Realizing she would need some help with a medium in which she had no experience whatsoever except for her long-ago magic show with Orson, she contracted Stella Adler in January 1956 to serve as her dramatic coach. Dolores was already thinking that the play *Anastasia* would be a good choice for her debut. It was the story of a woman chosen by a group of exiles to impersonate the daughter of Czar Nicholas of Russia, who along with his family had been executed by the Bolsheviks in 1918. While they are grooming her to claim his fortune, the exiles begin to wonder if in fact she *is* Anastasia, creating the play's tension. The ambiguousness of the lead character's identity makes the part very challenging, along with the fact that Anastasia ages in front of the audience's eyes from a teenager to an old woman.[49]

Adler was a renowned teacher and had worked with a series of outstanding actors, including Marlon Brando. She worked for years as a stage actress, though rarely on the screen, but by this time she was performing only rarely. A strong exponent of Method acting and a student of the works of Konstantin Stanislavsky, Adler was no understated instructor. Rather, her teaching was described as "passionate, scholarly and volatile, delivered with evangelical showmanship, wicked wit and pungent phrases." She was reported to keep "her students spellbound by raging, purring, cursing, cajoling and, from time to time, complementing." In particular, she did *not* subscribe to Stanislavsky's early notion that actors should bring their own experiences into their performances, an approach still promoted at that time by the renowned coaches Lee and Paula Strasberg, but she supported his later ideas "that the actor should create by imagination rather than by memory and that the key to success was 'truth, truth and the circumstances of the play.'" According to Adler, "The teacher has to inspire, to agitate. You cannot teach acting. You can only stimulate what's already there."[50]

Lolita was not intimidated. Adler worked with her for only two weeks at that time, but those two weeks led to a lifelong friendship and strong bonds of mutual caring and admiration. Arriving back in New York City, Adler wrote "Dear lovely Dolores, I miss you and I hope you miss me. I think you are beautiful and that is not too original a statement. I don't really know whether I miss looking at your face or I miss you. I am not going to talk about your character. I have a lovely scarf for you." (This from a no-nonsense woman who could tell other actresses, "You've got no talent! Nothing affects you!"[51] Obviously, she felt differently about Lolita, who soon went to New York to study with her further.)

Later, del Río continued preparing the role of Anastasia, with the Russian director Boris Taumarin and Lily Darvas, the Greek actress who would share the stage with her. In the summer of 1956, Dolores arranged through Producciones Visuales, the company she had formed with Lew, to open the play in summer stock at the Falmouth Playhouse in Massachusetts, and to continue with a tour of seven other theaters throughout New England.[52] Adler did not come cheap, developing friendship or no; the four weeks of coaching cost del Río almost $3,000, no small amount in 1956 and considerably more than Dolores herself would earn as salary from her tour. Although Dolores kept meticulous accounts in her own hand, it does not appear that from a financial point of view it was successful.[53]

However, as a move into a new medium and an extension of her performing career, the opposite was true. The benefits came to her as an artist. She loved the experience of being "face to face" with her audience. In an interview with a reporter in Matunuck, Rhode Island, one of the venues in which she performed, she explained that she fled Hollywood "in disgust over picture assignments that simply required her to wear pretty clothes," and that her acting in the theater was "a new part of my long, unending career." Her statement left out her disappointment with Orson Welles, but given the fluffiness of many of her later Hollywood roles it rings true. Her discussion of her theater appearances is also instructive. She had no intention of giving up acting as long as there was any way she could keep going, as her use of the term "unending career" makes clear. She also illuminated the current crisis in high-quality Mexican films, declaring "I think it is mostly a lack of distribution facilities." Finally, she emphasized the significance of performing on stage for her own acting: "I learned something every day. In rehearsals of course—but most of all when I go out there on stage before the public."[54]

Others acknowledged the quality of her performance by considering her for further theater productions. On August 18, 1956, the *New York Times* announced that the Theatre Guild was considering a production of George Bernard Shaw's *In Good King Charles's Golden Days*, with Dolores in the part of Catherine, the daughter of the King of Portugal. The report continued that Lawrence Langner, the co-administrator of the Guild, had seen her at the Westport Country Playhouse in *Anastasia* and "noted enthusiastically, 'She was sensational.'"[55] Unfortunately, the Theatre Guild project did not come to pass, but the discussion was indicative of her new credibility as a stage actress—and in English to boot. In 1958, she did a television program for the Guild, "The Public Prosecutor," with Walter Slezak.[56]

In fact, del Río continued to perform on the stage for many years, particularly in Mexico City and in Buenos Aires, in works by Dumas and Ibsen, among others. Her first production in Mexico City, in July 1958, was Oscar Wilde's *Lady Windermere's Fan*, which she had made as a film in Argentina several years earlier. She toured Mexico in the play, an enterprise that was both financially and critically successful, and she later took it to Buenos Aires. In her theater endeavors, her enormous fame in the United States and Mexico drew enthusiastic crowds with high expectations and a developed appreciation for her as an actress, a star, a personality, and a celebrity. Her great beauty, which never disappointed, and her empathy with the audience, along with her carefully coached and effective acting and stunning stage presence, led to a charismatic interaction that was memorable for all concerned.

The audience brought fantasy, images from the screen, an understanding of her worldwide fame and popularity, and, I think, particularly for

Mexicans, a sense that she had triumphed over audiences in the United States. These, coupled with her own comprehension of what the audience wanted and expected and her willingness to act to them directly and not just to the camera, led both to the success of these theater pieces and her own enormous satisfaction with the experience. She particularly seems to have enjoyed the shared enterprise with Lew, who was involved in production and direction, not just financing, on many of these projects. Her stage career lasted for fifteen years; she made one of her last appearances in Mexico City in 1970–71 in Alexandre Dumas's *The Lady of the Camellias,* the play that was the basis for the opera *La Traviata.*[57] She was directly instrumental in the choice and development of all of her theater roles, and it is obvious that she was setting high standards for herself.[58]

Though she was successful with *Anastasia,* her next stage production was still two years in the future. However, in December 1956, a very significant international offer came her way. At the suggestion of Robert Favre-Lebret, the organizer of the more and more prestigious Cannes Film Festival, she was invited to serve as its first female juror. The festival was less than five months away, scheduled for May 2–17, 1957. The French cultural attaché in Mexico, Jean Sirol, was enthusiastic about the prospect. In this capacity, she would be the first woman so honored in the ten years of the festival's existence, and he responded with excitement: "Your idea of inviting Dolores del Río to be a part of the jury at the next festival is excellent, and it fills me with joy. It involves not only a marvelous artist but also a very important and very sincere friend of our country." He went on to say that "I am convinced that she will accept."[59] He contacted her immediately, assuring her that the French members of the jury she would find at her side were a "group of individuals of great worth and of international reputation." He went on to emphasize that it would please him enormously if she would accept, not only because she was so well regarded in France but also because it would be such good public relations for Mexico.[60]

Almost a month later, she had not confirmed her willingness to serve, but Sirol wrote to Favre-Lebret that with all the publicity, it would now be difficult for her to refuse. Yet it was an interesting indication that in the mind of the attaché, it was particularly desirable for her to attend and would bring benefits for the festival as well as for her. This perception speaks to her enormous international prestige. In another communication to Favre-Lebret, he emphasized this point by attaching a report from the

Mexico City newspaper *Novedades* indicating in one-inch headlines that
"Dolores del Río has been designated a member of the jury of Cannes
Film Festival." It went on to say that she had just returned from New
York City, where she attended a memorial service for the Chilean poet-
ess and Nobel Prize winner Gabriela Mistral. She also went to an exhibit
of Salvador Dalí's work and saw a number of plays. The story included a
photograph of her with the artist, captioned "Dolores and Salvador are
great friends."[61] This schedule of intense cultural involvement with an
international intellectual and artistic elite was typical of her life at this
period of time, and Sirol's inclusion of the story was an interesting heads-
up to the Cannes organizers.

By February 4, she had apparently accepted, as Sirol happily announced
to journalist Moisés Vásquez that she was invited not only to indicate French
interest in the Mexican movie industry but particularly to honor Dolores herself, who, he averred, was well known in France for her wonderful
screen appearances.[62] By the end of March, Sirol was trying to work out
the details, as he wrote to Favre-Lebret that del Río would like to have a
secretary to work with her while she was at Cannes. The reply was brusque
and indicated that this request would be impossible to fulfill, since there
would be a secretary for the entire group. Quickly, however, he capitulated
and she had a secretary to accompany her.[63]

Positions as jurors were highly sought, as shown by a letter written to the
French ambassador to Spain from another of the organizers remarking that
Dolores would be the only representative of the Spanish-speaking cinema.
He further pointed out that unless the Spanish could come up with a name
of really brilliant stature, the fact that only four foreign jurors were allowed
would preclude anyone from their country.[64] No doubt, had she known of it,
del Río would have been gratified by this rebuff, after her poor treatment in
Spain during the filming of *Señora Ama*. The prestige involved in such an
invitation is underscored in another of Favre-Lebret's communications, in
which he mentioned that potential British jurors being considered were top
actors and directors Lawrence Olivier, Vivien Leigh, Alec Guinness, and
David Lean.[65] Ultimately, Michael Powell, the British director of notable
films such as *The Red Shoes*; George Stevens from the United States, who
would win the Oscar for best director for *Giant* at the Academy Awards in
March 1957; and Vladimir Voltchek, Czechoslovak screenwriter and director, were her fellow foreign jurors. The French members represented that

country's cultural and intellectual elite: writers and poets André Maurois, Jean Cocteau, Jules Romains, Maurice Genevoix, and Maurice Lehmann, along with filmmakers Marcel Pagnol and Maurice Lehmann, and finally Georges Huisman, the art historian who, as a member of the postwar French Cabinet a decade earlier, started the festival itself.[66] Del Río was doubly honored as the only woman and the only actor included, and then honored again when she was chosen as vice president of the jury.[67]

During her service at the festival, Dolores was working in the midst of the international artistic and cultural elite that surrounded and made up the film industry, a position of significance and power that she had long enjoyed in her home country. It seems clear, given her own careful notes about the movies she viewed, that she took her job very seriously. She took particular interest in films showing the horrors of violence and war. One that she particularly liked was *Kanal*, the Polish entry directed by Andrzej Wajda and described as "a symbolic depiction of hell on Earth, set in the last days of the Warsaw uprising in 1944." She opined that it was a "magnificent war film . . . It will be a finalist." Ultimately, it won a special jury prize. Her choice for best female actor was Giulietta Masina, for *Nights of*

Del Río and constant companion Lewis Riley, arriving at Cannes.
Bibliothèque du Film.

Cabiria, the Italian film from director Federico Fellini now recognized as a classic. Her comment on Masina's performance was that it was "one of the greatest interpretations that I have seen." For best male actor, she signaled as her choice John Kitzmiller, an African American who served in World War II and remained in Europe afterward. He had many roles in Italian cinema, working with Fellini and other directors. In this case, he was nominated for his work in a Yugoslav film called *Dolina miru* (*Peace Valley*). The story was dramatic; he played a pilot shot down behind German lines who encounters two children searching for the home of the boy's uncle in a valley that they believe is always peaceful. Kitzmiller and Masina were in due course winners. Del Río's highest praise was for William Wyler's *Friendly Persuasion* which was not the official U.S. entry; that was *Funny Face*, with Audrey Hepburn. Her comment on Wyler's film, which examined issues of Quaker resistance to Civil War violence, was that the direction was "*excelentísima*," that "One senses the master hand of an experienced director." In regard to leading man Gary Cooper, she noted that his acting was "*magnífica*" and full of "simple humanity." *Friendly Persuasion* was the eventual winner of the grand prize, the Palme d'Or, a great honor in the field of about fifty films.[68]

But it wasn't all work. She was wined and dined by Europe's royalty and its famous. She had invitations to lunch with the president of the festival; another lunch, this one in the countryside, given by the mayor of Cannes; a reception hosted by the vice minister of culture from the USSR; cocktails on one evening with the commanding officer and officers of the HMS *Bennington*, to meet the star and director of *Yangtse Incident*, and on another with L'Office Catholique International to be followed by mass (this latter indicated in tiny letters) for those who chose to participate. As she was once again in the good graces of U.S. authorities, Eric Johnston, the president of the Motion Picture Association of America, invited her to a reception for the American ambassador Amory M. Houghton.[69] Fellini was one of her conquests; he wrote "Let me say that you are wonderful and I feel for you a special sense of friendship and love . . . I leave with the memory of the light of your eyes and your smile. Thank you dear, thank you, all my kisses. Please write to me."[70] In a strange coincidence, her triumphant presence at the festival took place in the same month that Senator McCarthy died of cirrhosis of the liver.

A folder in her archive includes a card from "Commandant Paul-Louis Weiller, Commandant de la Légion de Honneur, Croix de Guerre, Medaille de la Résistance Francaise" who would later invite her to supper in Paris in honor of Sir Laurence and Lady Olivier (Vivien Leigh), both of whom were considered as jurors by the French but neither chosen, and another one from Lucien Gelly, the director of Cinematographie Française. A third was a hand-drawn remembrance of things past—a card with two beautiful slanted eyes, easily identifiable as Dolores's own—and a dove drawing along a banner inscribed with the word "always"—and signed Orson.[71] If, in fact, she saw him at this time, there is no reflection that I can find in the record.

The festival was a triumph for Dolores as a representative of Mexico and also for her personally. An appearance on U.S. television in the prestigious program *Schlitz Playhouse of Stars* quickly followed, a zany takeoff on the *Taming of the Shrew* with Dolores playing a prima donna actress named Dolores who became, in the course of thirty minutes, the handsome Cesar Romero's compliant wife.[72] Then she and Lew returned to Mexico City.

They took up residence at La Escondida but were soon shocked by the death of Diego Rivera, just three years after Frida. Del Río had returned from her travels with significant health problems of her own—both arthritis, which affected her ability to move and thus act, and bronchial difficulties, likewise problematic in that they affected her voice. She was cheered by a cover story for *Life En Español*, which announced at the side of her picture, "DOLORES DEL RIO a los 52 años" (Dolores del Río at 52). She looked as beautiful as ever, in a sexy black and white strapless dress and a demure pink gauze shawl.[73] By late July, she was back in Mexico City theaters, on the stage in *Lady Windermere's Fan*, and though it enjoyed a long run through the beginning of 1959 she was forced to take sick leave on at least one occasion. She made one more movie about the Mexican Revolution, *La Cucaracha*, with the old crowd of Armendáriz, Figueroa, and Fernández, and this time including her old rival María Félix, with whom she shared equal billing. Then she returned to the stage in Robert Sherwood's *Road to Rome*. Armendáriz was originally cast to play opposite her, which no doubt would have been a real thrill for theatergoers, seeing in person the romantic icons of the 1940s, but Armendáriz was unhappy with the director and left. Dolores, who was described "as happy as a child with new shoes" to work with Pedro again, must have been disappointed, the production was delayed, and costs mounted. His replacement, Wolf Rubinsky, lacked Armendáriz's chemistry, and the play closed immediately.[74] It was one of

Lolita and Lew, with longtime friends Gabriel Figueroa and his wife Antonieta.
CEHM CARSO.

her few utter failures. Yet Dolores was soon able to complete arrangements to go to Buenos Aires with *Lady Windermere.*

Meanwhile, she and Lew went to New York, where, after a decade of constant companionship, they were married on November 24, 1959.[75] The wedding did not attract much attention, probably because the principals wanted it that way. The ceremony itself actually took place in Newark in the law office of magistrate Harry Hazlewood, Jr., not in a public venue. It could not have been more discreet, suggesting that Dolores and her very Catholic family might have been concerned that her marriage to Cedric Gibbons (who had long since remarried) was still problematic in their minds. If so, Gibbons's death six months later removed even that potential impediment to the legitimacy of their union. Lew was described as a TV producer, and his home was given as New York. In the large picture of the two, Lew looked significantly older than Dolores. The article ran down her romantic past in detail, though not quite accurately: "The actress' [sic] first marriage, to Jaime Del Rio, ended in divorce in 1928. She married Cedric

Gibbons seven years later. They were divorced in 1942. She was engaged to Orson Welles, but they never married."[76] It was not a particularly cheerful litany, but this time, the third time, seemed to be the charm.

Yet even as she was moving into the last phase of her real-time life, del Río's celebrity was entering a new phase. Her 1940 Hollywood film, *The Man from Dakota*, was playing on television in New York City the very evening of her marriage. In late 1959 and early 1960, *Flying Down to Rio, Journey into Fear*, and *In Caliente* were all being shown on U.S. television, in cities across the country. Though she made only a few personal appearances on the American small screen, her younger image was being presented for a new audience as television, in its need for material, began to show many of her films.[77] A few months later, she appeared in an episode of *The Chevy Show* called "A Mexican Fiesta" with Gilbert Roland and Ricardo Montalbán— part of a series of television presentations advertised in a full-page ad taken out by NBC in the *Los Angeles Times* as being of "historic significance and cultural importance...."[78] Her fame and her face were beginning to recycle.

12   Icon

There are various ways to belong to a country.

Jaime Torres Bodet, *Estrella de día*[1]

[S]he is a figure composed of a presence and a set of discourses that symbolize an *iconic* identity.

Joanne Hershfield, *The Invention of Dolores del Río*[2]

DOLORES DEL RÍO died on April 11, 1983, a few days before Easter, in the home she shared with Lew Riley in Newport Beach, California. The cause was hepatitis, contracted years earlier, that had made a deadly turn into severe liver disease. She was seventy-eight, though the *New York Times* obituary fudged a bit and announced her age as seventy-seven.[3] The *Los Angeles Times* obituary reminded readers in its title that she was the "Exotic Queen of Films," reiterating the exoticism and association with royalty that had been an important part of her image since her arrival in Hollywood.[4] She had requested that her ashes be returned to her home country for interment with no fanfare, and her husband complied with her wishes, despite a great deal of ugly criticism from those who wanted an elaborate ceremonial remembrance. Rather furtively, he brought them back to Mexico, rushing through the airport in Mexico City to a waiting vehicle in order to avoid the public.[5]

During the months following her death, Lew discussed the possibility of leaving her home as a permanent memorial to Dolores, but after about a year of unsuccessful negotiations with the Regent of Mexico City he gave up. Consumed with grief, he had already moved into a hotel; now he asked Jaime Chávez to close up La Escondida and sell off her possessions. Among them were an inscribed silver dish from President Jimmy Carter to welcome her back to the United States to film *The Children of Sánchez* in 1978 and to honor her "lifelong achievement in the cause of Mexican-American cultural relations and friendship." There were also two medals that Orson Welles had won for elocution in high school.[6] We know how much the former meant to her, because she wrote to President Carter expressing her "gratitude for the honor you have bestowed upon me, and thus upon my country, with the citation and the beautiful words that accompany it. . . . I find it difficult to do justice to the feeling of admiration that I have for you and your great country, that not only honors its own artists but also those of other lands." We can also imagine that she believed it to be a vindication of her shunning by the State Department twenty-four years earlier. As for Orson's medals, we can only guess at their value to her.[7]

The more than two decades between her marriage and her last illness were filled with extensive honors, accelerating in the 1960s with, among others, the "Sarape" in 1965 from PECIME (the Association of Film Journalists of Mexico) for her international efforts on behalf of Mexican film; a special award from the Organization of American States in 1967 for her artistic achievements and her service to the cultural interactions of the American continent; the "Medalla de Oro" ("Gold Medal") from the Mexican association of press photographers for her "praiseworthy artistic work"; the presidency of the board of the international Cervantino Festival in Guanajuato from 1972 through 1976, a celebration of arts and music that she helped found and that continues until this day; and a flock of honors in 1975 celebrating her fifty years in film, followed in 1976 by a film festival in her honor at the Mexican Cineteca Nacional. She received recognition from other countries as well, notably Argentina and Venezuela.[8] She had also taken on as a special project the founding of day care centers throughout the country, open twenty-four hours a day for the convenience of working mothers and the safety of their children, a project she backed with her particular prestige.[9]

She suffered a profound loss in 1962 when her mother died, though she enjoyed continuing performances—fewer and fewer as the years wore on and her health became more problematic—and rewarding, devoted companionship. While she continued to have real-time, important experiences and interactions with the public, more and more she became iconic as her films, television performances, photographs, and various other images were reproduced and stories about her (accurate and not so accurate) spread worldwide.

Between the time of her marriage and her death, she made only eight more films: three in Mexico, two in the United States, one in Spain, one French-Italian film, and, fittingly, as her last film, *The Children of Sánchez*, a Mexican-U.S. co-production. The latter film was a great pleasure for her, as she finally got to work with that other great Mexican icon of U.S. film, Anthony Quinn. Interestingly, her two other U.S. films had to do with the insensitivities and injustices of the clash between the expanding U.S. presence in the American West and indigenous peoples. In *Flaming Star*, she was Elvis Presley's Indian mother, while he played a young man tragically torn by his loyalties to the two cultures of his parents. The reader will notice the similarity of plot to the film she was not permitted to make in 1954, *Broken Lance*.

The second, directed by John Ford, was *Cheyenne Autumn*; he wrote her, addressing her as "Mi Alma" ("My Soul" or "My Darling"), to tell her the role would be "extremely important." He signed it "Juanito," her pet name for him, indicating their continuing friendship. This time she played Sal Mineo's mother. The script was based loosely on the story of the tribe's attempt to flee the reservation where they had been placed, in an attempt to return to their northern Plains homeland. It was a confused mixture of tragic and comic scenes, though hers were of the former sort.[10] In both movies, she continued to be an effective film example of the pride and dignity of native peoples. Edwin Carewe would have been moved. She also made a handful of television appearances, and at least through the early 1970s she and Lew often worked together to put on theater pieces, in the capital and other cities. Far more important to her continuing image, however, were the television recycles of the film heritage that she left, now ubiquitous on both Mexican and U.S. small screens.

From the time of the real Dolores's arrival back in Mexico in the early 1940s, and particularly from her earliest successes in *Flor Silvestre* and *María Candelaria*, she assumed a place as one of Mexico's major actresses and figured in that country's Golden Age of Film, at the same time that these films highlighted the plight of indigenous peoples. It is interesting that in *Ramona*, then in *Flor Silvestre* and *Maria Candelaria*, and finally in *Flaming Star* and *Cheyenne Autumn* she played roles that highlighted the plight and mistreatment of native groups. Her own dark coloring made her believable in these roles, though physically—and paradoxically—she was less convincing in the Mexican productions than she was in the U.S. movies. She injected a nobility into these indigenous portrayals in her Mexican films that initially did not sit as easily with audiences in her homeland as her acting in the U.S. films did with viewers north of the border. Still, the international renown she eventually earned for *María Candelaria* in particular led to significant national pride in her home country, along with acceptance of the theme of the film and of the actress as diva.

Meanwhile, even when *Cheyenne Autumn* was released in 1964, U.S. reviewers were still focused almost entirely on her beauty, as these quotations reveal: "Dolores Del Rio, with a bit part in 'Cheyenne Autumn,' ran off with all the reviews simply because she still looks so beautiful at an age in the neighborhood of 60"; ". . . grown-up kiddies will find particular delight in Gilbert Roland and Dolores Del Rio among the Cheyennes and as beautiful as ever, both of them"; "still one of the most beautiful women on the screen, and after all these years!" "She's still a mighty handsome woman. . . ."[11] The movie reviewer for *Life Magazine* hated the film but reported more cheerfully that it was not without its virtues: "And it does have Dolores del Rio."[12]

Meanwhile, especially as health problems impinged on her, she spent more and more time in the United States, particularly in Newport Beach, where she and Lew could be close to the water and to friends in the film industry. Unlike the case of Charlie Chaplin, who lived permanently in Europe after denial of his visa in the 1950s, any resentments on del Río's part had long since faded, along with rumors about anti-American political activity. Just a year and a half before her death, in September 1981, she and Lew attended the Heritage Ball, given by Los Amigos Del Pueblo, celebrating the Spanish heritage of Los Angeles on the occasion of its bicentennial. She was an honored guest, introduced first by the association's president and then by her husband, who commented, "Let me warn you of one thing. Dolores loves California to the degree that she might want it back."[13]

The term *icon* fits her well. The Free Online Dictionary gives, among others, these definitions: "an image; a representation"; "a representation or picture of the sacred or sanctified Christian personage"; "an important and enduring symbol"; and "one who is the object of great attention and devotion; an idol."[14] These definitions work well with the idea of Dolores del Río (Dolores Del Rio), an object for reverence and sexual desire, a symbol of Mexico, the source of thousands of still and moving (and eventually speaking and even singing) images. Views and visions of del Río operated above and beyond the individual human being, but they changed over time and among individuals and groups. Factors such as gender, generation, and personal needs and dreams made a difference, and because of the continued availability of her films the young Dolores remained accessible for fantasy even as she aged. Certainly, notions of del Río differed according to space as well; as a lifelong border crosser in personal and professional terms, she was seen somewhat differently by Americans and Mexicans, with more hopes pinned on her in her native country than in the United States, except probably among U.S. Latinos. She led a rich, fulfilling, up-and-down life that was unusual largely because of her celebrity, her great wealth, her beauty, and ultimately her power to shape her own destiny.

It is important to explore this other aspect of del Río as a movie star, as a symbol of Mexican national identity, and as a woman whose images were disseminated, that is, the "presence" and "discourses" of her "*iconic* identity," on which Hershfield rightly insists. She was a celebrity in both countries within months of her arrival in Hollywood, yet the nature of that celebrity varied greatly between the two countries. Longtime del Río friend Marlene Dietrich pointed out her close association with her home country in an interview with a Mexican journalist, saying, "I believe that Dolores del Río is the symbol of Mexicans throughout the world. She is your symbol of beauty."[15]

Mexicans regularly followed reports about Dolores's publicity appearances and her more political ones, for example her meeting in 1929 with the American President Herbert Hoover.[16] Her U.S. fame gave her enormous cultural importance in Mexico. In this respect, Hershfield is insightful about Dolores's early career, in suggesting that "Del Río's star text was distinguished by a historically situated image of an exotic foreign woman who was attracted to (and attractive to) white men." Exotic, certainly; attractive, certainly. Hershfield is also correct that "When del Río arrived in Hollywood, the movie star was differentiated primarily by his or her physical image." Yet this attempt at historicizing is perhaps overstated; all movie stars, along with other figures in the visual media, are differentiated in this way. She further says that "Although female stars are defined primarily along the scale of sexual desirability, the color of del Río's skin and her facial characteristics marked her first of all as not white." On this point, I disagree; what is remarkable to me about del Río is that she was always coded white from her very first days in Hollywood, but she played roles, as all actors did, that were suitable to her particular coloring. She was never precluded from romantic roles with white men. As we have seen, the possibility of casting of her as indigenous was not even touched until she appeared in the film *Ramona*, and then repeated most importantly not in Hollywood but when she returned to Mexico. Indeed, during the early Hollywood years, she was more often portrayed as European than as Latin American, in great contrast to other stars such as Carmen Miranda and Lupe Vélez.[17] This early racial definition of Dolores as white, deriving not only from careful publicity upon her arrival in Hollywood but also from her great beauty and her social class, made important differences in what she achieved and how she achieved it.

One of the strangest myths is that she was not popular in Mexico.[18] Indeed, she was chosen to function as a star in Hollywood because the Latin American market was important to the studios and attractive Latin Americans would draw audiences south of the border. Her silent pictures were viewed widely in Mexico, and although they occasionally caused a scandal among others in her social class there, more importantly they led to a vision of her as a conqueror of their very problematic neighbor to the north. As Torres Bodet notes above, "There are various ways to belong to a country," and she was always insistent on her Mexican nationality, unlike Garbo and Dietrich, both of whom became U.S. citizens.

A view of her influence in her home country may be seen through three literary representations, two of them using her own name. The earliest, mentioned earlier, was Jaime Torres Bodet's novel, *Estrella del día*. Though identifying her by another name and describing her appearance differently, it is clearly modeled on her career and is a story about a young Mexican man obsessed with her screen image. This image is disseminated by Hollywood, but she is still seen by him as a real human being, not a Hollywood icon. He longs to encounter her, not only because he desires her romantically but also because he wants her clearly associated with his—and her—home country. The other two representations are not entirely favorable, though they do not question her status as a kind of national treasure.[19] These literary works by prominent Mexican intellectuals are interesting as they all look at the interaction between her iconicity and her reality, which fed back constantly into one another and interacted as well with her film images, both those in her continuing work and those produced in the past as they were shown again. This vision—iconicity, reality, produced images—is useful for analysis, but such a separation is artificial and used here only the better to illuminate the various aspects of her beauty, power, and celebrity.

The earliest of these, portraying her as the character Piedad Santelmo in Jaime Torres Bodet's *Estrella de día*, appeared in 1933. The author was a film critic only two years her senior who later gained fame as a poet and served as the Mexican secretary of education and as secretary of foreign affairs. Many years later, just a year before her death, she was, along with María Félix, the subject of a vicious and misogynistic attack in a play written in 1982 by the much younger novelist Carlos Fuentes, *Orquídeas en la luz de la luna* (*Orchids in the Moonlight*). It depicted them as gracelessly aging and living in a mythologized past of their greatest movie roles, with the action taking place on the day of Orson Welles's death. Del Río was shown as pottering around their shared apartment, dressed in braids and peasant clothes as she had been for her part in *María Candelaria*. Typically, always the perfect lady, the real Dolores chose to ignore the attack, while the real María stopped speaking to Fuentes. Del Río was further immortalized in 1988, five years after her death, in an essay by the prominent Mexican critic Carlos Monsiváis, focused largely on her beauty and specifically on her iconic status and the reasons for it. These three visions of Dolores, examined here, span fifty-five years.

Torres Bodet's *Estrella de día* (*Star of the Day*) is a fascinating study of the intersection of the very youthful del Río as the character Piedad, based largely on images in her films during her first years in Hollywood, with the imagination of the young protagonist, Enrique, a man of twenty-four (about the age of Piedad, twenty-three). He attempts to visualize her and also embody her by willing her back to Mexico, to relate the screen appearances to her actual living self. Finally, in the novella, he encounters the actual Piedad and must haltingly come to terms with the fusing of image and reality. At the time in which Torres Bodet wrote, in the late 1920s and early 1930s, the trajectory of Dolores's public persona in the United States was formed first by sexy roles (*What Price Glory?* and *Loves of Carmen*) and then increasingly by dewy romantic portrayals (*Ramona*, *Evangeline*), while in Mexico she was being noted as a source of national pride. He does not envision her as an English speaker, and so probably he either finished writing before her appearances in the talkies or ignored them.[20]

The novella, though in third-person, is written almost entirely from the point of view of Enrique, a young friend of Piedad's cousin who becomes obsessed with her when he sees her on the screen in her U.S. films. He travels throughout Mexico City, catching a showing of one film here and another there, longing for her actual presence, for an opportunity to encounter her in person. He also hopes for her homecoming because her choice of Mexico over the United States would be a reason for national pride. Torres Bodet shows Piedad, the idol, as created by her films, but he emphasizes as well that her personal reality in the novel is also twisted by a false biography. This reading was developed even before her arrival in Hollywood, a biography written by American publicists intended to "take away from her the least bit of reality, to steal from her a dear godfather, a small toy, not leaving intact the most fleeting memory of her childhood." Fortunately, as Torres Bodet fictionalized it, she did not speak English and was unaware of the falsification of the details of her real life; "she could not understand the degree to which notoriety demanded of her a prompt death, a total falsity, a silent and definitive betrayal."[21] He insists that in the publicity efforts to make her into a Mexican curiosity, her Hollywood handlers gave her "a shawl, a gourd," and this to a woman who "always requested the most European hats in the shops, to whom fruit was always served— even though it be pineapple, mangos, oranges—on . . . trays of crystal."[22] "A Mexican, my God, a Mexican . . . how could she be a Mexican? But she was, charmingly. And in her own way, intimate, tender, superfluous; and for this reason, impossible to falsify."[23] The author, through Enrique, contrasts the false image with the reality of her "patriotism: her own way of being, the religiosity of her mother, the soul of her small province, the song of her indescribable Mexico."[24]

As Enrique wanders around Mexico lost in his dreams of her, he begins to carry around a Hollywood guidebook, wondering where she is at the various hours of the day, focusing on her physical reality. But at four o'clock in the afternoon, he plunges into her iconic film appearances, so deceptively real. For the price of admission, she becomes his: "At this hour they opened the doors of the theater where they had hidden Piedad."[25] He realizes that he is "in love with a shadow," yet "the shadow he loved corresponded, point by point, with the existence of an indisputably real body, solid, precise, capable of hatreds, of scars, of sufferings, celebrated in Hollywood." When he discovers that she has returned to Mexico, and then miraculously encounters her in the Alameda Park, he concludes with joy that she has returned because "she was nostalgic for Mexico."[26]

The story is a vivid one, both of the youth in love with the icon and the young woman, the embodiment of the icon, who has her own life, her own wishes and desires. Of course, it is a fictional account, adding its own elements to del Río's symbolic incarnation. It is particularly important in that it shows the eagerness to claim her as Mexican by someone who was about her own age, as precocious in literature as she was in film. Even more interesting, at the same time she was undergoing construction in the United States as a celebrity in her publicity and in her films *Evangeline* and *Ramona* as an appealing and very young and innocent romantic heroine, in Mexico Torres Bodet sought to stress her humanity rather than her fame.

Almost fifty years later, the iconic view of her in her various roles, and particularly as María Candelaria, is exploited in Carlos Fuentes's 1982 play *Orchids in the Moonlight.* The piece opens with Dolores, dressed as María Candelaria, holding a cup of tea that she drops as she breaks into hysterical tears. When the character of María Félix appears, she asks what the problem is, and Dolores in distress answers that, "They didn't recognize me."[27] The play continues, exploring tensions between the two divas, now living together in Venice, California. María taunts Lolita, saying that she will get dressed for the "funeral of your ex-lover, if he can be called that," referencing Orson Welles's death, while keeping the day's newspaper from her so that she will not know who she's talking about.[28] This fiction by Fuentes was a deliberate and obvious affront to Dolores; Welles did not die until 1985, two years after Dolores. In the later stages of the play, the two women compete over a fan—a young man—who wanders to the door in search of Dolores.

Throughout the piece, Fuentes references films in which the two appeared, and dressing Dolores as María Candelaria, when, as Torres Bodet put it in his fictional account, she always sought out the latest European fashions in the shops, is one way of making us choose between the actual woman and the movie image. Both women in the Fuentes drama question whether the other is the actual star, a real person or an imposter, expressing the contradictions, the parallels, and the interactions between the film roles, their status as icons, and their imagined real lives. They attack each other on the basis of real vulnerabilities from the biographies of the lives they actually lived and with which Fuentes was familiar. Dolores accuses María of abandoning her son to become a film star, while María questions Dolores's virtue. When Dolores says she was "chased by the finest gentlemen," María answers, "Chased, but not chaste."[29] And both refer to the conflict between their realities and their images:

Dolores: the dream factory . . . which dreamed us up . . .
María: the centre of illusion . . . which turned out to be just another illusion . . .
Dolores: Our mirror . . .
María: Our mirage . . .[30]

These are images Fuentes uses extensively elsewhere, including in his novel *The Death of Artemio Cruz*, written decades earlier, in which the old revolutionary dies while looking at his disembodied reflection in the mirrored, fractured segments of his daughter's purse beside his bed. Yet Artemio is a composite figure, clearly a fictional character, though based on Fuentes's imagined lives of a number of male revolutionaries. In the play, however, he is using as characters two real women whom he knew and whom the Mexican public revered. He later described his intentions by suggesting that the play should be read as ambiguous, dreamlike, magic. Unsurprisingly, however, his subjects both hated the play, and to my knowledge it has been performed only once in Mexico with men, not women, in the principal roles—although a number of times outside of that country. Fuentes was pleased by the Mexican presentation, as he reported in 1992, because it had a "fringe, outsider quality . . . baroque, grotesque, cartoon-like at times, and very funny." He thought that it "worked as a comedy very well."[31] Yet Fuentes puts these words in Dolores's mouth at the end of the play: "The camera, Maria? Isn't the camera our salvation? Aren't all our prayers met by the movie camera? Isn't the camera our common altar, my love? . . . Let our movies run forever, uninterrupted."[32]

Fuentes's work was a harsh attack on the two women. By making them into figures dependent on the adulation of the public, he denigrated their great strength of character and powerful will, not to mention their continuing fame and prestige. He himself acknowledged that the play contained much "artificiality built into it because of the nature of the two women, who are artifice incarnate." He did emphasize, however, the not-quite-reality that he was trying to convey, as when the character Dolores points at the audience "which is there and is not there" and says "'they are not looking at us,' when the audience is doing nothing else, of course." He claimed that del Río "rehearsed it [the play] and wanted to do it for Mexican television, but then she died"--untrue, though del Río had made no public protest.

Félix was furious about the play, condemned the author (denominated "Mr. X") in *Vanity Fair* as "a horrible individual" who had "smeared" her, and branded him publicly as almost female in his nastiness. Though Fuentes claimed he had "no intention of offending," it seems incredible that he would not have understood that by portraying the women as two wrinkling, vicious, fame-obsessed women abandoned by their publics he was crossing the line into defamation.[33] Worse, he picked at old wounds, such as Dolores's affair with Orson Welles and María's rumored abandonment of her child. The play is rarely performed and thus has had little effect on the mythology of either woman, but it is a harsh comment on old age, fleeting beauty, and the insubstantial nature of celebrity, even though both of his protagonists were still beautiful, active, and major celebrities. Yet it moves toward Monsiváis's essay on Dolores, in which she is seen as a "face" and as a "Screen Goddess," a larger-than-life figure that is "at every showing . . . born again from the celluloid," listing her among those other immortals, Félix, Dietrich and Garbo, West, Monroe, Hepburn.[34]

It may be that Fuentes was rendering a kind of homage to Dolores and María. In an interview with the *New York Times*'s Arthur Holmberg before the first performance of the play at the American Repertory Theatre in Cambridge, Massachusetts, he insisted that

writing this play was a journey into the past and an evocation of two beautiful Mexican women who were important to me in my youth. . . . I loved these two actresses because they were strong and independent. They shattered all the macho myths. They were not what Latin women were supposed to be. They were not little dolls men could cuddle.

He further noted, in the same interview, that "Movies are bearers of the collective unconscious, the warehouse of modern myths . . . Hollywood manufactures the archetypes we need to understand our collective life." But as the author of the piece noted, "in one of the play's emotional climaxes, the two aging film beauties watch clips from their old movies. Their faces and bodies were once symbols of erotic fantasy onto which millions of mute spectators projected hidden desires. Past their prime, they no longer have any tangible relationship to those far-off images, and one cannot be sure if those shadows flickering across the wall promote self-definition or self-deception." Still, there is room for ambiguity. Joann Green, the director of the production, herself insisted that, "The vital fantasy of 'Orchids in the Moonlight' exists because of the *strength and beauty* of a bond between women. It is rare to have two such vibrant female presences stage center. These women reflect for each other the power of fame and glamour and the wisdom of revolution and nostalgia."[35] Thus Fuentes's work recognized female power, particularly the power of his two protagonists, but his own relationship to that power seems at best uncomfortable.

Although Fuentes's vision of Dolores was ambivalent, with his very attention and antagonism evidencing her significance, Carlos Monsiváis, the great essayist, provides a more balanced perspective several years after her death, still intent on her beauty. The very title of his essay, "Dolores del Río: The Face as Institution," sets the tone. He begins with a sentence fragment: "A dazzling face." Yet he, unlike Fuentes, who is focused on aging and decay, emphasizes the continuing beauty of that face: "Timeless—not because it is immune to the devastation of age but, rather, for the radiant effect it still has on those who contemplate it." Nevertheless, he portrays her as totally egocentric, "A woman, the possessor of a face, who in the preservation of her beauty finds the meaning of her artistic life." And he securely positions her as desiring the various processes—hairstyles, fashion, cosmetics, plastic surgery—that made her, already lovely, into the more stunning woman that she became: "For Dolores del Río, the need for beauty was a conscious desire and an endless victory."[36] He acknowledges her significance for Mexico in ways that evoke Torres Bodet's vision of Piedad: "In Mexico, Dolores del Rio's career in the United States is the [inevitable] cause of peripheral pride: she is the compatriot-who-has-made-it-in-Hollywood, the local girl who is a delight on the universal screen." Despite the fact that women in high society look at her with some disapproval, he notes that they imitate her, and that "she is declared an honorary member of that select club of Universal Mexicans."[37]

Pointing out the importance for Mexican film of her return in the early 1940s, he nevertheless expresses disappointment in the largely melodramatic nature of the parts she initially receives, ignoring the general awfulness of some of her last roles in Hollywood: "Dolores is confined to melodramas, the theatricalization of family torment as joy through tragedy, and the inevitable pact between the film industry and the public who, from such modest cartharses, extracts didactic conclusions."[38] However, Monsiváis recognizes her power in her best films, which he suggests are *La otra* (*The Other One*, also called "Double Destinée" in French) and *Doña Perfecta*, a judgment with which I concur. He points out that her dominance and cruelty in these two roles turns her away from the usual notion of Mexican femininity as "the inverted apology of *machismo*." He goes on: "Nature—implies the logic of the melodrama—made her the gift of beauty so that she could accomplish her desire to control."[39]

In making these judgments, he conflates the woman with the actress and her roles, as he applauds the escape from "her delirious succession of roles as the devastated and oppressed Long-Suffering Woman."[40] Speaking of her time in Hollywood, he suggests "glamour endows Dolores with the aura of being a woman of her time—modern, blamelessly happy, and without prejudice—who embodied and offered the public the chic atmosphere and up-to-date taste which were lacking in Mexico."[41] However, she possessed a sense of style and familiarity with European fashion before she ever went to Hollywood, and though she may have been a model in her movie roles for many Mexican women, the companions of her class were familiar with the same styles Dolores adopted. Probably, it seems to me, many women of Mexico's upper class were envious of her not because of her sense of style but because of her escape from the control of family, social strictures, and powerful men.

In the 1940s, just before her return to Mexico, writer Salvador Novo pointed out, and Monsiváis quotes,

If, at times, there surfaces a consolatory belief that talent is a form of beauty, with Dolores del Río we are in the presence of a case in which extraordinary beauty is only the material form of talent. She has been gifted with grace, elegance, a fresh and vibrant nimbleness that, being natural, seems exotic. The most important fashion magazines fight over her latest photograph in which she wears a simple hairdo that she has just made up and which, soon, families will begin to impose as the norm; a thick amethyst bracelet, the only adornment to quietly set off her tiara against her black hair; or the sandals in which she goes out to the garden to look at the frogs and ducks with which she has populated it; or the place in which she has placed the orchids on her suit. She creates herself . . . just like any artist creates their best work.[42]

It may be that Novo understood her the best of all these chroniclers. He was certainly more focused on the actual woman than he was on the icon, though he understood her widespread appeal. He became her next-door neighbor in Mexico City, when she returned to her native country years after he wrote the passage above. For decades he chronicled her activities in the regular column produced for the Mexico City periodical *Hoy*: hers was a life full of socializing with members of the Mexican cultural and political elite and with old friends from the United States and Europe as they came and went from Mexico and as she herself traveled back and forth. The great lady continued her glamorous life, performing professionally as opportunities arose or as she, often in collaboration with Lew, developed projects for herself. After her death, however, the Mexican attention to her memory was surprisingly sparse, though in recent years this is beginning to change. Unlike Dietrich in Germany and Garbo in Sweden, she has no museum; no public space, with the exception of a large statue of her as María Candelaria in Chapultepec Park, chronicles her memory. At the same time, the statue memorializes an indigenous woman of Mexico, albeit in an idealized version.

In the United States, by contrast, she has been memorialized in the years since her death through several important works of art, perhaps reflecting more comfort with the idea of a celebrity, particularly a female one, as a historically significant figure. Unsurprisingly and appropriately, two of these are public art, a mural and a statue, in Los Angeles; the third is an installation piece that has moved through several incarnations, the current one belonging to the Smithsonian.

The installation, a remarkable work of memory by Chicano artist Amalia Mesa-Bains, was first exhibited in 1984, shortly after del Río's death. Titled "Ofrenda for Dolores Del Rio," it took the form of the Day of the Dead altars common in Mexico and among persons of Mexican descent in the United States to celebrate and emphasize the continuing connection to deceased family members and admired persons. The Mesa-Bains work is dominated by beautiful fabrics—satin, lace, and gauze—and a backdrop all in a mauve pink, much like the gauzy veil she wore in her *Life en Español* cover thirty years earlier. In the center of the piece, the artist has placed a photograph of del Río wearing a shawl around her head, resonant of the images of the Virgin Mary that appear in many household shrines and on the altars of many Catholic, and particularly Latin American, churches. Over her head, clouds of gauze deepen the association with the Virgin, often seen in representations in which she hovers over the earth, the sky full of clouds emphasizing her numinous quality. Four photographs on each side of the fabric-draped central altar are reminiscent of paintings of the Virgin of Guadalupe, so powerful and so significant to Mexicans and persons of Mexican descent on both sides of the border, featuring cameos depicting her major miracles.

In this work, they show images of Dolores's films from both Mexico and the United States. This artistic language associates del Río directly with the most important female figure in the Catholic religion, a dazzling statement of her power and iconicity, yet at one and the same time a personal, intimate figure. This reality and intimacy is emphasized by a photograph of her parents, a doll, and the Mexican flag on the left-hand side of the table at the foot of the altar; on the right the focus is on her stardom, glamour, and physicality, with cosmetics, perfume bottles, and photographs of the male actors with whom she starred.

At the same time, the photographs and memorabilia show her as a border crosser, a person whose very identity is rooted in two cultures.[43] Jennifer González has noted that these juxtapositions suggest the "conflicting conditions of an identity split between a Mexican heritage and a Hollywood career." This point is interesting; I would argue that del Rio's identity was not "split" but rather integrated in her actuality as a Mexican with a career in Hollywood and her other myriad interactions with the United States. González further notes that "by transforming this historical figure into a canonized cultural icon, the artist adds del Rio to a pantheon of feminine role models with which she and other Chicanos can identify." She goes on to say, "The figure of Dolores Del Rio is the source of both mythological identification and historical recuperation."[44] Del Río, in Mesa-Bains's vision, takes on a numinous, almost sacred quality, while remaining quite obviously a representation of a real human being.

In another installation, "The Grotto of the Virgins" (1987), Mesa-Bains brings together *ofrendas* to del Río, Frida Kahlo—del Río's dear friend and artist and another powerful woman—along with the artist's own grandmother, Mariana Escobedo Mesa. In doing so, she leads the viewer to look for the similarities and parallels among these women significant to the artist. The artist herself has suggested that:

. . . the altar for Dolores del Rio in the Grotto of the Virgins reflects familial space and serves as an exercise for a personal definition and patriarchal challenge. The installations are devices of intimate storytelling developed through an aesthetic of accumulation, experience, reference, memory, and transfiguration. Historical

Alfredo de Batuc's stunning SPARC mural in tribute to Dolores. Photographed by Adam Avila. Copyright ©1990 by Alfredo de Batuc. Reproduced by permission.

works such as the Dolores del Rio altar contextualize a domestic icon of the cinema within the Hollywood/Mexicana dual worlds and act as well for my personal narrative of life events in the relations of power between women and society.

In the same essay, she goes on to say that struggles of the women in her installations "reflect the iconic battles of women and religion, women and society, and ultimately, women and the domination of patriarchy." Del Río is particularly significant in her view for her having challenged "the conventions of the *gente decente* [respectable people] of her age." She notes that her works "as a result of established themes of life and death . . . have mediated a pantheon of female figures," serving to "rehistoricize women." Moreover, "This canonization of icons counters the power of the Church and makes use of popularization through acclamation." Further, she asserts that she has chosen individuals "whose lives and work struggle against the power and domination of the masculine world," including del Río securely in this classification.[45] Judy Baca notes that

Mesa-Bains provides a visual and concrete case for the glorification of a secular icon of feminine glamour by circumscribing social space into a material memorial that also serves as a revision of history and a remembrance of the future. The evidence carefully selected and provided by Mesa-Bains in the installation . . . is used to say that Dolores del Rio is much more than just a movie star; she is a woman pioneer who broke through many barriers while maintaining her Chicano identity and feminine sensibilities.[46]

The most important piece of public art in the United States that features del Río is Alfredo de Batuc's Hollywood mural, inaugurated July 12, 1990. It is located at the northeast corner of Hollywood Boulevard and Hudson Avenue. The work was sponsored by the Social and Public Art Resource Center, a remarkable organization that has contributed to producing enormous numbers of public murals. It is directed by Baca, who is mentioned above in connection with Mesa-Bains's work. De Batuc reports that the idea for the mural was developed when he received a call for mural proposals from the SPARC project Great Walls Unlimited: Neighborhood Pride, a project "to produce public images that speak to the multi-ethnic communities" that make up Los Angeles.[47]

Hollywood was de Batuc's neighborhood, so he "thought it appropriate to honor this otherwise unacknowledged ethnic group, and at the same time salute the idea of the film Mecca." He wanted to "give the neighbor-hood a public picture that would be undeniably Mexican," because the very substantial Latino population of the area is generally ignored. As he noted, "Spurring my interest in choosing a Hollywood Mexican as the subject mat-ter was the dearth of information in mainstream media as regards to the participation of Mexicans in Hollywood cinema, an appalling omission akin to a well-planned boycott." Realizing that she was a "star of the first order, a household name," he proceeded with enthusiasm to produce a wonderfully colorful mural featuring a goddesslike del Río that resonates with Mexico's "devotional retablos," that is, "the popular illustrations of the supposed apparitions of Mary, the mother of Jesus, under the alias of Guadalupe."[48]

In choosing this form, he makes his mural reminiscent of Mesa-Bains's "Ofrenda" in form, though not at all in artistic conception or coloring. De Batuc has used a large central depiction of Dolores's authentic Mexican, pre-plastic surgery face. The four cameos illustrate some of her most im-portant roles—two U.S. productions, one Mexican, one U.S. movie filmed in Mexico—and are precisely reminiscent of the depictions of Guadalupe discussed in relation to the previous work. All of them are in black and white to contrast with the sunset colors, "fiery oranges to a passionate red to a dusky burgundy," of the background. The films shown, moving clockwise from the upper left, are her first big hit, *What Price Glory?* (1926); *Flying Down to Rio* (1933); *María Candelaria* (1943); and *The Fugitive* (1947). The work also references "orange crate label art," which featured "a sunny and colorful picture of pastoral bliss in a citrus paradise under a benign open sky"—a Southern California vision. It is contrasted with the snowy outline at the lower left of the volcano Ixtaccihuatl, the Sleeping Woman, visible from Mexico City whenever an opening in the smog permits. Thus both films and background combine Mexican and U.S. themes, accepting her binational personal history and continuing renown. "As an offering to this celluloid deity," de Batuc notes, he has included the flowers of the deserts of the Southwest as an allusion to her first Mexican movie, *Flor Silvestre* (*Wild Flower*), and two others, one U.S., one Mexican: *Bird of Paradise* (1932) and *Bugambilia* (1944).[49]

De Batuc's website also contains a brief biography of del Río. He, like Mesa-Bains, is aware that from her late teens she was testing the limits of behavior for well-to-do Mexican women, and he points out that she posed as the "justice" figure for Diego Rivera's first mural, "Creation," in 1922, at the

Escuela Nacional Preparatoria in Mexico City. Throughout the mural and his Artist's Statement as well as further discussion on his website, he shows her as binational, a part of two countries, like himself and many residents of Hollywood, Los Angeles, and California in general. The image therefore resonates not only with Dolores's own personal history but with that of many who view it. Moreover, she is a *successful* border crosser, triumphant in both societies.[50] The work highlights an iconic but real individual who was able to negotiate the challenges of the transitions they also face, moving back and forth between countries and cultures. Moreover, as the SPARC website presents the Neighborhood Pride Project, "For scholars, these murals hold the visual keys to give voice to those not included in the traditional historical recordings." I would suggest that this mural holds these keys for anyone who cares to read them. Mesa-Bains's and de Batuc's works share the sense of giving voice to binational Latinos and to Dolores herself.

A final tribute is the Hollywood La Brea Gateway, better known as the "Four Silver Ladies of Hollywood." It is located at the corner of Hollywood and La Brea streets at the western edge of the Hollywood Walk of Fame, which commemorates the town's most famous with sidewalk plaques. This gazebolike structure features sculptures of four of Hollywood's early female stars, although the figures are not greatly realistic in portraying these subjects. It shares this area with the stars on the Walk of Fame honoring the Beatles and Elvis Presley. The women are Dolores del Río, Mae West, Anna May Wong, and Dorothy Dandridge.[51]

It was designed by the production designer (now successful director) Catherine Hardwicke, a Texan from the border town of McAllen who had spent time in Mexico herself. Hardwicke's 1993 design was completed in 1994 by another sculptor; it is usually considered a tribute to racial and ethnic diversity in Hollywood, as well as an acknowledgment of women in the film industry. The women she chose were certainly diverse. West was always presented publicly as white but rumored to be African American, and Dandridge certainly was, while Wong was Chinese American and del Río Mexican. But it seems to me that the Four Silver Ladies form a wonderful monument to transgression. All transgressed the gender ideologies of their times, first by being female and powerful and then by not following their contemporary prescribed formula of respectability in marriage to one man. Wong never married at all, though she strongly protested against the strictures on interracial marriage in an article published in France in

1932. West's marriage to Frank Wallace was kept secret and damaged her career when it surfaced in 1935. Dandridge had two failed marriages, suffered vicious public criticism because of her affair with white director Otto Preminger, and died at forty-two of a barbiturate overdose despite her enormous success in nightclubs and in films. And del Río, of course, was fifty-five and had two previous marriages and a number of affairs before her happy union with Lew Riley—in which she was the dominant partner.

All played roles in which their sexuality was emphasized—yet another transgression, one that West, in particular, took to the level of great comic art as her scripts dodged around censors. As West said later, "It isn't what I do, but how I do it. It isn't what I say, but how I say it, and how I look when I do and say it." All walked on the edge of censorship by Hollywood authorities such as the Breen Office, the very sexuality that positioned them as star attractions subject to constant scrutiny. Wong, a third-generation Chinese American, and del Río both suffered some criticism from their home communities. Wong, whose ethnicity prevented her from kissing her white leading men, was accused of making films demeaning China, the Chinese, and Chinese Americans. Del Río faced problems in Mexico, particularly from her own class and even occasionally from the government, though her films were always popular with Mexican audiences.[52] And all of them were performing publicly by the time they were in their teens, a time of transition for women that Hardwicke, now a successful director, has examined in her films *Thirteen* (2003, a searing examination of the life of "a wholesome 13-year-old girl who abruptly falls into a world of drugs and sex"), *The Nativity Story* (2006, in which she directs Keisha Castle-Hughes playing the Virgin Mary "as a headstrong, thoughtful adolescent transformed by an unimaginable responsibility"), and her enormous hit *Twilight* (2008, in which the slightly awkward, new-girl-in-town teenage female protagonist falls in love with a vampire). It seems to me likely that Hardwicke is interested in honoring in these women not only ethnic and racial difference and audacious challenging of gender ideologies but also the courage to survive the difficult transition to fame—in a predominantly white society—at a very early age. Hardwicke has positioned del Río within a group of women whose strengths, challenges, failures, and successes had much in common with her own.

These representations and tributes to del Río show significant differences between the ways she is remembered in the United States and in Mexico. Although every taxi driver in Mexico City knows who she is, there is no major memorial to her in her home country. Yet she was acknowledged from her earliest arrival in Hollywood as a celebrity who brought luster to her origins. Torres Bodet's reviews of her work and his novel taking her as his protagonist, her connections from the mid-1920s until her death with other prominent Mexican intellectuals and artists, and her acknowledgment by second-generation Mexican Renaissance writers Fuentes and Monsiváis all show her strong identification with her place of origin and her position as a source of Mexican pride. Still, there is no major public acknowledgment of her own art or her cultural contributions to Mexico. This neglect has to some degree been repaired by an exhibit of photographs of del Río at Carlos Slim's Museo Soraya, now in a Mexico City shopping center pending construction of a permanent building in Chapultepec Park. The temporary exhibit was so popular with the public that it was remounted in another area after removal; hopefully, it will become a permanent part of the museum.

In contrast, Chicana artist Mesa-Bains, Mexican national Alfredo de Batuc (who lives and works in Los Angeles), and Texan border crosser Catherine Hardwicke have done stunning memorials to her in the United States. Mesa-Bains's work belongs to the Smithsonian; unfortunately, it is not currently exhibited but is viewable on their website. De Batuc's mural is a tribute from a fellow countryman that is constantly visible and accessible, and a source of pride and interest for not only the Mexicans and Mexican Americans who have crossed the border but also others fascinated by this strong and powerful Mexican woman. Hardwicke's gazebo places del Río among other talented and successful women of color at the very Gateway to the Hollywood Walk of Fame. She deserves these honors in both countries.

So how do the themes of this book—celebrity, beauty, and power—interact in her life, and how do they differ between the United States and Mexico, and even Europe and Latin America? Briefly, her dark beauty brought her to the attention of two powerful men who profoundly affected her future. The first was Jaime Martínez del Rio, in Mexico City, interested in the artistic prospects of the developing film industry, who was willing to use her beauty as a ticket to Hollywood. The other, Edwin Carewe, a Hollywood director, was looking for just such a dark beauty to serve his various sociological and artistic purposes: to make dark skin, at least that of indigenous peoples, legitimately erotic for whites, along with creating good films and developing a bankable female film star under his control. Dolores, because of her beauty, became the instrument of their ambitions, but her immediate celebrity and continued successes made it possible for her to leave both men behind and begin to develop what she herself wanted, an artistic career and a private life of autonomy and choice, of personal control reasonably free of male interference, obsession, and domination. Meanwhile, her celebrity as a screen beauty in the United States led to an admiration *for* and identification *with* her in Mexico as a woman who triumphed over what the Mexican public regarded as the domineering and arrogant country to the north.

As she aged and U.S. visions of beauty during World War II turned toward younger, blonder, and *not foreign* women, her U.S. celebrity was inadequate to provide her with a continuing career there. A return to Mexico changed all that. When she went home, her celebrity led to enormous power not only to continue her own career but also to aid the arts in many ways. She was an inspiration for the Mexican film industry and an indefatigable patron of art, music, and literature, related to movie production or not. Initially, despite her age, she played younger indigenous women, and these films were powerful in the sense that they made living human indigenous people—not just monuments from pre-Columbian civilizations—more valued and visible within Mexico and, as the movies were distributed abroad, around the world. Some of her later U.S. films did the same. Further, the power conferred on del Río and her collaborators by international recognition, particularly when *María Candelaria* won the Palme d'Or at Cannes, made it possible for them to continue high-quality filmmaking in Mexico and elsewhere for a few years.

In personal terms, her beauty and celebrity made it possible for her to make a great deal of money, both in the United States and later in Mexico. Another factor, her hard-headed intelligence when it came to finances and investments, led to the power that money brings in the cultural, social, and personal aspects of life. Of course, her beauty and celebrity contributed to her power to retain audiences and continue working, even as the structural position of the Mexican movie industry became more and more difficult in the late 1940s and 1950s. Then, as her films recycled in Mexico and in the United States through revivals, television showings, and eventually videotapes and DVDs, her beauty and celebrity continued to be appreciated and reinforced by younger viewers.

All contributed to her ongoing power as a cultural leader and as an icon of particularly Mexican and Latino/Latina devotion. Though she seems very rarely to have exercised her power in the crude sense of domination, her ability to realize her artistic desires—either through her own acting or by sponsoring other cultural activities through her financial resources and her continuing prestige and personal influence—remained substantial even as she aged. In the sense in which Rollo May understands power—as "the ability to cause or prevent change," as "the ability to affect, to influence, and to change other persons (or oneself)," and as "self-realization and self-actualization"—she was an immensely powerful woman. She had, by the time of her death, substantially influenced U.S. attitudes toward indigenous peoples and toward Mexicans more generally, though the racial category "Mexican" continues to be slippery, and deeply and negatively affected by the U.S. political process. She produced an enormous body of work in her more than five decades of active professional life in Mexico and elsewhere in Latin America, in the United States, and in Europe, and much of it survives. Del Río's life is a full and complex one of successes and failures, disappointments and joys. Yet she achieved "a life that was extremely meaningful, and, in the end, well-lived."[53]

Reference Matter

Notes

Chapter 1. Beauty, Celebrity, and Power in Two Cultures

1. Leo Braudy, *The Frenzy of Renown: Fame and Its History* (New York: Oxford University Press, 1986), 588.

2. Emily Leider, *Dark Lover: The Life and Death of Rudolph Valentino* (New York: Faber and Faber, for Farrar, Straus and Giroux, 2003), 4.

3. Dolores del Río interview with Elena Poniatowska (1964), in *Todo México* (Mexico City: Editorial Diana, 1993), Tomo II 20, 28–29, hereafter cited as *Todo II*; Spanish reads "cuento de hadas." *Sunday News*, London, Aug. 26, 1928, Dolores del Río Archive, Centro de Estudios de Historia de México CARSO, MXXIV 2/23. Archive hereafter cited as DDR followed by series number and document number. The reader is warned that the documents, in open plastic envelopes, can be removed easily, and even though as far as I can tell all are still available in the archive, some have been moved around

and may not be in the original envelopes. Others have been photocopied, particularly in the clippings file, and some of the dates and document numbers removed from these copies, making this problem particularly tricky. In my notes, where the dates are given but do not appear on the copies, they were taken from the originals when these were still available. In general, the documents, clippings, and photographs are in roughly chronological order and so should be relatively easy to locate.

4. Braudy, 588.

5. See Axel Madsen, *The Sewing Circle: Hollywood's Greatest Secret: Female Stars Who Loved Other Women* (Secaucus, N.J.: Birch Lane Press, 1995), 52; and Diana Mc-Clellan, *The Girls: Sappho Goes to Hollywood* (New York: St. Martin's Press, 2000), 214. Quotation from Elena Poniatowska, "Las burbujas de champaña en la copa de Marlene Dietrich" (interview), *Todo II*, 137.

6. Joanne Hershfield, *The Invention of Dolores del Río* (Minneapolis and London: University of Minnesota Press, 2000), xii.

7. Rollo May, *Power and Innocence: A Search for the Sources of Violence* (New York: Dell, 1972), 20, 99–100, 122.

8. Free Online Dictionary, Thesaurus and Encyclopedia, http://www.thefree dictionary.com/beauty, accessed Mar. 28, 2009.

9. *Webster's New World Dictionary* (New York: Warner Books, 1990), 53.

10. See Nancy Etcoff, *Survival of the Prettiest: The Science of Beauty* (New York: Anchor Books, 1999), 8–9; and David M. Buss, *The Evolution of Desire: Strategies of Human Mating* (New York: Basic Books, 2003), 52–55.

11. See, for example, David Ramón, *Dolores del Río: Historia de un rostro* (Mexico City: CCH Dirección Plantel Sur, 1993), cited hereafter as Ramón, *Historia*; Carlos Monsiváis, "Dolores del Río: The Face as Institution," in *Mexican Postcards*, edited, translated, and introduced by John Kraniauskas (London and New York: Verso, 1997).

12. Quotations from Joshua Gamson, *Claims to Fame: Celebrity in Contemporary America* (Berkeley: University of California Press, 1994), 15.

13. For a different view, see Hershfield, *The Invention*, in particular chap. 2, "Race and Romance," 17–32.

14. For the "chica moderna," see the excellent discussion in Joanne Hershfield, *Imagining la Chica Moderna: Women, Nation, and Visual Culture in Mexico, 1917–1936* (Durham, N.C.: Duke University Press, 2008), especially chap. 2, 44–72.

15. Birth certificate and baptismal certificate, Jaime Chávez Collection, Mexico City. Quotation from manuscript, "Second Chance," by Gladys Hall, Gladys Hall Collection, Academy of Motion Picture Arts and Sciences, hereafter cited as GH/MHL.

16. Charles L. Ponce de Leon, *Self-Exposure: Human-Interest Journalism and the Emergence of Celebrity in America, 1890–1940* (Chapel Hill and London: University of North Carolina Press, 2002), 7.

17. ProQuest Historical Newspapers, accessed May 20, 2010.

18. *Los Angeles Times* (hereafter cited as LAT), Sep. 29, 1925.

19. I am grateful to Chad Black, whose comments led me to this insight.

20. Hershfield, *The Invention*, 10–11, including quotation from *Photoplay*.

21. Hershfield, *The Invention*, xiii.

22. *Photoplay,* September 1932, 56. Hershfield, *The Invention*, ix, quotes part of the passage but locates it incorrectly.

23. *Photoplay,* August 1934, 34–35, 98–99.

24. Martha Menchaca, "Chicano Indianism: A Historical Account of Racial Repression in the United States," *American Ethnologist,* 20(3), August 1993, 583–584, 588.

25. See the discussion and quote in Mae Ngai, *Impossible Subjects: Illegal Aliens and the Making of Modern America* (Princeton and Oxford: Princeton University Press, 2004), 50–55.

26. Menchaca, 597–598.

27. Mark Reisler, "Always the Laborer, Never the Citizen: Anglo Perceptions of the Mexican Immigrant During the 1920s," *Pacific Historical Review,* 45(2), May 1976, 244.

28. Susan Courtney, *Hollywood Fantasies of Miscegenation: Spectacular Narratives of Gender and Race, 1903–1967* (Princeton and Oxford: Princeton University Press, 2005), 119.

29. Gary A. Greenfield, "Mexican Americans, Racial Discrimination, and the Civil Rights Act of 1866," *California Law Review,* 63(3), May 1975, 681. Irving G. Tragen, "Statutory Prohibitions Against Interracial Marriage," *California Law Review,* 32(3), September 1944, fn 12, 271.

30. John H. Burma, "Research Note on the Measurement of Interracial Marriage," *American Journal of Sociology,* 57(6), 1952, 587. "Constitutional Law. Equal Protection of the Laws. California Miscegenation Statute Held Unconstitutional," *Harvard Law Review,* 62(2), 1948, 307.

31. Peggy Pascoe, "Race, Gender, and Intercultural Relations: The Case of Interracial Marriage," *Frontiers: A Journal of Women Studies,* 12(1), 1991, 6.

32. Interview, *El Heraldo de México,* Mar. 8, 1966, DDR 1/371. Emphasis in the original. Spanish reads " . . . fue allá, en HOLLYWOOD donde empezó MI VIDA. Es decir, que me ENCONTRE A MI MISMA;" "LINEA RECTA, animado por el solo anhelo . . . llegar a ser reconocida MUNDIALMENTE como la ACTRIZ MAS IMPORTANTE DE MEXICO. . . ."

33. See the excellent article by Alicia L. Rodríguez-Estrada, "Dolores Del Río and Lupe Vélez: Images on and off the Screen, 1925–1944," in *Writing the Range: Race, Class, and Culture in the Women's West,* edited by Elizabeth Jameson and Susan Armitage (Norman and London: University of Oklahoma Press, 1997), 475–492. Yet it is important to note here that the feud between del Río and Vélez seems to have been a deliberate publicity stunt. See the widely disseminated article headlined "Fiery Lupe Registers Triumph in the Torrid Feud with Dolores," available in *Olean Times-Herald,* Olean, N.Y., Dec. 1, 1933.

34. See, for example, "Talk of London," *London Daily Express,* Aug. 25, 1928. DDR 2/18.

35. David Ramón, *Dolores del Río,* Vol. I: *Un cuento de hadas* (Mexico: Editorial Clío, 1997), 12. Cited hereafter as Ramón, DDR, followed by volume and page number.

36. Elizabeth Haiken, *Venus Envy: A History of Cosmetic Surgery* (Baltimore and London: Johns Hopkins University Press, 1997) 1–43, 46–55.

37. *Photoplay,* July 1927, 59. Quoted in Hershfield, *The Invention,* 13, with inaccurate citation.

38. See discussion and photograph in Haiken, *Venus Envy,* 73–74. The judgment that the image is almost identical to Dolores herself is my own.

39. Conversation with Carmen Parra, June 2008.

Chapter 2. Mexican Princess

1. Braudy, *The Frenzy of Renown*, 588.

2. Ramón, DDR I, 9.

3. Ramón, DDR I, 10. Paco Ignacio Taibo, *Dolores Del Río: Mujer en el Volcán* (Mexico, D. F.: Planeta, 1999), 19. Birth certificate and baptismal certificate, Jaime Chávez Collection, Mexico City.

4. See, for example, http://www.imdb.com/name/nm0003123/bio, accessed June 17, 2008.

5. Poniatowska, *Todo II*, 8. Spanish reads ". . . teníamos una carretela con dos caballos que eran la envidia de todos mis primos. Yo me subía a la carroza y me sentía como princesa. Mi mamá iba en la parte de atrás y yo la acompañaba a la iglesia, a hacer visitas, a la costurera . . . ¡Cómo me gustaban los regales de lazos, pulseras, arêtes! Las amigas de mi madre me daban dulces de leche mientras ellas tomaban té."

6. Ramón, I, 9–10. Spanish reads "un mundo idílico de landós, carretelas y banderas." See also http://en.wikipedia.org/wiki/Durango, accessed Apr. 14, 2009.

7. *El Heraldo de Mexico*, Mar. 8 1966, DDR 2/371. Spanish reads "A mi madre. El recuerdo mas luminoso de mi vida, junto al cual todos los demas se espuman y desapareen, pues ella, mi madre, llena toda mi vida y tambien mi recuerdo. . . ."

8. Salvador Novo, *La vida en México en el periodo presidencial de Manuel Avila Camacho* (Mexico: Empresas Editoriales, 1965), 361. Spanish reads "'su familia' consiste en su madre; en una madre que no vive sino para que su hija única sea feliz, y deja al excelente juicio de Dolores la forma de su felicidad."

9. Conversation with Carmen Parra, June 2008.

10. See, for example, DDR 1/411, July 9, 1956.

11. Poniatowska, *Todo II*, 9.

12. *El Heraldo de México*, Mar. 8, 1966, DDR 2/371. "Recuerdo la . . . Revolución que vino a romper *fulminantemente* ese mundo de paz. . . ." Emphasis in the original. Ramón, 10. Taibo, 30.

13. Poniatowska, Todo II, 9. Spanish reads ". . . salimos corriendo, muy de madrugada con otros señores importantes de Durango, porque al grito de '¡Ahí viene Pancho Villa!", todos huían. Contaban que Villa metía a la cárcel a todos aquellos que tuvieran que ver con el banco y que ¡nadie volvía a verlos! Mi mamá arregló el bastimiento para mi padre, que atravesó la Sierra Madre y se fue a los Estados Unidos. Nosotros tomamos el ultimo tren de Durango a la ciudad de México."

14. *El Heraldo de México*, Mar. 8, 1966, DDR 2/371. Spanish reads "hasta ese instante habia constituido mi primer pequeno mundo. . . ." See also Taibo, 22.

15. Poniatowska, *Todo II*, 9. Spanish reads " . . . con sus rebozos cruzados, a los soldados con su sombrero de anchas alas, las cananas, los rifles, el parquet, los caballos. En las estaciones me encontré, a cada parada, a los Emilio Fernández, a los Pedro Armendáriz de bigotes y calzón de manta, con quienes más tarde habría yo de filmar . . . tantas películas de la Revolución."

16. Ramón , I, 12. Spanish reads "la tierna luz"; "la paz, la justicia, y la belleza." See also Taibo, 22.

17. Taibo, 32.

18. Taibo, 30, 32. Ramón, DDR I, 10.

19. http://en.wikipedia.org/wiki/Durango, accessed Apr. 14, 2009.

20. Taibo, 25.

21. Taibo, 24–25.

22. *El Heraldo de México*, Mar. 8, 1966, DDR 2/371. Spanish reads ". . . a ese nuevo mundo. Aprendí a adaptarme, a tener amigos y *responsabilidades*." Emphasis in the original.

23. Ramón, DDR I, 11–12. Poniatowska, *Todo II*, 10.

24. Ramón, DDR I, 12–13.

25. Andrea Palma, interview, June 12 and June 17, 1975, Historia Oral—Cine Mexicano, PHO/2/24, Instituto José María Luis Mora. Spanish reads "patito feo," "criadas," "moscas en leche."

26. A copy of this portrait may be found in Ramón, DDR I, 14.

27. Taibo, 25. Spanish reads "ingenuas." Poniatowska, *Todo II*, 11, 15.

28. "La orquidea cruel," DDR 2/1 See also notes, photograph, DDR 3/53.

29. Aurelio de los Reyes, *Medio Siglo de Cine Mexicana (1896–1947)* (México: Editorial Trillas, 1987), 99, 108.

30. *Excelsior*, July 21 and July 22, 1920. Spanish reads "Sorprendente fué el espectáculo ofrecido anoche en el Teatro Iris"; "completo éxito"; "brillante aspecto, pues allí se hallaba congregada la 'elite' de nuestra sociedad"; "'Arlequinada'"; "interpretada por bellas y distinguidas señoritas de nuestro sociedad."

31. Palma, PHO/2/24. Spanish reads "Yo me caso con esa mujer o me muero"; "buen artista y muchísimo dinero"; "riquísimos." Del Río quotes in Taibo, 42. Spanish reads " . . . lo admiraba. Era un hombre del mundo . . . era cortés y atento y representaba para mí un hogar sereno. La diferencia de edad no me pareció inconveniente, sino por el contrario algo bueno, me aseguraba protección Yo era entonces, no lo olvide, muy joven."

32. DDR 2/371, Mar. 8, 1966. Spanish reads "su buen gusto, su exquisita caballerosidad, su admirable don de gentes."

33. *Excelsior*, Apr. 12, 1921. See also notes, back of photograph, DDR 3/53.

34. Notes, 3/53. See also La Duquesa del (indecipherable), Mar. 6 (no year), DDR 1/40.

35. Taibo, 41. Spanish reads "muy buen gusto."

36. See Notes, DDR 3/53. Taibo, 26, 44. Spanish reads "la catastrofe del algodón."

37. Taibo, 26. Quotation by Dolores reads in Spanish " . . . llamaron mucha atención."

38. Taibo, 26. Palma, PHO 2/24. Spanish reads "Esta educación nos marcó para siempre. Pero yo tenía la ventaja sobre mi prima de que cuando fui a Hollywood sabía inglés."

39. Taibo, 45. Poniatowska, *Todo II*, 16–17. Spanish reads "Se trataba de que Carewe conociera un hogar mexicana"; "Rodolfo Valentino femenino"; "una gran estrella."

40. Taibo, 50. Poniatowska, Todo II, 16–17. Spanish reads "el propio Jaime me llevó a Hollywood"; "Hollywood apenas empezaba. ¡Aún no se suicidaba nadie!" "Jaime era un hombre totalmente europeo, y veía con interés todo lo Nuevo. ¡Un hombre europeo sí hubiera permitido que su esposa fuera actriz! Así lo hizo Jaime"; "veía también para él la posibilidad de hacer guiones de cine, escribir, decorar, pintar, y se entusiasmó"; "Claro, la familia Martínez del Río se opuso, y toda la sociedad mexicana se nos echó encima"; "Las familias de abolengo, junto con los Martínez del Río, hicieron caer sobre nosotros una avalanche de críticas. A Jaime no pareció gran cosa.

. . . A mí, sea dicho la verdad, sí me afecto. Todavía ni nos íbamos a Hollywood y ya nos estaban haciendo pedazos." For Latin American demand, see *Film Daily Yearbook 1927* (New York and Los Angeles: John W. Alicoate, 1927), 957. Cited hereafter as FDY followed by year.

41. Taibo, 28. Spanish reads "Mi mama era mujer valiente, decidida, y a pesar de que a la familia le pareció un disparate que yo entrar en el cine de Hollywood, ella me apoyó. Había que ser muy valiente en aquellos años para dejar que una hija de familia acomodada entrar en el cine. Mi madre y yo fuimos un escándolo familiar."

42. Taibo, 43.

43. Ramón, DDR I,16. Taibo, 46. Laura Serna, "'As a Mexican I Feel It's My Duty': Citizenship, Censorship, and the Campaign Against Derogatory Films in Mexico, 1922–1930," *Americas*, 63(2), October 2006, pp. 225–245.

44. Braudy, 588.

45. Edward Weston, *The Daybooks of Edward Weston*, Vol. I: Mexico, edited by Nancy Newhall (Rochester, N.Y.: George Eastman House, n.d.), 52.

46. On Olín and Modotti, see Hayden Herrera, *Frida: A Biography of Frida Kahlo* (New York: Harper and Row, 1983), 31, 32, 58–59, 80, 85, 86.

47. Taibo, 49. Spanish reads "agresoras de lo que entonces se podía llamar el buen comportamiento social"; "porque estaba vergonzada que yo hubiera tomado parte de tal adefesio." See also Elena Poniatowska, *Tiníssima: A Novel*, translated by Catherine Silver (New York: Penguin Books, 1998), 76. Poniatowska positions her work as fiction but uses extensive primary documents in her re-creation of the story of Tina Modotti.

48. Taibo, 49. Spanish reads "De ropaje blanco, piel oscura, de tipo netamente indígena."

49. Taibo, 50.

50. De los Reyes, *Medio*, 92–93.

51. Gustavo A. García, "In Quest of a National Cinema: The Silent Era," in Joanne Hershfield and David Maciel, editors, *Mexico's Cinema: A Century of Film and Filmmakers* (Wilmington, Del.: SR Books, 1999), 5.

52. Taibo, 50. Spanish reads "En mis primeros años de matrimonio la naturaleza me negó como madre. Me repuse de lo que pudo haber sido traumático, haciendo cine."

53. Taibo, 42–43. Spanish reads "Mi marido parecía feliz, yo diría que divertido, ante lo que le parecía una aventura. El sabía de cine, yo no"; "Pero algunas veces, por la noche, me asustaba; no por las críticas familiares, sino porque yo jamás había actuado. Mis viajes con Jaime, he de decirlo, me habían quitado mucho de lo provincial y ya había estado en bailes importantes y lucido trajes elegantes, pero Hollywood. . . ." See also *Excelsior*, Apr. 12, 1921.

54. See Mariana Figerella, *Edward Weston y Tina Modotti en México: Su inserción dentro de las estrategias estéticas del arte posrevolucionario* (Mexico: Universidad Nacional Autónoma de México: Instituto de Investigaciones Estéticas, 2002), 12, 136. One of the photographs appears on 152.

55. Weston, *The Daybooks*, Vol. 1, 56.

56. Mildred Constantine, *Tina Modotti: A Fragile Life* (New York: Rizzoli, 1983), 154.

57. Ramón, DDR I, 17. Spanish reads " . . . tu decision es magnifica. Te voy a dar un gran baile de despedida y a él vendrán las mas grandes figuras de la sociedad."

58. This account of the festivities is taken from Ramón, DDR I, 70, and from Poniatowska, *Todo II*, 17. Spanish reads ". . . auguro tus éxitos en Hollywood, Dolores;" "Ahora a ver quién se atreve a cerrarte las puertas de su casa."

Chapter 3. Hollywood Baby Beauty

1. Monsiváis, 73.
2. LAT, Nov. 2, 1927.
3. LAT, Sep. 2, 1925. The particular script that Wilson was following is made clear in his discussion of her in a biographical sketch two years later. See Harry D. Wilson, "Official Biography of Dolores del Rio" (Hollywood: n.p., May 5, 1927), MHL, cited in Mary Caudle Beltrán, *Bronze Seduction: The Shaping of Latina Stardom in Hollywood Film and Star Publicity*, doctoral dissertation, University of Texas at Austin, 2002, 90–93.
4. Ramón, DDR I, 22.
5. Ramón, DDR I, 23.
6. Ramón, DDR I, 24. See quotations in Poniatowska, Tomo II, 18. Spanish reads "como siempre, un poco en las nubes. Vivía atrás de los sueños . . . ;" "¡Es como una espada que una trae adentro, como la columna vertebral!"
7. Ramón, DDR I, 24.
8. Taibo, 47. Leider, 153–172.
9. Leider, 5.
10. Poniatowska, 20. Spanish reads "Rodolfo Valentino es el hombre más hermoso que he conocido en mi vida. Llegaba a las fiestas vestido por los mejores sastres de Londres . . . y todas las mujeres se desmayaban a su paso. Tenía un charme enorme y esa especie de suavidad-casi-ternura, característica del hombre latino. Valentino jamás defraudó a su público. Como era un personaje de leyenda nunca rompió la ilusión que miles de mujeres tenían por él."
11. *Cinelandia*, September 1964. Spanish reads "una maravillosa inteligencia;" "una mujer a conquistar o una amistad a cultivar."
12. LAT, Sep. 9, 1925, and Sep. 27, 1925.
13. LAT, Sep. 13, 1925.
14. LAT, Sep. 15, 1925; two stories, Sep. 27, 1925.
15. LAT, Sep. 29, 1925. Ramón, I, 27. See also Adriana Williams, *Covarrubias* (Austin: University of Texas Press, 1994), 18–20.
16. Ramón, DDR I, 25. Photographs are available in DDR III.
17. Ramón, DDR I, 24.
18. LAT, Dec. 6, 1925.
19. LAT, Dec. 8, 1925. WAMPAS was the Western Association of Motion Picture Advertisers.
20. LAT, Dec. 13, 1925.
21. Ramón, DDR I, 25.
22. NYT, Dec. 15 and Dec. 19, 1925.
23. Ramón, DDR I, 24–25.
24. Taibo, 50–54. Spanish reads "es seguro que merece otra cosa"; "Es cierto que principia y que se nota que demasiado que principia, pero ¿no hemos notado también esto mismo en muchas otras actrices que ahora son estrellas?"

25. Jaime Torres Bodet, *Estrella de día* (Madrid: Espasa-Calpe, 1933).

26. LAT, Jan. 24, 1926. Ramón, DDR I, 27.

27. LAT, Feb. 7, 1926.

28. Jaime Martínez del Río to Edwin Carewe, Mar. 1, 1926, DDR 1/5.

29. Ramón, DDR I, 26. *The Whole Town's Talking*, UCLA Film and Television Archive VA 11334 M.

30. See Hershfield, *Imagining la Chica Moderna*.

31. Ramón, I, 26. Spanish reads "convertido cada vez en una especie de principe consorte." There is a discrepancy here in the sources; Del Rio's résumé, DDR/1/915, indicates that *Pals First* was shot before *The Whole Town's Talking*. LAT May 5 and June 9, 1926.

32. Taibo, 63–65.

33. Taibo, 63–65. Spanish reads ". . . yo solía llorar." Poniatowska, *Todo II*, 19. Quote in LAT, May 23, 1926. Calles to del Río, Sep. 14, 1926, DDR 1/6. LAT Aug. 17 and Aug. 18, 1926.

34. LAT, Aug. 1, Aug. 10, and Aug. 13, 1926.

35. LAT, Aug. 12, 1926.

36. Leider, 369. LAT, Sep. 5, 1926.

37. See figures on film distribution in Latin America in FDY 1927, 957, and FDY 1928, 941–943. De los Reyes, DDR, 40, 50. Taibo, 67–69. LAT June 9, 1926.

38. Ramón, I, 26.

39. Wilfred Sheehan to Sol Wurtzel, Sep. 17, 1926, Fox Legal Records, Box 521, UCLA Arts Special Collections. Collection hereafter cited as FX-FLR, followed by box number.

40. "What Price Glory?" Fox Produced Scripts 1034, Arts Special Collections, University of California, Los Angeles. Collection cited hereafter as FX-PRX, followed by a folder number.

41. P. S. Harrison, *Harrison's Reports and Film Reviews*, edited by D. Richard Baer, reprint ed. (Hollywood Film Archive, 1994), vol. 3, Oct. 4, 1926, 194. Cited hereafter as HRFR.

42. Blasting permit, City of Los Angeles, July 10, 1926, to Aug. 10, 1926, FX-FLR 916. *LAT*, May 29, 1959, MHL.

43. "Advance Information," William Fox Dramatic Productions for 1926–27, and Carthay Circle Theater advertisement, both in MHL.

44. *Fox Studio Mirror*, Dec. 7, 1926.

45. HRFR, Vol. 3, 194. Date of review is Dec. 4, 1926.

46. Ramón, DDR I, 27. Williams, *Covarrubias*, 18–20. NYT, Nov. 28, 1926.

47. FDY 1927, 697. Taibo, 69–70. NYT, Nov. 28, 1926.

48. LAT, July 17, 1927.

49. NYT, Oct. 16, 1927.

50. See, for example, Maggie Van Nostrand, "A Balloon in Cactus," http://www.mexconnect.com/articles/1015-a-balloon-in-cactus. Van Nostrand contends, "Today, we have plastic surgery and Botox, but Dolores Del Rio maintained her looks solely through a self-invented diet and exercise program, diligently followed."

51. Haiken, *Venus Envy*, 10.

52. Haiken, *Venus Envy*, 48, 60, 69.

53. Ramón, DDR I, 27–28. Contract between Inspiration Pictures, Inc., and Dolores Del Rio, Nov. 19, 1926, DDR 1/8.

54. Ibid.

55. http://www.imdb.com/name/nm0289297, accessed July 12, 2008.

56. Taibo, 88–91.

57. NYT, May 17, 1927. Flyer for *Resurrection*, DDR 3/3.

58. Taibo, 93. Spanish reads "de loar y ensalzar la magistral labor de Dolores del Río, artista mexicana que ha logrado imponerse contra todas las bajas pasiones y todas las intrigas y todos los obstáculos que se ponen a los que ansían llegar a la gloria y arrancar de su firmamento una estrella para orgullo de nuestra nacionalidad"; "su humilde traje de las mujeres rusas es la expresión universal y humana de la mujer burlada de cualquier raza, de cualquier arte, de cualquier época."

59. FDY 1927, 839.

60. DDR to Carewe, Jan. 19, 1927, FX-FLR-521.

61. Carewe to Sol Wurtzel, Jan. 21, 1927, and Wurtzel to Carewe, July 8, 1927, FX-FLR-521.

62. Carewe to Winfield Sheehan, May 5, 1927, and DDR to Sheehan, May 7, 1927, both in FX-FLR-521.

63. DDR to Carewe, May 7, 1927, FX-FLR-521.

64. Carewe to Sheehan, May 7, 1927, FX-FLR-521.

65. DDR to Sheehan, May 7, 1927, FX-FLR-521.

66. Carewe to Wurtzel, Oct. 24, 1927, FX-FLR-521.

67. LAT, Oct. 9, 1927.

68. Taibo, 82–87; Ramon, I, 32. See also Edwin Carew (sic) file, FX-FLR, UCLA Arts Special Collections.

69. Ugo Schneider Sartori, "Lettere a Dolores del Rio," unidentified clipping from mid- to late 1927 or early 1928, DDR 2/9.

70. Wurtzel to Carewe, July 8, 1927, FX-FLR-521.

71. Carewe to Dolores del Río, no date, DDR 1/133.

72. Taibo, 87. Palma, interview, PHO/2/24.

Chapter 4. Unwelcome Triangle

1. Carewe to del Río, Mar. 22, 1927, DDR 1/17.

2. Helen Hunt Jackson, *A Century of Dishonor: A Sketch of United States Government's Dealings with Some of the Indian Tribes*, reprint of the 1885 edition, foreword by Valerie Sherer Mathes (Norman and London: University of Oklahoma Press, 1995), 337.

3. Unidentified clipping, May 12, 1927, MHL. Toberman Mortgage signed by Dolores del Río and Jaime Martínez del Río, May 12, 1927, DDR 1/28. See also Ramón, I, 32.

4. LAT, July 10, 1927.

5. LAT, July 3, 1927.

6. *Photoplay*, July 1927, 59.

7. Sol Wurtzel to Carewe, Mar. 12, 1927; Carewe to Wurtzel, Mar. 13, 1927, FX-FLR-521.

8. Dolores Del Rio to Edwin Carewe, no date, DDR 1/18.

9. De los Reyes, 142. LAT Sep. 12, 1926.

10. Edwin Carewe to Dolores Del Rio, Feb. 28, 1927, DDR 1/9; Edwin Carewe to Jaime Del Rio, Mar. 3, 1927, DDR 1/11.

11. Edwin Carewe to Dolores Del Rio, Mar. 11, 1927, DDR 1/12; Dolores Del Rio to Edwin Carewe, Mar. 14, 1927, DDR 1/14.

12. LAT May 24, 1926. Schenck quoted in *FDY, 1928,* 825.

13. LAT, Feb. 21, 1926.

14. Balio, *United Artists,* 12–27.

15. *Moving Picture World,* Feb. 1, 1919, 607–8, quoted in Balio, *United Artists,* 13.

16. Quotes from Richard Rowland and Arthur Mayer, in Balio, *United Artists,* 14.

17. Balio, *United Artists,* 57.

18. LAT, Mar. 5 and Mar. 10, 1925. NYT Mar. 11, 1925.

19. Leider, 369.

20. See Carewe to DDR, Mar. 11, 1927, DDR 1/12; Mary Pickford Fairbanks to Madame Jaime Del Rio, Apr. 12, 1927, DDR 1/24.

21. John Considine to Winfield Sheehan, Mar. 12, 1927, FX-FLR-521.

22. Carewe to DDR, Mar. 14 (n.y.), DDR 1/96.

23. DDR to Edwin Carewe, Mar. 13, 1927, DDR 1/13; Edwin Carewe to DDR, Mar. 19, 1927, DDR 1/15.

24. Edwin Carewe to DDR, Mar. 22, 1927, DDR 117. LAT, Feb. 19 and Mar. 30, 1928. De los Reyes, DDR, 143.

25. DDR to Edwin Carewe, Mar. 24, 1927, DDR 1/18.

26. Edwin Carewe to DDR, Mar. 26, 1927, DDR 1/20.

27. Ramón, DDR I, 33.

28. Ramón, DDR I, 33–34. Unidentified clipping, Aug. 9, 1927, MHL.

29. LAT, Sep. 7, 1927. Unidentified clipping, June 8, 1928, MHL. Divorce decree, June 28, 1928, DDR 1/45.

30. Dolores Del Rio, "Achieving Stardom," and Edwin Carewe, "Directorial Training," in *Breaking into the Movies,* edited by Charles Reed Jones (New York: Unicorn Press, 1927), 28–35, 149–155.

31. Del Rio, "Achieving," 30, 32.

32. Unidentified clipping, Oct. 8, 1927, MHL.

33. Taibo, 98–99. Spanish reads "Cuando llegué al cine era una chica modesta y llena de esperanzas. Luché mucho antes de triunfar, pero conseguí abrirme paso. Y cuando mis aspiraciones se materializaron en realidad, caí bajo la zarpa de la calumnia. El amor de un hombre con quien jamás tuve nada que ver me amargó la vida para siempre. Por ese amor, al que mi voluntad era completamente ajena, tuve que divorciarme de mi primer esposo, Jaime del Río. Nos amábamos mucho, pero los injustificados celos de Jaime, obra de calumnia y de la maledicencia, fueron, poco a poco, destruyendo la armonía conyugal. El pobre murió lejos de mí, y según dicen, a consecuencia de nuestra separación. El tuvo la culpa de todo, es verdad, pero era bueno, buenísimo."

34. See, for example, *FDY 1928,* 839.

35. LAT, Sep. 26, 1927.

36. Unidentified clipping, June 8, 1928, MHL.

37. LAT, Mar. 31, 1927.

38. LAT, June 15, 1927.

39. NYT, Sep. 11, 1927.

40. LAT, Sep. 12, 1927.

41. Unidentified clipping, Nov. 4, 1927, MHL. Ramón, *Historia*, 87–93.

42. Ramón, *Historia*, 89.

43. LAT, Sep. 29, 1927.

44. LAT, Oct. 5, 1928.

45. LAT, Oct. 2, 1927 (for information on Finis Fox); June 19, 1927. See Chapter 1. On miscegenation, see Tragen, 271.

46. Dydia DeLyser, *Ramona Memories: Tourism in the Shaping of Southern California* (Minneapolis and London: University of Minnesota Press, 2005), 18, 30.

47. DeLyser, 80–81.

48. Carewe to Wurtzel, Oct. 18, 1917, FX-FLR-521.

49. Carewe to Wurtzel, Oct. 24, 1927 FX-FLR-521.

50. Lessing to Carewe, no date (probably Nov. 7 or Nov. 8, 1927), FX-FLR-521.

51. Wurtzel to Carewe, Oct. 25, 1927, FX-FLR-521.

52. Anna Schneider, memorandum, Nov. 1, 1927, FX-FLR-521.

53. Biography of Henry L. Gates, FX-FLR-521.

54. Unsigned letter to Carewe, Nov. 1, 1927, FX-FLR-521.

55. Carewe to Wurtzel, Nov. 2, 1927, FX-FLR-521.

56. Lessing to Carewe, Nov. 7, 1927, FX-FLR-521.

57. Carewe to Wurtzel, Nov. 7, 1927, FX-FLR-521. Emphasis in the original.

58. Wurtzel to Carewe, Nov. 9, 1927, FX-FLR-521.

59. Lessing to Carewe, Nov. 12, 1927, FX-FLR-521.

60. Unidentified clipping, Nov. 9, 1927, MHL.

61. Carewe to Wurtzel, Oct. 18 and Oct. 25, 1927; Wurtzel to Carewe, Oct. 24, 1927; Lessing to Carewe, no date; Lessing to Carewe, Nov. 7, 1927; in FX-FLR-521.

62. Carewe to Wurtzel, Nov. 10, 1927, FX-FLR-521.

63. Wurtzel to Carewe, Nov. 21 and Nov. 22, 1927; Carewe to Wurtzel, Nov. 10 and Nov. 29, 1927, all in FX-FLR-521.

64. LAT, Dec. 6, 1927.

Chapter 5. Pushing the Envelope

1. Fowles, *Starstruck*, 118.

2. Monsiváis, "Dolores del Rio," 76.

3. Jaime Martínez del Río to DDR, Dec. 5, 1927, DDR 1/1, also quoted in De los Reyes, 54. Spanish reads "No quiero causarte el menor trastorno, pues sé que te sientes muy mal. Vidita, tengo la cabeza hecha un verdadero lío y no puedo pensar, así que dejo que mi corazón hable. Estoy en un estado lastimoso, pues siente que se me ha caído el mundo encima. ¡Es horrible!"; "torpeza"; "Te quiero y te seguiré queriendo toda mi vida con toda mi alma. Cuando pienses en mí te ruego y pido que trates de no hacerlo con dureza. En fin no te puedo decir todo lo que quisiera, todo lo que siento porque mi estado de ánimo es tal que estoy medio loco."

4. Jaime Martínez del Río to DDR, Oct. 6, 1927, DDR 1/2. Spanish reads "pensando en ti—todo el tiempo"; "No se olvide al acostarse de echar una Ave María por mi, te aseguro que lo necesito."

5. Jaime Martínez del Río to DDR, Oct. 9, 1927, DDR 1/3. Spanish reads "frio terrible"; "Solo Dios sabe cuantos grados bajo cero"; "Cuidate mucho, gatita."

6. Jaime Martínez del Río to DDR, Dec. 28, 1927, DDR 1/31. Spanish reads "sentirse solo en medio de una ciudad tan llena de gente."

7. Jaime Martínez del Río to DDR, Feb. (n.d.) 1928, quoted in De los Reyes, 56. Spanish reads "No es justo que me dejen en esta zozobra y si comprendieras por lo que estoy pasando no lo harías." *Chicago Daily Tribune*, Jan. 1, 1928. Cited hereafter as CDT.

8. Taibo, 102, 108–109. LAT, Jan. 15, 1928.

9. LAT, Jan. 3, 1929.

10. See, for example, Mary Pickford Fairbanks to Madame Jaime Del Rio, Apr. 12, 1927, DDR 1/24; Poniatowska, *Todo México*, 20.

11. Unidentified clipping, Dec. 6, 1927, MHL. See also LAT, Dec. 7, 1927.

12. Unidentified clipping, Jan. 2, 1928, MHL.

13. Carewe to DDR, no date, DDR 1/199. This telegram is out of chronological order in the archive.

14. Unidentified clipping, Jan. 20, 1928, MHL.

15. Carewe to Wurtzel, Jan. 26, 1928; F. S. Modern, M.D., to William Fox Studios, Jan. 30, 1928, both in FX-FLR-521.

16. Agreement, Jan. 20, 1928, between Edwin Carewe and Dolores Asúnsolo Martínez del Río, DDR 1/38.

17. Unidentified clippings, Jan. 7, Jan. 20, Jan. 21, and Feb. 9, 1928, MHL.

18. James Ryan to Wurtzel, Feb. 9 and Feb. 20, 1928, FX-FLR-521.

19. NYT, Feb. 19, 1928. Emphasis mine.

20. LAT, Feb. 27, 1928.

21. LAT, Mar. 4, 1928.

22. LAT, Apr. 1, 1928.

23. WP, Feb. 12, 1928.

24. LAT, Apr. 15, 1928; Aug. 30, 1928.

25. Ramón, *Historia*, 96–97; unidentified clipping, Mar. 12, 1928, MHL.

26. Unidentified clipping, Mar. 22, 1928, MHL.

27. Unidentified clipping, Mar. 25, 1928, MHL.

28. De los Reyes, DDR, 58.

29. LAT, Mar. 13, 1928.

30. LAT, Mar. 25, 1928.

31. De los Reyes, 58. Ramón, DDR, I, 36. Taibo, 102. LAT, Apr. 1, 1928.

32. Unidentified clippings, Apr. 1 and Apr. 2, 1928.

33. Hershfield, 3. For Valentino, see for example Leider, chapters 8 and 9, 125–172.

34. Hershfield, xv.

35. This term appears in Hershfield, 10.

36. LAT, Feb. 26, 1928.

37. LAT, Mar. 20, 1928.

38. LAT, Mar. 25, 1928.

39. LAT, Apr. 11, 1928.

40. LAT, Apr. 4, 1928.

41. NYT, May 15, 1928.

42. Del Rio, "Achieving," 34–35. Ramón, *Historia*, 95. Taibo, 116; Spanish reads "horroroso." LAT, Oct. 2, 1927.

43. Taibo, 116, 118. Spanish reads "horroroso"; "Ya no era una mujer rusa dolorida, sino una mujer que se acercaba mucho a mí." Ramón, *Historia*, 88–89.

44. Ramón, DDR, I, 34–35. Taibo, 116. Spanish reads "horroroso." NYT, Mar. 30, 1928. *Atlanta Constitution*, cited hereafter as AC, Mar. 30, 1928. *Chicago Daily Tribune*, Mar. 30, 1928.

45. CDT, Mar. 30 and July 29, 1928.

46. CDT, July 5, 1928.

47. *Variety*, Apr. 25, 1928, in MHL. Taibo, 98–102.

48. Two unidentified clippings, Apr. 20, 1928, MHL. LAT, Apr. 21, 1928.

49. Unidentified clipping, Apr. 21, 1928, MHL.

50. Quoted in De los Reyes, 59. Spanish reads " . . . a medida que aumenta su éxito, disminuye la importancia del marido, quién poco a poco va perdiendo toda personalidad y convirtiéndose en una especie de fantasmón. Dolores, dicho sea en honor de la verdad, hizo cuanto estaba de su parte por resguardar mi amor propio, esforzándose siempre en darme el lugar que me correspondía; pero la batalla estaba perdida de antemano. Yo no me sentía feliz en aquel ambiente y Dolores lo comprendía."

51. Unidentified clipping, Apr. 23, 1928, MHL.

52. Unidentified clipping, Apr. 24, 1928, MHL.

53. Unidentified clipping, May 28, 1928, MHL.

54. See LAT, Sep. 22, Sep. 24, and Oct. 2, 1925; Feb. 28, May 20, and Aug. 29, 1926; June 17, 1927.

55. De los Reyes, *Dolores Del Río*, 62–63. Alvaro Obregón to Dolores del Río, May 12, May 28, and June 14, 1928, DDR/1/42, 43, 46. Spanish reads "emancipación," as in de los Reyes; "admirador y amigo," as in Obregón to del Río, June 14.

56. Ramón, *Historia*, 95.

57. De los Reyes, DDR, 143–145.

58. Tino Balio, *United Artists: The Company Built by the Stars* (Madison and London: University of Wisconsin Press, 1976), 40–41.

59. Ramón, *Historia*, 97.

60. WP, June 29, 1928.

61. Two unidentified clippings, May 29 and June 1, 1928, MHL.

62. Unidentified clipping, June 8, 1928, MHL. The actual divorce decree in her archive stated June 28, 1928, DDR 1/45. Spanish reads "la incompatibilidad tanto de caracteres como de carreras artísticas. . . ."

63. Two unidentified clippings, Aug. 2 and Aug. 3, 1928, MHL. For "highest what is," see Chapter 4.

64. *London Evening Standard, London Evening News*, Aug. 24, 1928, DDR 2/12.

65. *London Daily News and the Westminster Gazette*, Aug. 24, 1928, both in DDR 2/6.

66. *London Evening Standard*, Aug. 24, 1928, DDR 2/13. Capitalization as in the original.

67. *London Daily Sketch*, Aug. 25, 1928, DDR 2/17.

68. *London Daily Express*, Aug. 25, 1928, DDR 2/19.

69. *London Daily Mail*, Aug. 25, 1928, DDR 2/20.

70. *The Daily News and the Westminster Gazette*, Aug. 25, 1928, DDR 2/21.

71. *Cinelandia*, no date, DDR 2/80. Spanish reads ". . . ¿nos arruinará el cine sonoro?;" "todavía dubiosos"; "detestable"; "Una interesante 'pose' de 'nuestra' Dolores."

72. *London Daily Mail*, Aug. 29, 1928, DDR/3/25; *London Daily News*, Aug. 29, 1928, both in DDR 2/25.

73. Ramón, *Historia*, 99.

74. *L'Ami du Peuple*, Aug. 31, 1928, DDR 2/33.

75. *London Daily Mail*, Aug. 31, 1928, DDR 2/59.

76. Two unidentified clippings, Aug. 29 and Aug. 30, 1928, MHL. LAT, Dec. 5, and Dec. 8, 1928.

77. Unidentified clipping, Aug. 24, 1928, MHL.

78. Unidentified clippings, Sep. 17, 1928, DDR 2/81. German reads "Dolores ist hier!"

79. *La Settima Arte*, October 1928, DDR 2/40.

80. De los Reyes, DDR, 64.

81. *New York World*, n.d., DDR 2/56.

82. *El Latino-Americano*, Nov. 4, 1928, DDR 2/57. Spanish reads "un sombrerito mefistofélico negro"; "No estoy sola, estoy con mama, y con respeto a casamiento, no, no, y no."

83. De los Reyes, DDR, 64.

84. *Screenland*, November 1928, DDR 3/88; *Screen Book*, November 1928, DDR 3/89.

85. Four unidentified clippings, Dec. 4, 1928, MHL. De los Reyes, DDR, 66. LAT, Dec. 5, 1928.

86. Two unidentified clippings, Dec. 5, 1928, MHL.

87. LAT, Dec 5, 1928.

88. NYT, Dec. 6, 1928.

89. Unidentified clipping, Dec. 7, 1928, MHL. (Story itself datelined Berlin, Dec. 7.) Taibo, 110. AC, Dec. 8, 1928.

90. LAT, Dec. 8, 1928.

91. Taibo, 110–111. Spanish reads "Te adoro"; "¿Creen ustedes que Dolores viene?" "Mi Jaime."

92. Taibo, 111.

93. Taibo, 115. Spanish reads "Me quedé viuda después de divorciarme; así me sentía yo después de la muerte de Jaime"; "Hollywood no tiene compasión."

94. NYT, Dec. 9, 1928. LAT Dec. 9, 1928. AC Dec. 11, 1928.

95. Dr. Emil Kammerer to Dolores del Rio, Dec. 8, 1928, DDR 1/53. French reads "la plus grande stupéfaction"; "un parfait gentilhomme."

96. Unidentified clipping, Apr. 4, 1929, MHL.

Chapter 6. Fame and Its Perils

1. Gamson, *Claims to Fame*, 27.

2. Braudy, 9.

3. Ramón, *Historia*, 102.

4. *Evangeline* sheet music, DDR 3/90.

5. De los Reyes, 66. Spanish reads "el encuentro, la separación, la búsqueda y la perdida de la amada. . . ."

6. Unidentified clipping, Feb. 15, 1929, MHL.

7. See reports of runs in major cities for *Ramona* and *Revenge* in FDY 1929, 871.

8. Unidentified clipping, Apr. 3, 1929, MHL.

9. LAT Apr. 28, 1929.

10. LAT, Nov. 7, 1928.

11. Carewe to DDR, June 14, 1929, DDR 1/58.

12. Ramón, *Historia*, 104–105.

13. Ramón, DDR I, 37–38.

14. WP, June 28, 1929.

15. De los Reyes, 67. The author here is referencing reports in Mexico City publications *El Universal* and *Excelsior.*

16. WP, July 11, 1929.

17. *Variety,* July 31, 1929, MHL.

18. *Film Daily,* Aug. 4, 1929, MHL.

19. Unidentified clipping, September 1929, MHL.

20. Marques de Guadalupe to Dolores del Río, March 1929, DDR 1/54.

21. Federico Gamboa to Dolores del Río, Aug. 1, 1930, DDR 1/65. Spanish reads "un nuevo triunfo para Ud. en su trayectoria ascendente de estrella, un halago para nuestro México, y un beneficio para mi"; "Si la hipocresía de aquellas gentes opusiese reparos al asunto de SANTA, deje Ud. que la modifiquen a su gusto, siempre que no me la destrocen y cambien en cosa distinta."

22. Gregorio Martínez Sierra to Dolores del Río, July 20, 1930, DDR 1/64.

23. Taibo, 127–128.

24. Edwin Carewe to DDR, May 25, 1929, DDR 1/57.

25. Edwin Carewe to DDR, June 14, 1929, DDR 1/59. See also Carewe to DDR, no date, DDR 1/199, which is out of chronological order in the archive.

26. Ramón, *Historia*, 105.

27. LAT, Dec. 9, 1931.

28. Ramón, DDR I, 38.

29. Contract between Dolores Del Rio and Feature Productions, signed by DDR and John Considine, Jr., Oct. 28, 1929, DDR 1/ 62.

30. LAT Oct. 31, 1929, Dec. 9, 1931.

31. Ramón, *Historia*, 103. De los Reyes, 67.

32. LAT, Dec. 5, 1929.

33. Unidentified clippings, two from July 23 and July 24, 1930, May 23 and Sep. 17, 1931, MHL. LAT, Aug. 17, Aug. 18, and Sep. 21, 1926; Feb. 7, Feb. 10, and Mar. 10, 1927; and July 17, 1928.

34. Dolores Del Río as told to Gladys Hall, "Discoveries About Myself," Dec. 23 (no year), manuscript, MHL. Emphasis in the original.

35. Taibo, 128.

36. Ramón, *Historia*, 109.

37. Unidentified clipping, May 23, 1930, MHL. LAT, July 24, 1930.

38. Unidentified clipping, July 24, 1930, MHL.

39. Ramón, *Historia*, 110. De los Reyes, 70.

40. Scott Eyman, *Lion of Hollywood: The Life and Legend of Louis B. Mayer* (New York: Simon and Schuster, 2005), 209. *Toronto Star,* Mar. 21, 1986. Ramón, *Historia*, 119.

41. Eyman, 210.

42. Ramón, *Historia*, 111–112.

43. Ramón, *Historia*, 130.

44. Rodríguez Estrada, 475–484. Vélez soon moved on to *Tarzan* star Johnny Weissmuller, whom she married in 1933, but the explosive sexual publicity contin-

ued. Divorcing Weissmuller in 1939 after a marriage of violence, both physical and mental, she moved from man to man but married no one. Ultimately, Vélez wound up pregnant and alone, committing suicide in 1944. Rodríguez Estrada also attributes the different receptions of the two women to del Río's lack of ethnic identification and to Vélez's "sexual personification . . . distinctly meshed with her ethnicity."

45. NYT, Nov. 22, 1931. Cedric Gibbons, http://www.answers.com/topic/cedric -gibbons, accessed May 24, 2010.

46. Ramón, *Historia*, 116–117.

47. LAT, July 20, 1930.

48. Ramón, *Historia*, 123.

49. Unidentified clippings, two on Apr. 7 and Apr. 23, 1930, and one for Aug. 1, 1930, MHL; NYT, July 31, 1930; LAT, Aug. 1, 1930. Taibo, 132. Spanish reads "nada se sabía de esta relación."

50. LAT, Aug. 7, 1930.

51. Unidentified clippings, Aug. 1, Aug. 6, and Aug. 7 (2), 1930, MHL; NYT, Aug. 7, 1930; CDT, Aug. 7, 1930. See also photograph in De los Reyes, 70.

52. Unidentified clippings, Aug. 27 and Sep. 26, 1930, MHL. NYT, Aug. 27, 1930.

53. Barry Paris, *Garbo* (Minneapolis: University of Minnesota Press, 1994), 249. Taibo, 138. Spanish reads "una enfermedad delicada"; "El se portó como un matrimonio ideal."

54. NYT, Nov. 27, 1930.

55. Cedric Gibbons to DDR, n.d., DDR 1/1013.

56. Unidentified clippings, May 23 and Sep. 17, 1931, MHL; LAT, Sep. 17, 1931.

57. Unidentified clipping, Dec. 2, 1931, MHL.

58. Unidentified clipping, Dec. 3, 1931, MHL.

59. LAT, Dec. 9, 1931; Unidentified clippings, Dec. 7 and Dec. 8, 1931, MHL. Orthography as in the originals.

60. Unidentified clippings, Dec. 7 and Dec. 8, 1931, MHL.

61. Unidentified clipping, Dec. 8, 1931, MHL. See also LAT, Dec. 8, 1931.

62. Unidentified clipping, Dec. 15, 1931, MHL. LAT, Dec. 16, 1931.

Chapter 7. Second Chance

1. Fowles, *Starstruck*, 223.

2. Gladys Hall, "Second Chance," manuscript, June 22, 1931, MHL. Hall's manuscript is in draft, and many of the words are misspelled and almost unreadable, although decipherable in context. I have corrected the orthography for the quotes from this document.

3. Hall, "Second Chance."

4. Hall, "Second Chance."

5. Hall, "Second Chance."

6. Hall, "Second Chance." Emphasis in the original.

7. Hall, "Second Chance."

8. Taibo, 138–139. Spanish reads "Era hombre que me trataba de manera un poco paternal, cuidándome. Los dos habíamos tenido un gran amor que terminó tristemente. Muy triste. El era en la Metro toda una institución, incluso los obreros lo admiraban. Creo que su característica más visible era la elegancia, el comportamiento correcto y una educación muy sólida. Siempre sabía lo que quería y era capaz de imponer su punto

de vista artístico a estrellas que la gente consideraba intratable. No me dejó conocer la casa en la que viviríamos hasta que la dio por terminada. Entonces, me tomó en los brazos y entró conmigo. Yo le había dicho que adoraba la lluvia; así que me sentó en un sillón y fue a apretar unos botones; a través de los grandes cristales de un ventanal comencé a ver caer la lluvia. Había dispuesto un mecanismo para que yo tuviera lluvia cuando me apeteciera."

9. Taibo, 139. Fowles, *Starstruck*, 203.

10. See, for example, LAT Jan. 11 and Apr. 15, 1931, Dec. 27, 1933, and CDT Jan. 16, 1932.

11. Paris, 84–101, 155. Quote is from Diana McLellan, *The Girls: Sappho Goes to Hollywood* (New York: LA Weekly Books, 2000), 60.

12. Quoted in Paris, 98.

13. Quoted in Paris, 98.

14. LAT June 6, 1928.

15. LAT Jan. 3, 1929, and Jan. 7, 1930.

16. Stephen Bach, *Marlene Dietrich: Life and Legend* (New York: William Morrow, 1992), 97–121.

17. Quotes from Bach, 119.

18. Quotes from Bach, 119–120.

19. Quotes from Bach, 191.

20. Bach, 191–197.

21. Poniatowska, Tomo II, 21. Spanish reads "Es la figura más fabulosa del cine, es excepcionalmente inteligente y llena de complejos. Tiene pavor a la gente. No es ninguna pose o recurso publicitario, sencillamente, no deja que la gente llegue a ella porque le tiene pánico. Está dominada por el miedo . . . Tiene miedo de defraudarse a sí misma."

22. Interview with Alicia Rocha, *Cinelandia*, September 1964, in DDR 2/318. Spanish reads "Greta Garbo es la mujer más extraordinaria que—en el arte—haya cruzado por mi vida"; "Era como si tuviera diamantes en los huesos y su luz interior pugnará por salir por los poros de su piel"; "una niñez tremenda; y había pasado muchos hambres y frios en el cuerpo y en el alma y esto le había creado una enorme cantidad de timidez y complejos. . . . Una persona le había herido y las rosas nunca reponen el pétalo arrancado." Del Río frequently used the same image in speaking about Garbo; the researcher will find it elsewhere, as it appears in several of her interviews.

23. Poniatowska, Tomo II, 21. Spanish reads "lo contrario de Greta. Extrovertida, le encantan las fiestas, la publicidad, que la vean, los grandes romances y que todo el mundo se entere de sus cosas. Lo más dificil para una mujer es tener rodillas preciosas y Marlene además de esas piernas tan famosas tiene las rodillas más bellas que uno pueda imaginar. ¡Fantásticas!"

24. Paris, 135.

25. Bach, 203–207.

26. Bach, 130.

27. See Chapter 4 for indications of problems with Schenck; for Monroe, see Barbara Leaming, *Marilyn Monroe* (New York: Three Rivers Press, 1998), 25.

28. NYT, Nov. 30, 1930.

29. Feature Productions, to Dolores Del Rio, Sep. 30, 1930, DDR 1/68.

30. Ramón, *Historia*, 132.

31. NYT, Nov 6, 1980. For the nightmares, see Ramón, *Historia*, 130.

32. Brendan Gill, "Cedric Gibbons and Dolores Del Rio: The Art Director and the Star of *Flying Down to Rio* in Santa Monica," *Architectural Digest: Academy Awards Collector's Edition*, April 1992.

33. Eyman, 67–70, 134–135.

34. Ramón, *Historia*, 130.

35. Taibo, 142.

36. Gill, "Cedric," *Architectural Digest*.

37. NYT, Dec. 18, 1986.

38. Eyman, 209.

39. Ramón, *Historia*, 134.

40. Fernando Gamboa to Dolores del Río, Feb. 10, 1931, DDR 1/70. Spanish reads "Mi bella amiga"; "Dolores del Río, y sólo Dolores del Río, a la que desde aqui le beso los pies y por cuya completa salud se interesa cordialmente. . . ."

41. De los Reyes, 70, 121–122.

42. Quote in de los Reyes, *Medio*, 123. Spanish reads "Esa mujer que pecó por hambre y miseria y a la cual un amor redimió y consumió, viene a ser la esencia de un personaje fundamental: 'la sufrida mujer mexicana.'"

43. Phil Berg to Dolores del Río, Feb. 3, 1931, DDR 1/71; Raoul Walsh to Dolores del Río, Mar. 30, 1931, DDR 1/72.

44. Raoul Walsh, *Each Man in His Time: The Life Story of a Director* (New York: Farrar, Straus & Giroux, 1974), 188–189, 341.

45. *Sheboygan Press*, Apr. 6, 1931.

46. Budget of Production Cost, *The Dove*, RKO Production Files no. 37, UCLA Arts Special Collection. Archive hereafter cited as RKO-P-, followed by folder number.

47. See Daily Production Reports, Oct. 9 and Oct. 21, 1931, and Nov. 2, 1931, RKO-P-521.

48. NYT, Jan. 9, 1932.

49. NYT, Jan. 10, 1932.

50. Hall, "Second Chance." Florenz Ziegfeld to Cedric Gibbons, Dec. 16, 1931, DDR 1/75; and DDR to Ziegfeld, Feb. 17, 1931, DDR 1/77.

51. Taibo,154. NYT, May 9, 1932. LAT, May 10, 1932. Mora, 60, 70.

52. NYT, Feb. 7, 1932.

53. Ramón, *Historia*, 132.

54. *Bird of Paradise*, videotape, Hollywood Classics Collector's Edition, Madacy Entertainment Group, 1996.

55. LAT Mar. 18, Apr. 1, and Apr. 17, 1932.

56. LAT Apr. 23, 1932.

57. Carl J. Mora, *Mexican Cinema: Reflections of a Society 1896–1988* (Berkeley and Los Angeles: University of California Press: Revised Edition, 1989), 48.

58. Mora, 38.

59. *Memo from: David O. Selznick*, 74.

60. Ramón, *Historia*, 136.

61. The Reminiscences of Joel McCrea (Aug. 2, 1971), 6–7, in the Oral History Collection of Columbia University. Collection hereafter cited as OHC/CU.

62. Ramón, *Historia*, 136–137. Irene Mayer Selznick, *A Private View* (New York: Alfred A. Knopf, 1983), photograph section between pages 154 and 155.

63. Taibo, 138. Spanish reads "El mundo de cine es muy duro, está lleno de intrigas y maledicencias; Cedric parecía ajeno a todas estas cosas tan tristes. El matrimonio entre dos gentes del cine no es fácil. Cedric estaba rodeada de mujeres muy bellas y yo de galanes; era irremediable que los celos aparecieran de cuando en cuando."

64. Ramón, *Historia*, 137. Daily Production Reports, Feb. 6, 8, 10, and 13, 1932, RKO-P-16.

65. Daily Production Reports, Apr. 25, May 15, and May 16, 1932, RKO-P-521.

66. NYT, Aug. 7, 1932.

67. Taibo, *Historia*, 139. A somewhat different version of the Welles story appears in Simon Callow, *Orson Welles: The Road to Xanadu* (New York: Viking Press, 1995), 472. *Bird of Paradise* videotape, HCV-3–6119, Madacy Entertainment Group, 1996.

68. Taibo, 144–146. Spanish reads "un genio"; "Fuerte, moreno, concentrado"; "como una película dentro de una película"; "Tomaba un grupo de bailarinas y bailarines y los convertía en piezas de un espectáculo; en parte de un inmenso juego." Ramón, *Historia*, 137. NYT, Aug. 7, 1932. Reminiscences of Busby Berkeley (Aug. 4, 1971), 1–2, 6, OHC/CU.

69. Ramón, *Historia*, 139. NYT, Sep. 10, 1932.

70. *Bird of Paradise*, publicity handout, DDR 2/100.

71. See "The Hays Office," *Fortune Magazine*, vol. 18 (December 1938), reprinted in Tino Balio, editor, *The American Film Industry* (University of Wisconsin Press, 1976), 295–314. For Mae West, see the fascinating account in Jill Watts, *Mae West: An Icon in Black and White* (New York: Oxford University Press, 2001), 170–197; the quote from LAT appears on 170. For details on establishment of the Breen office, see http://en.wikipedia.org/wiki/Pre-Code_Hollywood, accessed May 25, 2010.

72. Watts, *Mae West*, 174.

73. Watts, *Mae West*, 181, 185.

74. LAT Nov. 6, 1932.

75. CDT Oct. 2 and Nov. 27, 1932.

76. Taibo, 158. Spanish reads "En México, el ya muy frágil prestigio social de Dolores fue destruido por la historia del baño en las islas del sur. Sobre todo porque la imaginación popular exageró la desnudez y aun las incidencias amorosas alrededor del baño. . . ." The supposed exclusion of the scenes from the Mexican cut of the film is noted in Taibo on 158.

77. NYT, June 19, 1932.

78. Princess Sushila of Kala to DDR, n.d., DDR 1/88.

79. Betty Lasky, *RKO, The Biggest Little Major of Them All* (Santa Monica: Round-table, 1989), 100.

80. *Flying Down to Rio* videotape, Nostalgia Merchants, Fox Hills Video, 1987.

81. LAT, Dec. 8, 1933; NYT, Dec. 22, 1933. Quote in NYT.

82. Budget of Production Cost, RKO-P-37.

83. Ramón, DDR I, 48.

84. See Selznick to B. P. Schulberg, Apr. 15, 1931, in *Memo*, 63 in regard to the limited roles he felt del Río could play. Hershfield, in *The Invention of Dolores del Río*, discusses the racialized portrait in *Bird of Paradise* at length, 25–32, but does not make the connection to Selznick's attitudes and his other films.

85. Raymond Durgnat and Scott Simmon, *King Vidor, American* (Berkeley: University of California Press, 1988), 138.

86. Ramón, DDR/I, 49. Spanish reads "un máximo símbolo sexual." See also Contract, DDR and P. A. Chase of Warner Brothers, Nov. 1, 1933, DDR 1/84. On Agua Caliente, see Paul J. Vanderwood, *Satan's Playground: Mobsters and Movie Stars at America's Greatest Gaming Resort* (Durham, N.C.: Duke University Press, 2010), 230–231. *Wonder Bar* videotape, M202557, MGM/UA Home Video, Turner.

87. NYT, Mar. 1, 1934.

88. WP Aug. 20, 1934.

89. Alfonso Reyes to DDR, Mar. 22, 1933, DDR 1/80. Spanish reads "que ya ha superado Ud. del todo con su vida y su gloriosa carrera"; "mi admiración y mi simpatía"; "el millón de adoradores"; "un importuno más"; "si no es mucho pedir."

90. Ramón, *Historia*, 150. Spanish reads "una mujer inconmensurablemente bella, famosa, rica, triunfadora, gloriosa, una mujer del brazo de un hombre guapísimo, refinado, un magnate de Hollywood."

91. See, for example, Vanderwood, 141.

92. Ramón, *Historia*, 150–153.

93. Ramón, *Historia*, 154. Spanish reads "hombres de ciencia, de literatos, de artistas, de hombres de armas"; "Porque es una mujer mexicana genuina, representativa de nuestra raza, de innegables dotes artísticas internacionalmente reconocidas. Porque su triunfo es de la belleza, la gracia y el encanto femeninos, en síntesis, perfumada y esplendorosa. Porque no ha necesitado para encumbrarse dañar a nadie. Su elevación a un tiempo grácil y vertiginosa se ha fincado en hacer vivir a las multitudes inapreciables horas de ensueño"; "la expression plástica y dinámica de la mujer ideal."

94. These were *The Widow from Monte Carlo, In Caliente, Madame DuBarry, I Live for Love*. DDR 1/915, 1978.

95. Taibo, 178. Poniatowska, 22–23.

Chapter 8. Affair

1. Alice Tildesley, "A Discussion of Love by Dolores Del Rio," press release, May 23, 1937, DDR 2/110.

2. Ramón, *Historia*, 207.

3. *Gallup Looks at the Movies: Increasing Profits with Continuous Audience Research* (Princeton: Audience Research Institute, 1941), 6, 14, 29. For quote, see Barbara Leaming, *If This Was Happiness: A Biography of Rita Hayworth* (New York: Viking, 1989), 29, 36.

4. Paris, 372–383; quotation on 383. See also Bach, chapters 12 and 13, 230–267.

5. Maria Riva, *Marlene Dietrich* (London: Bloomsbury, 1992), 438, 492. Bach, 230–231, 248–262.

6. André Soares, *Beyond Paradise: The Life of Ramón Novarro* (New York: St. Martin's Press, 2002), 235–238, 248–271.

7. Available in UCLA Film and Television Archive, VA16432M.

8. Gregory Black, *Hollywood Censored: Morality Codes, Catholics, and the Movies* (Cambridge: Cambridge University Press, 1994), 176–178.

9. Taibo, 169–172. Ramón, *Historia*, 157–160.

10. Ramón, *Historia*, 146. Harry Edington to Douglas Fairbanks Jr., Mar. 16, 1936,

and Fairbanks to Edington Mar. 16, 1936, DDR 1/97. See also Jack Gordean to DDR, no date but late 1937 or early 1938, DDR 1/140.

11. Ramón, *Historia*, 167.

12. Harry Edington to Douglas Fairbanks, Jr., Mar. 17, 1936, DDR 1/101; Edington to Dolores del Rio, Mar. 23, 1936, DDR 1/102; F. M. Guedalla to Dolores del Rio, Apr. 1, 1936; contract between Criterion Film Productions Ltd. and Miss Dolores Del Rio, Apr. 28, 1936, DDR 1/120.

13. Marcel Hellman to DDR, Apr. 21, 1936, DDR 1/117; Hellman to Dolores del Rio, Apr. 20, 1936, DDR 1/118.

14. Ramón, *Historia*, 168. Spanish reads "las personas inteligentes y cultivadas"; "la reina de Hollywood."

15. Del Rio to Beverly Hills Hotel, July (no day), 1936, DDR 1/129.

16. Jack Gordean to del Río, Dec. 9, 1937, DDR 1/130.

17. Quoted in Taibo, 177–180. Spanish reads "una gran pena me impide ser feliz"; "compañero tierno y respetuoso"; "Sabe dios que la culpa no tiene Cedric, que hizo todo lo posible porque olvidara mi pena. Cuando estoy a su lado soy desazón sin limites, por una intensa desesperación."

18. Quoted in Taibo, 178.

19. Phil Berg to Dolores del Rio, Mar. 26, 1936, DDR 1/103; Berg to del Rio, Mar. 6, 1936, DDR 1/104; Berg to del Rio Mar. 7, 1936, DDR 1/105; del Rio to Berg, Mar. 7, 1936, DDR 1/109; del Rio to Berg, Apr. 9, 1936, DDR 1/113; Berg to del Rio, May 16, 1936, DDR 1/126. See also Ramón, *Historia*, 169–170; de los Reyes, 151.

20. Jack Gordean, Famous Artists, to Dolores del Río, Dec. 9, 1937, DDR 1/130; Gordean to Dolores del Río, Dec. 21, 1937, DDR 1/131.

21. Ramón, *Historia*, 170–174.

22. *Lancer Spy*, UCLA Film Archive, VA22950M.

23. Berg to Dolores del Río, Jan. 3, 1937, DDR 1/143; Berg to del Río, Oct. 4, 1937, DDR 1/144; M. C. Levee to del Río, Mar. 1, 1938, DDR 1/146; Levee to del Río, Dec. 14, 1938, DDR 1/148; John Hyde to del Río, Nov. 3, 1939, DDR 1/161.

24. Gordean to del Río, Dec. 9, 1937, DDR 1/130.

25. Alice Tildesley, "A Discussion of Love by Dolores Del Rio," press release, May 23, 1937, DDR 2/110.

26. WP, Mar. 16, 1940; LAT, Mar. 16, 1940; *Los Angeles Herald*, Dec. 18, 1940, MHL. *Los Angeles Herald* cited in hereafter as LAH. See, for example, LAT May 31, Sep. 3, and Sep. 24, 1939.

27. Ramón, *Historia*, 181–184.

28. Ramón, *Historia*, 185. *Christian Science Monitor*, May 25, 1939, hereinafter cited as CSM. WP, July 26, 1936. LAT July 29, 39.

29. CSM Sep. 8, 1939.

30. LAT, Dec. 25, 1939; CDT, Dec. 26, 1939.

31. LAT, Jan . 14, 1940.

32. LAT, Jan. 14 and Feb. 4, 1940; WP, Mar. 27, 1940.

33. Diego Rivera to DDR, June 12, 1940, DDR 1/167. Spanish reads "Maravillosa Lolita"; "la muchacha mas preciosa que he vista en su (sic) vida y que eres tú"; "al mas afortunado de los hombres que es Orson Welles."

34. Quoted in Ramón, *Historia*, 198. Spanish reads "el más feliz de los locutores

de radio que envidian todos los pintores del mundo"; "La más linda, la más preciosa del oeste y del este y del norte y del sur, perdidamente enamorado de tí como los cuarenta millones de mexicanos y los ciento veinte de americanos que no pueden equivocarse."

35. Barbara Leaming, *Orson Welles* (New York: Viking, 1985), 206–207.

36. LAT, Jan. 23, 1940.

37. HRFR, Vol. 4, 154, and Vol. 5, 435, 439, 457, 467. See also www.imdb.com/name/nm0288986, nm0013688, and nm0289297, accessed Apr. 27, 2009.

38. LAT, Jan. 25, 1940.

39. Ramón, *Historia*, 189.

40. LAT, July 20, 1940.

41. Ramón, *Historia*, 188–190, 190. Spanish reads "La fuerza casi animal, magnética que Orson proyectaba acabó por seducir a la muy propia señora que por primera vez en su vida se vió en los brazos de un hombre que no era su marido."

42. Fay Wray, *On the Other Hand: A Life Story* (New York: St. Martin's Press, 1989), 136.

43. LAH, Dec. 18, 1940, MHL; LAT Mar. 16, 1940.

44. LAH, Dec. 18, 1940, MHL; LAT Mar. 16, 1940.

45. CDT, Mar. 25, 1940.

46. *Los Angeles Examiner*, Jan. 18, 1941, MHL. Hereafter cited as LAE. For quotations see also Wray, 136.

47. *News 4*, Jan. 18, 1941, MHL.

48. LAE, Dec. 31, 1940, MHL.

49. Dolores Del Rio Gibbons, Plaintiff, vs. Cedric Gibbons, Defendant, No. D 200 654, Final judgment of divorce, DDR 1/186. Ramón, *Historia*, 190–191.

50. Ramón, *Historia*, 188–189. De los Reyes, DDR, 152. *Kingsport Times*, Kingsport, Tenn., Mar. 31, 1940, for photograph; *Charleston Gazette*, July 22, 1940, for film announcement. Contract for *The Man from Dakota*, Loew's (producer), Feb. 13, 1940, DDR 1/161.

51. Ramón, *Historia*, 174–177. Spanish reads "la más exquisita belleza mexicana imaginable;" "del ideal de la belleza india o mestiza mexicana. . . ."

52. Herrera, *Frida*, 198–199, 278–279. Author's conversation with Arturo García Bustos, June 2007.

53. Frida Kahlo to DDR, Sep. 27, 1939, DDR 1/159. Kahlo to DDR, Mar. (no day), 1940, DDR 1/165. Spanish reads ". . . no pienses en ningún momento que es un abuso de mi parte el no haberte devuelto tu dinero"; ". . . no seas mala niña"; "Dime linda cómo estás y si pronto piensas venir a México. Todos te estrañamos *harto*"; "todavía lo quiero más que a mi vida. . . ."

54. Information and quotation in Simon Callow, *Orson Welles: The Road to Xanadu* (New York: Viking, 1995), 472–473; see also de los Reyes, DDR, 85; Taibo, 189.

55. LAT, June 14 and June 27, 1940.

56. Ramón, *Historia*, 198. Spanish reads "explosivo."

57. See Norman Krasna to Orson Welles, Feb. 17, 1941, DDR 1/171; King Vidor to Orson Welles, Feb. 15, 1941, DDR 1/172; Tim Durant to Orson Welles, Feb. 26, 1941, DDR 1/173; Frank Capra to Orson Welles, Mar. 22, 1941, DDR 1/174; Nunnally Johnson to Orson Welles, Mar. 24, 1941, DDR 1/175; Noel Coward to Orson Welles, Apr. 1, 1941, DDR 1/176; Sinclair Lewis to Orson Welles, May 2, 1941, DDR 1/178. See also Ramón, *Historia*, 192.

58. Leaming, *Orson*, 215–216.

59. CDT, May 7, 1941.

60. LAT, May 4, May 6, May 7, and May 9, 1941.

61. Last Will and Testament of Dolores del Río, L. Arnold Weissberger, Counselor at Law, Apr. 4, 1941, DDR 1/177.

62. Reminiscences of Jerome Zerbe (Aug. 15, 1979), 196–198, OHC/CU.

63. Orson Welles and Peter Bogdanovich, *This Is Orson Welles* (Da Capo Press: 1st paperback edition, 1998), 365.

64. Welles and Bogdanovich, 25–26, 38–39, 177–180.

65. Welles and Bogdanovich, 177–180. Callow, Vol. 2, 199.

66. Leaming, *Orson*, 204–206.

67. Leaming, *Orson*, 208–211. Welles and Bogdanovich, 86. Quotation in Callow, I, 550.

68. Quote in LAT, Oct. 3, 1941.

69. Ramón, *Historia*, 194–201. Quotation, on page 198, reads "que evita el melodrama y que consiste en una verdadera lección de guión cinematográfico y de traducción de una obra literaria al cine. . . ." Another of Dolores's biographers believes that Welles was not the author of the manuscript, found by Ramón among del Río's papers with a notation "Orson" in her hand in the margin of one of the interior pages. He thinks that the script was actually written by Chano Urueta, a prominent Mexican director who was deeply involved in trying to put the *Santa* project together, and that Orson commented on it rather than writing the script itself. See Taibo, 198–201. However, David Ramón encountered and published the script, with a convincing description of why he believed it to be Welles's work, in collaboration with del Río, Urueta, and Arturo de Córdova. See Orson Welles, *La Santa de Orson Welles*, David Ramón, editor (Mexico: Guadalupe Ferrer UNAM, 1991).

70. Ramón, *Historia*, 203–205. See also NYT, Feb. 14, 1941.

71. Santiago Reachi, *La revolución, Cantinflas, y Jolopo: Crónica de sucesos recientes, menos recientes, y futuros* (2nd edition: Mexico: Editores Asociados Mexicanos, 1982), 163–164. Seth Fein, "Myths of Cultural Imperialism and Nationalism in Golden Age Mexican Cinema," in *Fragments of a Golden Age: The Politics of Culture in Mexico Since 1940* edited by Gilbert Joseph, Anne Rubenstein, and Eric Zolov (Durham, N.C.: Duke University Press, 2001), 166–167.

72. Callow, Vol. 2, 12–13, 49–56. Leaming, *Orson*, 235. *Journey into Fear*, Editions Montparnasse, available at the Bibliothèque du Film, Paris.

73. Callow, Vol. 2, 43.

74. Leaming, *Orson*, 230. Charles Higham, *Orson Welles: The Rise and Fall of an American Genius* (New York: St. Martin's Press, 1985), 188–189.

75. Callow, Vol. 2, 44–45. Higham, 188–189.

76. Callow, Vol. 2, 103. See also LAT, May 5, 1943.

77. Higham, 178.

78. Callow, Vol. 2, 57–85, 104, 126, 128.

79. Trailer cutting continuities for *Journey into Fear*, no date, May 30, 1942, and Jan. 30, 1943, all in RKO-P-1673.

80. NYT, Aug. 9, 1942.

81. Callow, Vol. 2, 128–129.

82. CDT, Feb. 12, 1943.

83. *Journey into Fear*, Editions Montparnasse; available at the Bibliothèque du Film, Paris.

84. Ramón, DDR II, 15.

85. Welles and Bogdanovich, 164–166.

86. Higham, 189–190.

87. Leaming, *Orson*, 233–234. Ramón, *Historia*, 209.

88. LAT, Mar. 1, 1942.

89. *Charleston Daily Mail*, Apr. 22, 1942.

90. Higham, 200.

91. Leaming, *Orson*, 254. Ramón, *Historia*, 210.

92. Ramón, *Historia*, 208–210. Spanish reads "dejar de ser estrella y convertirme en actriz y eso solo lo podría hacer en México. Quise volver a México, un país que era el mío y que no conocía. Sentí la necesidad de regresar a mi país."

93. Leaming, *If This Was Happiness*, 29, 36, 84, 118–119.

Chapter 9. Return

1. Monsiváis, "Dolores del Río," 79.

2. Seth Fein, "Hollywood-United States Relations in Golden Age Mexican Cinema" (dissertation, University of Texas at Austin, 1996).

3. Aurelio de los Reyes, DDR, 92. Spanish reads "Una figura enorme, la máxima en el cine mexicano." Williams, *Covarrubias*, 56.

4. Frida Kahlo to DDR, Oct. 29 (n.y., though location and context suggest 1941); Frida Kahlo and Diego Rivera to DDR, Oct. 29 (n.y., as above), DDR 1/169, 1/170. Spanish reads "prometiste"; "ni para la niña ni para mí"; "Dolores maravillosa"; "Cuando llegó Diego se molestó muchísimo porque te había escrito yo en los términos que te escribí, pues todo lo que gana con su trabajo me lo da a mí y no me falta nada. Y quedó indignado"; "Quedo indignado por que Fridita recibió los mil pesos que mandaste para 'la niña enferma' y que debía devolverte inmendiatamente, lo que hago con el cheque adjusto. . . . Escusa a una enferma y recibe los saludos mas atentos de tu atto. Diego Rivera."

5. J. C. Orozco to DDR, Oct. 8, 1941, DDR 1/184; Orozco to DDR, Nov. 21, 1941, DDR 1/185. Spanish reads "su última visita a México"; "ex-templo de Jesús"; "simpática y verdaderamente agradable."

6. Ramón, DDR II, 12–13.

7. LAT, Sep. 4, 1967; Jan. 15, 1974.

8. De los Reyes, DDR, 126.

9. Ramón, DDR II, 11–14.

10. See, for example, "Directores del cine mexicano: Emilio Fernández," http://cinemexicano.mty.itesm.mx/directores/indio_fernandez.html, accessed Jan. 8, 2009; and Maggie Van Ostrand, "A Balloon in Cactus: Emilio Fernández, One of a Kind," www.mexconnect.com/articles/1015-a-balloon-in-cactus.

11. Beatriz Reyes Navares, *The Mexican Cinema: Interviews with Thirteen Directors*, introduction by E. Bradford Burns, translated by Elizabeth Gard and Carl J. Mora (Albuquerque: University of New Mexico Press, 1976), 14.

12. Poniatowska, *La mirada*, 42. Adela Fernández, *El Indio Fernández: vida y mito* (Mexico: Panorama Editorial, 1986), 233–235. See also Van Nostrand.

13. Julia Tuñon, *En su propio espejo* (Mexico: Universidad Autónoma Metropolitana, Unidad Extapalapa, 1988), 63. Spanish reads "... hubo un momento en que estos gentes tuvieron que abrir un contacto y, por medio de Dolores y por medio del cine y por medio de pintores se refugiaron. ..."

14. Elena Poniatowska, *Todo Mexico*, Tomo III: *La mirada que limpia* (Mexico: Editorial Diana, 1996), 13–16, 29–30, 74. Cited hereafter as Poniatowska, *La mirada*. NYT, Apr. 30, 1997.

15. Ramón, DDR II, 13–14. Poniatowska, *La Mirada*, 216–217.

16. Poniatowska, *La mirada*, 31.

17. Williams, *Covarrubias*, 56.

18. Poniatowska, *La mirada*, 42.

19. For more on Mexican immigration into the United States during these years, see Linda B. Hall and Don M. Coerver, *Revolution on the Border: The United States and Mexico, 1910–1920* (Albuquerque: University of New Mexico Press, 1988), 126–141.

20. LAT, June 19, 1963. NYT, June 19, 1963.

21. Receipt from Films Mundiales, Feb. 26, 1943, DDR 1/190. Ramón, DDR II, 15.

22. Paco Ignacio Taibo I, *"Indio" Fernández: El cine por mis pistolas* (Mexico: Joaquín Mortíz/Planeta, 1986), 75. Spanish reads "una gran fama y categoría de estrella."

23. *Flor Silvestre*, Alter's Collection: ¡Viva México! DVD Alterfilms.

24. Ramón, DDR II, 15. Tuñon, *En su propio espejo*, 37. Spanish reads "una cosa militar ... todos los soldados y los oficiales y los jefes ... se mueven bajo una autoridad y es el que concibe todo lo que va a ejecutar, ¿no?"

25. Leah Brenner, "The Film Scene Down Mexico Way," NYT, Mar. 7, 1943.

26. Ramón, DDR II, 15.

27. De los Reyes, DDR, 93. Spanish reads "un baño de agua helado ... una exposición de pintura y no de la exhibición de una película." Ramón, DDR II, 16. Reyes Navares, 18.

28. Ramón, DDR II, 16. Spanish reads "no se preocupe, Lolita, lo que pasa es que a nosotros el público no nos quiere porque somos comunistas, esto es puramente circunstancial."

29. Eduardo Iturbide to DDR, Apr. 29, 1943, DDR 1/191. Spanish reads "... despues de haberlo hecho en mejor medio, con todos los elementos y verdaderamente bien dirigida, tendrías aquí muy pocas probabilidades de éxito;" "fracaso;" "Sábado de Gloria;" "tu justa y gran vanidad de una mujer internacional hermosa y chic;" "Dolores, has vuelto a ser mexicana, la mejor mexicana, por lo que has sabido mostrar ante México entero."

30. Reyes Navares, 18.

31. Ramón, DDR II, 15.

32. Ramón, DDR II, 16–17.

33. WP, Mar. 29, 1943.

34. LAT, Apr. 15 and Nov. 10, 1943.

35. De los Reyes, DDR, 97. Spanish reads "Las diferencias sociales no se acaban con las buenas intenciones."

36. Tuñon Pablos, *En su propio*, 48. Spanish reads "muy artificiosa ... pero era preciocísima, la mujer más bella y además hablaba precioso. Era muy disciplinada, muy dedicada y concentrada en su labor. Ella tenía una técnica del tiempo silencioso, muy exagerado, de teatro."

37. Reyes Navares, 18.

38. Ramón, DDR II, 16. Spanish reads "A México ya regresa con entusiasmo sincero a desarrollar el arte que cuesta y deja dinero."

39. Ramón, DDR II, 16. Spanish reads "Es su regalo de día de santo, una historia de cine. Pos a ver si le gusta, es su próxima película, se llama *Xochimilco*. Es de usted, es de su propiedad, si alguien quiere comprarla que se la compren a usted."

40. See the discussion in David A. Brading, "Manuel Gamio and Official Indigenismo in Mexico," *Bulletin of Latin American Research*, 7(1), 1988, 75–89.

41. Taibo, *"Indio"*, 84. Spanish reads ". . . el pueblo indígena [es] el que mata a la joven y destroza toda posibilidad de vida féliz entre la pareja. La condición de honestas, pacíficos e ingenuos, no se muestra sino en las dos figuras principales y el resto del pueblo parece comportarse como todo pueblo inculto e infeliz"; ". . . de forma nueva, con seres bellos y con una cargo lírica singular. . . ."

42. Susan Dever, *Celluloid Nationalisms and Other Melodramas: From Post-Revolutionary Mexico to Fin De Siglo Mexámerica* (Albany: State University of New York Press, 2003), 34.

43. Leaming, *If This*, 29, 36.

44. Ramón, DDR II, 20–21. Spanish reads "a la actriz, pero no a la mujer."

45. WP, Sep. 13, 1943.

46. Reyes Navares, 18–19.

47. Reyes Navares, 18–19. Taibo, *"Indio"*, 81. Spanish reads " . . . yo no compartía en esta película con entusiasmo. Yo pensaba que la historia de *María Candelaria* era falsa. Modifiqué lo que pude, muchas veces contra el criterio de Emilio. Lo que más me molestaba de *María Candelaria* era su folclorismo."

48. Ramón, DDR II, 20–21. Spanish reads "Dolores del Río logra su máxima altura, su consagración como actriz poderosamente dramática . . . no pierde su tinte sombrío de mujer perseguida." Fernando de Fuentes to DDR, Jan. 21, 1944; Emilio Portes Gil to DDR, Jan. 21, 1944; Spanish reads "magistral" in both cases. Alfonso Reyes to DDR, Jan. 27, 1944, Spanish reads "Nunca vi mejor film mexicano, y nunca la vi a Vd. en una realización más hermosa. Estoy conmovido y—no se porqué—orgulloso." John Steinbeck to DDR, Jan. 28, 1944, Spanish reads "magnífica"; DDR 1/196, 1/1 95, 1/197, 1/198.

49. Stokowski to DDR, June 10, 1944, DDR 1/203.

50. LAT, Sep. 27, 1944.

51. LAT, Mar. 12, 1945; Jan. 29 and July 13, 1946.

52. LAT, Sep. 21 and Oct. 7, 1946.

53. See Fernández, *El Indio Fernández*, 249; Taibo, *"Indio,"* 216; de los Reyes, DDR, 99.

54. Mora, 62.

55. http://www.pardo.ch/jahia/home/2006, accessed Apr. 1, 2007.

56. Poniatowska, *La mirada*, 41. Spanish reads "Lo metí al cine."

57. Poniatowska, *La mirada*, 110. Spanish reads "era tremendo con su pistola."

58. Poniatowska, DDR, 30. Spanish reads " . . . no supo salirse a tiempo del cine mexicano. Nosotros debemos dejarle el lugar a los jóvenes para que haya una renovación. No podemos repetir una y otra vez hasta la saciedad lo que bien hicimos. ¡Lo hicimos muy bien! ¡Qué bueno! No tiene sentido volverlo hacer. La época de oro del cine mexicano de 'tipo indigenista o mexicanista,' si quieres llamarlo así, ya pasó. Ahora debemos ir hacia otra etapa que pueda ser igualmente buena, pero distinta."

59. Poniatowska, *La mirada*, 56.

Chapter 10. Resurrection

1. Fowles, *Starstruck*, 87.

2. Monsiváis, "Dolores del Río," 82.

3. Anne Rubenstein, "Bodies, Cities, Cinema: Pedro Infante's Death as Political Spectacle," in *Fragments of a Golden Age*, edited by Gilbert Joseph, Anne Rubenstein, and Eric Zolov (Durham, N.C.: Duke University Press, 2001), 209–212.

4. Francisco Peredo Castro, *Cine y propaganda para Latinoamérica: México y Estados Unidos en la encrucijada de los años cuarenta* (Mexico: Universidad Autónoma de México, 2004), 202. Spanish reads "'escuela mexicana de cine'; "se convirtieron en lujoso artículo de exportación'; "'buen salvaje.'"

5. NYT, June 19, 1963; LAT, June 19, 1963.

6. *Las abandonadas*, DVD, ¡Viva México! Cine en 35 mm, Alter Films. For Armendáriz's suicide, see NYT, June 19, 1963; LAT, June 19, 1963.

7. Ramón, DDR II, 24–25. Spanish reads "llanto incontenible."

8. Taibo, *El Indio*, 89.

9. Peredo Castro, 296.

10. Tuñon Pablos, *En su propio espejo*, 79. Spanish reads "mis escaleras eran en gran función dramática para mí, para presentar a las personas, para verlas por primera vez, así, bajando. . . ."

11. LAT, Jan. 12, 1946.

12. Salvador Novo, *La vida en México en el periodo presidencial de Manuel Avila Camacho* (Mexico: Empresas Editoriales, 1965), 289–290.

13. LAT, Jan. 15, 1946.

14. Ramón, DDR II, 21–22. Novo, *Avila Camacho*, 288.

15. De los Reyes, DDR, 103. Spanish reads "imagenes de la visión que tiene de Dolores;" "contradigan su intención de retratar la reprimida vida de una joven, hija de minero de Guanajuato, que vive en una casa provinciana de pequeñas dimensiones."

16. Novo, *Avila Camacho*, 363–364.

17. LAT, Jan. 2, 1946.

18. Ramón, DDR II, 23–24.

19. LAT, Sep. 24, 1946.

20. Peredo Castro, 294–295.

21. Peredo Castro, 300–302.

22. Peredo Castro, 301–302.

23. Ramón, DDR II, 25. Spanish reads "no quiero genios."

24. LAT, Sep. 2, 1946.

25. Fein, 168.

26. Gustavo García, *Pedro Armendáriz*, Vol. II (Mexico: Clío, 1997), 16–17. Hereafter cited as García, PA followed by volume and page number. See also NYT, July 7, 1944.

27. Taibo, *Indio*, 102.

28. NYT, Jan. 1, 1945.

29. Novo, *Avila Camacho*, 332–335.

30. Ramón, DDR II, 25–26. Callow, Vol. 2, 285. Novo, *Avila Camacho*, 359.

31. *La selva de fuego*, Grandes Idolos: Dos Películas Colección, Mexcinema video de México, s.a.de c.v.

32. *Joplin Globe*, Aug. 24, 1945.

33. DDR to Films Mundiales, Oct. 10, 1944; Bugambilia account sheet for DDR; Mauricio de la Serna and Jesús Grovas for Grovas, to DDR, July 9, 1945; contract, "The Power and the Glory," DDR 1/204, 209, 210, 217.

34. CDT Oct. 7, 1944.

35. WP, Nov. 10, 1944.

36. NYT, Jan. 15, 1945.

37. Manuscript, *Bugambilia* by Rodolfo Usigli, DDR 1/208. Spanish reads "Nada más me reconcilia/tu belleza con mi suerte . . . /¡Eres mi adorno y mi muerte,/planta de bugambilia!"

38. CSM, Jan. 4, 1946.

39. LAT, July 13, 1946.

40. *La otra*, DVD Videosuenos, 2002. Roberto Gavaldón, interview, PHO/2/81. Spanish reads "muy disciplinada, muy profesional. . . ."

41. LAT, Nov. 25, 1947.

42. LAT, Sep. 26, 1946.

43. Tag Gallagher, *John Ford: The Man and His Films* (Berkeley: University of California Press, 1986), 201–204.

44. Ronald L. Davis, *John Ford: Hollywood's Old Master* (Norman and London: University of Oklahoma Press, 1995), 185–192.

45. Emilio García Riera, *Emilio Fernandez, 1904–1986* (Mexico: Cineteca Nacional de México), 104.

46. NYT, Feb. 16, 1947.

47. LAT, Dec. 29, 1946.

48. See Cooper to DDR, Apr. 1, 1936; DDR to Cooper, Apr. 5, 1936; DDR 1/107, 108.

49. Charles FitzSimons, quoted in Davis, *John Ford*, 195. Lasky, *RKO*, 74.

50. Davis, *John Ford*, 195.

51. Quoted in Davis, *John Ford*, 195–198.

52. LAT, Dec. 21, 1946.

53. LAT, Feb. 21, 1947

54. Davis, *John Ford*, 196.

55. LAT, Feb. 10, 1947.

56. LAT, Feb. 5 and Feb. 10, 1947.

57. Taibo, *Indio*, 113. Spanish reads "taciturno e irritable."

58. Davis, *John Ford*, 197–198.

59. NYT, Feb. 16, 1947.

60. Quote in Davis, *John Ford*, 196.

61. NYT, Feb. 16, 1947; LAT, Feb. 21, 1947.

62. LAT, Mar. 29, 1947.

63. NYT, Dec. 26, 1947; Davis, *John Ford*, 76.

64. LAT, Feb. 21, 1947.

65. LAT, Dec. 26, 1947.

66. NYT, Dec. 28, 1947.

67. LAT, Mar. 29, 1948.

68. *Le Figaro*, no date. French reads ". . . la lenteur souvent périlleuse de son rythme," ". . . se égale certainement aux oeuvres qui leura exceptionelles qualities recommandant á la memoire." DDR 2/147.

69. *La Capital* (Rosario, Argentina), May 12, 1960. Spanish reads "John Ford. Es maravilloso." DDR 2/239.

70. Ford to del Rio, no date, DDR 1/218.

71. LAT, July 28, 1948; NYT, July 28, 1948.

72. LAT, June 4, 1948.

73. García Riera, *Emilio*, 104–107. Spanish for Reachi quotations originally published in *Esto*, Feb. 7, 1947, reads, "luminosidades;" "han dejado a muchos productores en la calle." Spanish for Fernández quotes, originally published in *Esto*, Aug. 29, 1947, reads "Hay que tener muy presente que el cine es la única industria que da a la gente del país y del extranjero una visión permanente y significativa de lo que es México;" "Mi cine es ambición y patriotismo, porque yo vengo de abajo. Era un chiquillo cuando ya andaba partiéndo el pecho en la Revolución. De mi familia, mi padre es el único qu ha pasado a mejor vida 'de muerte natural.' Y eso, llevando en el cuerpo treinta y tantos plomazos. ¡Comprendan ustedes por qué no puedo hacer películas mariconas o estériles! ¡No las siento! ¡No las siento!" "México es un niño y hay que enseñarle, valiéndonos del cine, cuáles son sus errores; hay que afinar sus virtudes. . . ."

74. García Riera, *Emilio*, 104.

75. LAT, Mar. 2, 1947. See also WP, Mar. 13, 1946.

76. NYT, May 4, 1947.

77. Ramón, DDR II, 29.

78. Ramón, DDR II, 29–30.

79. CDT, Apr. 1, 1948.

80. Salvador Novo, *La vida en México en el periodo presidencial de Miguel Alemán* (Mexico: Consejo Nacional para la Cultura y las Artes, 1994), 100–101. Spanish reads "denigrante"; "el bíblico tema de la persecución de los justos y del abuso de la fuerza"; "el cine es el más típico y el menos indicado para aprender historia ni documentar hechos."

81. Del Río to Mentasti, June 16, 1948, DDR 1/269. Spanish reads "Esto me garantiza un magnifico [sic] lanzamiento y distribucion [sic] de la pelicula [sic]."

82. Ramón, DDR II, 29–30. Spanish reads "como trofeo"; "mítica y fabulosa."

83. Ramón, DDR II, 31.

84. Ramón, DDR II, 33.

85. Rivera to del Río, Jan. 16, 1947, DDR 1/223. Spanish reads ". . . a darle la buena suerte—y a todos, y a mi el placer de verte tan maravillosamente linda como siempre"; "respetuosamente adorada amiga."

Chapter 11. Diva

1. Monsiváis, 87.

2. Carlos Fuentes, quoted in Arthur Holmberg, "Carlos Fuentes Turns to Theater," NYT June 6, 1982.

3. CDT, Aug. 5, 1956.

4. Novo, *Alemán*, 102, 151, 163, 265.

5. Ramón, DDR II, 30–31, 35–36.

6. Ramón, DDR II, 35–36; LAT, June 1, 1951, Apr. 13, 1983.

7. LAT, Nov. 14, Nov. 27, and Nov. 28, 1949.

8. Latin American soap operas usually have a specified number of episodes, rather than going on indefinitely. Ramón, DDR II, 42–43.

9. CDT Dec. 6, 1952.

10. WP, June 2, 1955. LAT May 3, 1955. For Novo's reports, see Salvador Novo, *La vida en México en el periodo presidencial de Adolfo Ruíz Cortines* (Mexico: Consejo Nacional para la Cultura y las Artes, 1996), Tomo II, 46, and Tomo III, 6–9, for example.

11. Ramón, DDR II, 43. IMDB, accessed Sep. 28, 2011.

12. "Cronología," by Fernando Mejía Barquero, in *Televisa: El quinto poder*, Fernando Mejía Barquero et al. (México: Claves Latinoamericanos, 1985), 25.

13. Ramón, DDR II, 44. *Reportaje*, http://www.imdb.com/title/tt0046236/, accessed Feb. 13, 2009. DVD, "The Report: Reportaje," Classics of Mexican Cinema, Vanguard Cinema Release.

14. Quote from imdb.com/title/tt0046808/, accessed Jan. 26, 2009.

15. Jack Gordean to DDR, Jan. 6, 1954, DDR 1/328. See also LAT, May 11, 1949, and *The Washington Post and Times Herald*, Mar. 30, 1954, for example.

16. Del Río to Gordean, Jan. 12, 1954; del Rio to Gordean, Jan. 25, 1954, DDR 1/329 and 1/330.

17. Twentieth Century Fox Film Corporation (no name) to Dolores Del Rio (sic), Jan. 28, 1954, DDR 1/331.

18. LAT Feb. 24, 1954; CDT Feb. 25, 1954.

19. Gordean to DDR, Feb. 22, 1954, DDR 1/334.

20. Three drafts, designated "Carta '1,'" "Carta '2,'" "Carta '3,'" DDR 1/327. Spanish reads "Debo confesar que esa determinación me asombró"; "A ese pueblo debo, en buena parte, el desarrollo que he alcanzado en el arte cinematográfico"; "Soy una mujer cristiana que solo aspira a vivir en paz con Dios y con los hombres"; "católica."

21. Spanish reads "En algunas ocasiones, requerida por mis compatriotas, he brindado mi solidaridad para actos patrióticos y humanitarios de ayuda a los debiles y a los perseguidos, con intenciones exclusivamente humanitarias, ya que jamas he militado en actividades políticas."

22. Spanish reads "Nunca he pertenecido a ningun partido politico, y cuando he aportado mi modesta colaboración para aliviar el dolor en sus multiples manifestaciones, ha sido siempre sin fines sectarios ni políticos, sino con el proposito de servir a mi patria o a la humanidad."

23. DDR to Embajador de los Estados Unidos de América, Feb. 26, 1954, DDR 1/335.

24. Lawrence S. Wittner, *One World or None: History of the World Nuclear Disarmament Movement Through 1953* (Stanford, Cal.: Stanford University Press, 1993), 180–184.

25. See "International Review of the Red Cross," ICRC Statement 1950, http://www.icrc.org/eng/resources/documents/misc/5kylur.htm, accessed Feb. 6, 2009; and "Joseph McCarthy, "http://history.sandiego.edu/GEN/20th/1940s/huac.html, accessed Feb. 8, 2009.

26. Leaming, *Marilyn Monroe*, 176–180. For Chaplin, see "Celebrities in Switzerland: Charlie Chaplin," http://switzerland.isyour.com/e/celebrities/bios/33.html, accessed Apr. 26, 2009.

27. Ramón, DDR II, 38, 45.

28. DDR to Veada Cleveland, Mar. 1, 1954, DDR 1/336. Dip. Lic. Rodolfo Echeverría Alvarez to José Gorostiza Alcalá, Mar. 1, 1954, DDR 1/337. Spanish reads "rumores

absurdos"; "pretextos absurdos que no pueden prevalecer ni frente a nuestra Agrupación ni frente a la personalidad de nuestra compañera Dolores del Río dedicada unica y exclusivamente a sus labores artísticas."

29. NYT, Mar. 3, 1954.

30. Assistant treasurer, Twentieth Century-Fox Film Corporation, to DDR, Mar. 4, 1954, DDR 1/338.

31. "Excerpt from Drew Pearson broadcast—March 7, 1954," DDR 1/340.

32. Arnold Weissberger to DDR, Mar. 11, 1954, DDR 1/343.

33. Spencer Tracy to DDR, Mar. 5, 1954, DDR 1/345.

34. CGT, Mar. 8, 1954. Guenther Reinhardt, *Crime Without Punishment: The Secret Soviet Terror Against America* (New York: Hermitage House, 1952), 92–94.

35. CGT, Apr. 3, 1954.

36. CSM, Apr. 20, 1954.

37. DDR to Colgate-Palmolive, May 4, 1954, DDR 1/346.

38. Vicente Sánchez Gavito to DDR, June 6, 22, 1954, DDR 1/348.

39. Mora, 76–77, 97–99.

40. Mora, 99.

41. Fernando de Fuentes to DDR, July 1 and Aug. 21, 1954, DDR 1/361 and 1/359.

42. *Excelsior*, July 1, 1954. Spanish reads "terror rojo."

43. *Excelsior*, July 5 and July 6, 1954.

44. Herrera, *Frida*, 431–432.

45. Ramón, DDR II, 48.

46. Plot summary is based on *Señora Ama*, Grandes Idolos: Dolores del Río, Mexcinema video de México, VHS videotape rather than on Benavente's play. The reproduction, particularly of the sound, is quite poor and makes the plot difficult to follow.

47. Diana Films, Mar. 1, 1957, DDR 1/461. Julio Bracho, interviews, I and II, PHO/2/23.

48. *Daily Variety*, Aug. 8, 1995, reprinted column from Aug. 8, 1955.

49. http://www.imdb.com/title/tt0048947/plotsummary, accessed Feb. 20, 2009.

50. L. Arnold Weissberger to Stella Adler, Jan. 12, 1956, DDR 1/351. NYT, Dec. 22, 1992; and LAT, Dec. 22, 1992.

51. Stella Adler to DDR, Feb.12, 1956, DDR 1/351. Flint, LAT Dec. 22, 1992.

52. Ramón, DDR II, 48.

53. Expense sheets, DDR's handwriting, DDR 1/352.

54. CGT, Aug. 5, 1956.

55. NYT, Aug. 18, 1956.

56. DDR 1/915.

57. See list of performances in DDR 1/915.

58. DDR 1/915.

59. Jean Sirol to Robert Favre-Lebret, Dec. 26, 1956, Folder FIFA 476 B78, Bibliothèque du Film, Paris, France. Cited hereafter as Bifi. French reads "Votre idée de demandara a Dolores del Rio de faire participante du jury du prochain Festival es excellente et me remplit de joie. Il s'agit non seulement d'une merveilleuse artiste mai également d'une tres grande e tres sincere amie de notre pays."

60. Sirol to DDR, Dec. 26, 1956, DDR 1/460. French reads "personnes de grande valeur et de réputation internationale."

61. Sirol to Favre-Lebret, Jan. 22, 1957, FIFA 476 B78, Bifi. French reads "Je crois qu'il sera maintenant tres dificile de refuser." *Novedades*, Jan. 22, 1957. Spanish reads "Dolores y Salvador son muy grandes amigos."

62. Notes for "Extra" interview, Feb. 4, 1957, FIFA 468, B81, Bifi.

63. Sirol to Favre-Lebret, Feb. 4, 1957, FIFA 456 B78, Bifi.

64. R. Crevenne to Mons. Defourneaux, ambassador to Spain, Mar. 21, 1957, FIFA 456 B78, Bifi.

65. Favre-Lebret to Philippe Erlanger, Feb. 11, 1957, FIFA 456 B78.

66. Jean Sirol to DDR, Apr. 6, 1957, DDR 1/462.

67. DDR 1/915.

68. "Festival International du Film: Reglement," with del Río's handwritten notes, DDR 2/215. Del Río quotes read "magnífica película de guerra. . . . Será finalista"; "Una de las más grandes interpretaciones que he visto"; "Se siente la mano maestra de un viejo director"; "sencilla humana." The quote describing *Kanal* is from http://www .imdb.com/title/tt0050585/. See also http://www.imbd.com/title/tt0049150 and www .imbd.com/name/nm0457839/bio. Online sources accessed Jan. 16, 2009.

69. Invitations, DDR 2/203, 2/206, 2/207. Memorabilia de Cannes, DDR 1/193.

70. Federico Fellini to DDR, n.d., DDR 1/1021.

71. Memorabilia de Cannes, DDR 2/193.

72. *Schlitz Playhouse of Stars*, "An Old Spanish Custom," UCLA Film and Television Archive, VA11411 T.

73. *Life en Español*, July 14, 1958.

74. See Salvador Novo, *La vida en México en el periodo presidencial de Adolfo López Mateos*, Vol. 1 (Mexico: Consejo Nacional para la Cultura y las Artes, 1997), 123, 128–129, 163.

75. Ramón, DDR II, 52.

76. LAT Nov. 25, 1959. Cedric Gibbons, IMDB, http://www.imbd.com/name/ nm0316539/, accessed Aug. 24, 2006.

77. NYT Nov. 24, 1959; WP Dec. 20, 1959; CGT Jan. 2 and Feb. 6, 1960.

78. LAT Mar. 1, 1960.

Chapter 12. Icon

1. Torres Bodet, *Estrella*, 29.

2. Hershfield, xii.

3. NYT, Apr. 13, 1983. Ramón, DDR III, 60–61.

4. LAT, Mar. 12, 1983.

5. Conversation with Luisa Riley, June 2010.

6. Conversations with Jaime Chávez, August 2007 and June 2010.

7. For text, see Jimmy Carter, the White House, Nov. 7, 1978, DDR 1/910. DDR to Jimmy Carter, Dec. 1, 1978, DDR 1/913.

8. "Dolores del Río 1925–1978," DDR 1/915. Spanish reads "su loable labor artística."

9. Conversations with Patricia Moran and Jaime Chávez, August 2010.

10. John Ford to DDR, Feb. 26, 1963, DDR 1/584. De los Reyes, 163–167. *Flaming Star*, Cinema Classics Collection, Twentieth Century Fox Home Entertainment, DVD 2005. *Cheyenne Autumn*, Warner Home Video, DVD 2007.

11. Quotations from Sheila Graham and the *Des Moines Tribune*, Oct. 22, 1964;

New York Herald Tribune, Dec. 24, 1964; *New York Telegraph,* Dec. 24, 1964; *Chicago Tribune,* Dec. 24, 1964, DDR 2/326, 2/346, 2/347, 2/348.

12. Clipping, no date, *Life Magazine,* DDR 2/349.

13. LAT, Sep. 21, 1981.

14. http://www.thefreedictionary.com/icon, accessed Mar. 8, 2009.

15. Poniatowska, *Todo II,* 137. Hershfield, xii.

16. De los Reyes, 67. The author here is referencing reports in Mexico City publications *El Universal,* June 28, 1929, and *Excelsior,* July 14, 1929.

17. Hershfield, xii–xv.

18. See for example, Hershfield, 52–55.

19. Torres Bodet, *Estrella de Dia.* Carlos Fuentes, "Orchids in the Moonlight," in *Latin American Plays,* edited and translated by Sebastian Doggart, including an interview with Fuentes also by the editor (London: Nick Hern Books, 1996), 101–174. Monsiváis, "Dolores del Río," 71–87.

20. See, for example, Taibo, 93, for Enrique del Llano's comment on her status as a source of "pride of our nationality."

21. Torres Bodet, 24–26. Spanish reads "quitarle un atisbo de realidad, a robarle un padrino querido, un juguete pequeño, a no dejarle intacto el más leve recuerdo de infancia"; "insistieron en escribir su nerviosidad exagerada, sus vertigos, los desmayos frecuentes de su memoria"; "no le permitía comprender hasta qué punto la notoriedad exigía de ella una muerte pronta, un total engaño, una traición silenciosa y definitiva."

22. Spanish reads "un rebozo, una jícara"; "¡A ella, que pedía siempre en las tiendas los sombreros más europeos! ¡A ella, que servía siempre las frutas—aunque fuesen piñas, mangos, naranjas—en bandejas anónimas de cristal!"

23. Spanish reads "Una mexicana. ¡Dios mío! Una mexicana . . . ¿Como se puede ser mexicana? Piedad lo era, preciosamente. Pero lo era a su modo, íntimo, tierno, superfluo; por eso mismo infalsificable."

24. Spanish reads "su patriotismo: su ambiente propio, la religiosidad de su madre, el alma de su provincia discreta, la canción de su México indescriptible."

25. Spanish reads "A esa hora se abrían las puertas del teatro donde le aguardaba Piedad."

26. Torres Bodet, 136–138. Spanish reads "enamorado de una sombra"; "la sombra que amaba correspondía, punto por punto, con la existencia de un cuerpo indiscutible, sólido, justo, capaz de odios, de cicatrices, de sufrimientos, célebre en Hollywood"; "Tenía nostalgia de México."

27. Fuentes, 105.

28. Fuentes, 113.

29. Fuentes, 127.

30. Fuentes, 129.

31. Sebastian Doggart, interview with Carlos Fuentes, July 1992, in *Latin American Plays,* Doggart, 169–174.

32. Fuentes,163.

33. Doggart, interview with Fuentes, 171.

34. Monsiváis, "Dolores del Río," 71.

35. "Carlos Fuentes Turns to Theater," by Arthur Holmberg, NYT June 6, 1982. Emphasis mine.

36. Monsiváis, 71.

37. Monsiváis, 78.

38. Monsiváis, 83.

39. Monsiváis, 82.

40. Monsiváis, 81.

41. Monsiváis, 78.

42. Quoted in Monsiváis, 79.

43. An excellent discussion of the Ofrenda and of Mesa-Bains's other installations is available in Jennifer A. González, *Subject to Display: Reframing Race in Contemporary Installation Art* (Cambridge: MIT Press, 2007), 122–131, though the interpretation offered above the endnote is my own.

44. González, 124–127.

45. Mesa-Bains, 311.

46. Judy Baca, "Amalia Mesa-Bains' Domesticana: Material Transformation of the Social Space Through Chicana Rasquachismo," http://sparcmurals.org/ucla/index .php?option_content&task=view&id=321&Itemid=74, accessed Feb. 16, 2009.

47. http://www.sparc.org, accessed June 4, 2009. SPARC is the Social and Public Arts Resource Center in Los Angeles and specializes in the promotion of public art.

48. http://www.debatuc.com, accessed May 1, 2009.

49. http://www.debatuc.com, accessed May 1, 2009.

50. Artist's Statement, http://www.debatuc.com/doloresdelrio.html., accessed Apr. 30, 2009.

51. http://en.wikipedia.org/wiki/Hollywood Walk_of_Fame, accessed June 5, 2009. See also http://www.bigorangelandmarks.blogspot.com/2008_10_01_archive .html, accessed June 2, 2009.

52. For Dandridge, see http://www.imdb.com/name/nm0199268/bio, accessed June 5, 2009. For Wong, see the outstanding biography, Graham Russell Gao Hodges, *Anna May Wong: From Laundryman's Daughter to Hollywood Legend* (New York: Palgrave Macmillan, 2005), xiv–xxiii, 136–137, 163–164. On West, see Watts, 3–4, 13–14, 51–52, 201–203. On Hardwicke, see http://www.imdb.com/find?s=all&q=Catherine +Hardwicke&x=15&y=11, accessed June 2, 2009; http://movies.yahoo.com/movie/ contributor/1800196628/bio, accessed May 20, 2009; NYT Aug. 20 and Oct. 5, 2003, Nov. 5 and Dec. 1, 2006.

53. May, *Power and Innocence*, 20, 99–100, 122. The quotation is from one of the anonymous reviewers.

Filmography

1. *Joanna* (1925). Producer: Edwin Carewe. Director: Edwin Carewe.
2. *High Steppers* (1926). Producer: Edwin Carewe. Director: Edwin Carewe.
3. *Pals First* (1926). Producer: Edwin Carewe. Director: Edwin Carewe.
4. *The Whole Town's Talking* (1926). Producer: Universal Pictures-Jewel; Carl Laemmle. Director: Edward Laemmle.
5. *What Price Glory?* (1926). Producer: William Fox. Director: Raoul Walsh.
6. *Resurrection* (1926). Producer: Inspiration Pictures–Edwin Carewe Productions/ United Artists. Direction: Edwin Carewe.
7. *The Trail of '98* (1927). Producer: Metro-Goldwyn-Mayer Movietone. Director: Clarence Brown.
8. *The Loves of Carmen* (1927). Producer: William Fox. Director: Raoul Walsh.
9. *Ramona* (1927). Producer: Inspiration Pictures. Director: Edwin Carewe.
10. *No Other Woman* (1927). Producer: William Fox. Director: Lou Tellegen.
11. *The Gateway of the Moon* (1928). Producer: William Fox. Director: John Griffith Wray.
12. *The Red Dancer* (1928). Producer: William Fox. Director: Raoul Walsh.
13. *Revenge* (1928). Producer: Edwin Carewe Productions. Director: Edwin Carewe.
14. *Evangeline* (1929). Producer: Edwin Carewe Productions/Feature Productions. Director: Edwin Carewe.
15. *The Bad One* (1930). Producers: Joseph Schenck and John W. Considine, Jr. Director: George Fitzmaurice.
16. *The Girl of the Rio* (1931). Producer: RKO Radio Pictures. Director: Herbert Brenon.
17. *Bird of Paradise* (1932). Producer: David O. Selznick. Director: King Vidor.
18. *Flying Down to Rio* (1933). Producer: Merian C. Cooper for RKO Radio Pictures. Director: Thornton Freeland.
19. *Wonder Bar* (1934). Producer: Robert Lord, Warner Brothers. Director: Lloyd Bacon.
20. *Madame DuBarry* (1934). Producer: Warner Brothers. Director: William Dieterle.
21. *In Caliente* (1935). Producer: Warner Brothers. Director: Lloyd Bacon.
22. *I Live for Love* (1935). Producer: Brian Foy. Director: Busby Berkeley.
23. *The Widow from Monte Carlo* (1936). Producer: Brian Foy. Director: Arthur Greville Collins.
24. *Accused* (1936). Producers: Marcel Hellman and Douglas Fairbanks, Jr., for Criterion Films. Director: Thornton Freeland.

25. *The Devil's Playground* (1937). Producer: Columbia Pictures. Director: Erle C. Kenton.

26. *Ali Baba Goes to Town* (1937). Producer: Darryl F. Zanuck. Director: David Butler.

27. *Lancer Spy* (1937). Producer: Darryl F. Zanuck. Directors: Gregory Ratoff/Irving Pichel.

28. *International Settlement* (1938). Producer: Sol M. Wurtzel. Director: Eugene Ford.

29. *The Man from Dakota* (1940). Producer: Edward Chodorov. Director: Leslie Fenton.

30. *Journey into Fear* (1942–1943). Producer: Orson Welles/Mercury. Director: Norman Foster.

31. *Flor Silvestre* (1943). Producer: Agustín J. Fink. Director: Emilio Fernández.

32. *María Candelaria* (1943). Producer: Agustín J. Fink. Director: Emilio Fernández.

33. *Bugambilia* (1944). Producer: Felipe Subervielle. Director: Emilio Fernández.

34. *Las abandonadas* (1944). Producer: Felipe Subervielle. Director: Emilio Fernández.

35. *Selva de fuego* (1945). Producers: Jesús Grovas and Mauricio de la Serna. Director: Fernando de Fuentes.

36. *La otra* (1946). Producer: Mauricio de la Serna. Director: Roberto Gavaldón.

37. *The Fugitive* (1947). Producers: John Ford and Merian C. Cooper. Director: John Ford; co-director Emilio Fernández.

38. *Historia de una mala mujer* (1948). Producer: Argentina Sono Film. Director: Luís Saslavsky.

39. *La malquerida* (1949). Producer: Felipe Subervielle. Director: Emilio Fernández.

40. *La casa chica* (1949). Producer: Jacobo Derechin. Director: Roberto Gavaldón.

41. *Deseada* (1950). Producers: Clemente Guizar Mendoza and José Baviera. Director: Roberto Gavaldón.

42. *Doña Perfecta* (1950). Producer: Francisco de P. Cabrera. Director: Alejandro Galindo.

43. *Reportaje* (1953). Producer: Miguel Alemán, Jr. Director: Emilio Fernández.

44. *El niño y la niebla* (1953). Producer: Ricardo Beltri. Director: Roberto Gavaldón.

45. *Señora Ama* (1954). Producers: Producciones Diana Films/Fernando de Fuentes and Union Films. Director: Julio Bracho.

46. *Torero* (1956). Producer: Manuel Barbachano Ponce. Director: Carlos Velo.

47. *¿A dónde van nuestros hijos?* (1956/1958). Producer: Cinematográfica Filmex-Azteca. Director: Benito Alazraki.

48. *La Cucaracha* (1958). Producers: Unifilmes Cimex/Películas Rodríguez. Director: Ismael Rodríguez.

49. *El pecado de una madre* (1960). Producers: Películas Nacionales/Producciones Brooks. Director: Alfonso Corona Blake.

50. *Flaming Star* (1960). Producer: David Weisbart. Director: Donald Siegel.

51. *Cheyenne Autumn* (1964). Producer: John Ford/Bernard Smith Productions. Director: John Ford.

52. *La dama del alba* (1966). Producer: Films Rovira Beleta. Director: Francisco Rovira Beleta.

53. *Casa de mujeres* (1966). Producer: Producciones Amador. Director: Julián Soler.

54. *More Than a Miracle* (*C'era una volta*) (1967). Producers: France and Italy: MGM Champion (Rome)/Les films Concordia (Paris)/Co-production: Carlo Ponti. Director: Francesco Rossi.

55. *Río Blanco* (1967). Producer: Hermanos Galindo. Director: Roberto Gavaldón.

56. *The Children of Sanchez* (1977). Producers: Conacine/Carmel Enterprises. Director: Hall Bartlett.

Bibliography

Archives

Academy of Motion Picture Arts and Sciences, hereafter cited as MHL.

Bibliothèque du Film, Paris, France.

Dolores del Rio Archive, Centro de Estudios de Historia de México CARSO, MXXIV. Series 1: Documents. Series 2: Clippings. Series 3: Photographs.

Fox Legal Records, UCLA Performing Arts Special Collections, cited as FX-FLR, followed by folder number.

Fox Produced Scripts 1034, Performing Arts Special Collections, UCLA Arts Special Collections, cited as FX-PRX, followed by folder number.

Jaime Chávez Collection, Mexico City.

Oral History Collection of Columbia University. Collection hereafter cited as OHC/CU.

Programa de Historia Oral, Instituto José María Luis Mora, Mexico, DF. Cited as PHO followed by interview number.

RKO Production Files, UCLA Performing Arts Special Collections. Cited as RKO-P-, followed by folder number.

Books and Articles

The American Film Industry, edited by Tino Balio. University of Wisconsin Press, 1976.

Baca, Judy. "Amalia Mesa-Bains' Domesticana: Material Transformation of the Social Space Through Chicana Rasquachismo," http://sparcmurals.org/ucla/index .php?option_content&task=view&id=321&Itemid=74, accessed Feb. 16, 2009.

Bach, Stephen. *Marlene Dietrich: Life and Legend.* New York: William Morrow & Co., 1992.

Balio, Tino. *United Artists: The Company Built by the Stars.* Madison: University of Wisconsin Press, 1976.

Black, Gregory. *Hollywood Censored: Morality Codes, Catholics, and the Movies.* Cambridge: Cambridge University Press, 1994.

Brading, David A. "Manuel Gamio and Official Indigenismo in Mexico." *Bulletin of Latin American Research*, 7(1), 1988, 75–89.

Braudy, Leo. *The Frenzy of Renown: Fame and Its History.* London and New York: Oxford University Press, 1986.

Burma, John H. "Research Note on the Measurement of Interracial Marriage." *American Journal of Sociology*, 57(6), 1952, 587.

Buss, David M. *The Evolution of Desire: Strategies of Human Mating.* New York: Basic Books, 2003.

Callow, Simon. *Orson Welles: The Road to Xanadu.* Vol. 1. New York: Viking, 1995.

Callow, Simon. *Orson Welles: Hello Americans,* Vol. 2. New York: Viking, 2006.

Caudle Beltrán, Mary. *Bronze Seduction: The Shaping of Latina Stardom in Hollywood Film and Star Publicity.* Doctoral dissertation, University of Texas at Austin, 2002.

Constantine, Mildred. *Tina Modotti: A Fragile Life.* New York: Rizzoli, 1983.

"Constitutional Law: Equal Protection of the Laws. California Miscegenation Statute Held Unconstitutional." *Harvard Law Review,* 62(2), 1948, 307.

Courtney, Susan. *Hollywood Fantasies of Miscegenation: Spectacular Narratives of Gender and Race, 1903–1967.* Princeton and Oxford: Princeton University Press, 2005.

Davis, Ronald L. *John Ford: Hollywood's Old Master.* Norman and London: University of Oklahoma Press, 1995.

de los Reyes, Aurelio. *Medio Siglo de Cine Mexicana 1896–1947.* Mexico: Editorial Trillas, 1987.

de los Reyes, Aurelio. *Dolores del Río.* Mexico: Grupo Condumex, 1996.

del Río, Dolores. "Discoveries About Myself," as told to Gladys Hall, Dec. 23, 1929. Manuscript, Gladys Hall Collection, MHL.

del Río, Dolores. "Second Chance." Interview with Gladys Hall, June 22, 1931. Manuscript, MHL.

del Río, Dolores. Interview with Alicia Rocha. *Cinelandia,* September 1964.

del Río, Dolores. Interview with Elena Poniatowska, ca. 1964, in *Todo México.* Mexico City: Editorial Diana, 1993, Tomo II, cited as Poniatowska, *Todo II.*

DeLyser, Dydia. *Ramona Memories: Tourism in the Shaping of Southern California.* Minneapolis and London: University of Minnesota Press, 2005.

Dever, Susan. *Celluloid Nationalisms and Other Melodramas: From Post-Revolutionary Mexico to Fin De Siglo Mexamérica.* Albany: State University of New York Press, 2003.

"Directores del cine mexicano: Emilio Fernández," http://cinemexicano.mty.itesm.mx/directores/indio_ fernandez.html, accessed Jan. 8, 2009.

Doggart, Sebastian. Interview with Carlos Fuentes, July 1992. *Latin American Plays: New Drama from Argentina, Cuba, Mexico, and Peru,* translated and introduced by Sebastian Doggart. London: Nick Hern Books, 1996.

Durgnat, Raymond, and Scott Simmon, *King Vidor, American.* Berkeley: University of California Press, 1988.

Etcoff, Nancy. *Survival of the Prettiest: The Science of Beauty.* New York: Anchor Books, 1999.

Eyman, Scott. *Lion of Hollywood: The Life and Legend of Louis B. Mayer.* New York: Simon and Schuster, 2005.

Fein, Seth. *Hollywood and United States-Mexico Relations in the Golden Age of Mexican Cinema.* Dissertation, University of Texas at Austin, 1996.

Fein, Seth. "Myths of Cultural Imperialism and Nationalism in Golden Age Mexican Cinema." In *Fragments of a Golden Age: The Politics of Culture in Mexico Since 1940,* edited by Gilbert Joseph, Anne Rubenstein, and Eric Zolov. Durham, N.C.: Duke University Press, 2001.

Fernández, Adela. *El Indio Fernández: vida y mito.* Mexico: Panorama Editorial, 1986.

Figerella, Mariana. *Edward Weston y Tina Modotti en México: Su inserción dentro de las estrategias estéticas del arte posrevolucionario*. Mexico: Universidad Nacional Autónoma de México: Instituto de Investigaciones Estéticas, 2002.

Film Daily Yearbook. New York and Los Angeles: published by John W. Alicoate, 1927–1934.

Fowles, Jib. *Starstruck: Celebrity Performers and the American Public*. Washington and London: Smithsonian Institution Press, 1992.

Fuentes, Carlos. "Orchids in the Moonlight." In *Latin American Plays: New Drama from Argentina, Cuba, Mexico, and Peru*, translated and introduced by Sebastian Doggart. London: Nick Hern Books, 1996.

Gallagher, Tag. *John Ford: The Man and His Films*. Berkeley: University of California Press, 1986.

Gallup Looks at the Movies: Increasing Profits with Continuous Audience Research. Princeton: Audience Research Institute, 1941.

Gamson, Joshua. *Claims to Fame: Celebrity in Contemporary America*. Berkeley: University of California Press, 1994.

García, Gustavo. *Pedro Armendáriz*, Vol. II. Mexico: Clío, 1997.

García, Gustavo A. "In Quest of a National Cinema: The Silent Era." In Joanne Hershfield and David Maciel, editors, *Mexico's Cinema: A Century of Film and Filmmakers*. Wilmington, Del.: SR Books, 1999.

García Riera, Emilio. *Emilio Fernandez, 1904–1986*. Mexico: Cineteca Nacional de México.

Gill, Brendan. "Cedric Gibbons and Dolores Del Rio: The Art Director and the Star of *Flying Down to Rio* in Santa Monica." *Architectural Digest: Academy Awards Collector's Edition*, April 1992.

González, Jennifer A. *Subject to Display: Reframing Race in Contemporary Installation Art*. Cambridge: MIT Press, 2007.

Greenfield, Gary A. "Mexican Americans, Racial Discrimination, and the Civil Rights Act of 1866." *California Law Review*, 63(3), 1975, 681.

Haiken, Elizabeth. *Venus Envy: A History of Cosmetic Surgery*. Baltimore and London: Johns Hopkins University Press, 1997.

Hall, Linda B., and Don M. Coerver. *Revolution on the Border: The United States and Mexico, 1910–1920*. Albuquerque: University of New Mexico Press, 1988.

Harrison, P. S. *Harrison's Reports and Film Reviews*, edited by D. Richard Baer. Reprint edition: Hollywood Film Archive, 1994, cited as HRPR with publication data.

Herrera, Hayden. *Frida: A Biography of Frida Kahlo*. New York: Harper and Row, 1983.

Hershfield, Joanne. *The Invention of Dolores del Río*. Minneapolis and London: University of Minnesota Press, 2000.

Hershfield, Joanne. *Imagining la Chica Moderna: Women, Nation, and Visual Culture in Mexico*. Durham, N.C.: Duke University Press, 2008.

Higham, Charles. *Orson Welles: The Rise and Fall of an American Genius*. New York: St. Martin's Press, 1985.

Hodges, Graham Russell Gao. *Anna May Wong: From Laundryman's Daughter to Hollywood Legend*. New York: Palgrave Macmillan, 2005.

Jackson, Helen Hunt. *A Century of Dishonor: A Sketch of United States Government's Dealings with Some of the Indian Tribes*, reprint of the 1885 edition, foreword by Valerie Sherer Mathes. Norman and London: University of Oklahoma Press, 1995.

Lasky, Betty. *RKO: The Biggest Little Major of Them All*. Santa Monica: Roundtable, 1989.

Leaming, Barbara. *Orson Welles.* New York: Viking, 1985.

Leaming, Barbara. *If This Was Happiness: A Biography of Rita Hayworth.* New York: Viking, 1989.

Leaming, Barbara. *Marilyn Monroe.* New York: Three Rivers Press, 1998.

Leider, Emily. *Dark Lover: The Life and Death of Rudolph Valentino.* New York: Faber and Faber for Farrar, Straus & Giroux, 2003.

Madsen, Axel. *The Sewing Circle: Hollywood's Greatest Secret: Female Stars Who Loved Other Women.* Secaucus, N.J.: Birch Lane Press, 1995.

May, Rollo. *Power and Innocence: A Search for the Sources of Violence.* New York: Dell, 1972.

McClellan, Diana. *The Girls: Sappho Goes to Hollywood.* New York: St. Martin's Press, 2000.

Memo from: David O. Selznick. Selected and edited by Rudy Behlmer with an introduction by S. N. Behrman. New York: Viking Press, 1972.

Menchaca, Martha. "Chicano Indianism: A Historical Account of Racial Repression in the United States," *American Ethnologist,* 20(3), 1993, 583–584, 588.

Mesa-Bains, Amalia. "*Domesticana*: The Sensibility of Chicana *Rasquachismo.*" In *Chicana Feminisms,* edited by Gabriela Arredondo et al. Durham, N.C., and London: Duke University Press, 2003.

Monsiváis, Carlos. "Dolores del Río: The Face As Institution." In *Mexican Postcards,* edited, translated, and introduced by John Kraniauskas. London and New York: Verso, 1997.

Mora, Carl J. *Mexican Cinema: Reflections of a Society 1896–1988.* Berkeley and Los Angeles: University of California Press: Revised edition, 1989.

Ngai, Mae. *Impossible Subjects: Illegal Aliens and the Making of Modern America.* Princeton and Oxford: Princeton University Press, 2004.

Novo, Salvador. *La vida en México en el periodo presidencial de Manuel Avila Camacho.* Mexico: Empresas Editoriales, 1965.

Novo, Salvador. *La vida en México en el periodo presidencial de Miguel Alemán.* Mexico: Consejo Nacional para la Cultura y las Artes, 1994.

Novo, Salvador. *La vida en México en el periodo presidencial de Adolfo Ruíz Cortines.* Mexico: Consejo Nacional para la Cultura y las Artes, 1996.

Paris, Barry. *Garbo.* Minneapolis: University of Minnesota Press, 1994.

Pascoe, Peggy. "Race, Gender, and Intercultural Relations: The Case of Interracial Marriage." *Frontiers: A Journal of Women Studies,* 12(1), 1991, 6.

Peredo Castro, Francisco. *Cine y propaganda para Latinoamérica: México y Estados Unidos en la encrucijada de los años cuarenta.* Mexico: Universidad Autónoma de México, 2004.

Ponce de Leon, Charles L. *Self-Exposure: Human-Interest Journalism and the Emergence of Celebrity in America, 1890–1940.* Chapel Hill, N.C., and London: University of North Carolina Press, 2002.

Poniatowska, Elena. *Todo Mexico,* Tomo II and Tomo III. Mexico: Editorial Diana, 1996.

Ramón, David. *Historia de un rostro.* Mexico City: CCH Dirección Plantel Sur, 1993.

Ramón, David. *Dolores del Río,* 3 volumes. Mexico: Editorial Clío, 1997. Cited as Ramón, DDR, followed by volume number and page number.

Reachi, Santiago. *La revolución, Cantinflas, y Jolopo: Crónica de sucesos recientes, menos recientes, y futuros.* 2nd edition: Mexico: Editores Asociados Mexicanos, 1982.

Reisler, Mark. "Always the Laborer, Never the Citizen: Anglo Perceptions of the Mexican Immigrant During the 1920s." *Pacific Historical Review,* 45(2), 1976, 244.

Reyes Navares, Beatriz. *The Mexican Cinema: Interviews with Thirteen Directors,* introduction by E. Bradford Burns, translated by Elizabeth Gard and Carl J. Mora. Albuquerque: University of New Mexico Press, 1976.

Riva, Maria. *Marlene Dietrich.* London: Bloomsbury, 1992.

Rodríguez, Clara E. *Heroes, Lovers, and Others: The Story of Latinos in Hollywood.* Washington: Smithsonian Books, 2004.

Rubenstein, Anne. "Bodies, Cities, Cinema: Pedro Infante's Death as Political Spectacle." *Fragments of a Golden Age,* edited by Gilbert Joseph, Anne Rubenstein, and Eric Zolov. Durham, N.C.: Duke University Press, 2001.

Selznick, Irene Mayer. *A Private View.* New York: Knopf, 1983.

Serna, Laura. "'As a Mexican I Feel It's My Duty': Citizenship, Censorship, and the Campaign Against Derogatory Films in Mexico, 1922–1930." *Americas,* Vol. 63 #2 October 2006.

Soares, André. *Beyond Paradise: The Life of Ramón Novarro.* New York: St. Martin's Press, 2002.

Taibo I, Paco Ignacio. *"Indio" Fernández: El cine por mis pistolas.* Mexico: Joaquín Mortíz/Planeta, 1986.

Taibo I, Paco Ignacio. *Dolores Del Río: Mujer en el Volcan.* Mexico, D. F.: Planeta, 1999.

Televisa: El quinto poder. Fernando Mejía Barquero et al. Mexico: Claves Latinoamericanos, 1985.

Torres Bodet, Jaime. *Estrella de día.* Madrid: Espasa-Calpe, 1933.

Tragen, Irving G. "Statutory Prohibitions Against Interracial Marriage." *California Law Review,* 32(3), 1944, 271.

Tuñon, Julia. *En su propio espejo.* Mexico: Universidad Autónoma Metropolitana, Unidad Ixtapalapa, 1988.

Van Ostrand, Maggie. "A Balloon in Cactus: Emilio Fernández, One of a Kind," http//www.mexconnect.com/mex_/travel/mvanostrand/mvo0205/html.

Vanderwood, Paul J. *Satan's Playground: Mobsters and Movie Stars at America's Greatest Gaming Resort.* Durham, N.C.: Duke University Press, 2010.

Walsh, Raoul. *Each Man in His Time: The Life Story of a Director.* New York: Farrar, Straus & Giroux, 1974.

Watts, Jill. *Mae West: An Icon in Black and White.* New York: Oxford University Press, 2001.

Welles, Orson, and Peter Bogdanovich. *This Is Orson Welles.* 1st paperback edition. New York: Da Capo Press, 1998.

Weston, Edward. *The Daybooks of Edward Weston.* Vol. I: Mexico, edited by Nancy Newhall. Rochester, N.Y.: George Eastman House, n.d.

Williams, Adriana. *Covarrubias.* Austin: University of Texas Press, 1994.

Wittner, Lawrence S. *One World or None: History of the World Nuclear Disarmament Movement Through 1953.* Stanford, Cal.: Stanford University Press, 1993.

Wray, Fay. *On the Other Hand: A Life Story.* New York: St. Martin's Press, 1989.

Newspapers and Magazines
L'Ami du Peuple, Paris
Atlanta Constitution
La Capital, Rosario, Argentina
Charleston Daily Mail
Charleston Gazette

Chicago Daily Tribune
Christian Science Monitor
Cinelandia
El Heraldo de México, Mexico, DF
El Latino-Americano, New York City
El Universal, Mexico, DF
Excelsior, Mexico, DF
Le Figaro, Paris
Film Daily
Fox Studio Mirror
Joplin Globe
Kingsport Times, Kingsport, Tennessee
Life en Español
Life
London Daily Express
London Daily Mail
London Daily News and the Westminster Gazette
London Daily Sketch
London Evening News
London Evening Standard
Los Angeles Examiner
Los Angeles Herald
Los Angeles Times
Moving Picture World
New York Times
New York World
News 4
Photoplay
Screen Book
Screenland
La Settima Arte
Sheboygan Press
Sunday News, London
Olean Times-Herald
Variety
Washington Post

Interviews and Reminiscences
Roberto Gavaldón, interview, PHO/2/81, Instituto José María Luis Mora.
Andrea Palma, interview, June 12 and June 17, 1975, Historia Oral—Cine Mexicano, PHO/2/24, Instituto José María Luis Mora.
Reminiscences of Busby Berkeley, Aug. 4, 1971, OHC/CU.
Reminiscences of Joel McCrea, Aug. 2, 1971, OHC/CU.
Reminiscences of Jerome Zerbe, Aug. 15, 1979, OHC/CU.

Index

Page numbers in italic type refer to illustrations.

Lightning Source UK Ltd.
Milton Keynes UK
UKHW010348210521
383974UK00013B/218